FRETBOARD BIOLOGY
COMPREHENSIVE GUITAR PROGRAM

"The Knowledge without the College"™

LEVEL 5

This textbook accompanies the Level 5 course at Fretboardbiology.com

©2022 Joe Elliott. Please do not distribute or reproduce this material. This program represents a lifetime of work teaching guitar players like you how to be better musicians. If you think this program is great, please encourage your friends to sign up for the course and go through it with you. They will get more out of the program, and you will feel better knowing that you aren't hurting fellow artists by just giving away their work. Thank you.

Music Biology Publishing

Copyright © 2022 Joe Elliott

All rights reserved. Except as permitted under the U.S. Copyright Act of 1976, no part of this book may be reproduced in any manner whatsoever without written permission from the publisher, except in the case of brief quotations in critical articles or reviews.

The paper used in this publication meets the minimum requirements of the American National Standards for Information Services - Permanence of Paper for Printed Library Materials,
ANSI Z39.48-1984.

ISBN 13: 978-1-7362942-4-6

DEDICATION

I would like to dedicate this to all the great teachers out there who are passing along their knowledge and experience.

ACKNOWLEDGMENTS

In any project like this, it is hard to thank all of the people who have been instrumental in its development and success. I've been fortunate to have the support and friendship of many people along the way. I've somehow been wise enough to listen to those who know more than me, too. I encourage everyone to live that way.

I would like to start by thanking my wife, Eileen, for all the support, encouragement, and freedom to take on this monstrous project—and the faith that it would be a success—as well as all the years of putting up with the stresses of being married to a professional musician. My interest in music was fostered and supported by my parents, Jack and Marian Elliott, who always had a house full of big band and classical music, and my older siblings, Dave, Mary, and Dan, who exposed me to a lot of great music growing up like the Trashmen, The Beatles, The Stones, Sergio Mendes, Chicago, Sly, and Crosby, Stills, and Nash.

There were several people who were very influential in my development as a musician and educator that I would like to acknowledge: Fred Brush for showing so many great musicians to me in my formative years. Glen Johnston for exposing all of us "Montana Boys" to the real musicians in person at Montana State. Kent Erickson for drilling me on theory on our long road trips. Carl Schroeder for your unique way of getting your points across back in the day when I was in your classes in LA. You certainly shaped my way of teaching and managing a classroom. Keith Wyatt for the steady example of professionalism in guitar education. Combining great guitar talent with an organized mind is a great combination for any student. Scott Henderson for your relentless intolerance of mediocrity. You still scare me into working harder. Don Mock for being such an egoless sharer of your knowledge and gifts. You'll probably never know how many lives you affected with your pragmatic approach. Howard Roberts for all the lives you changed teaching guitar players real-world skills and shaping the most innovative guitar program that's ever existed. Bruce Buckingham for feeding me the right information at the right time. Eric Paschal for always finding the best in all your students. And Dan Gilbert for the energy you pumped into every class and the motivation to practice more than I've ever practiced.

For this project I was very fortunate to be surrounded by a team of amazing and intelligent musicians and specialty experts such as Ricky Peterson, Sean Nilson, Eliot Briggs, Bill Lafleur, Luke Elliott, Carter Elliott, John Krogh, Harry Chalmiers, Kevin Sullivan, Tony Axtell and the McNally Smith College of Music "guitar department in exile"—Tim Lyles, Paul Krueger, Chris Olson, Mike Salow, Dave Singley, and Eva Beneke—for test-driving this Fretboard Biology method for seven years.

None of this would have happened without the dedicated work of my business partner in the Fretboard Biology program, Todd Berntson, and his wife, Monique. There's a lot of skill and talent in that duo and it was only through Todd's insistence that this project was launched.

Lastly, I would like to thank all the great musicians and students I have had the pleasure to work with over the past 40 years.

TABLE OF CONTENTS

LEVEL 5 INTRODUCTION   1

UNIT 1   3

- Theory - Suspended Chords, Add2 / Add9 Chords, 6 Chords, 6/9 Chords, Power Chords, Harmonic Minor Scale
- Fretboard Logic - Pattern II & Pattern IV Harmonic Minor Scales, Chord-Fingering Exercise
- Rhythm Guitar - Introduction to Latin Rhythm Guitar: Bossa Nova
- Chart Reading - Introduction to Chart Reading
- Improvisation - Soloing with the Patterns II & IV Harmonic Minor Scales
- Practice - Practice Routine Development

UNIT 2   41

- Theory - Harmonizing the Harmonic Minor Scale with Triads, Minor Modal Interchange
- Fretboard Logic - Patterns I, III, and V Harmonic Minor Scales, Augmented Triads, Augmented Triad Arpeggios
- Rhythm Guitar - Bossa Progression in A Minor
- Chart Reading - Basic Information: Title, Tempo, Style, Clef, Key Signature, and Time Signature
- Improvisation - Soloing with the Harmonic Minor Scale over the V7 Chord
- Practice - Continue Practice Routine Development

UNIT 3   65

- Theory - Harmonizing the Harmonic Minor Scale with 7th Chords, the VII°7 Chord
- Fretboard Logic - Diminished Chords, Diminished Triad Arpeggios
- Rhythm Guitar - Samba Rhythm Guitar
- Chart Reading - Slash Marks, Importance of Clarity in Charts
- Improvisation - Soloing with the Harmonic Minor Scale over the V7 Chord
- Practice - Continue Practice Routine Development

UNIT 4 — 87

- Theory - The V7 Chord, the Tritone
- Fretboard Logic - The V-I Resolution
- Rhythm Guitar - Samba Rhythm Guitar
- Chart Reading - Section Markings: Rehearsal Letters, Bar Numbers
- Improvisation - Soloing with the Harmonic Minor Scale over the V7 Chord
- Practice - Continue Practice Routine Development

UNIT 5 — 113

- Theory - The VII°7 Chord, Inversions of Diminished 7 Chords
- Fretboard Logic - Diminished 7 Chords and Arpeggios
- Rhythm Guitar - Salsa Rhythm Guitar, Montuno, Tumbao, Clave
- Chart Reading - Repeat Tools: One-Bar and Two-Bar Repeats, Simile, Multiple-Measure Rests
- Improvisation - Soloing with the Harmonic Minor Scale over the VII°7 Chord
- Practice - Continue Practice Routine Development

UNIT 6 — 136

- Theory - The Imi(ma7) Chord
- Fretboard Logic - Minor(Major 7) Chords and Arpeggios
- Rhythm Guitar - Introduction to Odd Meter
- Chart Reading - More Repeat Devices: Repeat Signs, Endings, Repeat Until Cue
- Improvisation - Soloing with the Harmonic Minor Scale over the Imi(ma7) Chord
- Practice - Continue Practice Routine Development

UNIT 7 — 161

- Theory - The ♭IIIma7(+5) Chord
- Fretboard Logic - Major 7(+5) Chords and Arpeggios
- Rhythm Guitar - Odd Meter: 5/8 Time
- Chart Reading - Jump Marks: D.C. and D.S.
- Improvisation - Soloing with the Harmonic Minor Scale over the ma7(+5) Chord
- Practice - Continue Practice Routine Development

UNIT 8   195

- Theory - Primary Dominant, Functioning and Non-Functioning Dominants
- Fretboard Logic - In-Position Arpeggios in Harmonic Minor
- Rhythm Guitar - Odd Meter: 7/8 Time
- Chart Reading - Ensemble Rhythm Figures, Signature Riff Notation, Top Note of a Voicing Notation, Transpositional Markings
- Improvisation - Soloing with the Harmonic Minor Scale In-Position
- Practice - Continue Practice Routine Development

UNIT 9   223

- Theory - Secondary Dominants, the Dominant ♭9 ♭13 Scale
- Fretboard Logic - Patterns I-V Dominant ♭9 ♭13 Scale
- Rhythm Guitar - Odd Meter: 11/8 Time
- Chart Reading - Dynamics, Accents, Markings that Affect Time
- Improvisation - Soloing over Secondary Dominants in Major Keys
- Practice - Continue Practice Routine Development

UNIT 10   269

- Theory - Harmonic Analysis of Secondary Dominants
- Fretboard Logic - In-Position 7th Chord Voicings for the Harmonized Harmonic Minor Scale
- Rhythm Guitar - Odd Meter: 13/8 Time
- Chart Reading - The Chart Checklist, Analyzing Charts, Memorization
- Improvisation - Soloing over Secondary Dominants in Minor Keys
- Practice - Continue Practice Routine Development

APPENDICES   317

LEVEL 5 INTRODUCTION

Fretboard Biology Level 5 builds on the material in the previous levels. If you haven't completed those levels, go back and make sure that you are confident in all the material. In Level 5, the Harmonic Minor Scale and its use will command a lot of attention. New and more advanced harmonic concepts result from this study.

What's in Level 5

- In the Theory modules, you will learn how to construct the Harmonic Minor Scale and to harmonize it with both triads and 7th chords. This will result in chords that are new to you and that creates a need for chord-scale solutions. There are a group of chords that don't fall into the categories you've learned so far: triads or 7th chords. We will categorize them simply as 'Other Chord Types'.

- In the Fretboard Logic modules you will learn the Harmonic Minor Scale patterns as well as the chords and arpeggios, some of them new, that result from harmonizing it. You'll learn to see the both the arpeggios and chords of the harmonized Harmonic Minor Scale 'in-position'. You will learn to see the scales, arpeggios, and chords of the parallel Natural and Harmonic Minor Scales superimposed on one another. You will also learn about using scales as 'chord scales' and that will include the Dominant ♭9 ♭13 Scale. You will learn chord voicings for the 'Other Chord Types' that are introduced in the Theory modules.

- The first five Rhythm Guitar modules will give you an introduction to the vast world of Latin music. In Units 6 through 10, the focus will be about playing in odd meters.

- In Level 5, you will be introduced to new Chart Reading modules. Reading a chord chart is an essential skill and Level 5 dedicates 10 units to the topic. It's important to understand the core elements of chord charts and how to approach them.

- In the Improvisation modules you will learn to transition between Natural Minor and Harmonic Minor Scale patterns, much like you did with modal interchange in Level 4. In many progressions, specific chords require special accommodation, and in this Level the focus will be on how the Harmonic Minor Scale is a solution.

Let's get started.

UNIT 1

Learning Modules

> **Theory** - Suspended Chords, Add2 / Add9 Chords, 6 Chords, 6/9 Chords, Power Chords, Harmonic Minor Scale

> **Fretboard Logic** - Pattern II & Pattern IV Harmonic Minor Scales, Chord-Fingering Exercise

> **Rhythm Guitar** - Introduction to Latin Rhythm Guitar: Bossa Nova

> **Chart Reading** - Introduction to Chart Reading

> **Improvisation** - Soloing with the Patterns II & IV Harmonic Minor Scales

> **Practice** - Practice Routine Development

THEORY

Level 5 Theory will start with chord types that are different than triads and 7th chords. Throughout this Level you will also study the Harmonic Minor Scale and how it's used. There is also extensive study on the harmonized Harmonic Minor Scale, the resulting chords, and how they are used in music.

Chords

We begin with chords. There are chord types used in popular music that don't fit into the standard categories like triads, 7th chords, inversions, or what are called 'extended chords'. Extended chords will be discussed in a later level, but in short, they are 7th chords with additional notes added.

In this Module you will learn about some of these 'other chord types'. This is kind of a catch-all group. What all of these chords have in common is that they don't fit into the categories you have already learned. Here are the chord types you will learn in this Module:

- Suspended chords
- Add2 chords, sometimes called add9 chords, or even just '2' chords
- 6 chords
- 6/9 chords
- Power chords

Suspended Chords

There are a variety of chords that use the word 'suspended' in their name. You have already learned a little bit about them.

Sus4 Chord

Among the types of suspended chords, the most common is the suspended 4th chord, which is commonly called sus4 or even just sus. You will remember that we touched on the sus4 chord way back when we first learned about triads. A sus4 chord is built by replacing the third in a major or minor triad with a perfect 4th.

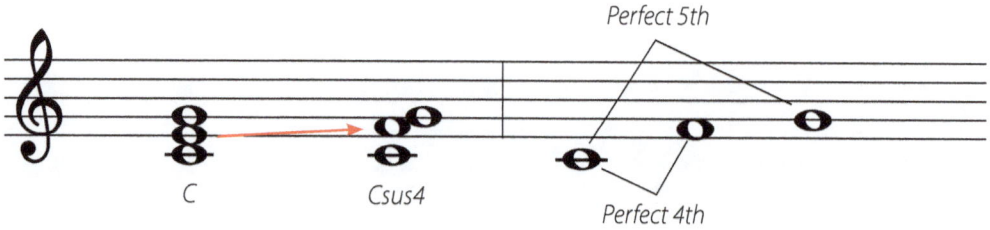

It is spelled Root-perfect 4th-perfect 5th. The common chord symbol is sus or sus4. If you see just 'sus' written on a chord chart, it means sus4. Csus and Csus4 are the same. Suspended chords create a feeling that the harmony is in unresolved suspense before resolving to a major or minor triad. Usually the 4th in a sus chord resolves down to the 3rd.

Sus4 Chord Resolves to a Triad

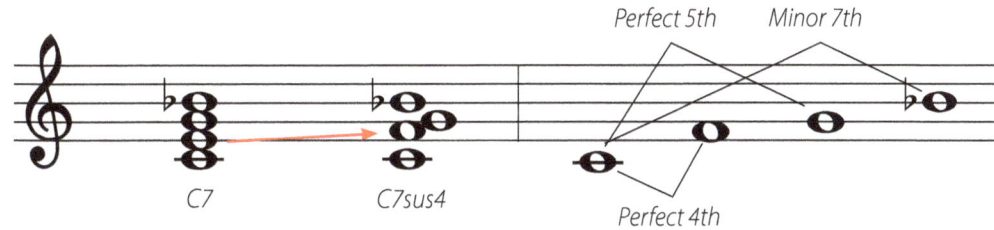

It is important to note that a suspended chord does not always resolve to a major or minor triad. There are times when a sus chord just stands alone.

And again, the possible chord symbols are: Csus or Csus4.

Dominant 7sus4 Chord

7th chords are not discussed much in this Unit but we should at least look at dominant 7sus4 chords, sometimes called 7sus chords. The 7sus4 chord is built by replacing the third of a dominant 7 chord with a perfect 4th. It is spelled Root-perfect 4th-perfect 5th-minor 7th. The chord symbol is 7sus or 7sus4.

Like the Sus4 chords, 7sus4 chords typically resolve to either a major or minor triad.

7sus4 Chord Resolves to a Triad

Possible chord symbols are: C7sus or C7sus4.

Sus2 chord

The common interpretation of a Sus2 chord is for a major 2nd to replace the 3rd of a triad. The root-position closed voicing is spelled Root-major 2nd-perfect 5th. Sus2 chords can be used in a major or minor context because there is no 3rd. In fact, they are sort of 'quality neutral' when heard all alone and out of the context of a tune.

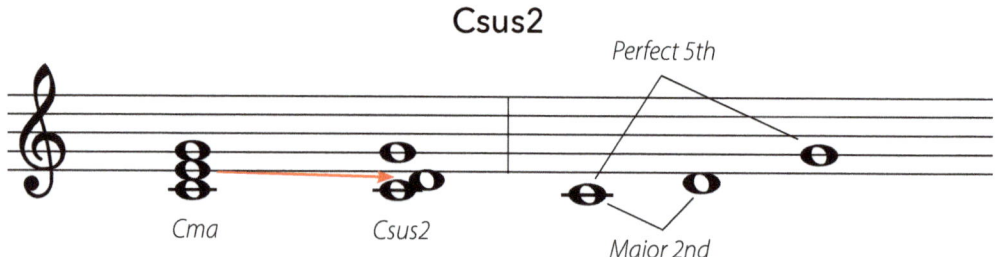

When using a Sus2 chord in the context of a tune, a quality of major or minor is implied by the scale degree of the root. The quality of the chord that would normally be built on that scale degree is implied.

For example, in the key of A minor, a minor quality is implied for Asus2 because A is the 1st scale degree and a minor chord is built on I in minor.

Chord symbol is: Asus2.

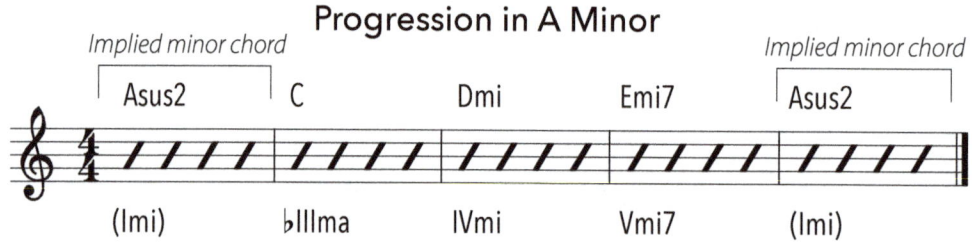

Here is another example. In the key of A minor, the quality of major is implied for Csus2 because C is the 3rd scale degree and a major chord is built on ♭III in minor.

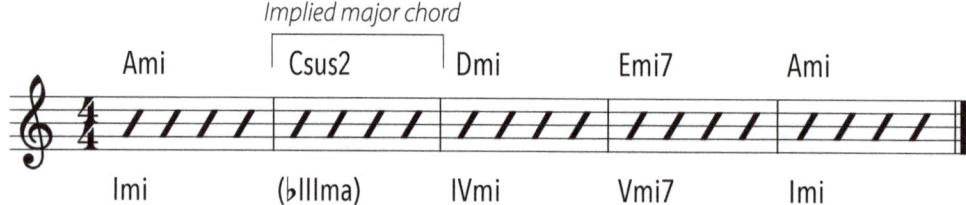

Chord symbol is: Csus2.

This symbol is used regardless of whether a major or minor triad is implied.

Sus6/4 Chord

The suspended 6/4 is also called a Sus6/4. In a Sus6/4 chord, a perfect 4th replaces the 3rd and a major 6th replaces the 5th It's sort of a double suspension. The voicing is normally followed by a major triad.

The root-position closed voicing is spelled Root-perfect 4th-major 6th. When it resolves to a major triad, the 4th resolves down a half step to the major 3rd and the major 6th resolves down a whole step to the 5th.

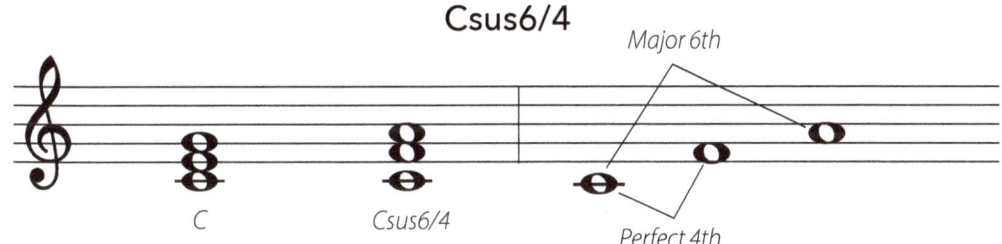

There is also another popular way to write the Sus6/4 chord as a slash chord. Examine Csus6/4 closely. It is spelled C-F-A. If you look at it a little differently you will see that it's an F triad, F, A, and C, with C or the 5th in the bass. That makes it a 2nd inversion F chord, right?

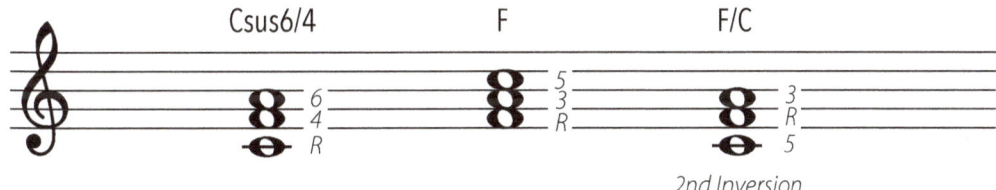

Remember that an inversion can be written as a slash chord. In this case, it is F/C. That means an F triad over a C bass note, a 2nd inversion F major triad. So you can see that the Csus6/4 is the same as F/C. You will see this chord written both ways.

Possible chord symbols are: Csus6/4 and F/C.

Sus2/4 Chord

Another sort of double-suspended chord is the Sus2/4. In a Sus2/4 chord, a perfect 4th replaces the 3rd. The 2 or major 2nd is also present in sort of a Sus2 role. The root-position closed voicing is spelled Root-major 2nd-perfect 4th.

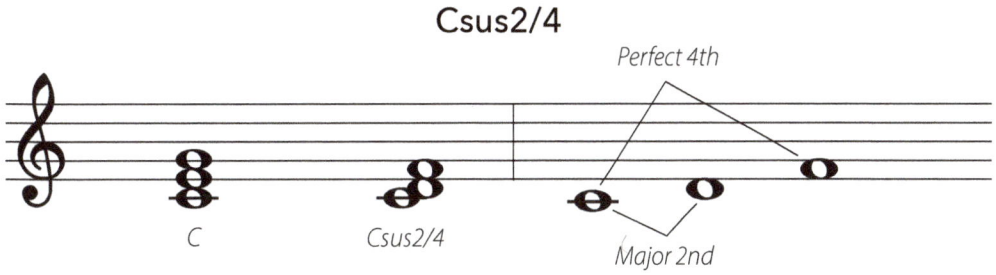

The voicing is normally followed by a major triad. When it resolves to a major triad, the 4th resolves down a half step to the major 3rd and the major 2nd resolves down a whole step to the root—even though the root is probably also being played in another voice in a lower octave.

Possible chord symbols are: Csus2/4 and C2sus4.

Add2 Chords

An Add2 chord is sometimes called an Add9 chord or sometimes just a 2. It's not a 2 chord as in 'a chord built on the 2nd scale degree' that we think about with harmonized scales, but instead, a 2 is a chord with a major 2nd added above the root. Don't confuse these with Sus2 chords. Sus2 chords have no 3rd; Add2 chords have 3rds.

An Add2 chord is a triad only, with an added major 2nd (or 9th). I need to explain the term '9th'. The 9th is the same pitch as a 2 but technically up an octave. If you count to 9, you see that it is the octave of 2: 1, 2, 3, 4, 5, 6, 7, then 8 is the octave of 1, and 9, the next note higher, is the octave of 2. You will learn much more about these larger intervals like 9ths, 10ths, 11ths, and so on, in a later level.

To construct an Add2 chord, add a major 2nd to a major triad. The root-position closed voicing is spelled Root-major 2nd-major 3rd or minor 3rd-perfect 5th. Built on a C root, Cadd2 is spelled C-D-E-G.

Cadd2 or C2

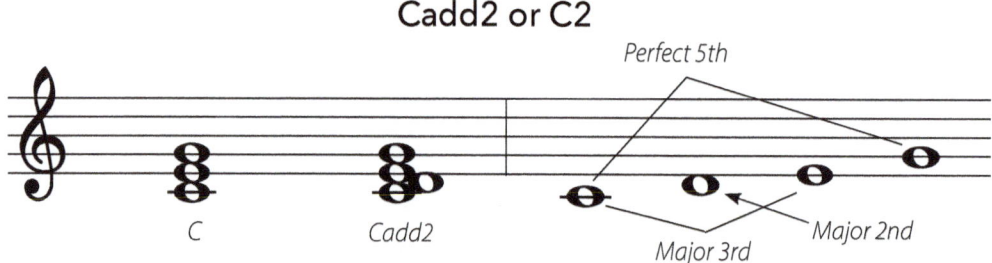

Possible chord symbols are: Cadd2, Cadd9, or simply C2.

To construct a minor Add2 chord, add a major 2nd to a minor triad. The root-position closed voicing is spelled C-D-E♭-G.

Cmi(add2) or Cmi2

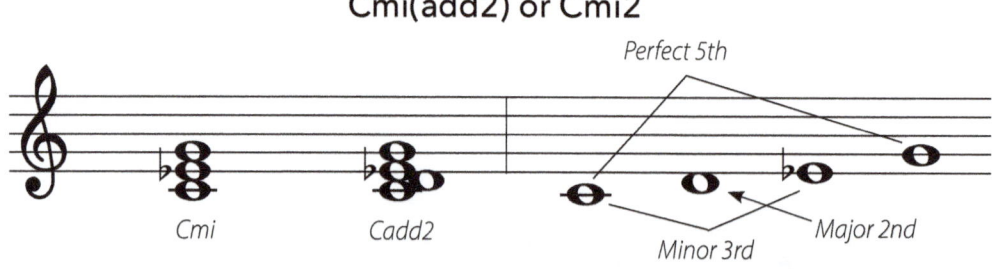

Possible chord symbols are: Cmi(add2), Cmi(add9), or simply Cmi2.

As you know, in reality, chords don't have to be voiced in numerical order. For example, a C2 could be voiced Root, 5th, 2nd, 3rd or Root, 3rd, 5th, 2nd or any of the other possible combinations of the numbers. However, the 2nd/9th is never voiced in the bass.

As an important side note, Add2 or Add9 chords should not be confused with Ma9, Dom9, or Mi9 chords. The distinction is that those contain a 7th. And they sound remarkably different. You will learn those chords further along in this course.

6 Chords

6 chords are major or minor triads with an added major 6th. To construct a 6 chord, add a major 6th to a major triad. The root-position closed voicing is spelled Root-major 3rd or minor 3rd-perfect 5th-major 6th. Built on a C root, the root-position closed voicing C6 is spelled C-E-G-A. The chord symbol is C6.

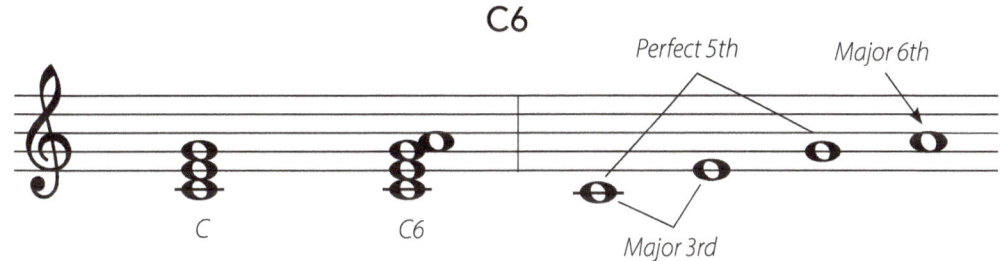

To construct a minor 6th chord, add a major 6th to a minor triad. The root-position closed voicing Cmi6 is spelled C-E♭-G-A. The chord symbol is Cmi6. And remember that the 6th is a major 6th.

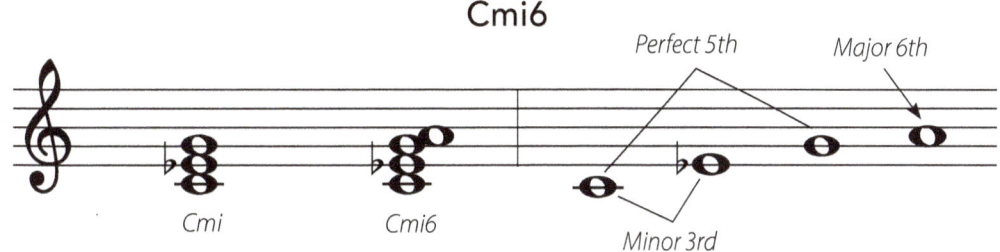

Again, chords don't have to be voiced in numerical order; that is, root position and closed voiced. For example, a C6 can be voiced in any of the other possible combinations of the numbers. However, the 6th is never in the bass.

6 chords should not be confused with Ma13, Dom13, or Mi13 chords. All of those chords have a 7th. And note that the 6th is a major 6th, even on the Mi6 chord.

6/9 Chords

6/9 chords are major or minor triads with an added major 6th and major 9th, which you know is a 2nd. The root-position closed voicing is spelled Root-major 3rd or minor 3rd-perfect 5th-major 6th-major 9th.

Built on a C root, the root-position closed voicing for C6/9 is spelled C-E-G-A-D. The chord symbol is C6/9, with a slash mark separating the 6 and 9. Don't confuse this with the slash chords discussed in an earlier unit. Know that there are some notable inconsistencies in chord symbol notation. There is no way around it. It's just the way it is. You just have to learn what they are and I'll point them out as we go. There is a whole module dedicated to chord symbol notation coming up.

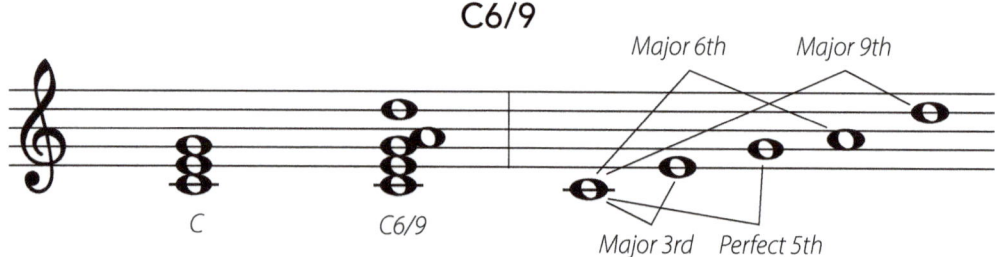

To construct a minor 6/9 chord, add a major 6th and a major 9th to a minor triad. The root-position closed voicing for Cmi6/9 is spelled C-E♭-G-A-D. The chord symbol is Cmi6/9.

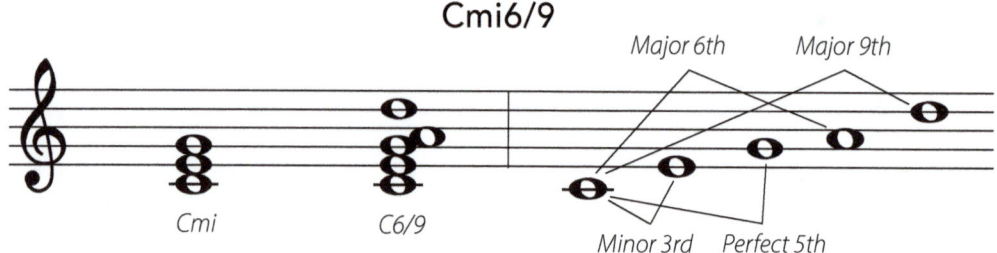

6/9 chords should not be confused with Ma13, Dom13, or Mi13 chords. Those all contain a 7th.

Power Chords

Power chords contain only a root and a perfect 5th. These chord tones may be repeated in multiple octaves. Since they have no 3rd, they technically have no 'quality', but a major or minor quality is normally implied by the context.

The implied quality of a power chord—that is, major or minor—can be determined by looking at the key signature. In other words, the key of the song determines the quality of the chord built on the scale degree of the root of the power chord. So if you learn a song in B minor and there's a B5, meaning a power chord built on B, a Bmi chord is implied by the prevailing key. That is because the I chord in the key of B minor is Bmi. If in the same song in the key of B minor there is an E5 chord, E is the 4th scale degree and the IV chord in the minor key is minor, so an Emi chord is implied by the prevailing key.

You might also determine the quality by looking at the melody notes, examining the root movement, noting what quality chord another instrument in the band is playing, or all the above.

As for notating power chords, sometimes the C5 symbol is used. Back in the day, before anybody thought to notate a power chord with the number 5, somewhere in the music where the full chord symbols were used on the chart there would be instructions to use power chords.

This old notation is still used today. A great thing about that is that a guitarist can see the implied chord quality while knowing to voice only a root and fifth.

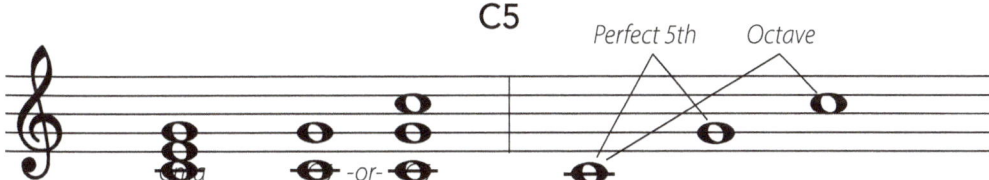

Possible chord symbols are: C5, C (with 'power chord' written above), or Cmi (with 'power chord' written above).

Chord Identification

Take a moment to practice identifying some chords. They might be Sus chords, Add2 chords, 6 chords, 6/9 chords, or power chords. Write the appropriate chord symbol above the staff. All chords are in root position.

Chord Construction

(Answer key on page 306)

Take a moment to build a few Sus chords, Add2 chords, 6 chords, 6/9 chords and power chords. Write these in root position.

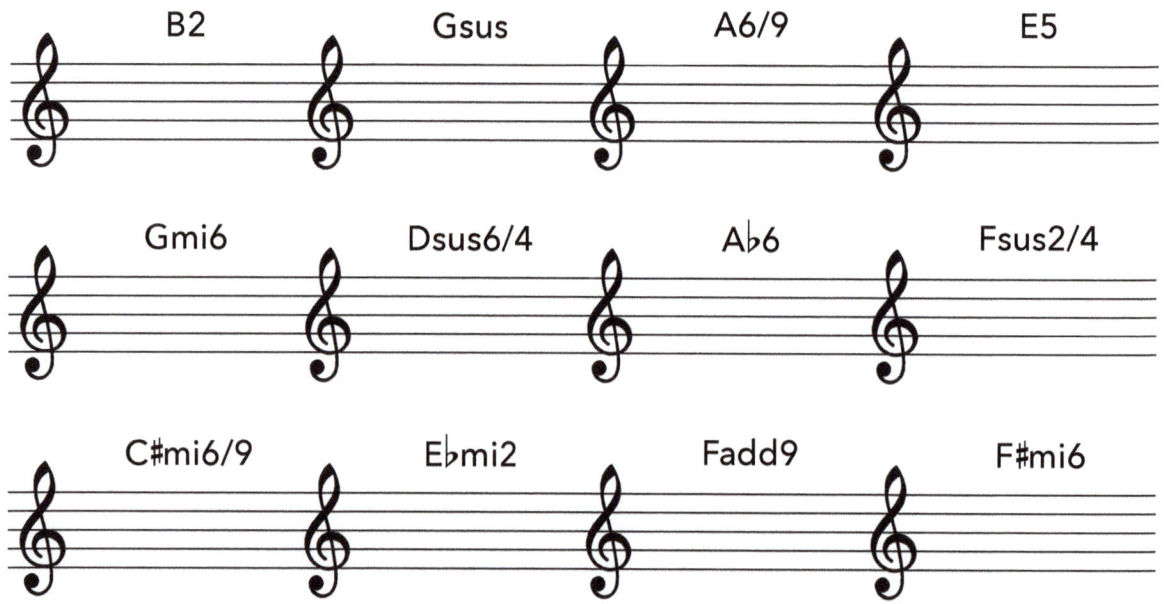

(Answer key on page 306)

Scales

Let's turn our attention to scales. Through the previous levels, you have learned the diatonic systems that exist with Major and Natural Minor Scales. Remember that the term 'diatonic harmony' means that all melody notes and all of the chords are either from the seven-note Major Scale or the Minor Scale.

You have been introduced to two exceptions to diatonic harmony so far in this course:

1. The concept of modal interchange
2. The introduction of the dominant V chord that sometimes occurs in minor keys

From this point forward, you will be introduced to more exceptions to the diatonic systems. To get started, let's revisit a topic we discussed in the previous Level: the leading tone. The 7th degree of the Major Scale is also called the leading tone because of its strong pull toward the tonic, that is, the 8th scale degree or the octave of 1.

It's easy to feel this 'leading-tone effect' by playing the C Major Scale ascending and then pausing on the 7th degree before playing the 8th degree. It is natural to want to hear the scale resolve up one half step to the tonic.

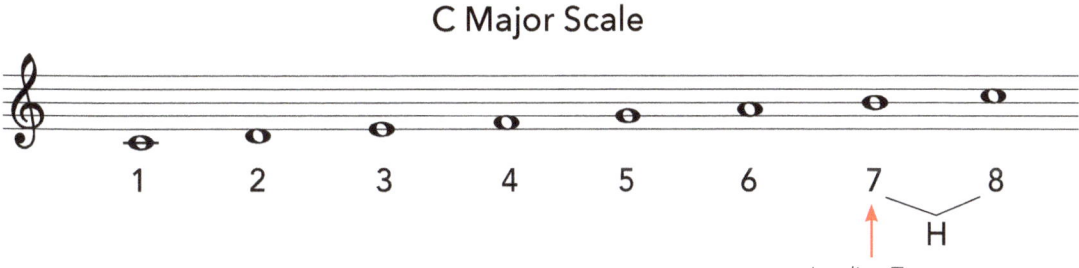

Now, let's try this in Natural Minor. Play the C Natural Minor Scale ascending and pause on the 7th degree. This is a flat 7th. Do you notice that you didn't feel the same strong attraction to the tonic that you felt with the major 7th (the leading tone) in the Major Scale? The ♭7 of the Natural Minor Scale just doesn't offer the same sense of urgency as the leading tone.

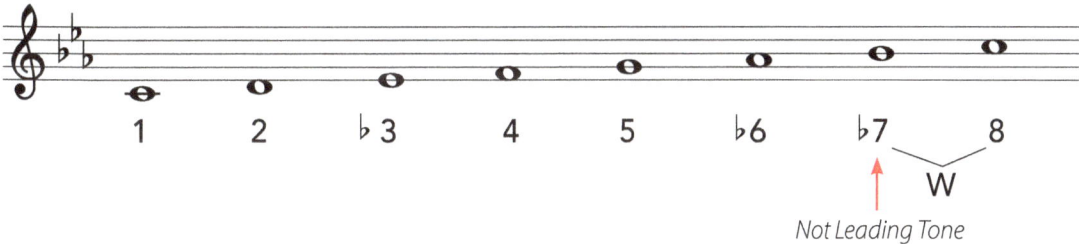

Now, play the C Minor Scale but change the 7th from a minor 7th to a major 7th. As you play it, pause on this major 7th and feel the leading-tone effect. You should now feel a real sense of urgency to resolve up a half step to 8 which is 1 (the tonic). This version of the Minor Scale with a major 7th instead of a minor 7th has a name. It's called the Harmonic Minor Scale.

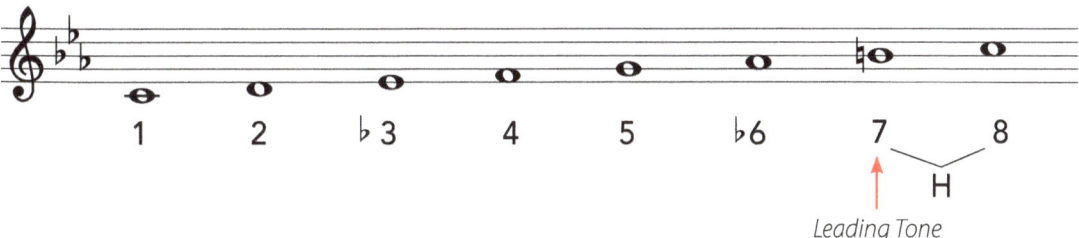

The Harmonic Minor Scale can be the basis for a composition but in popular music is more commonly used as a solution for isolated chords in a more broad minor context. That will be discussed a whole lot more later.

The Harmonic Minor Scale is spelled like this:

1 Ma2 Mi3 P4 P5 Mi6 Ma7 Octave

The Harmonic Minor Scale is constructed using this formula:

W H W W H A2 H

The easiest way to build a Harmonic Minor Scale is to start with the Natural Minor Scale and raise the 7th a half step. Notice the wide interval between the minor 6th and the major 7th, the augmented 2nd. That is a big gap in a seven-note scale. Play the scale ascending and descending. Do you think the increased distance is more noticeable ascending or descending?

Compare the C Natural Minor Scale and the C Harmonic Minor Scale.

C Natural Minor Scale

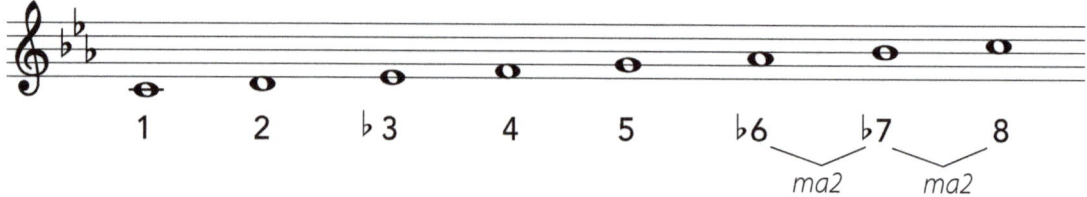

C Harmonic Minor Scale

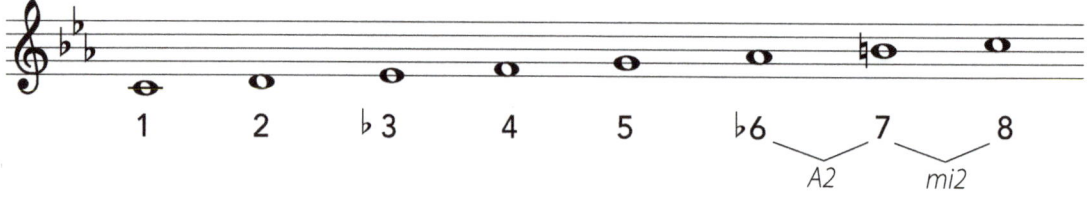

Harmonic Minor Scale Key Signatures

You might be wondering about key signatures and the Harmonic Minor Scale. Here's how this works. Contemporary compositions are not normally written 'in' Harmonic Minor. By that I mean that it's not very common for a song to be written where all the notes belong to the Harmonic Minor Scale. It is more common for a song to be primarily in Natural Minor but use Harmonic Minor only over some isolated chords in the progression.

However, if you were to write a key signature for a Harmonic Minor Scale, use the key signature for the Natural Minor Scale and apply the appropriate accidental on the staff each time the 7th appears, to make the 7th degree a major 7th.

Here are a few examples:

D Harmonic Minor Scale

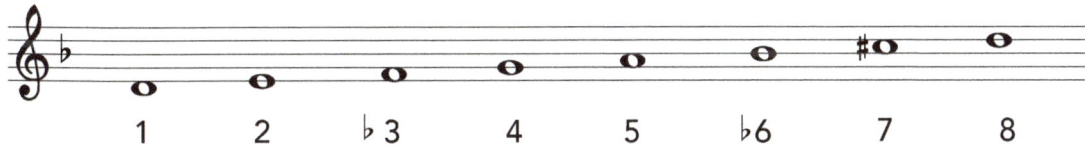

E Harmonic Minor Scale

F Harmonic Minor Scale

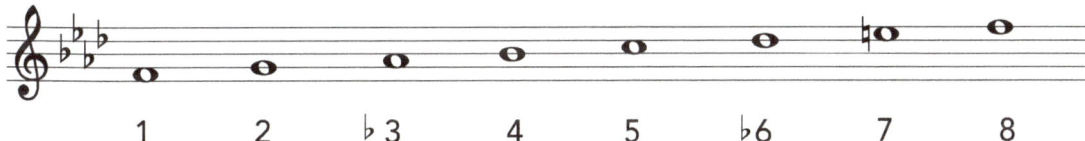

C# Harmonic Minor Scale

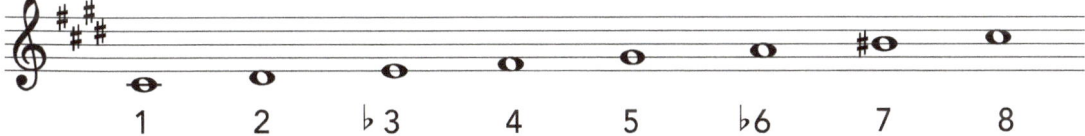

Notice in each example that the key signature is for the Natural Minor Scale, and the appropriate accidental is applied to make the 7th degree a major 7th.

Be sure you remember that a leading tone is the major 7th degree of a scale and that the leading tone pulls the listener to the tonic. That half-step attraction is powerful. The Major Scale has a major 7th scale degree so it has a leading tone. However, the Natural Minor Scale has a minor 7th scale degree so it does not have a leading tone. But if we raise the 7th scale degree of the Natural Minor Scale a half step so that it is a major 7th, we have a leading tone!

The different version of the Natural Minor Scale that results from having a major 7th is called the Harmonic Minor Scale. Note that there's an augmented 2nd between the minor 6th and major 7th.

FRETBOARD LOGIC

The Level 5 Fretboard Logic modules will focus on the Harmonic Minor Scale. You learned how to construct the Harmonic Minor Scale in the Theory Module. You learned the best way to build the scale is to raise the 7th of a Natural Minor Scale one half step. Harmonic Minor was referenced earlier in the program when you learned about the Harmonized Natural Minor Scale. You learned that often a V7 chord replaces the diatonic Vmi7 chord. Let's convert the Patterns II and IV Natural Minor Scales to Harmonic Minor Scales.

Pattern II Minor Scales

Here are the Pattern II Minor Pentatonic and Natural Minor Scales with the scale degrees numbered. In the diagram to the right, the 7th is raised from a minor 7th to a major 7th. The result is a Pattern II Harmonic Minor Scale.

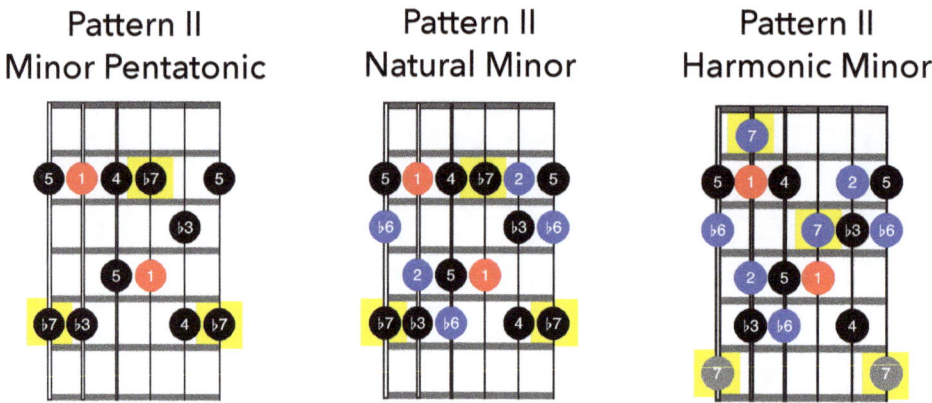

Pattern IV Minor Scales

Next, here are the Pattern IV Minor Pentatonic and Natural Minor Scales with the scale degrees numbered. In the diagram to the right, the 7th is raised from a minor 7th to a major 7th. The result is a Pattern IV Harmonic Minor Scale.

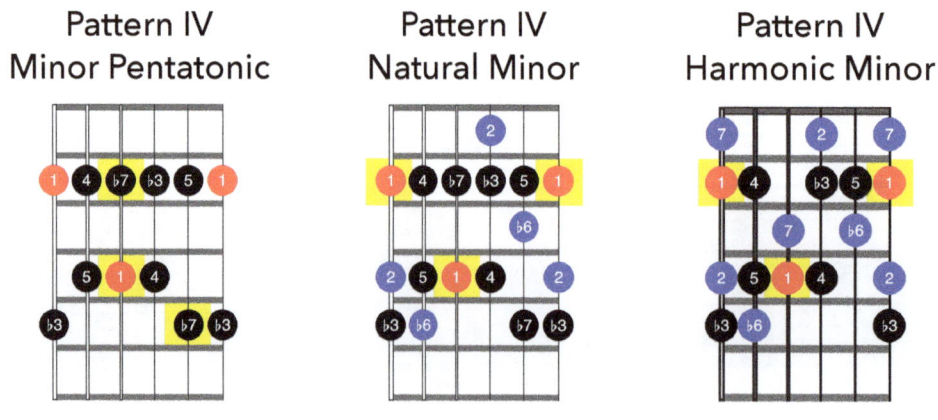

Chords

In the Theory Module you learned about other chord types: suspended chords, Add2, sometimes called Add9 or even just 2 chords, 6 chords, 6/9 chords, and power chords. In this Unit you will learn these chords and their practical application. By now, your familiarity with the Octave Shape Family Tree and the chord interval formulas presented in Theory make it possible for you to figure out these chords without any assistance.

Even though I will present many of them here, I encourage you to go through each of the five octave shapes and test what you've learned so far. By this, I mean that you should figure out the voicing for each of these chord types within each of the octave shapes, according to the formulas, and then check your results with voicings presented here.

One important goal of this course is for you to be self-reliant on the fretboard. The combination of theory knowledge and command of the octave shape system is powerful. Don't underestimate it. The Theory modules teach you the 'why', plus the formulas for scales, arpeggios, and chords. The Fretboard Logic modules teach you the 'how' and 'where' on the fretboard. To help you develop self-sufficiency when it comes to several chord types, let's do a simple chord-fingering exercise.

Chord-Fingering Exercise

In this exercise, you will be presented with five patterns of either a triad or 7th chord, and you will have to come up with a fingering for various chord types that are derived from those chords. For example, if you are presented with this:

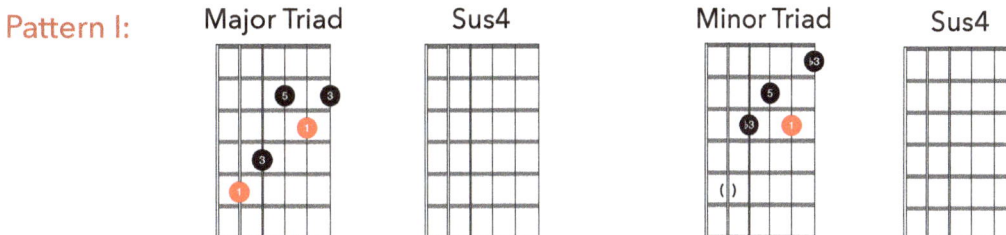

Pattern I: Major Triad   Sus4   Minor Triad   Sus4

You would write in the fingering for a Pattern I Sus4 chord based on a major triad, and then a minor triad, and draw a line between the notes that are different, to highlight how the Sus4 chord is different from the major or minor triad.

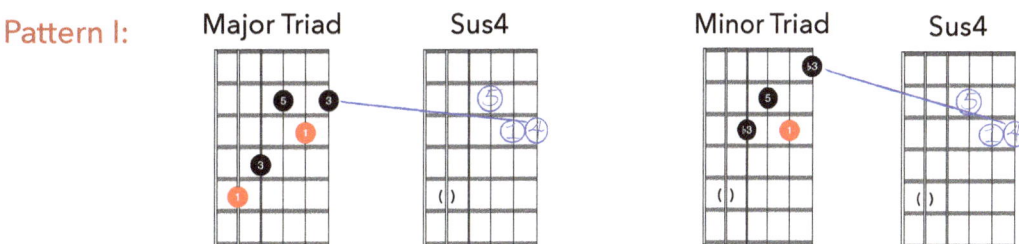

Pattern I: Major Triad   Sus4   Minor Triad   Sus4

Finally, play each chord in the set so you can hear the relationship between them. Try this exercise in all octave shapes.

Sus4 Chords

The most common suspended chord is the Sus4 or Sus chord. As we just mentioned in the last Module, a Sus4 chord is built by replacing the 3rd in a major or minor triad with a perfect 4th. The root-position closed voicing is spelled Root-perfect 4th-perfect 5th. There are different voicings depending on the octave shape. The common chord symbol is Csus or Csus4. Know that if you see just 'Sus' written on a chord chart, it means Sus4. Csus means Csus4.

Sus4 Chord Exercise

Take a moment to figure out the sus4 chord voicings for each of the five octave shapes. Then play each of these voicings to get a sense of their relationship to the other chords and to hear what they sound like. Once you have come up with your own voicings, you can check the answer key in the Appendix to see whether you came up with the same fingerings.

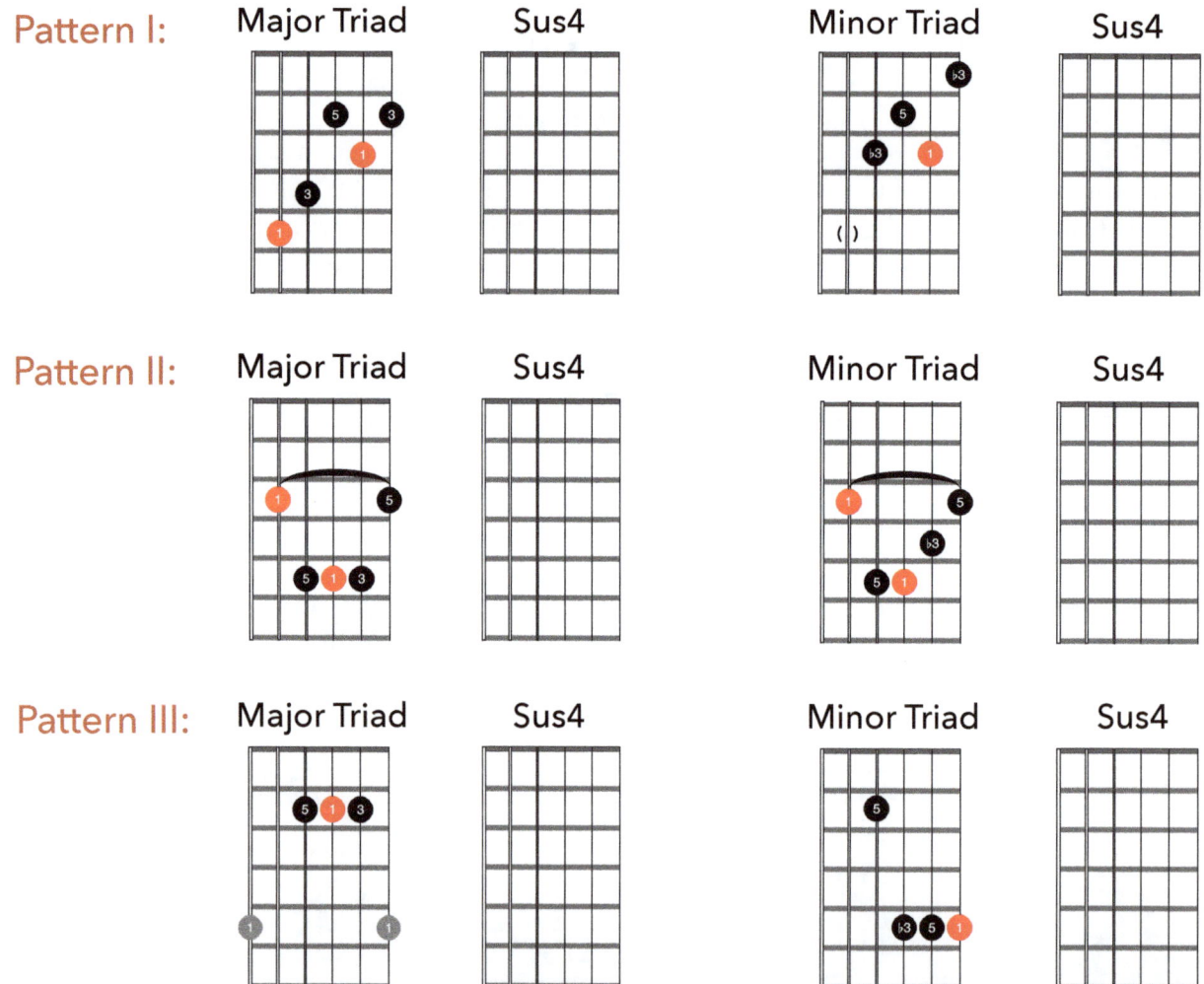

Fretboard Biology   Level 5 • Unit 1: Fretboard Logic   19

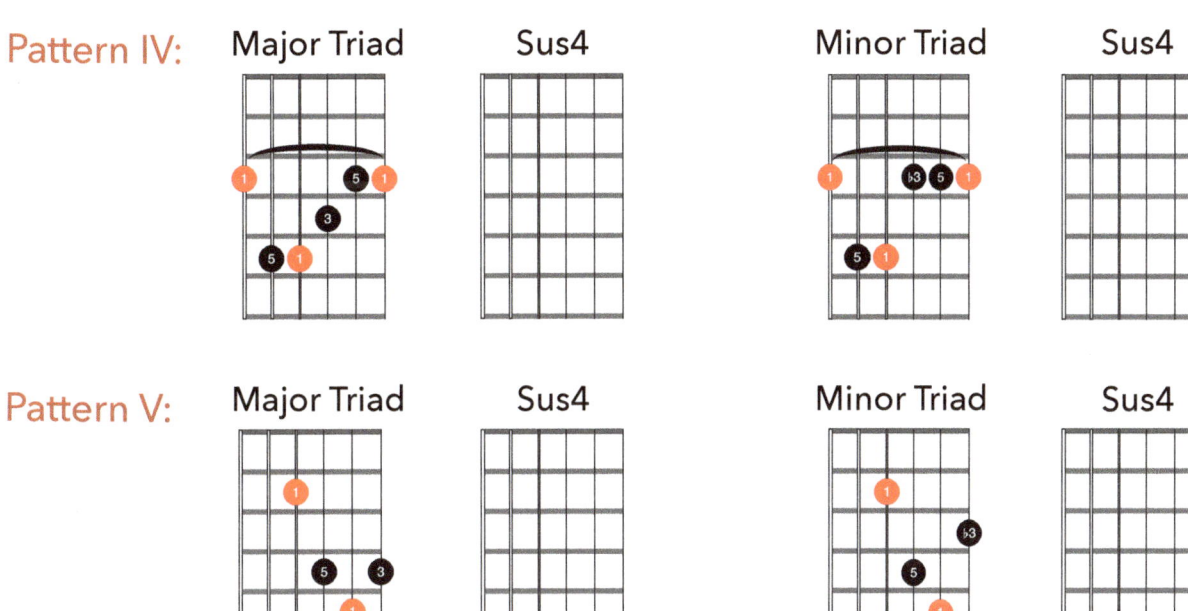

(Answer key on page 307)

Dom7sus4

A Dom7sus4 chord is built by replacing the third in a dominant 7 chord with a perfect 4th. The root-position closed voicing is spelled Root-perfect 4th-perfect 5th-minor 7th. There are different voicings depending on the octave shape. The chord symbol is C7sus or C7sus4.

7sus4 Chord Exercise

Take a moment to figure out the 7sus4 chord voicings for each of the five octave shapes. Once you have figured them out, play each of these voicings to get a sense of their sound and how the fingerings relate to other chords. Finally, when you have come up with your own voicings, check the answer key in the Appendix.

Pattern I: Dom 7   7sus4   Minor 7   7sus4

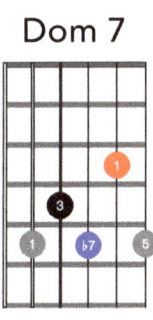 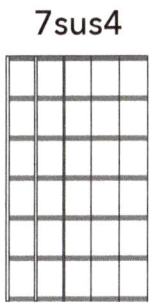 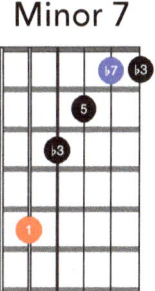 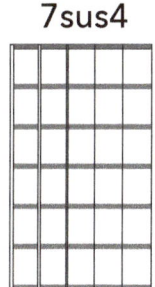

20 Level 5 • Unit 1: Fretboard Logic Fretboard Biology

Pattern II: Dom 7 7sus4 Minor 7 7sus4

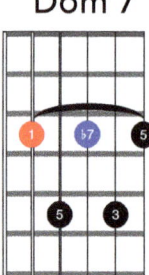 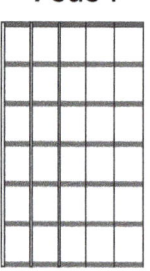 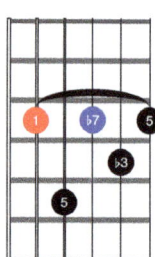 

Pattern III: Dom 7 7sus4 Minor 7 7sus4

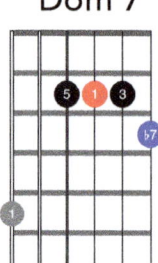 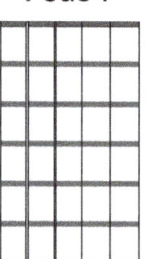 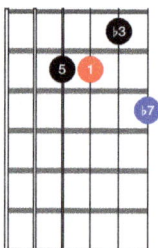 

Pattern IV: Dom 7 7sus4 Minor 7 7sus4

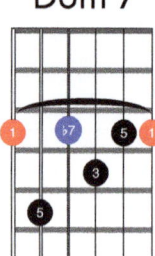  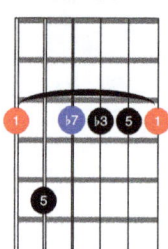 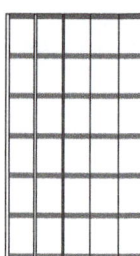

Pattern V: Dom 7 7sus4 Minor 7 7sus4

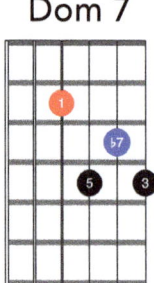 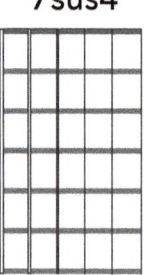 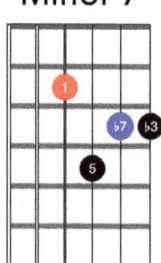 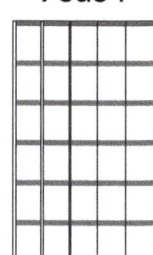

(Answer key on page 308)

Sus2 Chords

The common interpretation of a Sus2 chord is for a major 2nd to replace the 3rd of a triad. The root-position closed voicing is spelled Root-major 2nd-5th. There are different voicings depending on the octave shape. Sus2 chords can be used in a major or minor context because they have no 3rd.

Sus2 Chord Exercise

Take a moment to figure out the Sus2 chord voicings for each of the five octave shapes. I strongly suggest that you first try to figure these out yourself before looking at the diagrams in the Appendix.

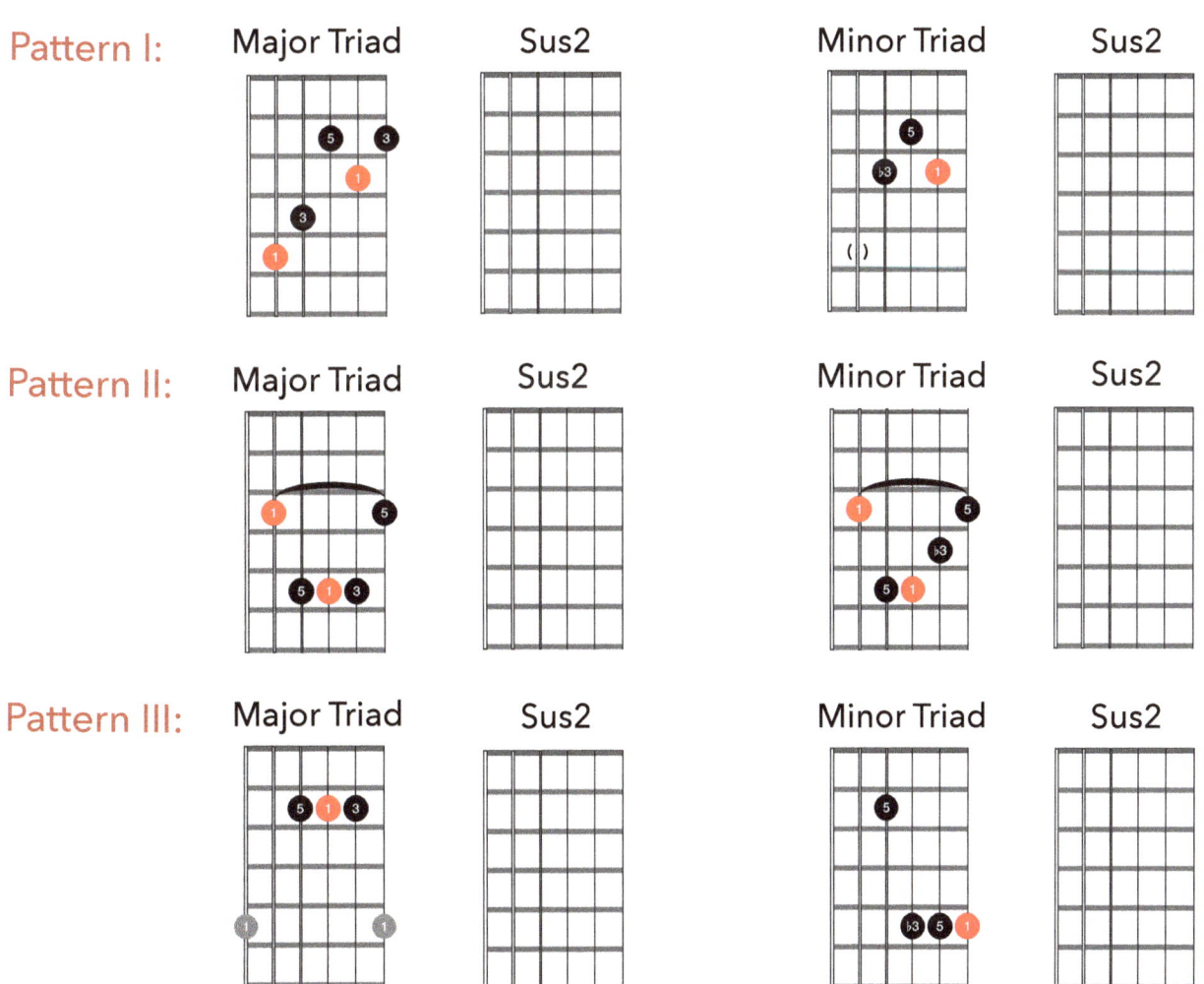

Pattern IV: Major Triad   Sus2   Minor Triad   Sus2

Pattern V: Major Triad   Sus2   Minor Triad   Sus2

(Answer key on page 309)

Sus6/4 Chords

You learned about this chord in the Rock Rhythm Guitar modules in an example associated with the Rolling Stones. In a Sus6/4 chord, the 4th replaces the 3rd and the 6th replaces the 5th in sort of a double suspension. The voicing is normally followed by a major triad.

The root-position closed voicing is spelled Root-perfect 4th-major 6th. The voicing varies depending on the octave shape. When it resolves to a major triad, the 4th resolves down a half step to the major 3rd and the major 6th resolves down a whole step to the 5th.

Sus6/4 Chord Exercise

Take a moment to figure out the Sus6/4 chord voicings for each of the five octave shapes. I strongly suggest that you first try to figure these out yourself before looking at the diagrams in the Appendix.

And remember that the Sus6/4 chord is sometimes written as a slash chord, as was discussed in the Theory Module. Think of Csus6/4. It would be C (the root), F (the Sus4), and A (the Sus6). If you look at it a little differently you'll see that it's an F triad, F, A, and C, with the C or the 5th in the bass. That makes it a 2nd inversion F chord, F/C.

Fretboard Biology — Level 5 • Unit 1: Fretboard Logic

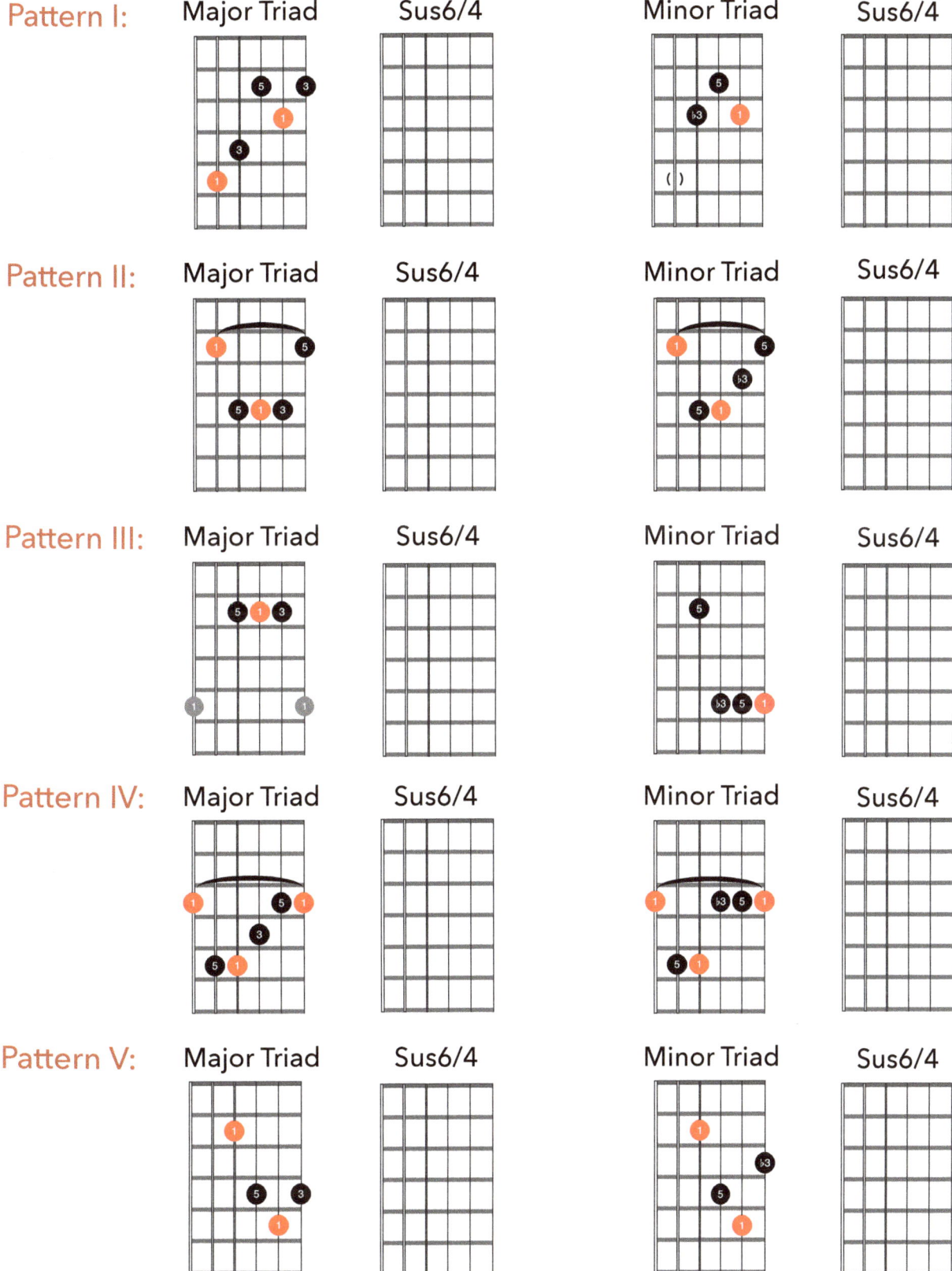

(Answer key on page 310)

Sus2/4 Chords

In a Sus2/4 chord, the 4th replaces the 3rd as does the 2 (major 2nd). It's spelled Root-major 2nd-perfect 4th. The voicing is normally followed by a major triad.

When it resolves to a major triad, the 4th resolves down a half step to the major 3rd and the major 2nd resolves down a whole step to the Root—even though the root is probably being played in another voice in a lower octave. There are different voicings depending on the octave shape.

Sus2/4 Chord Exercise

Take a moment to figure out the Sus2/4 chord voicings for each of the five octave shapes on your own before looking at the diagrams in the Appendix.

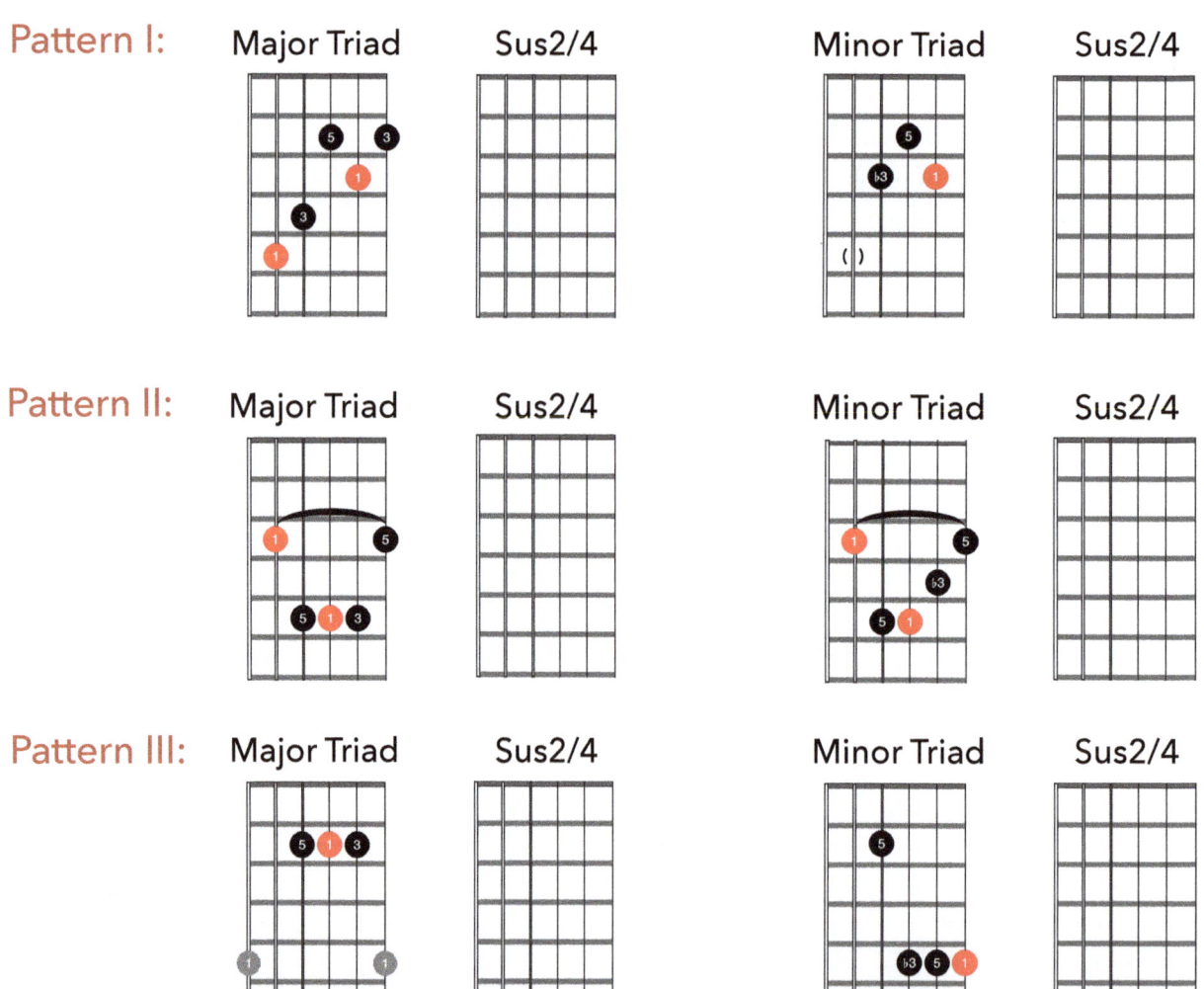

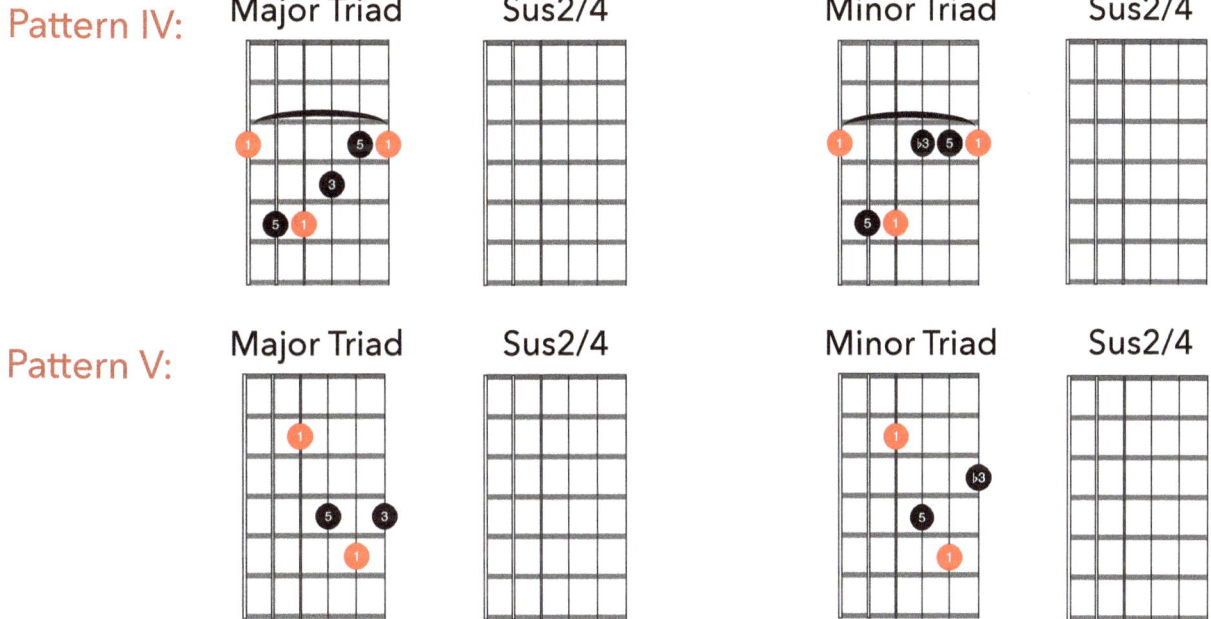

(Answer key on page 311)

2 Chords (Add2)

Add2, Add9, or a chord just labeled '2' are different ways to label the same chord. The Add2 chord is a triad only, with a major 2nd (major 9th) added: Just add a major 2nd to a major or minor triad. For major, the root-position closed voicing is spelled Root-major 2nd-major 3rd-perfect 5th. Possible chord symbols are Cadd2, Cadd9, or simply C2. For minor, the root-position closed voicing is spelled Root-major 2nd-minor 3rd-perfect 5th. Possible chord symbols are Cmi add2, Cmi add9, or simply Cmi2.

2 Chord Exercise

Take a moment to figure out the Add2 chord voicings for each of the five octave shapes on your own before looking at the diagrams in the Appendix.

An important side note: the Add2 or Add9 chords should not be confused with Ma9, Dom9, or Mi9 chords. Those contain a 7th, while the Add2 or Add9 chords do not. And they sound remarkably different. You will learn those later in this course.

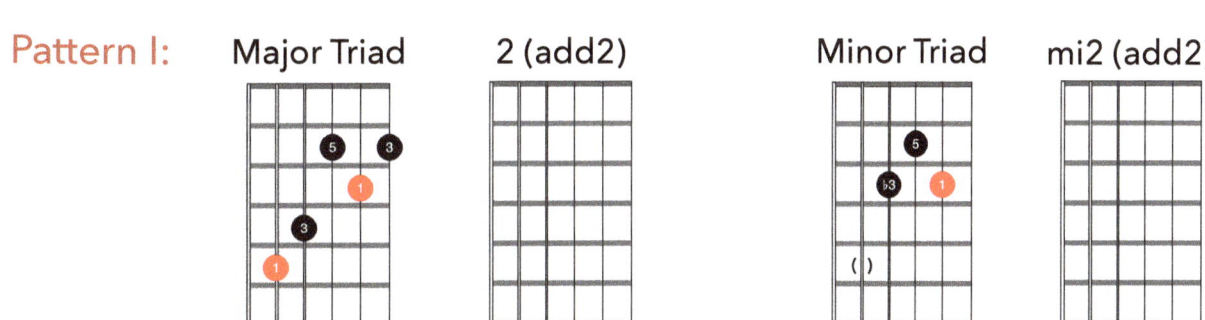

Pattern II: Major Triad   2 (add2)   Minor Triad   mi2 (add2)

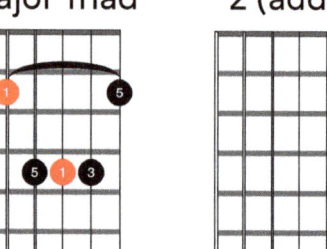
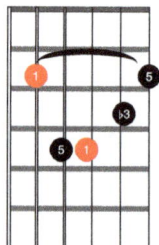
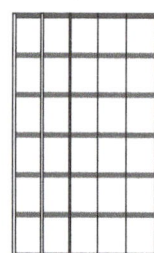

Pattern III: Major Triad   2 (add2)   Minor Triad   mi2 (add2)

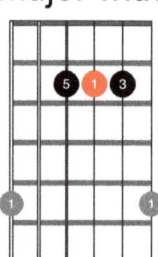
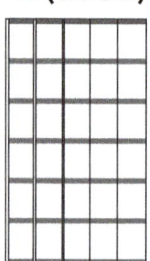
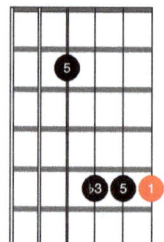
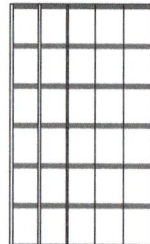

Pattern IV: Major Triad   2 (add2)   Minor Triad   mi2 (add2)

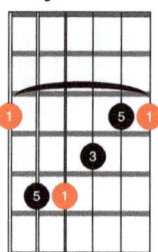
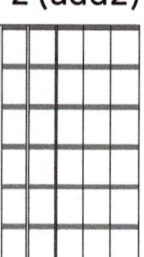
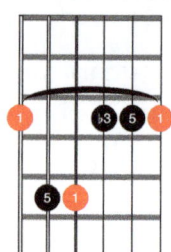
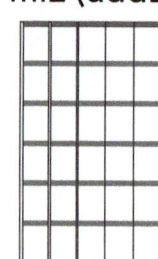

Pattern V: Major Triad   2 (add2)   Minor Triad   mi2 (add2)

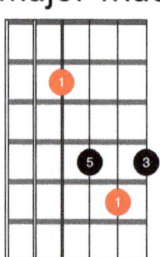
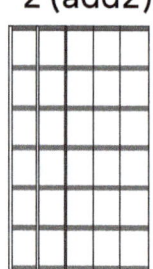
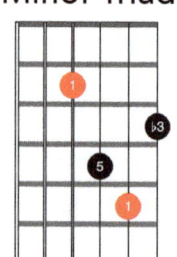
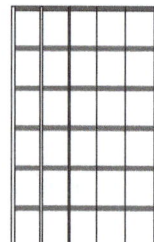

(Answer key on page 312)

6 Chords

Add a major 6th to a major or minor triad to construct 6 chord. For major, the root-position closed voicing is spelled Root-major 3rd-perfect 5th-major 6th. There are different voicings depending on the octave shape. For minor, the root-position closed voicing is spelled Root-minor 3rd-perfect 5th-major 6th.

6 chords should not be confused with Ma13, Dom13, or Mi13. Those all have a 7th. In all cases, the added 6th is a major 6th, even on the minor 6 chord.

6 Chord Exercise

Figure these out yourself before looking at the diagrams in the Appendix.

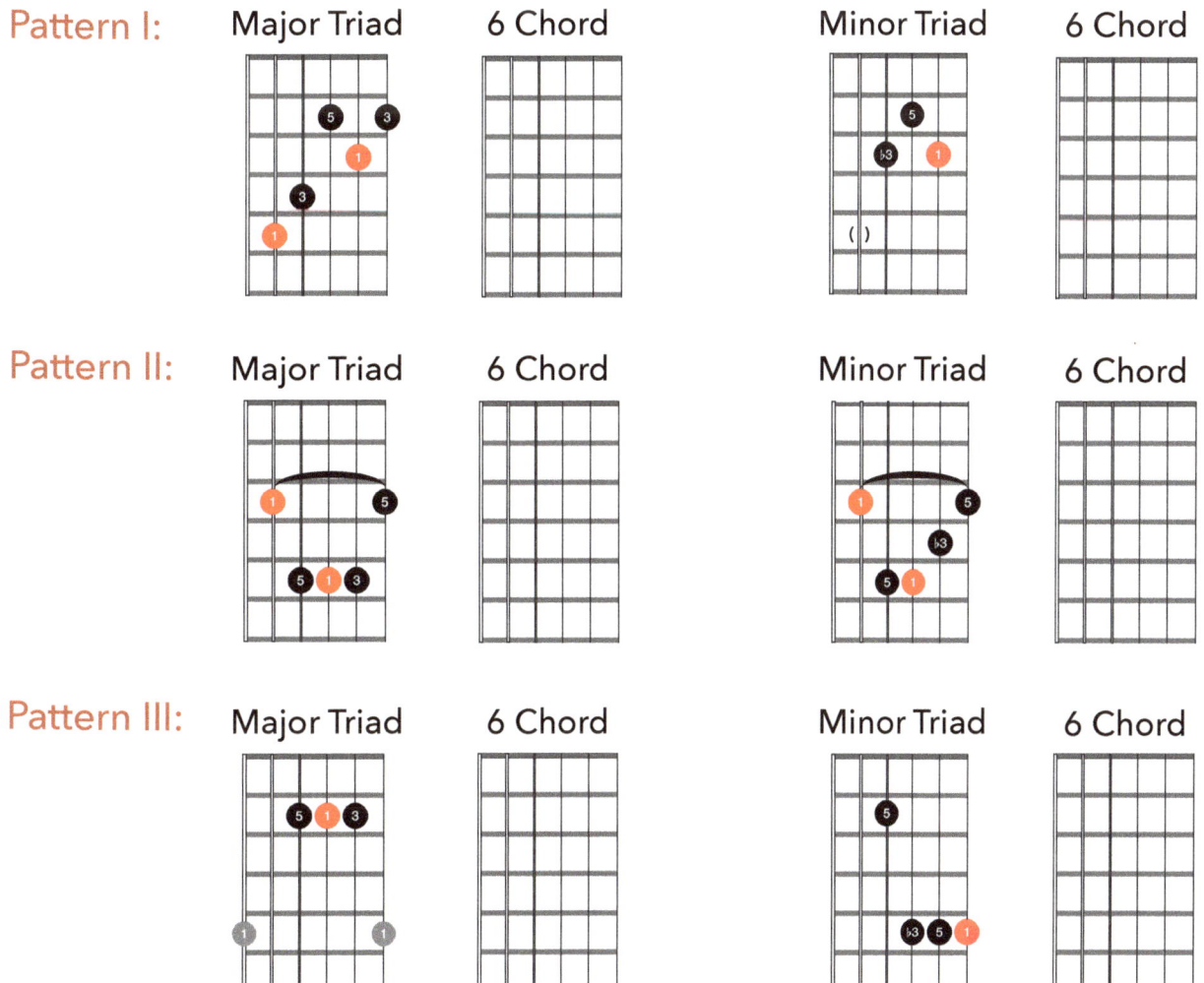

Pattern IV: Major Triad   6 Chord   Minor Triad   6 Chord

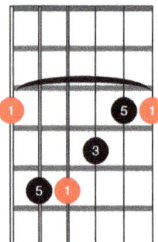 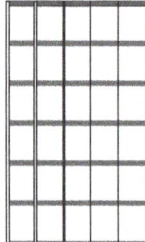 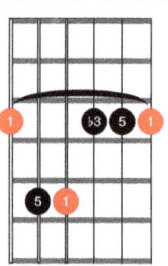 

Pattern V: Major Triad   6 Chord   Minor Triad   6 Chord

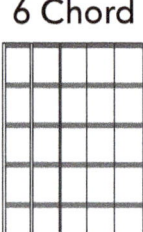 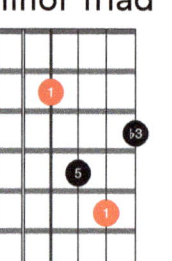 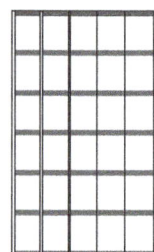

(Answer key on page 313)

6/9 Chords

Add a major 6th and major 9th to a major or minor triad to construct a 6/9 chord. Again, remember that a 9th is the same as a 2nd. For major the root-position closed voicing is spelled Root-major 3rd-perfect 5th-major 6th-major 9th. Voicings vary depending on the octave shape. For minor, the root-position closed voicing is spelled Root-minor 3rd-perfect 5th-major 6th-major 9th.

6/9 Chord Exercise

Figure these out yourself before looking at the diagrams in the Appendix.

Pattern I: Major Triad   6/9 Chord   Minor Triad   6/9 Chord

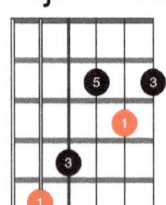 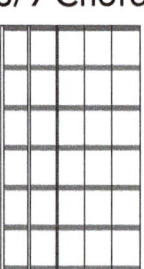 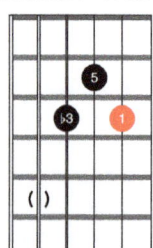 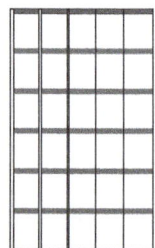

Fretboard Biology — Level 5 • Unit 1: Fretboard Logic

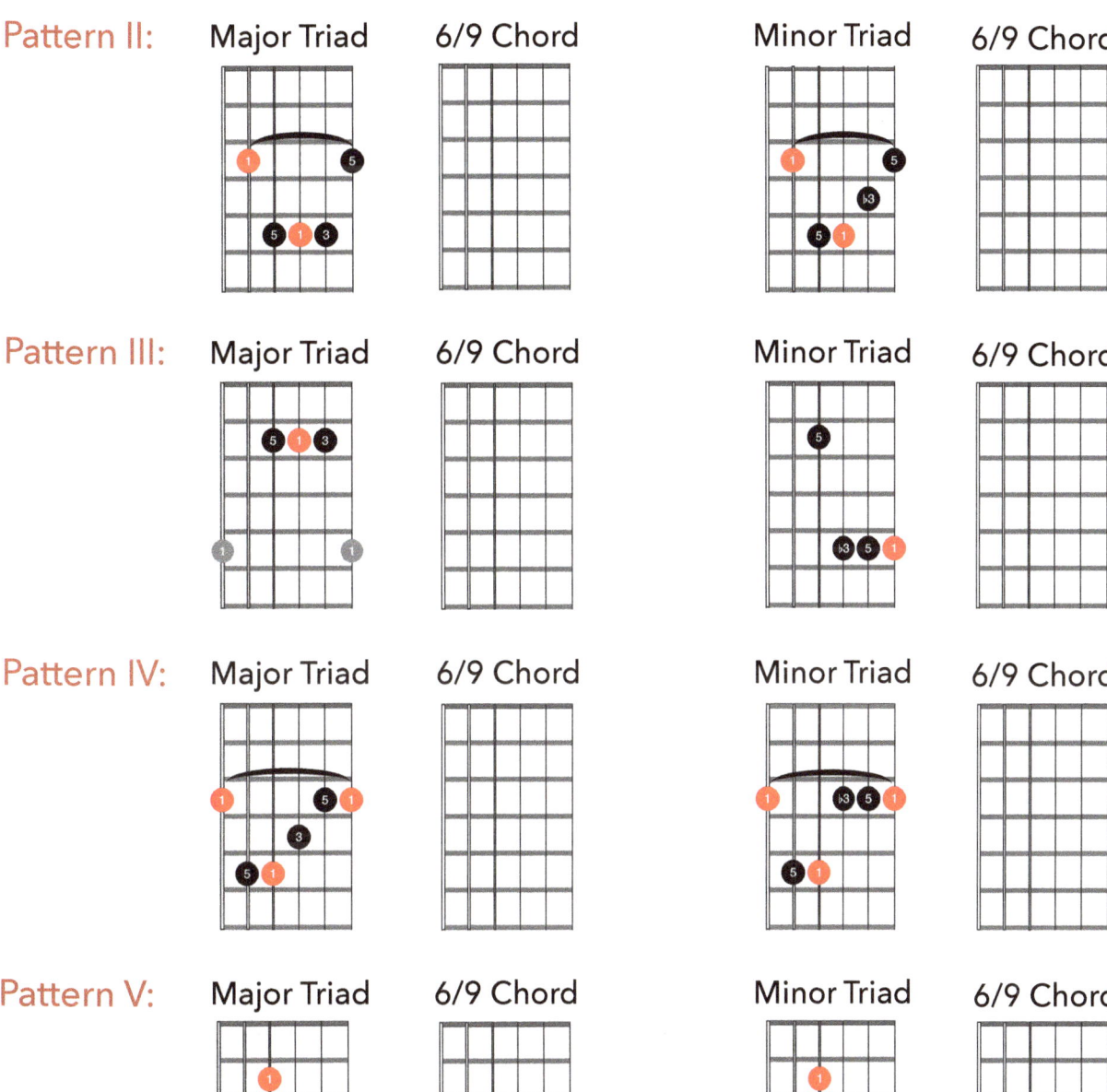

(Answer key on page 314)

Power Chords

Power chords contain only the root and perfect 5th. These two chord tones may be repeated in multiple octaves. The common chord symbol is C5. The 'old way' power chords were notated was to write 'power chords' above a section on the chart and then write regular chord symbols.

Power Chord Exercise

Figure these out yourself before looking at the diagrams in the Appendix.

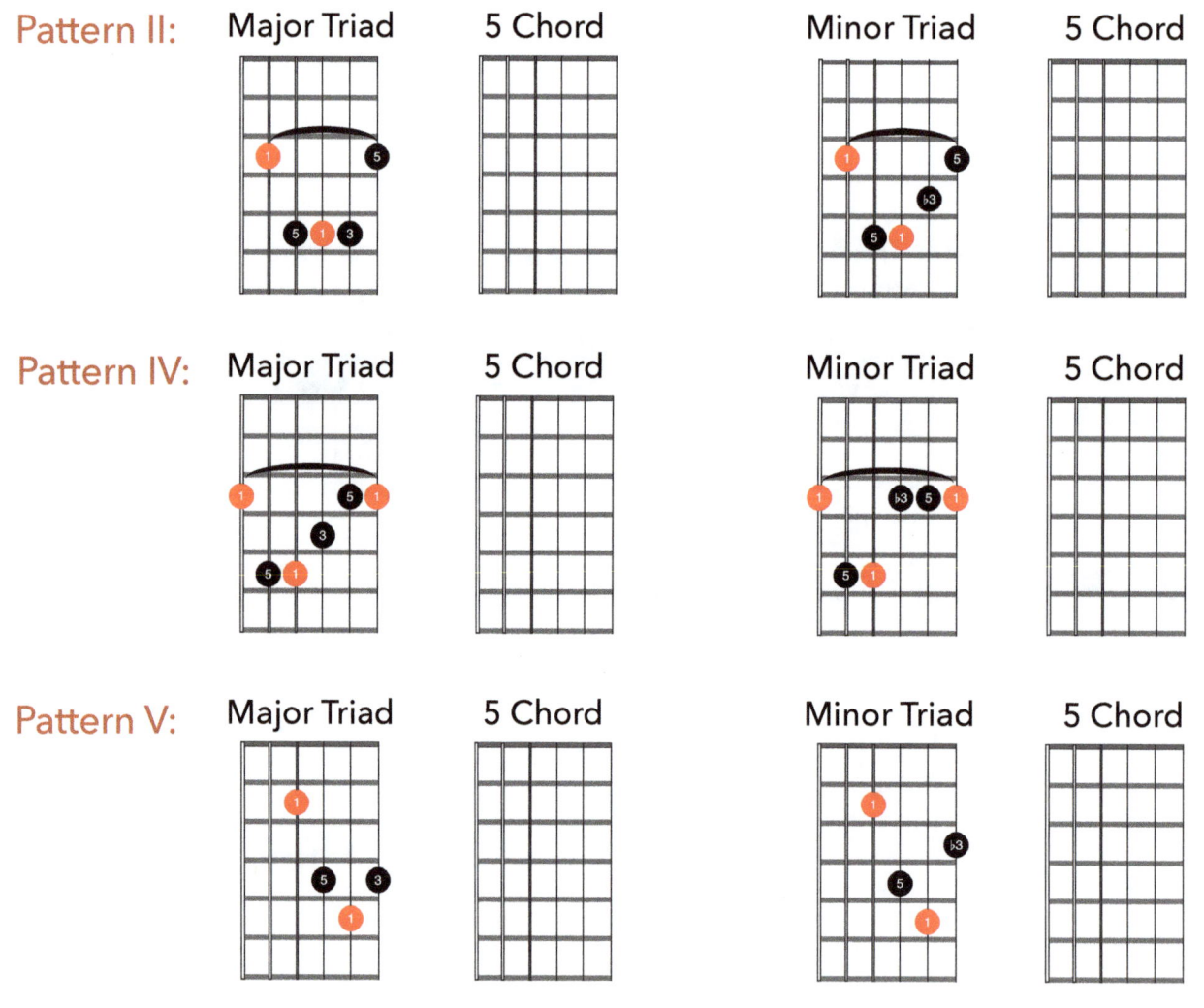

(Answer key on page 315)

RHYTHM GUITAR

Latin Rhythm Guitar

'Latin Music' as a genre label is a broad generalization and is better labeled as Afro-Latin music. This next series of five Rhythm Guitar Modules is an introduction to the two Afro-Latin music styles that have influenced Western popular music the most: Afro-Brazilian and Afro-Caribbean (sometimes labeled 'Salsa'). These two broad style categories are different from one another and each deserves significant study beyond what these Modules provide; these Modules are designed to be merely introductions.

Remember that all genres represent a culture or subculture and to even approach authenticity you must invest a lot of time to listening, studying, and performing. The blended culture in America has mixed Afro-Latin music with styles like Rock, Funk, and Jazz, often without much thought about the purity of each Afro-Latin genre.

Afro-Brazilian

We begin with Afro-Brazilian music. The next few units focus on the two grooves that have influenced American popular music the most: Samba and Bossa Nova. Samba predates the Bossa Nova, but for study purposes the Bossa Nova, or just 'Bossa', as it's normally called, is introduced first. A Bossa is slower than a Samba and felt in four. A Samba is generally faster than a Bossa and is felt in 2/2 (or 'cut time').

Let's begin by learning to play a Bossa comping pattern that's used when playing in a rhythm section. Take a look.

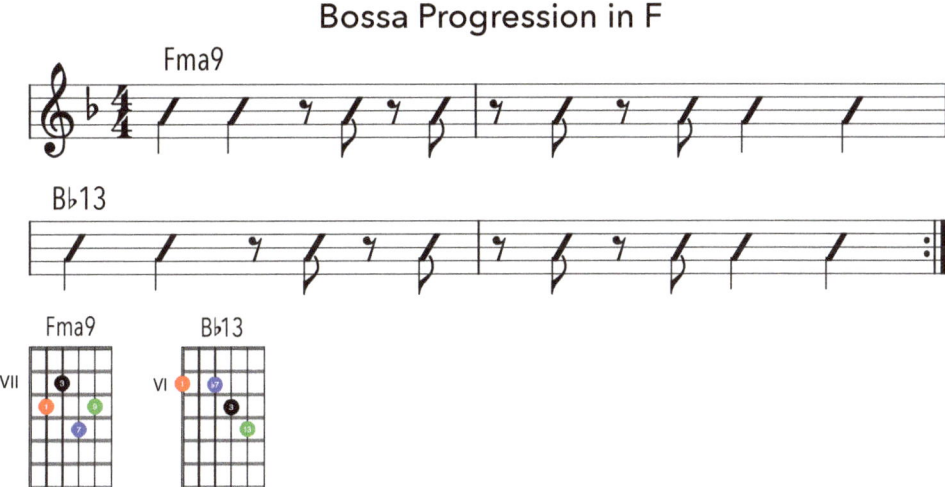

This four-bar example is in the key of F and uses a Pattern II Fma9 voicing and a Pattern IV B♭13 voicing. Even though we haven't formally learned Ma9 and 13th chords, you have played examples that use them in previous Rhythm Guitar modules.

The rhythm pattern in this example is a good starting place for Bossa comping, but variations are common. The part played in this example would be used when playing with a rhythm section.

Your picking hand can play this two ways:
- Bare picking hand, using fingers 1, 2, and 3
- Using a pick playing all downstrokes

Let's discuss the detail of each hand. With your fretting hand, there are two choices. You can play the entire four-note version shown in the diagram or you can focus on the three-string set of the 2nd, 3rd, and 4th strings. Be aware that your fretting hand can just avoid the notes on the 5th and 6th strings if you prefer.

It's not a requirement, but it is common to omit roots that are voiced on the 5th and 6th stings. This helps keep the lower register clearer for the bass part.

Focus on the 2nd, 3rd, and 4th Strings

Fma9

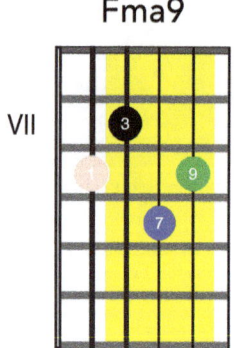

Bb13

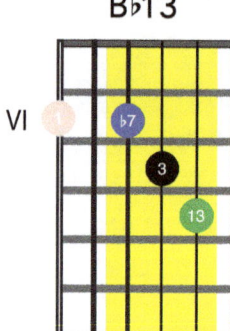

Here are the two ways to use your picking hand. First, learn the 'fingers-only' technique:
- Hold your 1st, 2nd, and 3rd fingers in a soft-claw formation and curl your knuckles slightly.
- Place your 1st finger on the 4th string, 2nd finger on the 3rd string, and 3rd finger on the 2nd string.
- Place your fingertips slightly under the strings so that the strings ring when you pull up.

It may take some time to develop a touch for this articulation.

Next, play the part with a flat pick. I suggest using all downstrokes for the sake of consistency. You can certainly use alternate picking but I find I can get a more consistent sound with all downstrokes.

Again, the part played in this example is appropriate for use with a rhythm section. Regardless of the chords played in a song, these picking-hand techniques are applicable. This rhythm pattern is a place to start and can be varied if the musical situation calls for it. There is so much beautiful Bossa Nova music and a simple online search can open the door to a whole world of great music. In the next Rhythm Guitar Module, you'll learn to play a Bossa Nova pattern in a situation when there is no bass player.

CHART READING

In this series of Chart Reading modules, you will learn some important skills for reading chord charts. A chord chart is a minimal representation of a song that usually fits on one or two pages. It usually has these components:

- Title
- Style
- Key signature
- Time signature
- Form
- Chord changes
- Any rhythm figures played by the whole band
- Any signature bass, guitar, or keyboard riffs

If you can read and write a chord chart, you can learn songs faster and have a permanent record for future use. I have literally thousands of charts filed away from hundreds of gigs, bands, and shows. Having them cataloged and stored away is a huge time saver. If I'm preparing for a show and already have the song charted out from a gig a year ago or even 10 or 20 years ago, I don't have to start from the beginning when learning it.

Guitarists are notoriously bad readers, or, in most cases, can't read at all. It's just not the way most guitar players learn to play. Because of this, guitar players are usually intimidated by the very idea of reading. Reading a chord chart is the minimal reading skill any musician should have and it's well within your reach, even if you have never tried to read.

Reading a chart and writing a chart are two very important skills and are huge time savers. Level 5 delves into chart reading. After you have some knowledge and experience with reading, learning the rules for writing charts is much easier.

Imagine this scenario: You play in a band and the leader schedules a two-hour rehearsal. The leader instructs the band to learn five songs. Each musician listens to the songs and learns their parts on their own at home. Then everyone shows up at the rehearsal to put the songs together. Because there's no common road map for the songs, rehearsing the songs becomes tedious and maybe even contentious because each musician has learned the songs slightly differently or to different degrees of detail. There may be disputes about some of the chords or parts. Working on specific sections is challenging because there is no common agreement about how the songs are organized. Precious time is wasted trying to agree on the sections, transitions, or other important components of the songs. By the time the frustrating two-hour rehearsal has ended, only two or maybe three of the five songs are rehearsed, and those are not very good.

Now imagine a very different scenario: The band leader instructs the band to learn five songs, but in this scenario, the band leader provides each musician with a basic chord chart. Each musician listens to the songs and learns their parts at home using the chart for each song as a guide. The chart provides all the components listed above: the title, style, key signature, time signature, form, chord changes, any rhythm figures played by the whole band, and any signature bass, guitar, or keyboard riffs. Everyone shows up at the rehearsal to put the songs together. Because the musicians are all using the same chart as a guide, rehearsing the songs is efficient. The road map, that is, the form, is the same for everyone. If the sections of the songs are labeled with rehearsal letters like A, B, C, and so on, the band leader can quickly direct the band to a particular section.

If each musician has done their homework using the charts as guides, rehearsing goes smoothly. The leader can rehearse the sections, transitions, or other important components of each song. By the time the two-hour rehearsal has ended, all five songs are rehearsed.

You should be able to read a chord chart and use it to learn the song.

Let's discuss two terms that need some clarification: reading and sight reading. These are related but different skills. A couple of other terms also need definition.

Reading

Reading music means that you are able to decipher notated music and transfer that information to your instrument. You may not be fast at it but you are able to associate written music with your instrument. Having this skill opens many doors. You are able to learn notated music whether you have heard it or not. If a leader asks whether you can read a chord chart, you can say yes.

Reading a chord chart is one part of reading. Reading single notes or lines on guitar is another part of reading. A lot more guitarists learn to read chord charts than single note lines, and that is understandable.

Sight Reading

Sight reading music means you can read and perform music simultaneously. This skill requires a lot of practice. Very few guitarists are skilled sight readers. It's just not the way most guitarists learn. But in larger cities where there are show gigs, theatre gigs, and certain types of session work, there is demand for guitarists who can sight read.

Lead Sheets

Sometimes there is confusion about what a chord chart is versus a lead sheet. Lead sheets have the melody line notated and the chord symbols written above the staff. There are instrumental lead sheets that you might see in the Real Book and there are vocal lead sheets that include the lyric below the staff.

Chord Chart

A chord chart is what was described earlier in this Module. It essentially shows the chords and the form. The Chart Reading modules in this Level are dedicated to reading charts but not to writing them properly.

You will see some well-written charts in your life but you will probably see far more that are poorly written. It is important for me to present examples that are realistic, and that includes things that are technically wrong. There are many situations where the creator of the chart gets 'creative' in their notation. There are often special notes written in the chart that don't fall into any special category. There's also a lot of innocent misuse of the tools you learn in these modules.

The message is simple: Learn what is presented as 'correct' in this course but understand that in real life, most charts will not be written 'by the book', so keep an open mind and be on your toes.

Fretboard Biology — Level 5 • Unit 1: Improvisation

IMPROVISATION

The focus of the Level 5 Improvisation modules is on the use of the Harmonic Minor Scale. In this Unit's Fretboard Logic Module you learned the Patterns II and IV Harmonic Minor Scale. You recall that the Harmonic Minor Scale is most easily understood as a Natural Minor Scale with a raised 7th scale degree. In other words, the scale has a major 7th, which you know is a leading tone. Because the Natural Minor Scale is a derivative of the Minor Pentatonic Scale, the Harmonic Minor Scale can also be referenced to the minor pentatonic shell. The 7th is different, but the general shape is the same.

In this Module, you will learn how the Harmonic Minor Scale is used as the source of notes in a key-center way. We will start with a two-bar progression in the key of A minor. A quick analysis shows Ami as Imi and E7 as V7.

Progression in A Minor

The A Harmonic Minor Scale is appropriate for both chords, although in practice G#, the leading tone and major 7th, is the 'money note' for the E7. It is one of the important notes to target as the first note played on the E7, along with the other chord tones of E7, which are E, B, and D. I won't say to NOT play G# on the Ami; it will sound fine if you do. But you can consider it like the punch line of a joke to be delivered at the most effective time, which is on E7.

Locate the Pattern IV A Harmonic Minor Scale in 5th position.

Pattern IV A Harmonic Minor Scale

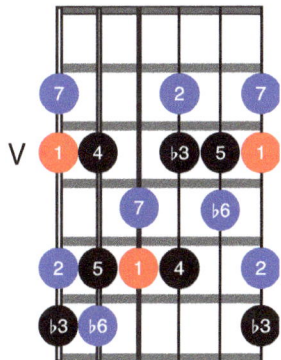

To begin, run the scale ascending and descending to get a feel for it. Next, create motifs and improvise using the storytelling devices you have used since Level 1. Experiment with avoiding G# over the Ami chord and withholding it for the E7.

Next, locate the Pattern II A Harmonic Minor Scale in 12th position.

Pattern II A Harmonic Minor Scale

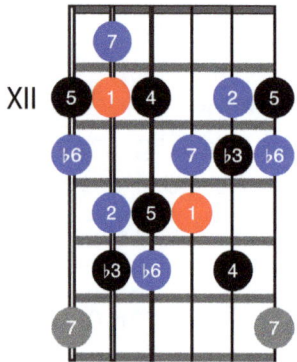

As before, run the scale ascending and descending and then create motifs and improvise using the storytelling devices you know. And again, experiment with avoiding G# over the Ami chord and withholding it for the E7.

Add this progression to your practice routine. Your goal is to move freely within the Harmonic Minor Scale, and be in control of when you use the leading tone. The primary goal of combining Theory knowledge with Improvisation is to remove any mystery about what notes you can choose when soloing over a single chord or group of chords.

The information in this Module was presented to you in Patterns II and IV because those are the places that are most comfortable for most guitarists. But know that these concepts should eventually be learned in other patterns as well.

Level 5 Unit 1 • Improv Demo

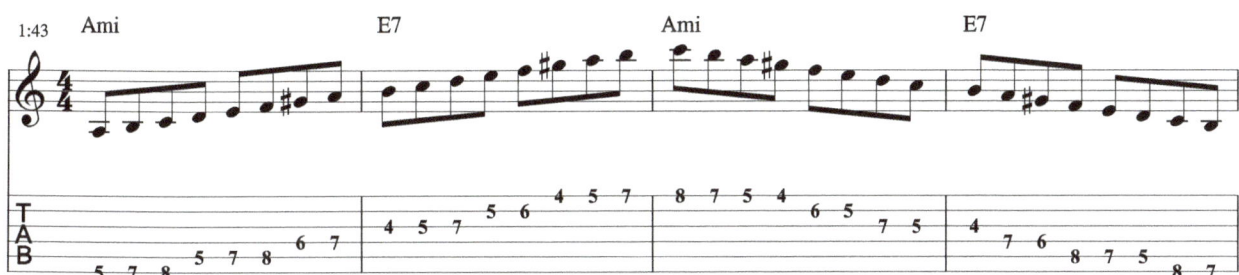
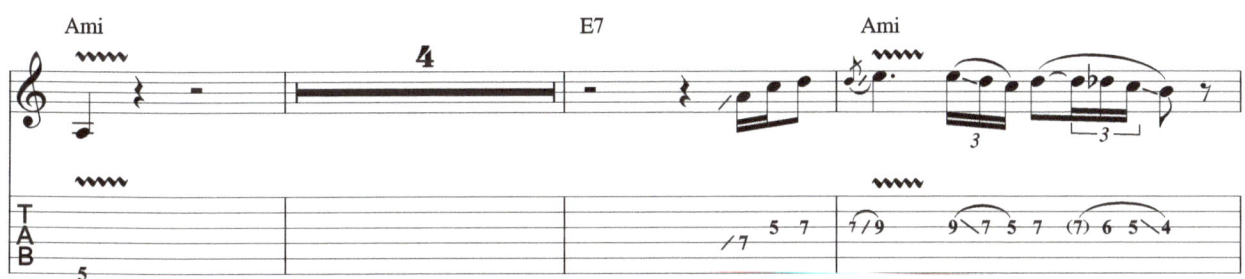
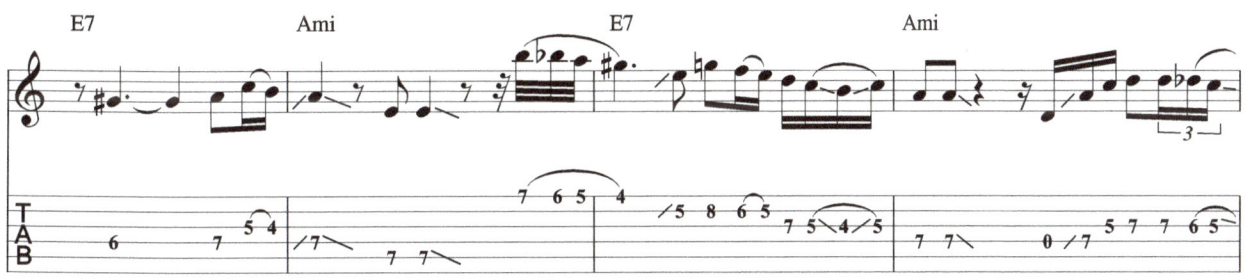
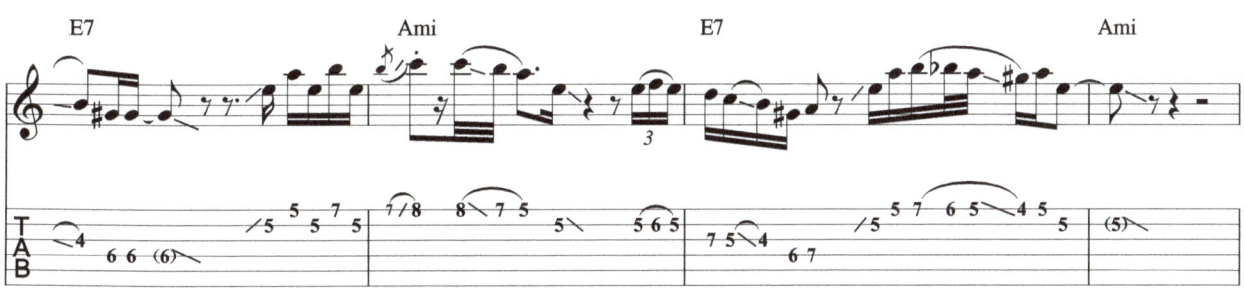

PRACTICE

Theory

- ❑ Go to the tabs below the Theory video on the website and complete the quiz.
- ❑ Learn to spell suspended chords, Add2 / Add9 chords, 6 chords, 6/9 chords, and power chords.
- ❑ Learn the Harmonic Minor Scale.

Fretboard Logic

- ❑ Learn the Pattern II and Pattern IV Harmonic Minor Scales.
- ❑ Go through the chord fingering excerise to see if you can figure out the chord voicings. Check your answers in the Appendix.

Rhythm Guitar

- ❑ Learn the basics of the Bossa Nova genre.
- ❑ Practice playing the Bossa progression in F.

Chart Reading

- ❑ Understand the basic components of a chart.

Improvisation

- ❑ Practice playing solos over the progression in A minor using the Pattern IV and Pattern II A Harmonic Minor Scales.

UNIT 2

Learning Modules

> **Theory** - Harmonizing the Harmonic Minor Scale with Triads, Minor Modal Interchange

> **Fretboard Logic** - Patterns I, III, and V Harmonic Minor Scales, Augmented Triads, Augmented Triad Arpeggios

> **Rhythm Guitar** - Bossa Progression in A Minor

> **Chart Reading** - Basic Information: Title, Tempo, Style, Clef, Key Signature, and Time Signature

> **Improvisation** - Soloing with the Harmonic Minor Scale over the V7 Chord

> **Practice** - Continue Practice Routine Development

THEORY

In Unit 1 you learned to build a Harmonic Minor Scale. The easiest way to think of it is as a Natural Minor Scale with a raised 7th. But to fully understand how the Harmonic Minor Scale is used, you need to harmonize it. Remember what harmonizing a scale means? It means to build chords on each scale degree of a scale using only notes from the scale. Harmonizing the Harmonic Minor Scale reveals some interesting and useful alternatives to the chords from the harmonized Natural Minor Scale.

Let's first harmonize the Harmonic Minor Scale with triads. Look at the C Harmonic Minor Scale. The scale degrees are numbered.

C Harmonic Minor Scale

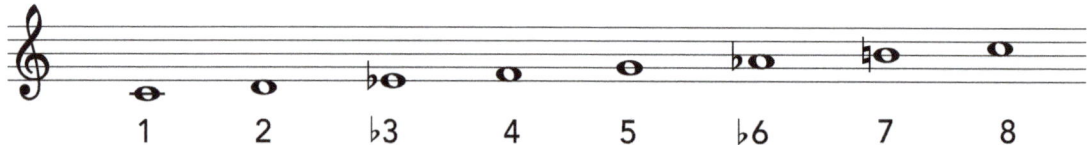

Next, let's harmonize the C Harmonic Minor Scale with triads by building a diatonic 3rd and 5th above each scale tone. You have harmonized enough scales by this point and don't need a step-by-step explanation. Remember that you build a triad on each scale degree using only notes from the scale. Next, determine the quality of each triad by comparing the intervals in each triad to the triad formulas.

Let's study the analysis of each chord.

C Harmonic Minor Scale Harmonized with Triads

Remember that chord symbols are represented with Roman numerals followed by the quality. A flat sign is used before III and VI and sometimes a natural sign is used before VII to draw attention to the difference from the ♭VII in the Natural Minor Scale.

Here is the list of chords created by harmonizing the C Harmonic Minor Scale:
- The I chord is minor
- The II chord is diminished
- The ♭III chord is augmented
- The IV chord is minor

- The V chord is major
- The ♭VI chord is major
- The VII chord is diminished

Let's compare the harmonized Natural Minor and Harmonic Minor Scales.

C Natural Minor Scale Harmonized with Triads

Imi II° ♭IIIma IVmi Vmi ♭VIma ♭VIIma Imi

C Harmonic Minor Scale Harmonized with Triads

Imi II° ♭III+ IVmi Vma ♭VIma (♮)VII° Imi

Which chords are the same as the Natural Minor Scale? The Imi, IIdim, IVmi, and ♭VIma.

Which chords differ from the Natural Minor Scale? Only those that contain the 7th of the scale are different: ♭III+, Vma, and VII°. These chords are different than the III, V, and VII in Natural Minor because they contain the leading tone from the scale.

Harmonized Chords of Natural Minor and Harmonic Minor

MINOR:	Imi	IIdim	♭IIIma	IVmi	Vmi	♭VIma	♭VIIma
	Cmi	D°	E♭	Fmi	Gmi	A♭	B♭
HARMONIC:	Imi	IIdim	♭III+	IVmi	Vma	♭VIma	(♮)VIIdim
	Cmi	D°	E♭+	Fmi	G7	A♭	B°

Take special note of the Vma and VII°. These are the most commonly used chords 'borrowed' from the Harmonic Minor Scale for isolated use in a song in a minor key. Understanding how and which chords from Harmonic Minor are used in a progression that is primarily Natural Minor is a focus of this Unit, so let's dig into this a little deeper.

Why should we care about comparing the harmonized C Natural Minor Scale and the harmonized C Harmonic Minor Scale? Well, you can think of C Natural Minor and C Harmonic Minor as parallel minor scales. They share the same tonic and most of the same notes.

Minor Modal Interchange

In Level 6 we'll study other parallel minor scales as well; scales like Dorian or Melodic Minor. It's common for a song to be in C Natural Minor but temporarily shift into Harmonic Minor for a chord or two. This is why we call it a kind of 'minor modal interchange' and it's very common. That means a song primarily in Natural Minor might 'borrow' melody notes or chords from its parallel Harmonic Minor Scale. We'll dedicate a whole unit to this soon.

FRETBOARD LOGIC

In Unit 1 you learned the Patterns II and IV Harmonic Minor Scales. In this Module you will learn the Patterns I, III, and V Harmonic Minor Scales by converting the Natural Minor Scales.

Pattern I Minor Scales

Here are the Pattern I Minor Pentatonic and Natural Minor Scales with the scale degrees numbered. In the diagram to the right, the 7th is raised from a minor 7th to a major 7th. The result is a Pattern I Harmonic Minor Scale.

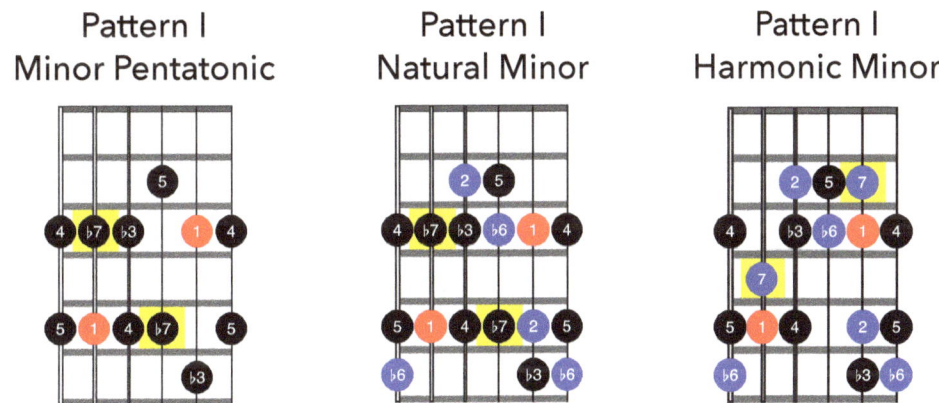

Pattern III Minor Scales

Here are the Pattern III Minor Pentatonic and Natural Minor Scales with the scale degrees numbered. In the diagram to the right, the 7th is raised from a minor 7th to a major 7th. The result is a Pattern III Harmonic Minor Scale.

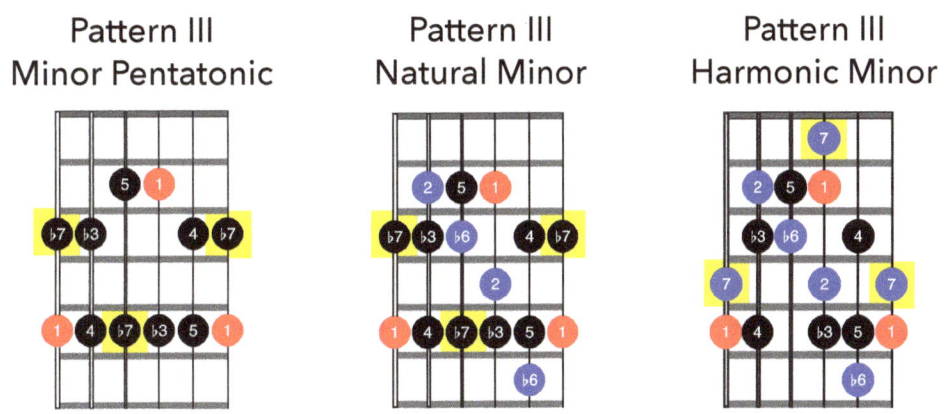

Pattern V Minor Scales

Here are the Pattern V Minor Pentatonic and Natural Minor Scales with the scale degrees numbered. In the diagram to the right, the 7th is raised from a minor 7th to a major 7th. The result is a Pattern V Harmonic Minor Scale.

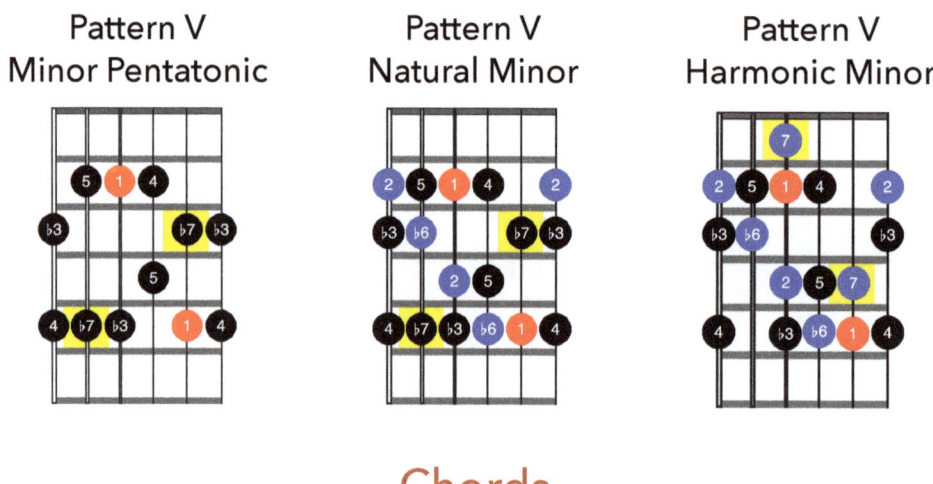

Chords

Back in Level 2 you learned how to build and identify four types of triads: major, minor, augmented, and diminished. Major, minor, and diminished triads have gotten a lot of attention but there has been little attention given to augmented triads. Let's spend a bit more time on them now.

Augmented Triads

You will remember that we touched on the augmented triad way back when we first learned about triads. An augmented triad can be built by changing the perfect 5th of a major triad to an augmented 5th.

Notice the internal intervallic structure of an augmented triad:

- The interval from the root to the major 3rd is a major 3rd. That is two whole steps.
- The interval from the from the major 3rd to the augmented 5th is a major 3rd. That's two whole steps.
- The interval from the augmented 5th to the octave of the root is a diminished 4th which is the enharmonic equivalent major 3rd. That is two whole steps.

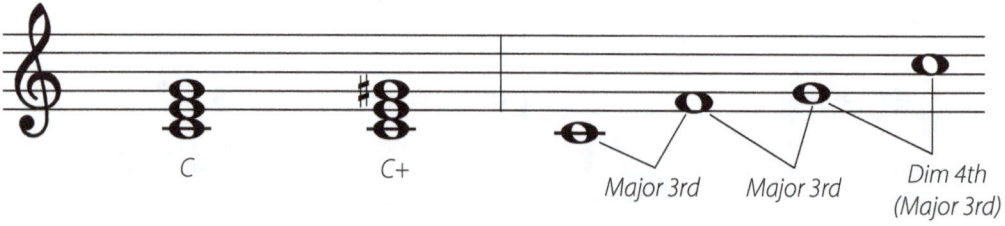

Here is another important point about the internal intervallic structure:

- The interval from the root to the augmented 5th is an augmented 5th.
- The interval from the from the major 3rd to the octave of the root is an augmented 5th.

The word 'symmetry' or 'symmetrical' is often used to describe the repeating interval structure of a scale or chord. So an augmented chord is referred to as a 'symmetrical chord'. These two repeating interval patterns offer some interesting geometric possibilities on the fretboard.

Here are the simple augmented triad chord shapes. Think back to the Super Shapes in Level 2. These three-string and four-string shape layouts should remind you of the Super Shapes.

Augmented Three-String Shapes

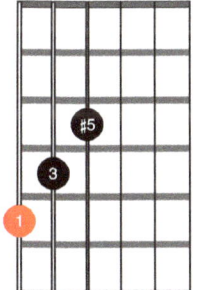 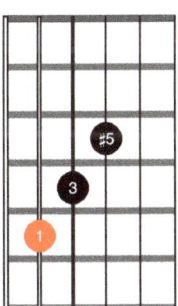  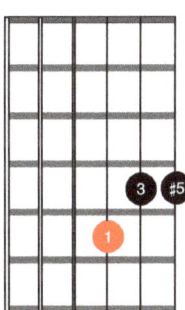

Augmented Four-String Shapes

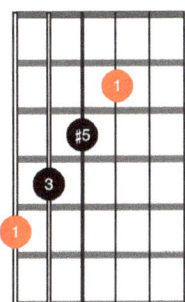 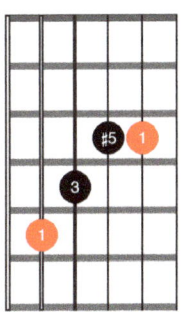 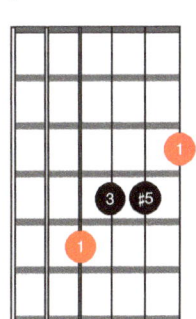

It is also interesting to see all of the possible notes of an augmented chord across the entire fretboard. From this matrix any number of fingerings can be derived.

Augmented Chords

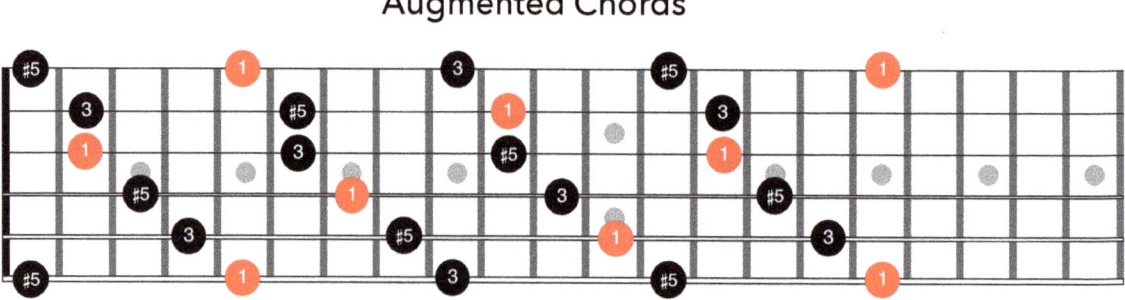

Augmented Triad Arpeggios

All of the information about augmented triad chords applies to augmented triad arpeggios. The arpeggio shapes can be played in a variety of ways, but let's examine them within the octave shape system.

Augmented Triad Arpeggios

This information is important but it is an encyclopedia-like approach to the augmented triad chord and arpeggio location and fingering possibilities on the entire fretboard. I would not dedicate a lot of time to the physical practice of learning all of these augmented chord and arpeggio shapes. There are simply too many other things to practice to devote a lot of time to the augmented triad chords and arpeggios. So it is far more important that you know how to construct them on the fretboard. Your goal should be to create the information in the diagrams in this Unit on your own based on your knowledge.

RHYTHM GUITAR

In this Module you will continue learning to comp in the Bossa Nova style. The example in this Module is used when there is no bass player; it incorporates the bass part.

This four-bar example is in A Dorian minor and uses a Pattern IV Ami7 voicing and a Pattern II D9 voicing. Even though you haven't formally learned 9th chords, you have played examples that use them in previous Blues, Funk, and R&B Rhythm Guitar units.

The rhythm pattern in this example uses the same rhythm pattern presented in the last Unit, but adds the half-note bass part normally played by a bass player. Do not use this part in a situation where a bass player is playing. You will just get in the way (and the bass player will not be happy).

Bossa Progression in A Minor

Before we work on the rhythm, let's talk about where you place your fretting hand and picking hand fingers.

- With your fretting hand, play the Ami7 as a barre chord. Notice that the root is voiced on the 6th string at the 5th fret. The 5th is voiced on the adjacent string; the 5th string at the 7th fret. These two notes will be used to play the bass part for this chord.

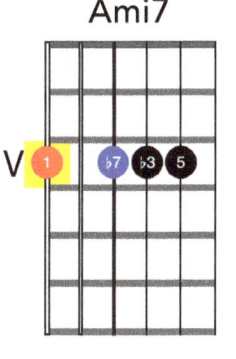

Root on 6th String

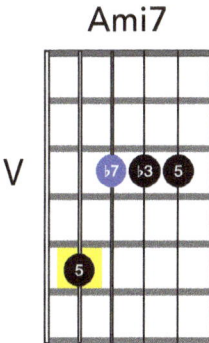

5th on 5th String

- Next play the D9 chord. The root of the D9 chord is played at the 5th fret of the 5th string. The 5th of the D9 can be played, also at the 5th fret, on the 6th string. These two notes will be used to play the bass part on the D9.

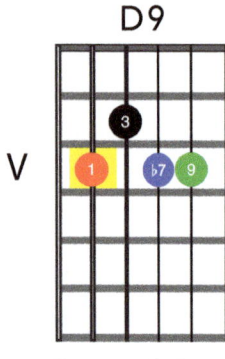 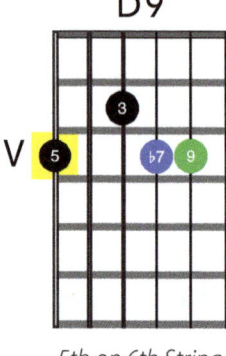

Root on 5th String   *5th on 6th String*

With both the Ami7 and D9, the bass part for the entire example can be played on the 6th and 5th strings. And this makes sense because the bass part should be in a low register.

- With your picking hand, assign your thumb to the 6th and 5th strings to play the bass part with half notes. The chord tones for the bass part are the root and 5th only.
- Start by playing an Ami7 with your fretting hand. With your picking hand, place your thumb on the root on the 6th string.
- Then arrange your 1st, 2nd, and 3rd fingers in a soft-claw formation. Slightly curl your knuckles.
- Place your 1st finger on the 4th string, 2nd finger on the 3rd string, and 3rd finger on the 2nd string. Place your fingertips slightly under the strings so the strings ring when you pull up. Your thumb will alternate between the root and 5th: Root on the 6th string and 5th on the 5th string. Your picking hand is now in position to play the part on Ami7.
- Next play D9 with your fretting hand. With your picking hand, start by placing your thumb on the 5th string. That's the root.
- Keep your 1st, 2nd, and 3rd fingers in the claw formation on the 4th, 3rd, and 2nd strings. Your thumb will alternate between the root on the 5th string and 5th on the 6th string. That's the opposite of the Ami7 chord. Your picking hand is now in position to play the part on the D9.

This is a two-bar phrase repeated over and over. The bass part is half notes only and the comping rhythm pattern is played on top. The challenge is developing the independence between your thumb and other the fingers of your fretting hand.

Fretboard Biology

Level 5 • Unit 2: Rhythm Guitar

Let's go step by step through the Ami7 part to begin.

- In measure one play both thumb and claw on beat one. Your thumb plays the root on the 6th string.

- On beat two, play claw only.

- On beat three, play thumb only on the 5th string; that's the 5th of the chord.

- On the 'and' of three, play claw only.

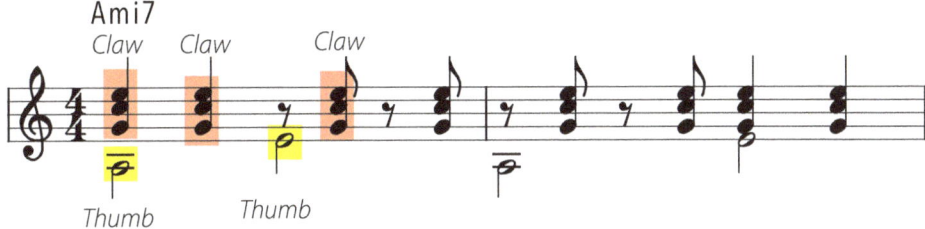

- On the 'and' of four, play claw only.

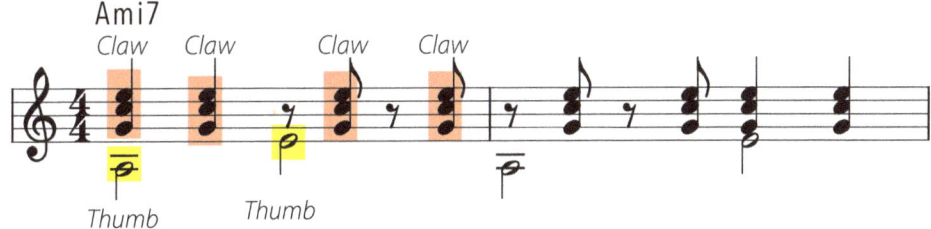

Review the first measure. Practice that much in isolation as much as you need. The independence between your thumb and claw is important.

Now let's look at the second measure.

- Begin measure two with thumb only. Play the root on the 6th string on beat one.

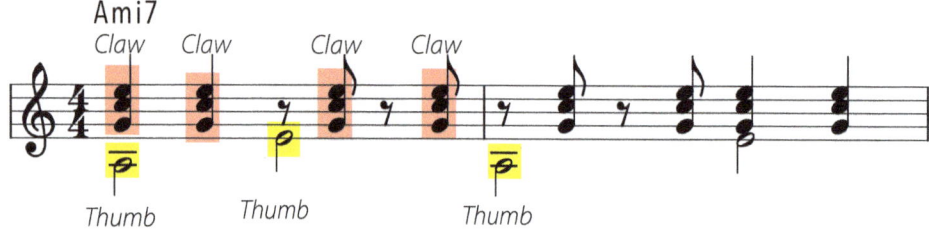

- On the 'and' of one, play claw only.

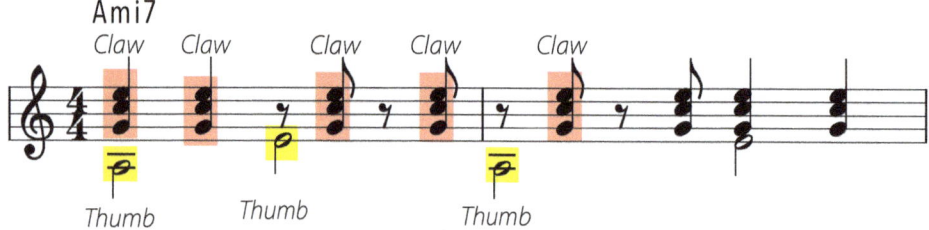

- On the 'and' of two, play claw only.

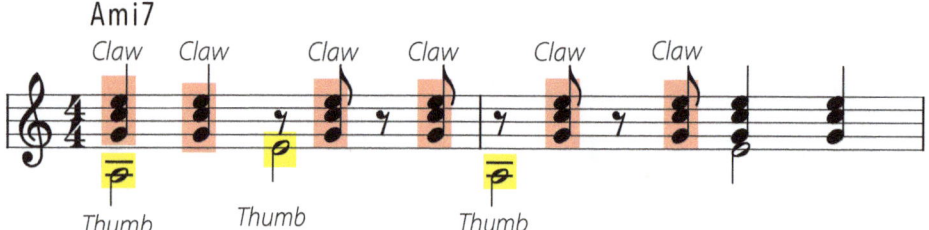

- On beat three, play both thumb and claw. Thumb plays the 5th on the 5th string.

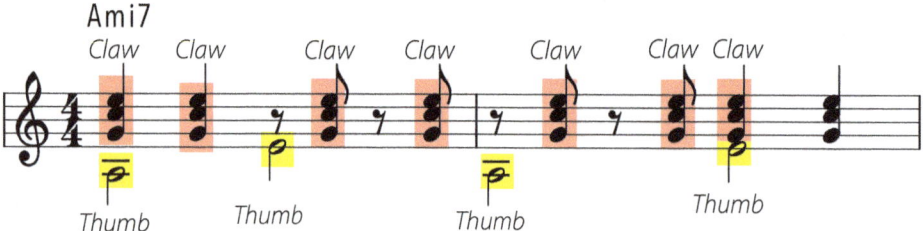

- On beat four, play claw only.

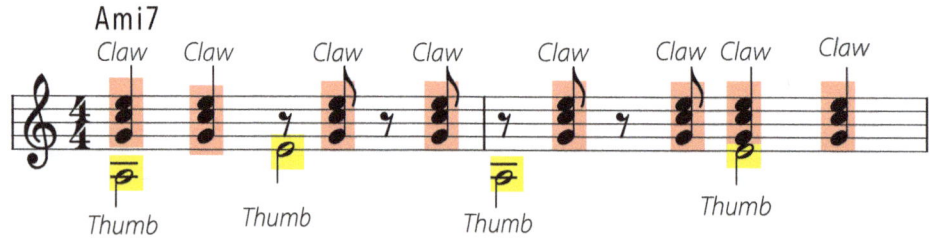

Practice the second measure as much as you need. The independence between thumb and claw is important. Now put both measures together. This is the whole two-bar phrase on Ami7. It's normal to spend a day or more getting comfortable with this before moving on to D9. The phrase will be the same on D9, but the bass notes will be different.

- In measure one of the D9, play both thumb and claw on beat one. Your thumb plays the root on the 5th string.

- On beat two, play claw only.

- On beat three, play thumb only on the 6th string; that's the 5th of the chord.

- On the 'and' of three, play claw only.

- On the 'and' of four, play claw only.

Review the first measure. Practice that in isolation as much as much as you need. The independence of your thumb and fingers is important.

Now let's look at the second measure.

- Begin measure two with thumb only on beat one, playing the root on the 5th string.

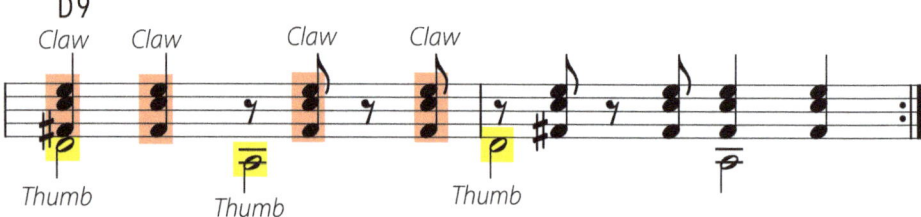

- On the 'and' of one, play claw only.

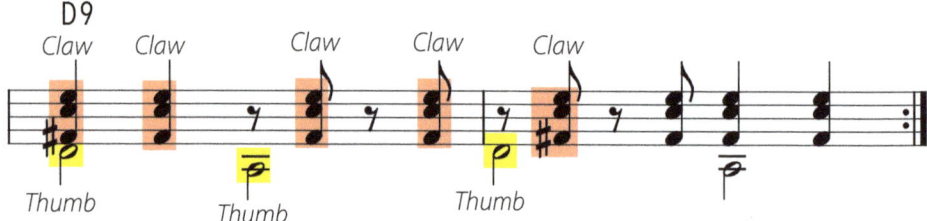

- On the 'and' of two, play claw only.

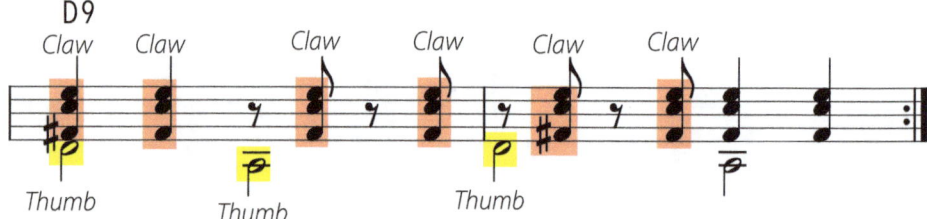

- On beat three, play both thumb and claw. Your thumb plays the 5th on the 6th string.

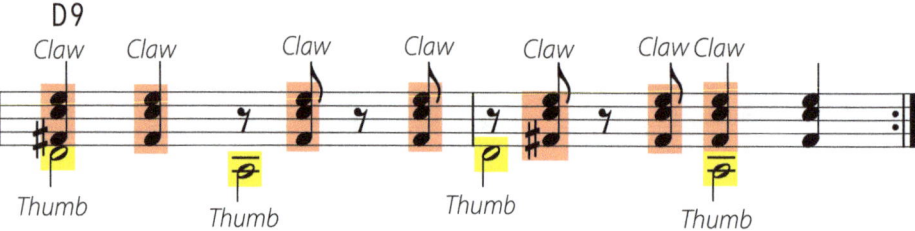

- On beat four, play claw only.

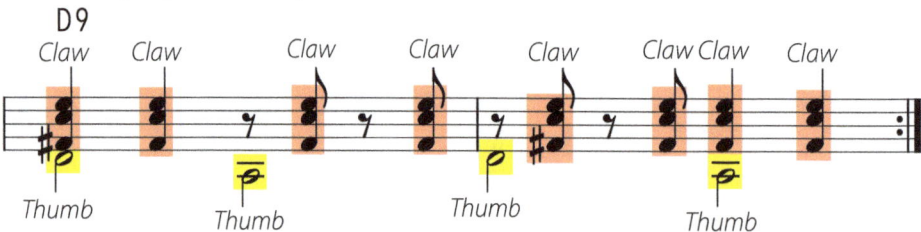

Review the second measure. Practice the part in isolation as much as you need. Then put both measures together. After practicing the two measures on D9, put the entire example together at a very slow tempo. Don't play this faster than you can play it accurately. When you have it under your fingers, turn on the on the metronome at a very slow tempo, perhaps 60-70 bpm. Over days, weeks, or months, work up to about 132 bpm. Regardless of the chords played in a song, these picking-hand techniques are applicable.

CHART READING

When you first look at a chart, be aware of the 'get-started' instructions. The top left area of a chord chart or any piece of music has important preliminary information that gets you ready to play.

Let's take a look at this information:

- **Title**: Songs are usually referred to by name. The song title is usually the first thing written at the top of the page. Sometimes the name of the songwriter or artist is written to the right of the title.

- **Tempo**: The tempo marking is usually in the upper left corner somewhere below the song title. It's shown with a note value (usually a quarter note or 8th note), an equal sign (=), and a number representing 'beats per minute' which is often written as 'BPM'.

- **Indication of Style**: Adjacent to the tempo, either on the left or the right, is the indication of style. This could be a one-word description like Rock, Swing, Shuffle, or Samba, or a multiple-word description like 16-Note Shuffle. Sometimes there's even a reference to another song or band as in "a la Stones" or "a la Cowboys Don't Cry".

- **Clef Sign**: Sometimes chord charts have a treble clef sign and sometimes a bass clef. The decision is based on what kind of figures may need to be written on the chart. For example, if there's a signature bass riff that the song relies on, the appropriate choice is to use a bass clef. If there's a signature guitar riff that the song relies on, it's appropriate to use a treble clef.

    If the same riff is played in different octaves by the bass and guitar, pick one clef or the other and one person will have to decipher the clef they normally don't read.

    You can also use different clef signs for different sections. For example, if a song opens with signature guitar riff, start with a treble clef. If there's a signature bass riff later in the chart, switch to bass clef.

- **Key Signature**: The key signature is written directly to the right of the clef sign.

- **Time Signature**: The time signature is written directly to the right of the key signature.

Think of the 'get started instructions' as the first thng on your checklist when you look at a chart fotr the first time. There will be more information that you will need to pay attention to when you encounter a chart, but these things will orient you to the style, tempo and key of the song.

Make it a habit of looking at all this information as the first thing you do when reading a chart for the first time. As you read more charts, you'll be able to scan and absorb all of this information in a few seconds. In a sight-reading environment, that's usually all the time you have. As soon as you've absorbed this information, your eyes need to scan the form of the song. It's critical to plan how your eyes will move through the sections of a chart. That is the focus of some of the modules coming up.

IMPROVISATION

The focus of the Level 5 Improvisation modules is the use of the Harmonic Minor Scale. In the Unit 1 Improvisation Module, the Harmonic Minor Scale was used as the source of notes in a key-center kind of way on a two-bar progression in the key of A minor. While the A Harmonic Minor Scale is appropriate for both chords, you learned that G#, the leading tone, is the 'money note' for E7 and is an important note to target as the first note played on the E7. In a way, that suggests perhaps holding back from playing that note and using it exclusively on the E7. Remember that E7 is based on an E major triad.

In this Module, the goal is to be more specific and selective with note choices, particularly on the Vma chord. Let's analyze the following progression in B minor. Play this progression and focus on the Vma chord and how strong the leading tone in the Vma sounds.

Progression in B Minor

Next, let's look at the harmonized B Natural Minor and Harmonic Minor Scales and think about which scale contains each chord.

B Natural Minor Scale Harmonized with Triads

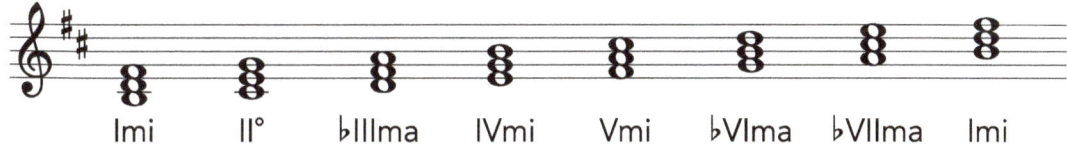

B Harmonic Minor Scale Harmonized with Triads

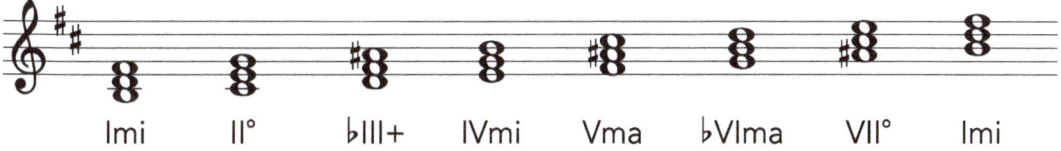

Bmi is the Imi and Emi is the IVmi in both B Natural Minor and B Harmonic Minor Scales. This means that both the B Natural Minor and B Harmonic Minor Scales are appropriate note sources for these chords.

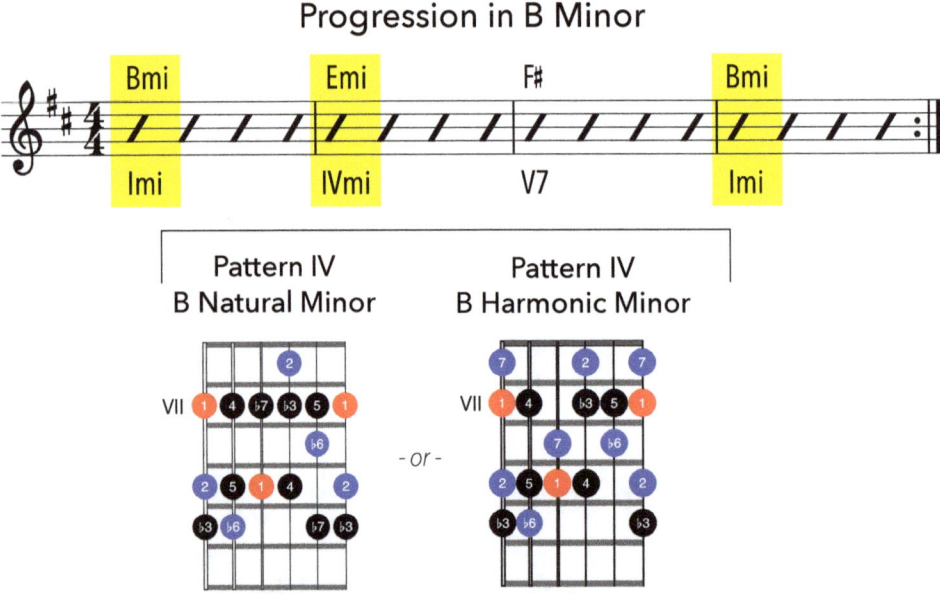

F# is the Vma in B Harmonic Minor Scale but does not belong to the B Natural Minor Scale. This means that the B Harmonic Minor Scale is the appropriate note source for this chord. And from the viewpoint of chord tones, it's good to point out that the F# major triad chord tones are:

- F#: The root of the F# chord and 5th of the B Harmonic Minor Scale.
- A#: The 3rd of the F# chord and major 7th of the B Harmonic Minor Scale.
- C#: The 5th of the F# chord and 2nd (or 9th) of the B Harmonic Minor Scale.

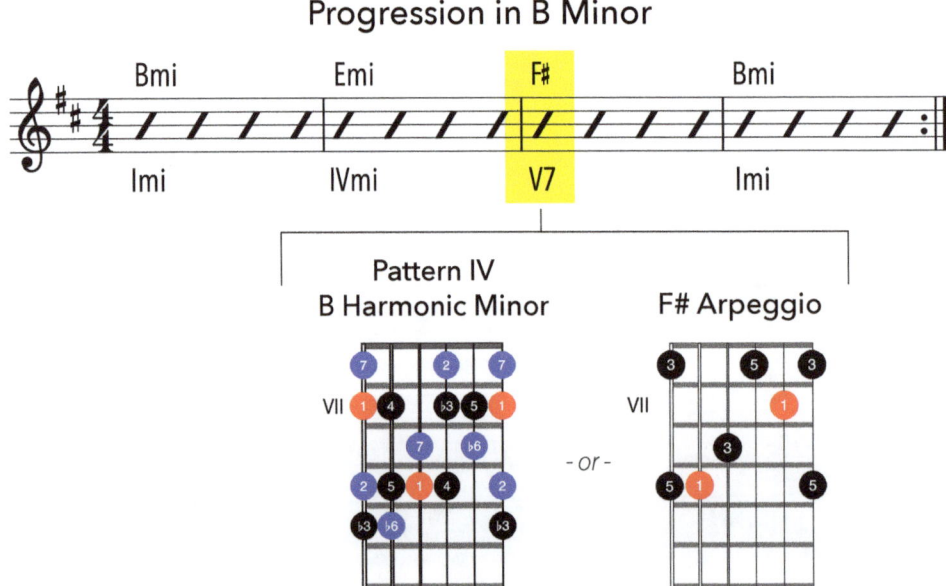

The goal of your practice for this Module is to target the chord tones of the Vma, F#ma, on at least the first beat of the 3rd measure when it's played. You have a choice on the first two chords between using B Natural Minor or B Harmonic Minor.

- Locate the Pattern IV B Natural Minor and B Harmonic Minor Scales on the fretboard. To begin, run the scales ascending and descending.
- Also locate the F# major arpeggio found within the Pattern IV B shape. That is a Pattern I major triad shape.
- Next, create motifs and improvise using the storytelling devices you have used since Level 1. Experiment using the F# major arpeggio over F#.

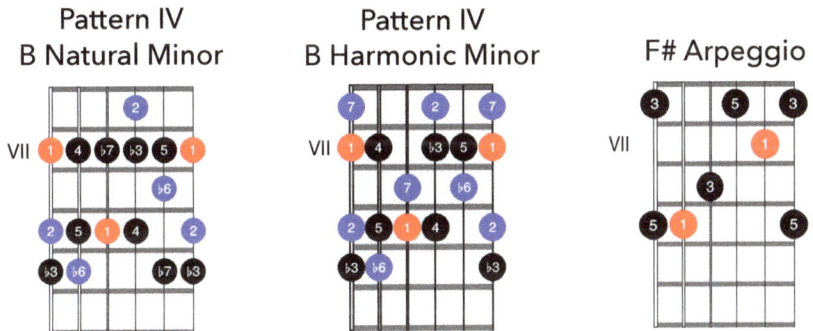

- Now locate the Pattern II B Natural Minor and Harmonic Minor Scales. To begin, run the scale ascending and descending.
- Also locate the F# major arpeggio found within the Pattern II B shape. That is a Pattern IV major triad shape.
- Next, create motifs and improvise using the storytelling devices you have used since Level 1. Experiment using the F# major arpeggio over F#.

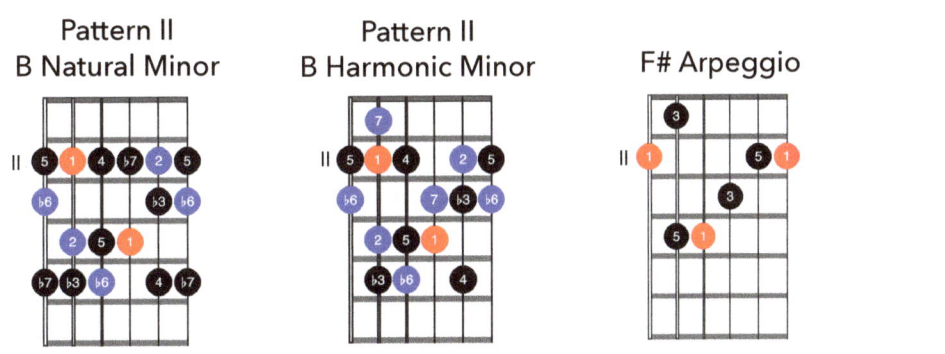

In this Module, you used the Patterns IV and II Octave Shapes because those are the most comfortable for most guitarists, but these concepts should eventually be learned in other Patterns as well. Add this progression to your practice routine. Your goal is to move freely through the both the Natural Minor and Harmonic Minor Scales and the Vma arpeggio, and to be in control of when you use the leading tone.

Level 5 Unit 2 • Improv Demo

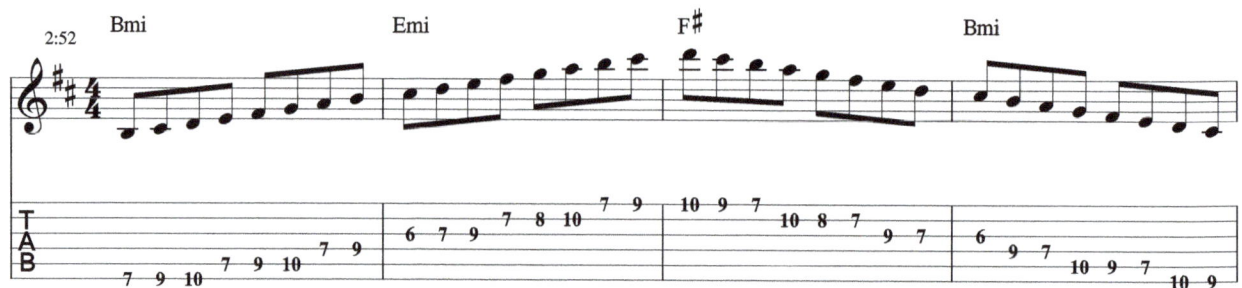
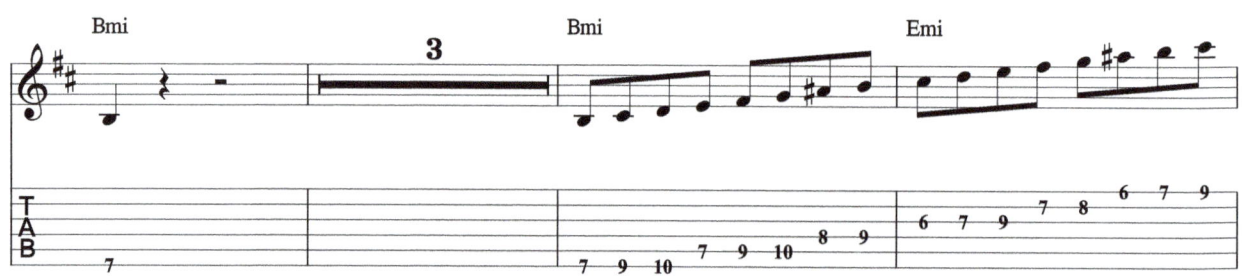
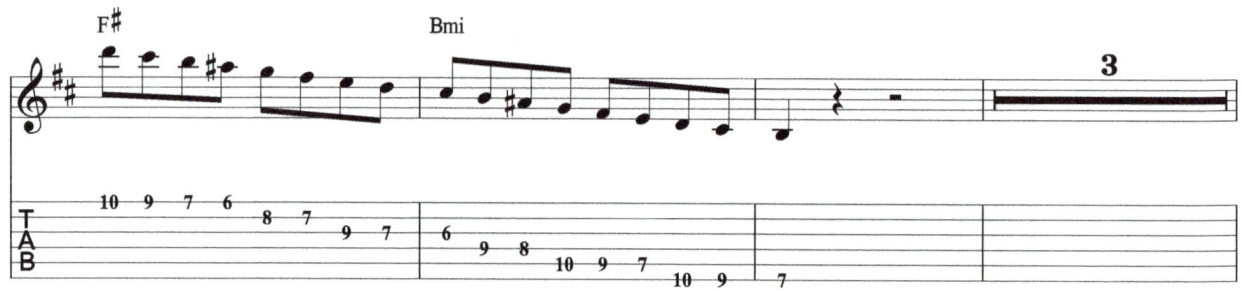

Fretboard Biology
Level 5 • Unit 2: Improvisation

61

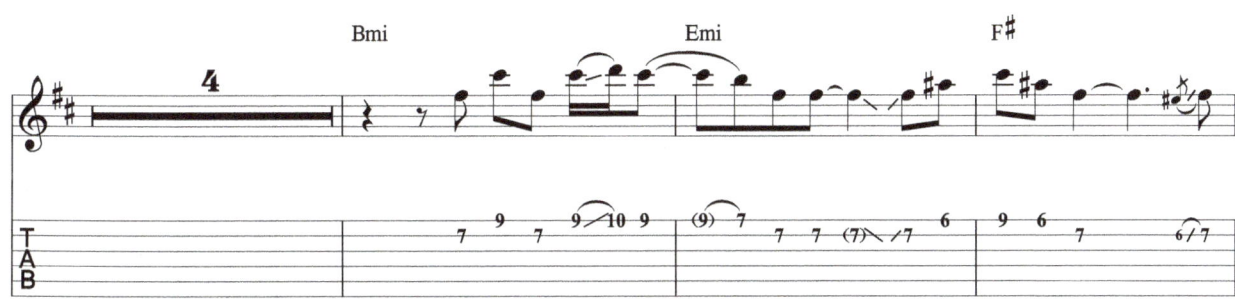
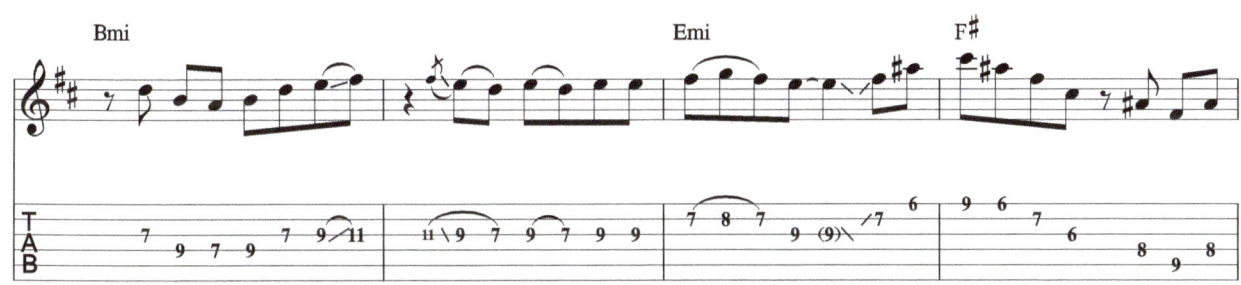

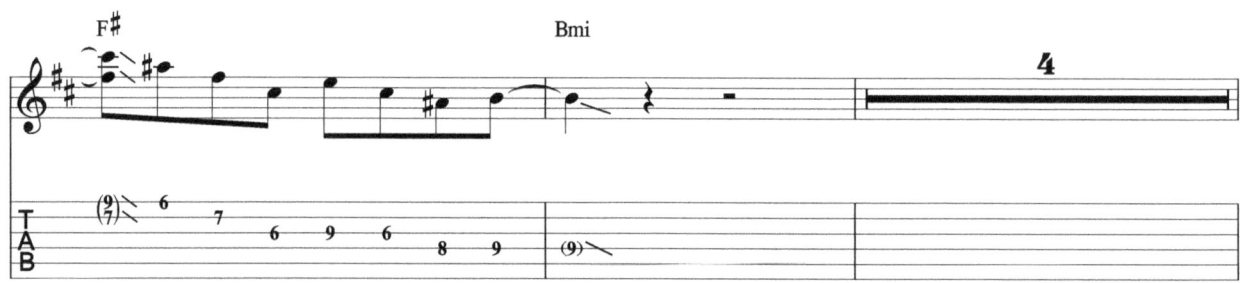
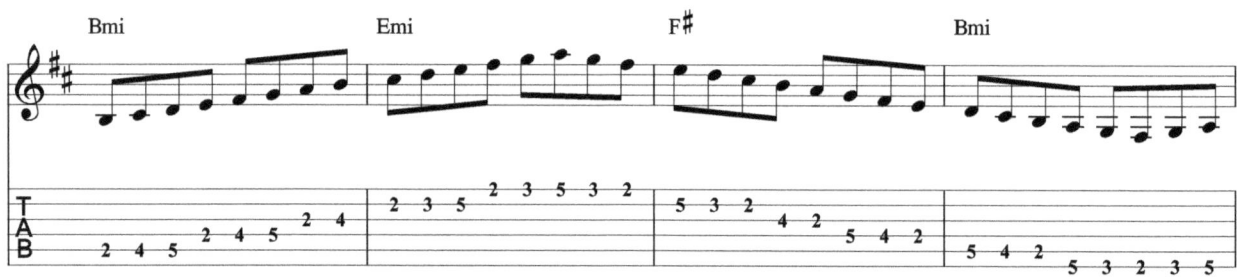
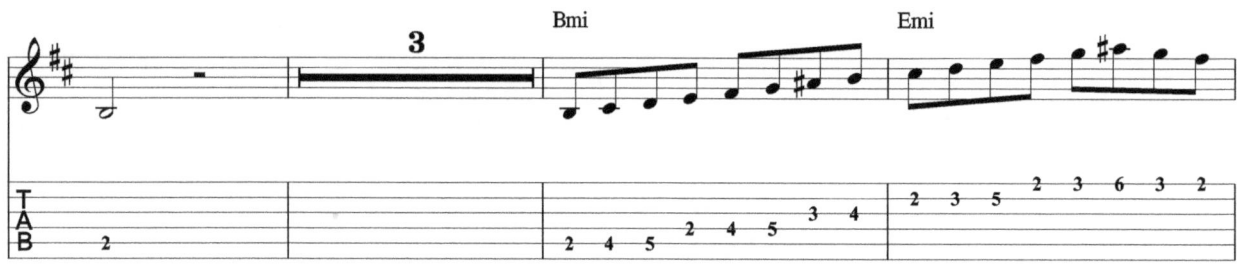

Fretboard Biology — Level 5 • Unit 2: Improvisation

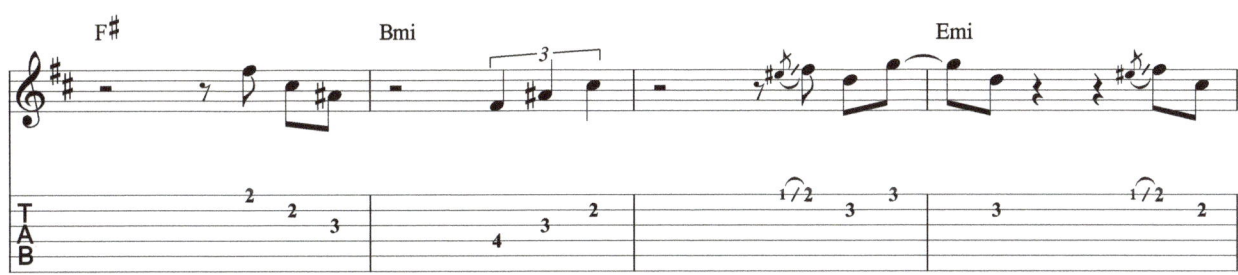

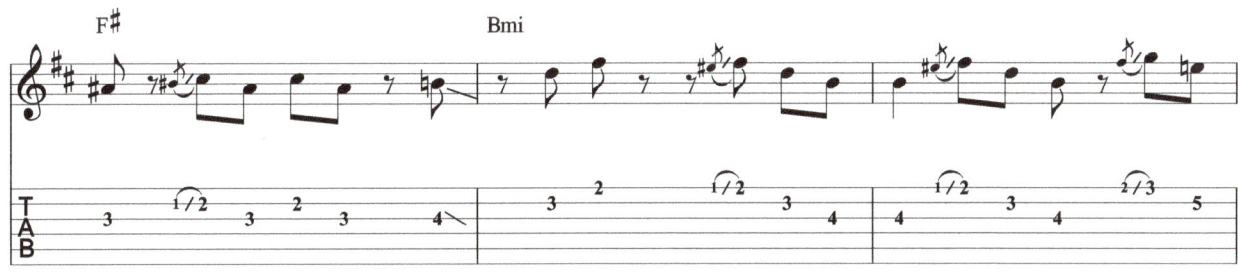

PRACTICE

Theory

- ☐ Go to the tabs below the Theory video on the website and complete the quiz.
- ☐ Learn the Harmonic Minor Scale harmonized with triads.

Fretboard Logic

- ☐ Learn the Patterns I, III, and V Harmonic Minor Scales.
- ☐ Learn the augmented triads and triad arpeggios.

Rhythm Guitar

- ☐ Practice playing the Bossa progression in A minor.

Chart Reading

- ☐ Understand the 'get-started' instructions on a chord chart.

Improvisation

- ☐ Practice playing solos over the progression in B minor using the Pattern IV and Pattern II Natural Minor and Harmonic Minor Scales and the F# in-position arpeggio.

UNIT 3

Learning Modules

> **Theory** - Harmonizing the Harmonic Minor Scale with 7th Chords, the VII°7 Chord

> **Fretboard Logic** - Diminished Chords, Diminished Triad Arpeggios

> **Rhythm Guitar** - Samba Rhythm Guitar

> **Chart Reading** - Slash Marks, Importance of Clarity in Charts

> **Improvisation** - Soloing with the Harmonic Minor Scale over the V7 Chord

> **Practice** - Continue Practice Routine Development

THEORY

In the last Unit you learned how to harmonize the Harmonic Minor Scale with triads. You also compared the triads of the harmonized Natural Minor Scale with the triads of the harmonized Harmonic Minor Scale. As mentioned in the last Unit, this is relevant because it's common for a song to be written in Natural Minor, but temporarily shift into Harmonic Minor for a chord or two. It's a kind of minor modal interchange and is very common. That means a song based in Natural Minor might borrow melody notes or chords from its parallel Harmonic Minor Scale. This will be an ongoing theme and we will explore this with various other minor scales as we get further into the program.

In this Unit you'll learn to harmonize the Harmonic Minor Scale with 7th chords. And just a reminder, the easiest way to think of the Harmonic Minor Scale is as a Natural Minor Scale with a raised 7th. Harmonizing the Harmonic Minor Scale with 7th chords reveals some interesting and useful chords that are different than what you have seen so far.

Let's start by looking at the C Harmonic Minor Scale with the scale degrees numbered.

C Harmonic Minor Scale

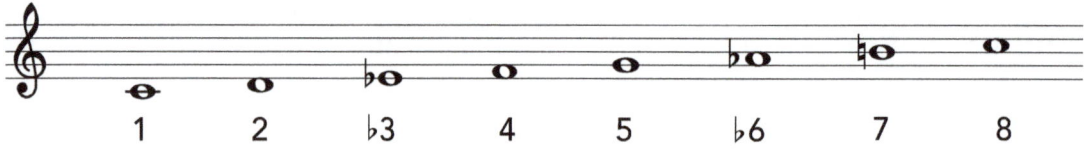

Next, let's harmonize the scale with 7th chords by building a diatonic 3rd, 5th, and 7th above each note of the scale. You have harmonized enough scales by this point and don't need a detailed explanation but I will point out a few things as we go.

Remember, the process is to build a 7th chord on each scale degree using only notes from the scale. Then, determine the quality of each 7th chord by comparing the intervals in each chord to the interval formulas for 7th chords.

Harmonized C Harmonic Minor Scale with 7th Chords

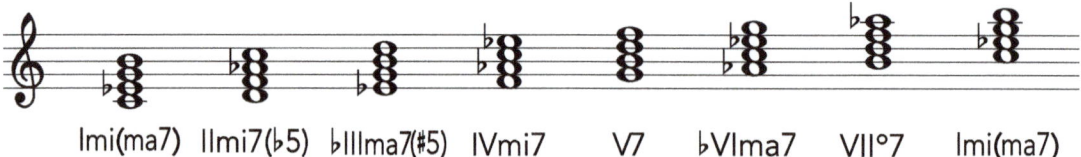

Imi(ma7)   IImi7(♭5)   ♭IIIma7(♯5)   IVmi7   V7   ♭VIma7   VII°7   Imi(ma7)

In the process of harmonizing the Harmonic Minor Scale with 7th chords, there will be several chords with interval formulas that are new.

Let's study the analysis of each chord in the harmonized scale.

Imi(ma7)

The I chord has a minor 3rd, perfect 5th, and major 7th. This may be new to you. You know that a minor triad with a minor 7th is a minor 7 chord, but this has a major 7th. Spoken, this chord is 'minor major 7th'. The chord symbol is Mi(Ma7). This interval formula is probably new to you. Memorize the formula: Root, minor 3rd, and perfect 5th, major 7th. The easiest way to think of is as a minor triad with a major 7th. Alternatively, you could think of it as a Mi7 chord whose 7th has been raised a half step.

Imi(ma7)

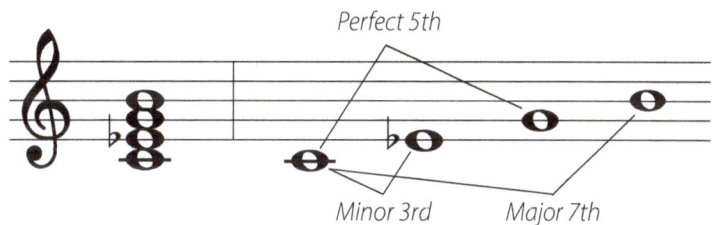

In the chord symbol, 'Mi' refers to the quality of the core triad and 'Ma7' refers to the quality of the 7th. The (Ma7) is parenthesized in this symbol. This is a great sounding chord and you will learn voicings and arpeggios soon and how it is used in songs. Add this 7th chord with a quality that's new to you to your list.

IImi7(♭5)

The II chord has a minor 3rd, diminished 5th, and minor 7th, which should be a familiar chord to you. The II chord is IImi7(♭5).

IImi7(♭5)

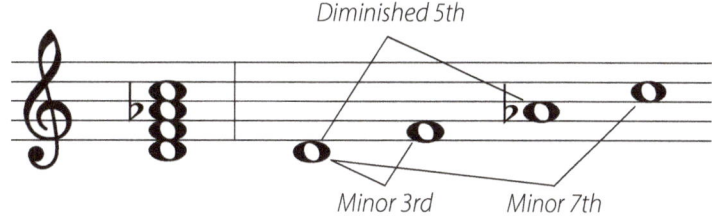

bIIIma7(#5)

The bIII chord has a major 3rd, an augmented 5th, and a major 7th. You can see this as a Ma7 chord with an augmented 5th or as an augmented triad with a major 7th. This an interesting sounding chord. You will learn voicings and arpeggios soon and, most importantly, how it is used in songs. It sounds a little stressful when played alone but will make sense when you learn how it is used in the context of a song.

There are several ways this chord name is written and spoken:

- Ma7(#5): This is because it is a major 7 chord with a raised or sharp 5th.
- Ma7(+5): This is because it is a major 7 chord with a raised 5th; '+' is another way to notate '#' in a chord symbol.
- Augmented major 7: This is another way the chord is named when spoken about. It would still be written Ma7(#5) or Ma7(+5).

This chord is normally called 'major seven sharp five' when spoken. The most common chord symbol is Ma7(+5).

IVmi7

The IV chord has a minor 3rd, perfect 5th, and minor 7th. You know this chord. It's a minor 7 chord. The IV chord in the harmonized Harmonic Minor Scale is IVmi7.

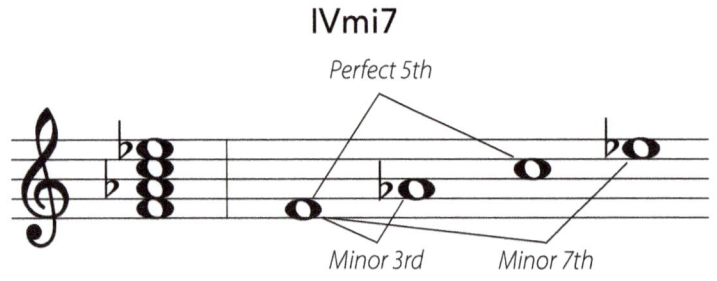

V7

The V chord has a major 3rd, perfect 5th, and minor 7th. You already know this chord and interval formula. It's a dominant 7 chord. So, the V chord in the harmonized Harmonic Minor Scale is V7.

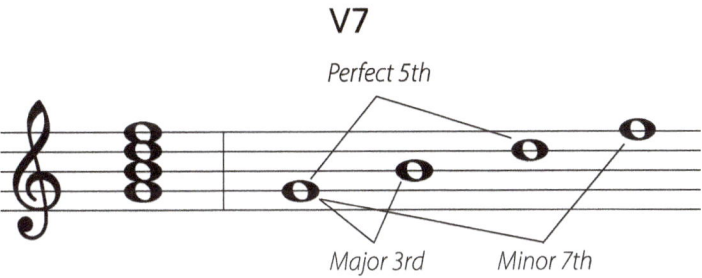

bVIma7

The bVI chord has a major 3rd, perfect 5th, and major 7th. You know this chord and interval formula. It's a Ma7 chord. The bVI chord in the Harmonic Minor Scale is bVIma7.

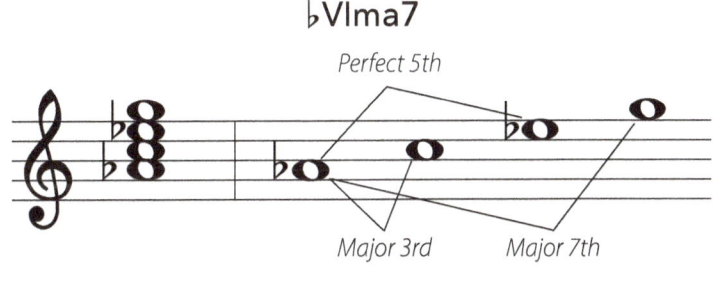

VII°7

The VII chord has a minor 3rd, diminished 5th, and diminished 7th. This formula is new to you. I suggest you see it as a diminished triad with a diminished 7th. Spoken, this chord is 'diminished seven'. The chord symbol is °7. The VII chord is VII°7.

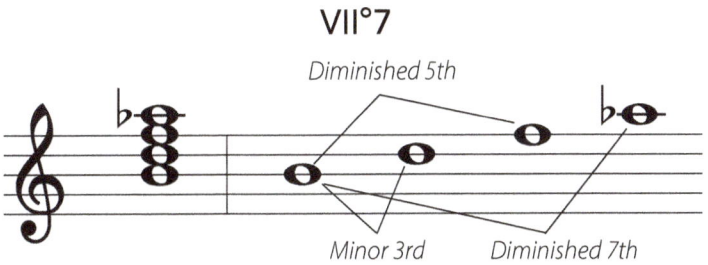

Let's look deeper into the interval called a diminished 7th by looking at several other diminished intervals. This is the first time this program has shown a diminished 7th interval so it's important to look closer. Remember that a diminished interval is one half step smaller than a perfect or minor interval. Let's look at a few.

Diminished 3rd

The first one shown here is rare and theoretically possible. The interval one half step smaller than a minor 3rd is a diminished 3rd. It's the enharmonic equivalent of a major 2nd but because the letters used are a 3rd apart, it has to be called a 3rd.

Diminished 3rd

Diminished 3rd (Enharmonic Major 2nd)

Diminished 4th

This next one is also rare and theoretically possible The interval one half step smaller than a perfect 4th is a diminished 4th. It's the enharmonic equivalent of a major 3rd but because the letters used are a 4th apart, it has to be called a 4th.

Diminished 4th

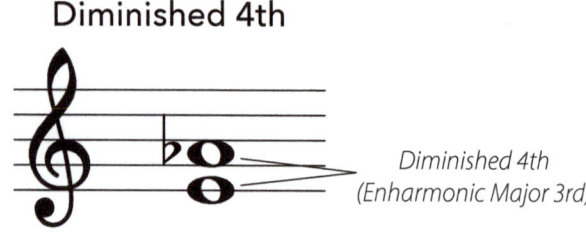

Diminished 4th (Enharmonic Major 3rd)

Diminished 5th

The interval one half step smaller than a perfect 5th is a diminished 5th. This is already familiar to you. It is the enharmonic equivalent to an augmented 4th.

Diminished 5th

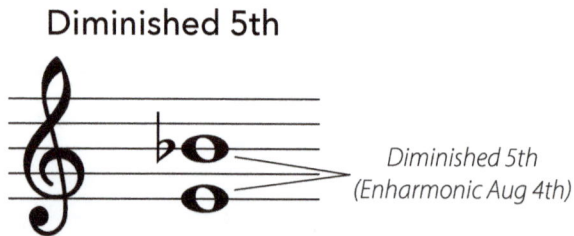

Diminished 5th (Enharmonic Aug 4th)

Diminished 7th

Likewise, the interval one half step smaller than a minor 7th is a diminished 7th. It is the enharmonic equivalent of a major 6th but because the letters used are a 7th apart, it has to be called a 7th.

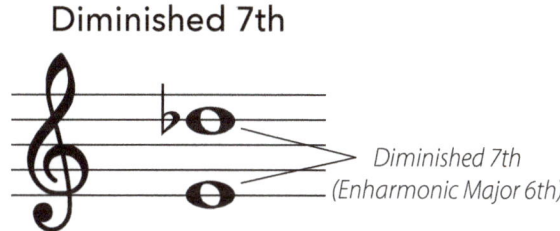

Just to be completely clear, look at the diminished 7th interval another way.

- Use B as the starting note. The major 7th above B is A#.

- Start with B again. The minor 7th above B is A natural. You know that a minor 7th is a half-step smaller (lower) than a major 7th.

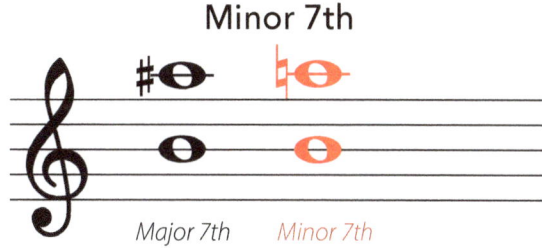

- Start with B again. A diminished 7th is a half-step smaller (lower) than a minor 7th. The diminished 7 above B is A♭. And again, it's the enharmonic equivalent of a major 6th but because the letters used are a 7th apart, it has to be called a 7th. (A major 6th above B is G#. G# and A♭ are enharmonic equivalents.)

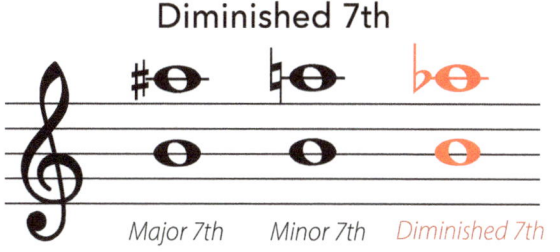

A diminished 7th chord is an interesting sounding chord and has so many really interesting uses. Entire books have been written about diminished chords and scales. You will learn diminished chord voicings and arpeggios soon and, most importantly, how they are used in songs. The diminished 7th chord sounds stressful and dissonant when played alone, but this dissonance will make sense when you learn how the chord is used in context. This is another chord and interval formula that is new to you. Add it to your list.

The VII°7 Chord

We will talk about the VII°7 in greater detail in a later unit, but I wanted to touch on it briefly here. The VII chord has a minor 3rd, diminished 5th, and diminished 7th. Examine the intervals between chord tones. They are all the same; they're all minor 3rds. Because of the reoccurring interval pattern, this is called a symmetrical chord.

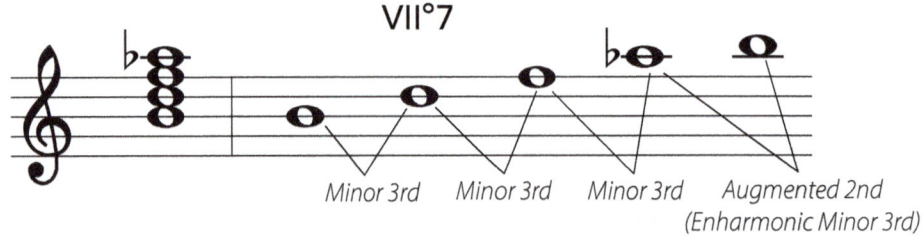

Note the similarity to the Mi7(♭5) chord, but make no mistake—this chord is different and is used very differently. Here are a Bdim7 and Bmi7(♭5) side by side. Notice that both are built on a diminished triad.

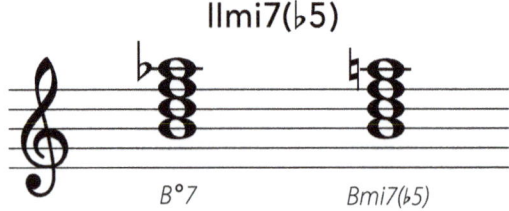

- Bdim7 is a diminished triad with a diminished 7th.
- Bmi7(♭5) is a diminished triad with a minor 7th.

The difference between the two chords is the 7th.

There are other sort of 'slang' names for both of these chords that are pretty common. Get used to hearing them:

- The Mi7(♭5) chord is sometimes called a 'half-diminished' chord or simply 'half-diminished'.
- The diminished 7 chord is sometimes called a 'fully-diminished' chord.

Now let's return to the harmonized Harmonic Minor Scale. As always, chord symbols are represented with Roman numerals followed by the quality. A flat sign is used before III and VI because compared to the major scale, those scale degrees are lowered one half step.

Pay special attention to the VII chord. In Natural Minor we get used to it being ♭VII. In Harmonic Minor, it's built on the major 7th so sometimes a parenthesized 'courtesy natural sign' is used before VII to denote the difference from the ♭VII in the Natural Minor Scale.

Harmonized C Harmonic Minor Scale with 7th Chords

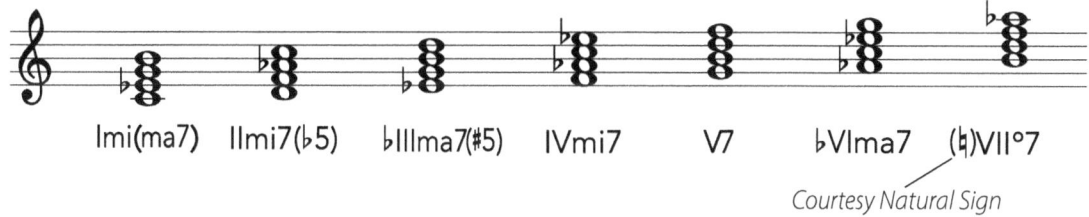

Imi(ma7)   IImi7(♭5)   ♭IIIma7(♯5)   IVmi7   V7   ♭VIma7   (♮)VII°7

Courtesy Natural Sign

Memorize the qualities for the harmonized Harmonic Minor Scale. Let's compare the harmonized Natural Minor and Harmonic Minor Scales. Again, this is important because it is common to be in Natural Minor but temporarily shift into Harmonic Minor for a chord or two.

Harmonized 7th Chords of Natural Minor and Harmonic Minor

MINOR:	Imi7	IImi7(♭5)	♭IIIma7	IVmi7	Vmi7	♭VIma7	♭VII7
	Cmi7	Dmi7(♭5)	E♭ma7	Fmi7	Gmi7	A♭ma7	B♭7
HARMONIC:	Imi(ma7)	IImi7(♭5)	♭IIIma7(♯5)	IVmi7	V7	♭VIma7	VII°7
	Cmi(ma7)	Dmi7(♭5)	E♭ma7(♯5)	Fmi7	G7	A♭ma7	B°7

Which chords are the same in both Natural Minor and Harmonic Minor? The IImi7(♭5), IVmi7, and ♭VIma7.

Which chords differ between the Natural Minor and Harmonic Minor Scale? The Imi(ma7), ♭IIIma7(♯5), V7, and VII°7.

Remember that the V7 and VII°7 are the chords most commonly 'borrowed' from Harmonic Minor for isolated use in a song in minor.

FRETBOARD LOGIC

You have learned five patterns of the Harmonic Minor Scale, so let's take a look at all the notes of the Harmonic Minor Scale available on the fretboard. This graphic shows the combination of all five patterns and how they all connect.

Harmonized Minor Scales

I recommend that you reference the Harmonic Minor Scale shapes with the octave shapes and Minor Pentatonic shells you learned in Level 1. Keep in mind that one difference with the Minor Pentatonic Scale is the major 7th of the Harmonic Minor Scale as opposed to the minor 7th of the minor pentatonic shell. But the essence of the shell is there and making this association will speed up your learning.

Diminished Chords

Back in Level 2 you learned how to build and identify four types of triads: major, minor, augmented, and diminished. Let's take a moment to focus on diminished triads.

Here are the simple diminished triad chord shapes on the fretboard:

Diminished Three-String Shapes

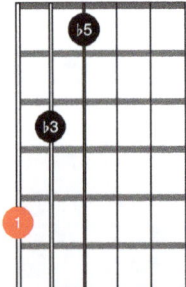 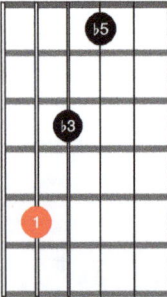 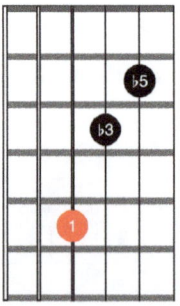 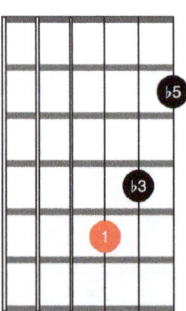

It is also interesting to see all of the possible notes of diminished chords across the entire fretboard. From this matrix any number of fingerings can be derived.

Diminished Chords

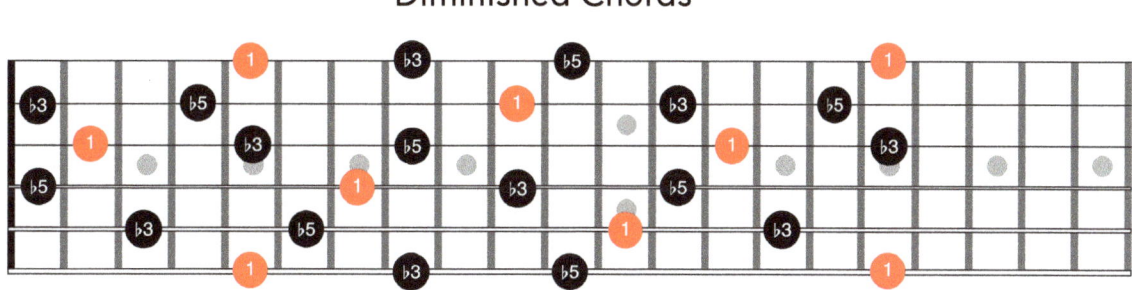

Diminished Triad Arpeggios

All of the information about diminished triad chords can be applied to diminished triad arpeggios. The arpeggio shapes can be played a variety of ways but think of them as if they were introduced as chords.

Diminished Triad Arpeggios

As stated in the last Unit, this information is important, but you should not dedicate a lot of time to the physical practice of learning all of these diminished chord and arpeggio shapes. It is far more important that you simply know how to construct them on the fretboard. There are too many other things to practice to devote a lot of time to memorizing the diminished triad chords and arpeggios. Your goal should be able to create the information in the diagrams in this Unit based on your knowledge.

RHYTHM GUITAR

Samba

In this Module you'll be learning to comp in the Samba style. Samba actually predates Bossa Nova, but because a Bossa is slower and physically less demanding, it was introduced first. A Bossa is felt in 4 because the tempo is usually medium to slow. A Samba is generally faster than a Bossa and is felt in 2 (2/2 or 'cut time'). Writing, reading, and therefore feeling up-tempo music in cut time relaxes the feel. If you are counting in fast 4, the feel can become frantic and and not very graceful. Compare a fast 1, 2, 3, 4 to a relaxed 1, 2, 1, 2. The quarter notes go by at the same speed in cut time (2/2) but the pulse, now in 2, feels better.

The rhythm pattern in this example is a good starting place for Samba comping, but variations are common. It is essentially the same rhythm pattern as the Bossa, just played in cut time. The part played in this example is appropriate for use when playing in a rhythm section. This two-bar example is played on E9 to E9sus. Although we haven't formally studied dominant 9 chords, know that E9 is E7 with a 9th, and therefore E9sus is like E7sus with a 9th.

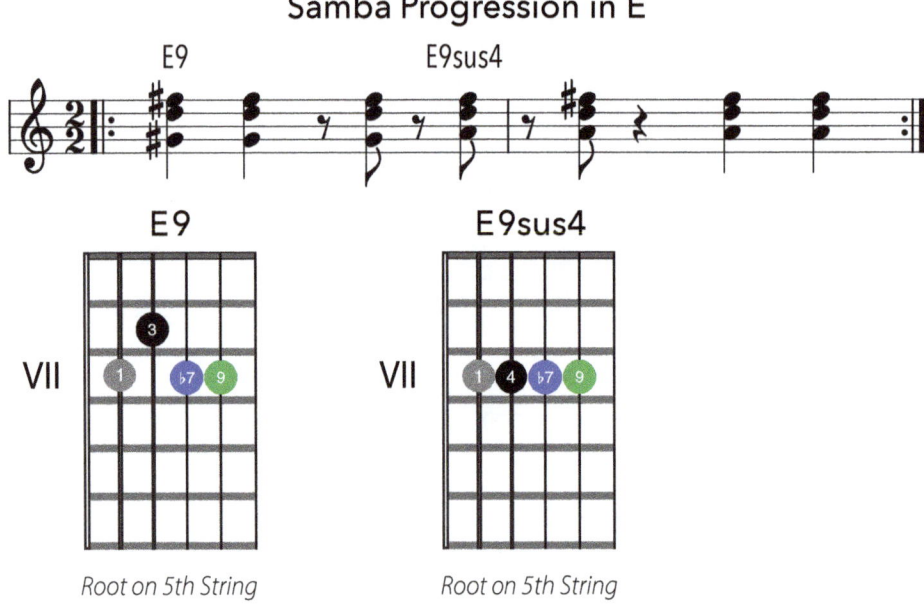

As in the last Unit, we will talk about how to use your picking hand to play the examples. There are two ways you can do it. The first way is to use your bare fingers and the second way is to use a pick using alternate picking. Let's get into the detail of each hand.

With your fretting hand, you have two choices. You can play the entire four-note version shown in the diagram, or you can focus on the three-string set of the 2nd, 3rd, and 4th strings.

Be aware that your fretting hand can avoid the notes on the 5th and 6th strings. It is not a requirement, but sometimes it is a good choice to omit the roots that are voiced on the 5th and 6ths strings. The reason for this is to keep the lower register clear for the bass part.

Start by using the 'fingers-only' technique as you did in the last Unit, and then try it out with a flat pick.

With fingers only:

- Hold your 1st, 2nd, and 3rd fingers in a soft-claw formation: 1st finger on the 4th string, 2nd finger on the 3rd string, and 3rd finger on the 2nd string.
- Pluck the strings simultaneously to make the chord ring.

Now play the part with a flat pick. The faster the tempo, the more likely it is you'll need to use alternate picking to keep the feel relaxed. If you use all downstrokes, the effort you need to use could make it feel frantic.

Sambas are fun to play and usually move along pretty quickly. You need to be on your toes. Whatever you do, don't drag. The feel needs to be light and aggressive all at the same time. Be as efficient as possible with your picking hand to avoid having it sound frantic and/or heavy.

In the next Unit, you'll learn to play a Samba when there is no bass player.

CHART READING

You learned about the 'get-started' instructions, so next up is learning to read the body of the chart. Much of reading a chord chart is about navigation. Musicians often refer to the chart as the 'road map' because it is important to know how your eye travels across the page or pages. Let's focus on something you'll see frequently: slash marks.

Slash Marks

Most chord charts use what are called 'slash marks' written in the staff. These are not to be confused with slash chords. Slash marks are diagonal lines that slant upward from left to right connecting the second and fourth lines of the staff. This is sometimes called 'slash notation'. When slash marks don't have stems, they are marking only where the quarter note pulse is, in most cases. In other words, they are only showing where the quarter notes are and not directing you to literally play quarter notes.

Placement of Chord Symbols with Slash Marks

The placement of a chord symbol above the slash mark on the staff shows the rhythmic placement of the chord. For example, in 4/4 time, the chord symbol for a chord played on beat one is placed directly above the slash mark on beat one. The chord symbol for a chord played on beat three is placed directly above the slash mark on beat three. The chord symbol for a chord played on beat four is placed directly above the slash mark on beat four, and so forth.

Slash Marks with Stems

When slash marks have stems, their meaning changes from just marking where the quarter note is to notating the actual rhythm they represent. Think of the slash as a note head that is not assigned to a specific note on the staff. The slash shows where the chord written above the staff should be played rhythmically.

- A slash mark with a stem pointing down is a quarter note.
- A slash mark with a stem pointing down and a flag is an 8th note.
- A slash mark with a stem pointing down and two flags is a 16th note, and so on.

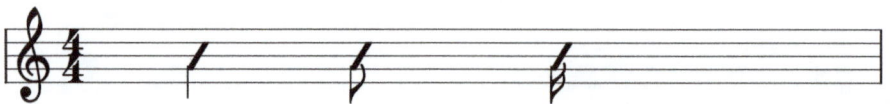

Stems on slash marks usually extend downward. This keeps the corridor directly above the staff clear for the chord symbols.

Slash Marks with Stems and Beams

Groups of 8th and 16th notes as well as triplets can be beamed together. Because the stems extended downward, the beams lie slightly below the staff so they aren't hidden by or confused with the lines of the staff.

Combinations

It is common for charts to switch back and forth between slash marks with stems and slash marks without stems. If you see slash marks in a measure or even part of a measure, you are not being instructed to play a specific rhythm. But when you see stems, stems and flags, half notes, or whole notes, you are being instructed to play the specific rhythm shown.

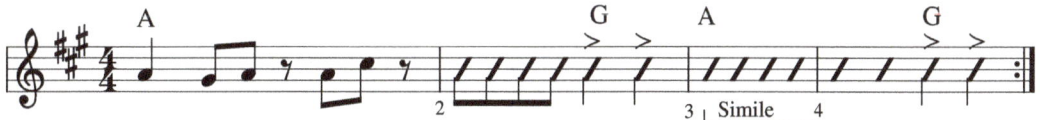

Slash Notation for Half Notes and Whole Notes

There are different styles of writing half notes and whole notes with slash notation but what all styles have in common is some sort of 'enclosed' shape. It could be a triangle, diamond, parallelogram, or circle. In the next Level when we learn to write charts I will suggest you start with a slash mark as the left side of a triangle and then complete the shape with the other two sides to the right.

- For a whole note in slash notation, there is no stem.
- For a half note, the stem is attached to the left side and extends downward.

Half Note and Whole Note Slash Marks

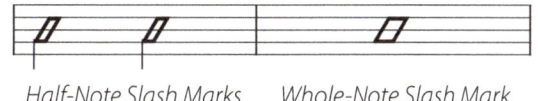

Half-Note Slash Marks   Whole-Note Slash Mark

No Slash Marks

You will see chord charts with blank measures with no slash marks and just the chord symbol above. This is not rare, and sometimes the intent of the creator of the chart is to leave room for the individual musicians to write in what is unique to their parts. This can very useful.

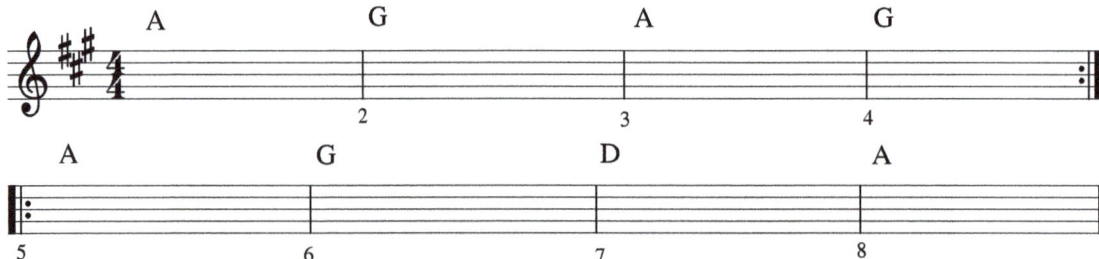

Clarity

People who are good at writing charts are doing their best to help the musician who has to read the chart. Unfortunately, not everyone takes the extra few minutes here and there to make a chart that is easy to read. Whether you use the chart at home to learn a song, take it to a rehearsal to use for a guide there, or use it on the gig, it is important that it's easy to read. A musician should use their brain power to play the music, not decipher a poorly-written chart. But brace yourself for bad charts: You will see plenty of them. There have been instances where I've rewritten a poorly-written chart that was given to me so that I had one less thing to worry about when performing.

Remember that great artists don't always provide great charts. I've worked with amazing, well-known musicians who have atrocious charts. There's an expression musicians use when talking about a well-written chart: "That chart reads itself". As you read more and more charts, you will see what a difference a well-written chart can make.

IMPROVISATION

The first two Level 5 Improvisation Modules led you toward the idea of being selective about when and where to use the leading tone of the Harmonic Minor Scale. The suggestion is to perhaps 'save it' for the V chord which, as you know, contains the leading tone, the major 7th of the scale. The leading tone is an impactful note that brings out the essence of the V major or V7 chord.

The focus in this Module is to be very intentional about the use of the Harmonic Minor for specific chords. In effect, this is a kind of modal interchange within the minor world. A progression may call for shifting between the parallel Natural Minor and Harmonic Minor Scales. Let's analyze the following progression in G minor. Play this progression and focus on the V7 chord and how strong the leading tone in the V7 sounds.

Progression in G Minor

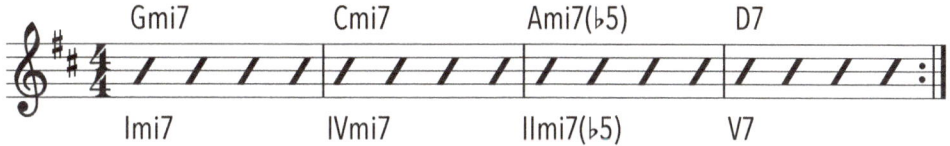

Next, let's take a look at the harmonized G Natural Minor and Harmonic Minor scales side by side.

G Minor Scale Harmonized with 7th Chords

G Harmonic Minor Scale Harmonized with 7th Chords

We can see that the Gmi7 is the Imi7 in G Natural Minor but does not belong to the G Harmonic Minor Scale. This means that the G Natural Minor Scale is the appropriate note source for this chord.

Progression in G Minor

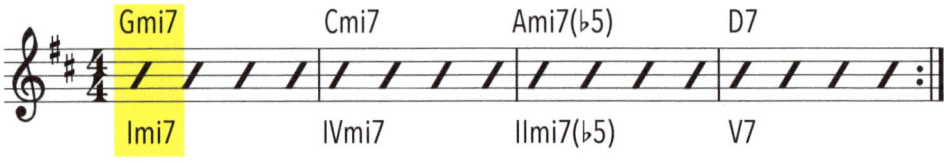

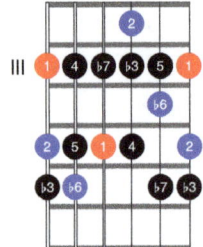

Pattern IV
G Natural Minor

Cmi7 is the IVmi7 in both the G Natural Minor and G Harmonic Minor Scales. This means that either the G Natural Minor or Harmonic Minor Scale is an appropriate note source for this chord.

Ami7(♭5) is the IImi7(♭5) in both the G Natural Minor and G Harmonic Minor Scales. This means that either the G Natural Minor or Harmonic Minor Scale is an appropriate note source for this chord.

Even though both the G Natural Minor and G Harmonic Minor Scales can be played on IVmi7 and IImi7(♭5), I suggest using G Natural Minor for both. This saves the impact of the leading tone for the critical V7 chord.

Progression in G Minor

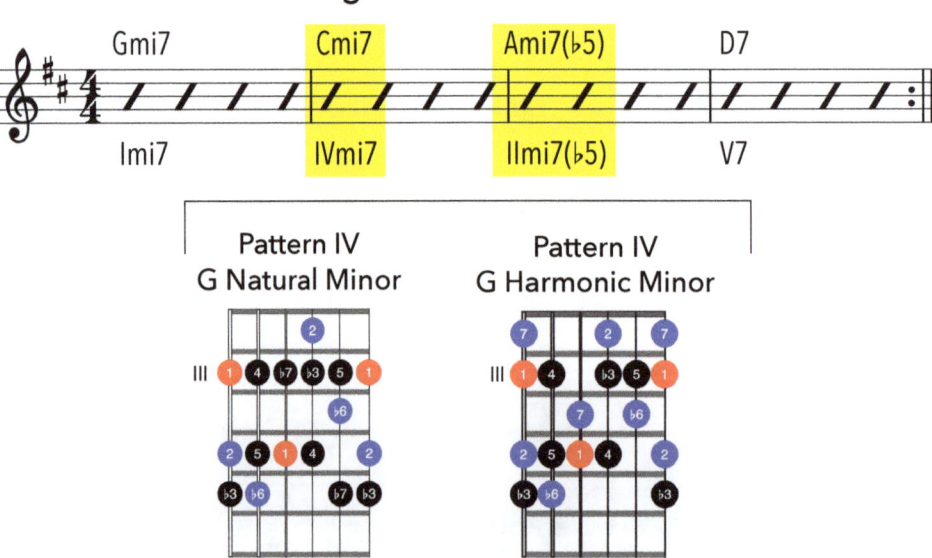

D7 is the V7 in the G Harmonic Minor Scale but does not belong to the G Natural Minor scale. This means that the G Harmonic Minor Scale is the appropriate note source for this chord.

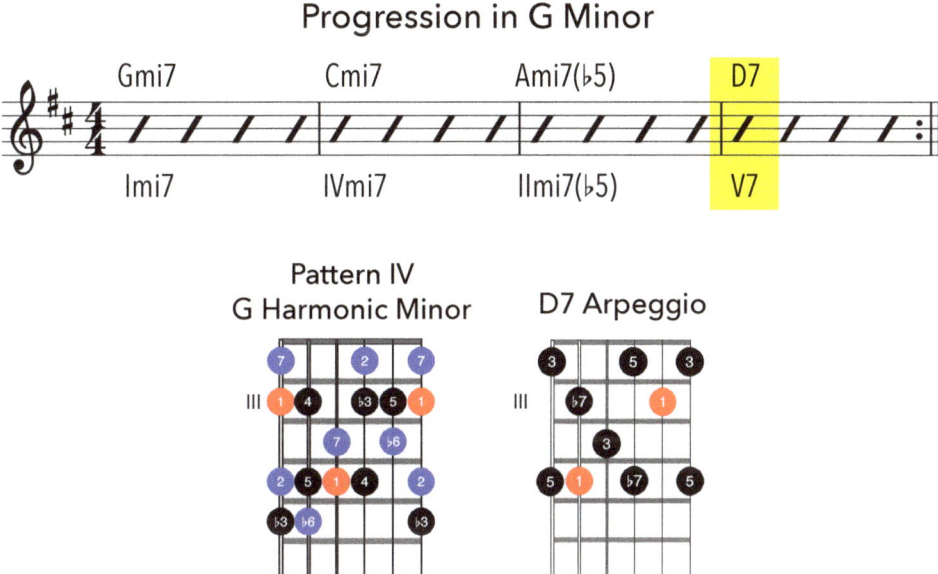

The goal of your practice for this Module is to target the chord tones of the V7 on at least the first beat of the 4th measure when it's played.

- Locate the Pattern IV G Natural Minor and Harmonic Minor Scale patterns in 3rd position.
- Locate the V7 arpeggio in the same vicinity. That will be an Octave Shape I D7 in 2nd position.
- Create motifs and improvise using the parallel scales and the V7 arpeggio on D7.

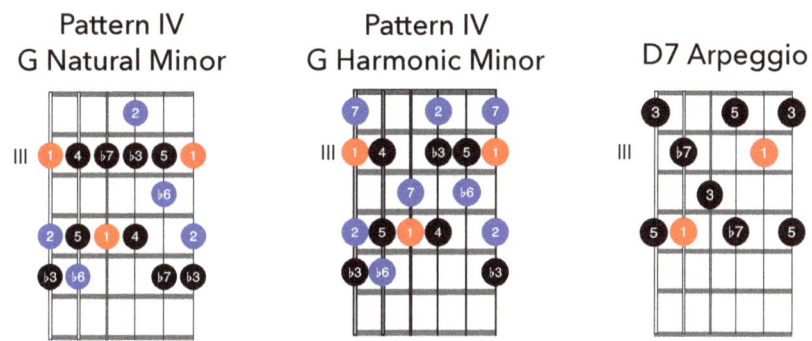

The information in this Module was presented to you in the Pattern IV Octave Shape area because it's the place that's most comfortable for most guitarists. But know that these concepts should eventually be learned in other patterns as well. Your goal is to transition freely between the Natural Minor and Harmonic Minor Scales and be in control of the V7 arpeggio.

Level 5 Unit 3 • Improv Demo

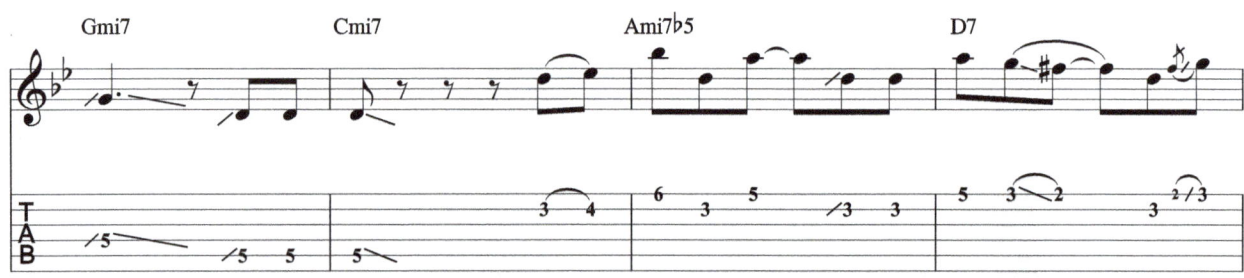

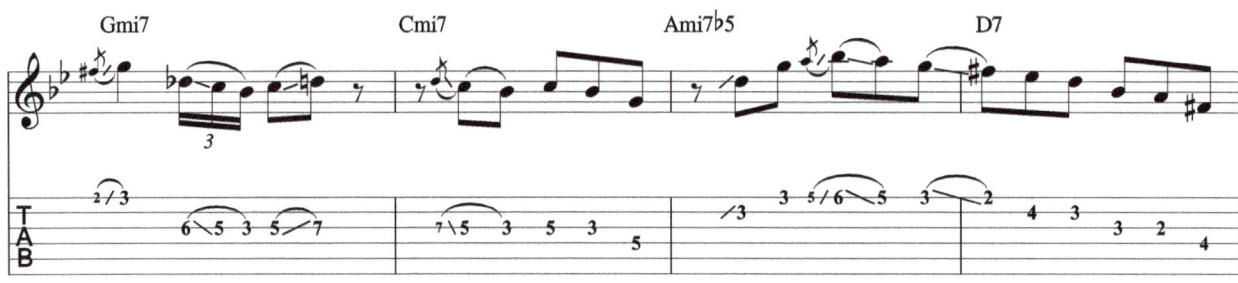

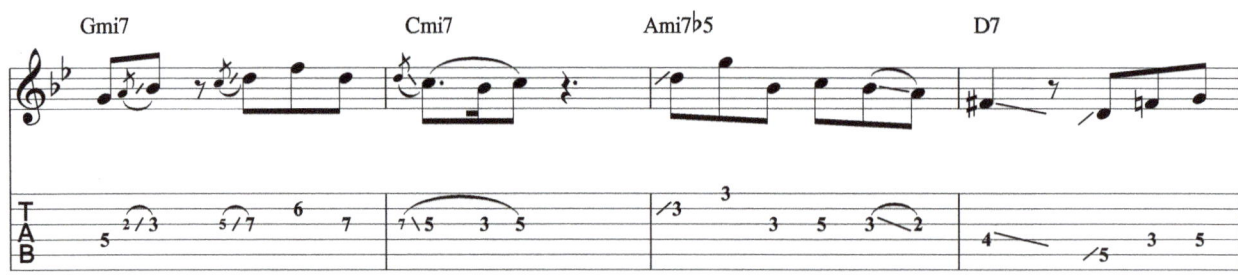

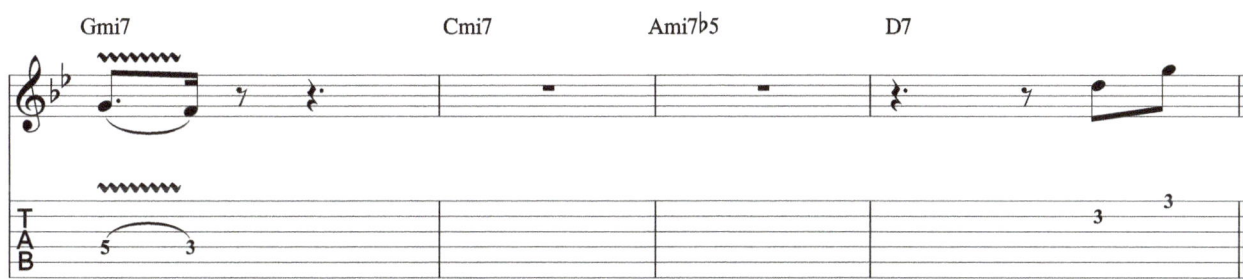
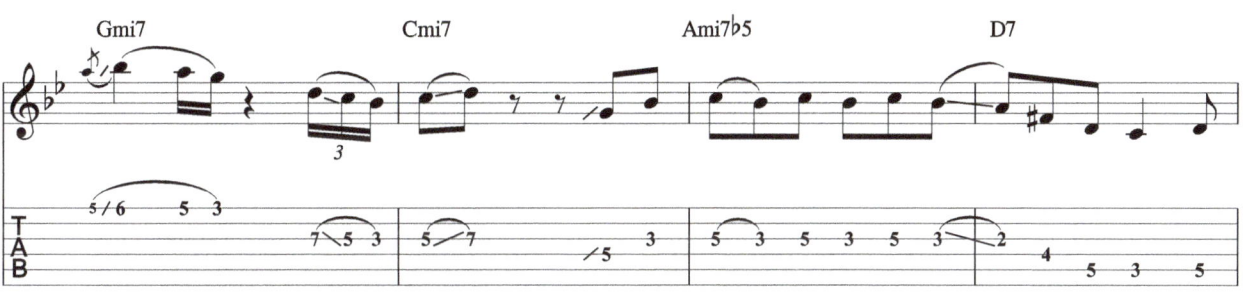
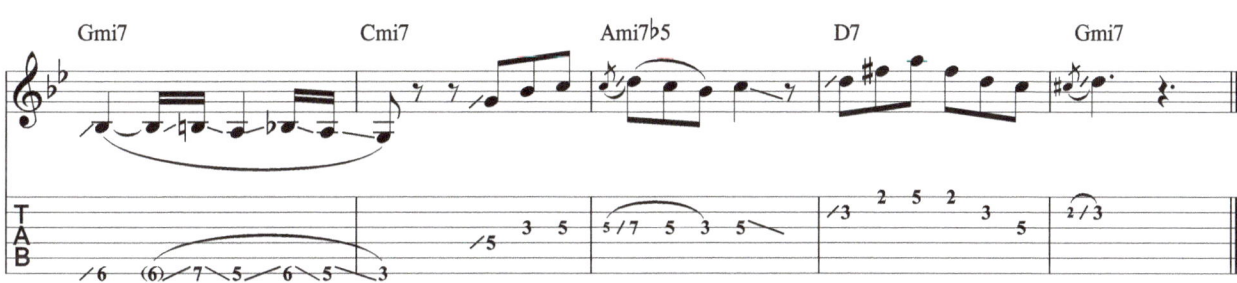

PRACTICE

Theory

- ☐ Go to the tabs below the Theory video on the website and complete the quiz.
- ☐ Learn the Harmonic Minor Scale harmonized with 7th chords.
- ☐ Learn the new chords that occur when harmonizing the Harmonic Minor Scale.
- ☐ Learn about the VII°7 Chord.

Fretboard Logic

- ☐ Learn the voicings for diminished chords and diminished triad arpeggios.

Rhythm Guitar

- ☐ Practice the Samba rhythm pattern over the progression in E.

Chart Reading

- ☐ Understand how slash marks and slash marks with stems are used in a chart.
- ☐ Understand the importance of clarity in a chart.

Improvisation

- ☐ Practice playing solos over the progression in G minor using the Pattern IV Natural Minor and Harmonic Minor Scales, and the D7 in-position arpeggio.

UNIT 4

Learning Modules

> **Theory** - The V7 Chord, the Tritone

> **Fretboard Logic** - The V-I Resolution

> **Rhythm Guitar** - Samba Rhythm Guitar

> **Chart Reading** - Section Markings: Rehearsal Letters, Bar Numbers

> **Improvisation** - Soloing with the Harmonic Minor Scale over the V7 Chord

> **Practice** - Continue Practice Routine Development

THEORY

In the last Unit you learned the Harmonic Minor Scale harmonized with 7th chords.

Harmonized C Harmonic Minor Scale with 7th Chords

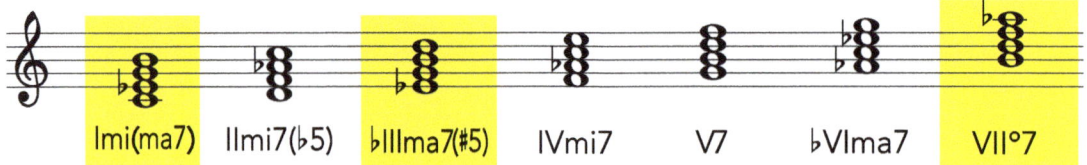

Imi(ma7)   IImi7(♭5)   ♭IIIma7(#5)   IVmi7   V7   ♭VIma7   VII°7

In the process of harmonizing the scale you learned these chords:

- Mi(Ma7), a minor triad with a major 7th
- Ma7(+5), an augmented triad with a major 7th
- Dim7, a diminished triad with a diminished 7th

Along with learning to harmonize the scale, you learned that the Harmonic Minor Scale is not usually the basis for entire compositions. What is more common is minor modal interchange, meaning that songs written in minor keys use mostly melody notes and chords from Natural Minor but have some melody notes and some chords borrowed from the parallel Harmonic Minor Scale.

Let's compare the C Natural Minor and C Harmonic Minor Scales again. We have done this before in previous units, but let's take another look. Notice what is different between the two scales. It is the major 7th right? Because of this single difference, you can think of these as 'parallel minor scales'.

C Natural Minor Scale

1 2 ♭3 4 5 ♭6 ♭7 8

C Harmonic Minor Scale

1 2 ♭3 4 5 ♭6 7 8

Next, take another look at the table below that compares the harmonized Natural Minor and Harmonic Minor Scales using 7th chords. We did this in the last Theory Module, but let's look at this again. This comparison is important so you see which chords are the same and which are different.

Harmonized 7th Chords of Natural Minor and Harmonic Minor

MINOR:	Imi7	IImi7(♭5)	♭IIIma7	IVmi7	Vmi7	♭VIma7	♭VII7
	Cmi7	Dmi7(♭5)	E♭ma7	Fmi7	Gmi7	A♭ma7	B♭7
HARMONIC:	Imi(ma7)	IImi7(♭5)	♭IIIma7(♯5)	IVmi7	V7	♭VIma7	VII°7
	Cmi(ma7)	Dmi7(♭5)	E♭ma7(♯5)	Fmi7	G7	A♭ma7	B°7

In the next series of units we will examine each of the chords that are different in harmonic minor and study how each one is used in progressions.

- Imi(ma7)
- ♭IIIma7(+5)
- V7
- VII°7

The V7 Chord

This Unit focuses on the V7 chord from Harmonic Minor that is often used in a Natural Minor setting. Some of this is a review because the use of V7 in minor was introduced back in Level 3. There is a lot of critical detail about dominant 7 chords in this Module, so go through this information carefully.

Composers and songwriters often change the V chord in minor keys from a minor 7 chord to a dominant 7 chord. This is because the V7 chord contains the leading tone, which is the 3rd of the V7. Remember that a leading tone is the major 7th scale degree of a scale and it has the powerful effect of leading the ear up one half step to the tonic.

The diatonic V chord in Natural Minor Scale is minor 7 so there is no leading tone effect. Therefore, the sound of the diatonic Vmi7 resolving to Imi is not as strong as the V7 resolving to Imi.

The V Chord in Natural Minor and Harmonic Minor

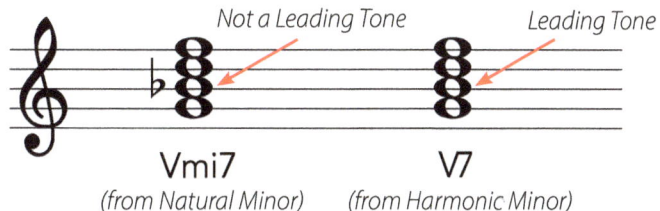

Let's break down the dominant 7 chord a little more. A really important characteristic of a dominant 7 chord is the interval in the interior of the chord between the major 3rd and minor 7th.

Take a look at the G7 chord and notice the interval between the major 3rd, B, and flatted 7th, F. The interval is a diminished 5th and it's very dissonant, which means that it's unsettled and makes the listener anxious for resolution.

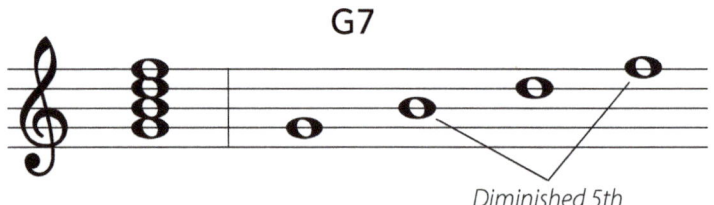

Resolution happens by resolving a dissonant interval to a consonant interval. The diminished interval resolves like this:

- The 3rd of the G7, B, resolves up a half step to the tonic, which is the root of the I chord.

The 3rd Resolves to the Tonic

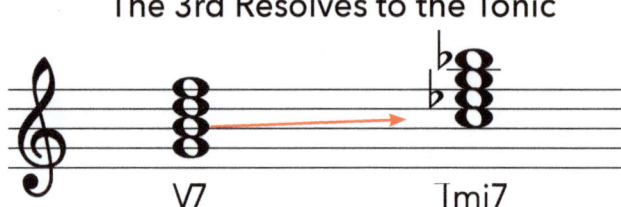

- In a minor context, the ♭7 of the G7, F, resolves down a whole step to E♭, the minor 3rd of a Cmi chord. In a major context, the F resolves down a half step to E, the major 3rd of a Cma7 chord.

The ♭7 Resolves to the Minor 3rd   The ♭7 Resolves to the Major 3rd

- The root of the G7, G, resolves up a 4th, to the C, the root of the Cmi7 chord.

The Root Resolves to the 3rd

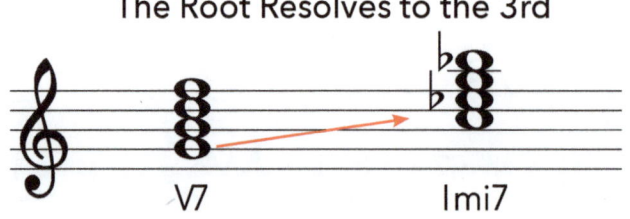

You may have noticed that the Cmi7 (Imi7) chord in this example is voiced above the G7 (V7) chord, so it makes sense that it would sound like there was an upward resolution to the Imi7 chord. But what happens if the Imi7 chord is voiced an octave lower?

Would it still sound like the 3rd, b7, and root of the V7 are 'resolving up' to the notes of a Imi7 chord that is voiced lower than the V7?

Yes, it would. Even if the V7 chord resolves to Imi7 chord voiced in a lower register, the ear still perceives an upward resolution.

The important point to remember here is that in addition to the 3rd of the V7 being the leading tone of the key, the interval of a diminished 5th between the 3rd and b7 adds to the tension and therefore the need for resolution. When a V7 chord resolves to I, the stress of the diminished 5th interval gives way to a sense of resolution on the I chord, whether the I chord is major or minor.

The Tritone

You may have heard the term 'tritone' before. A diminished 5th is often referred to as a tritone. The 'tri' in tritone refers to the three whole steps in a diminished 5th or its enharmonic equivalent, the augmented 4th. For example, there are three whole steps between B and F. 'Tritone' is a very popular term, often used in place of 'diminished 5th'.

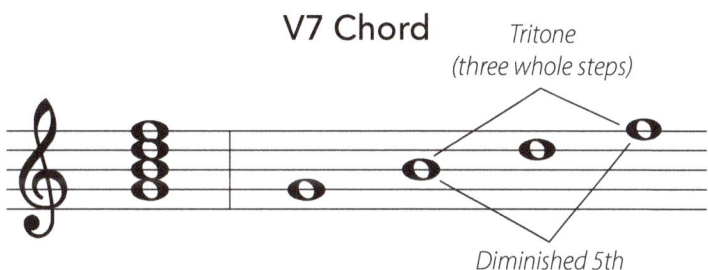

Now that you know a little more about how and why a V7 chord resolves to a I chord, it's time return to the discussion of how it's used in a minor key. Because the V7 chord is from the parallel Harmonic Minor Scale, melodies played over the V7 chord should shift to Harmonic Minor for the duration of the V7 chord.

Take a look at this progression.

Progression in C Minor

Cmi7	Ebma7	Dmi7(b5) G7	Cmi7
Imi7	bIIIma7	IImi7(b5) V7	Imi7

The Cmi7, Ebma7, and Dmi7(b5) are all diatonic to C Natural Minor. Therefore, the source of notes for melodies over those chords is the C Natural Minor Scale. And remember that the term 'melodies' applies to improvised lines, too.

The G7, however, comes from the C Harmonic Minor Scale. So for the duration of the G7 chord, the source of melody notes is the C Harmonic Minor Scale. This really isn't a radical physical difference—that is, the B (leading tone) of the C Harmonic Minor Scale versus the B♭ of the C Natural Minor Scale. It's only one note, but it does make a harmonic difference.

FRETBOARD LOGIC

The V-I Resolution

In the Theory Module we looked more closely at how functioning dominant chords resolve to both I major and I minor. In this Module we will take the Fretboard Logic point of view of this V-I resolution.

You learned the two most important things about a functioning dominant 7:

- The 3rd of a functioning dominant is the leading tone of the next chord. It resolves up a half step to the root of the next chord.

- There is a tritone interval between the major 3rd and minor 7th of a functioning dominant. The tritone is a dissonant interval which means it is unsettling. The 3rd again resolves up a half step and the minor 7th resolves down to the major 3rd of I major or the minor 3rd of I minor.

Let's get a visual look at the V-I resolution on the fretboard, and physically feel what it's like to play it and hear what it sounds like. So get out your guitar and play these:

V-I Resolution to Major

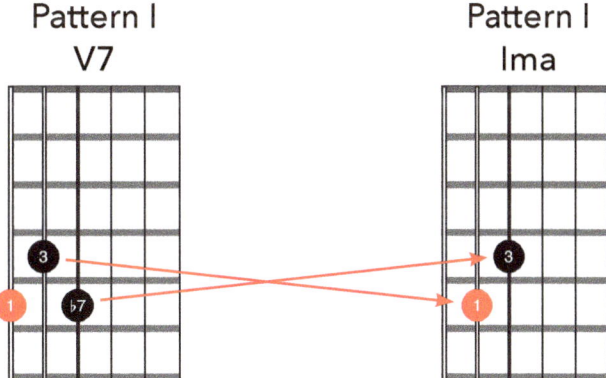

This example is based on the skeleton of a Pattern I major triad. It's preceded by its V7. Notice how the 3rd of V7 resolves up a half step to the root of the I chord and the ♭7 resolves down a half step to the major 3rd.

Next, play these:

V-I Resolution to Minor

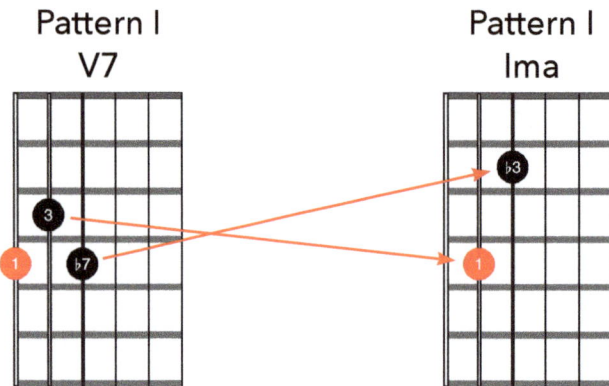

This example is based on the skeleton of a Pattern I minor triad. It's preceded by its V7. Notice how the 3rd of V7 resolves up a half step to the root of the I chord and the ♭7 resolves down a whole step to the minor 3rd.

Play this:

V-I Resolution to Major

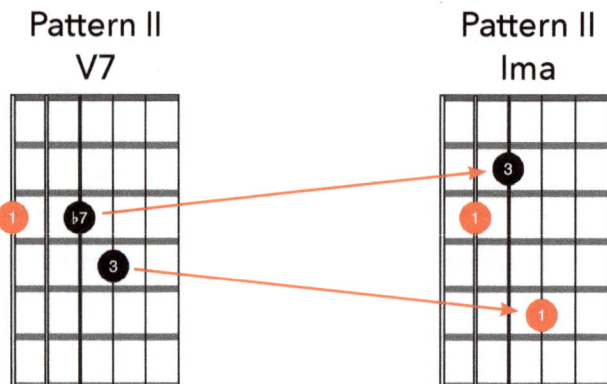

This example is based on the skeleton of a Pattern II major triad. It's preceded by its V7. Notice how the 3rd of V7 resolves up a half step to the root of the I chord and the ♭7 resolves down a half step to the major 3rd.

Now play this:

V-I Resolution to Minor

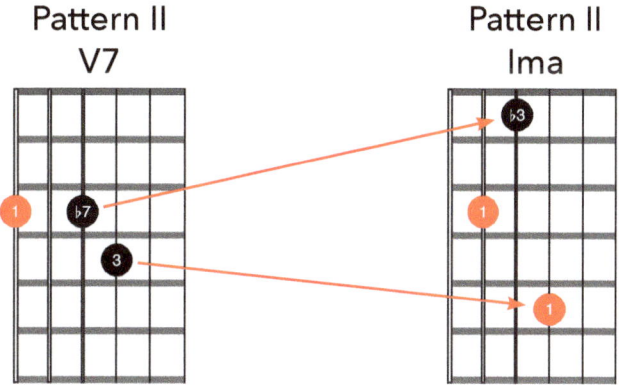

This example is based on the skeleton of a Pattern II minor triad. It's preceded by its V7. Notice how the 3rd of V7 resolves up a half step to the root of the I chord and the b7 resolves down a whole step to the minor 3rd.

Play this:

V-I Resolution to Major

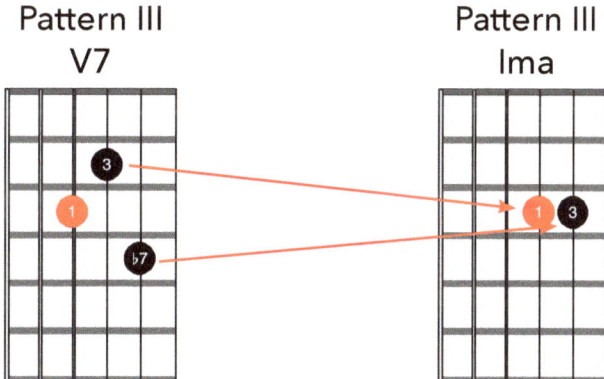

This example is based on the skeleton of a Pattern III major triad. It's preceded by its V7. Notice how the 3rd of V7 resolves up a half step to the root of the I chord and the b7 resolves down a half step to the major 3rd.

Now play this:

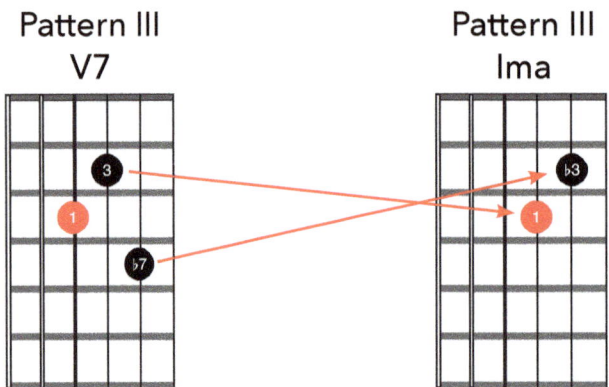

This example is based on the skeleton of a Pattern III minor triad. It's preceded by its V7. Notice how the 3rd of V7 resolves up a half step to the root of the I chord and the ♭7 resolves down a whole step to the minor 3rd.

Play this:

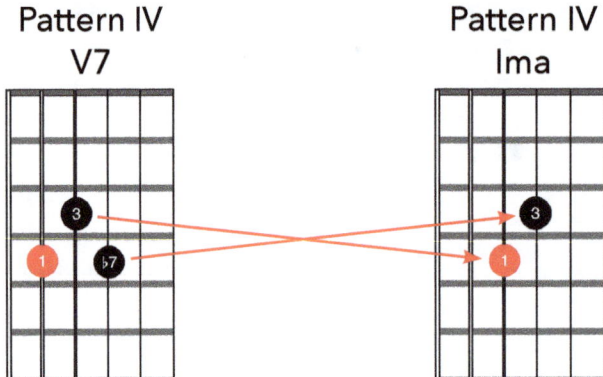

This example is based on the skeleton of a Pattern IV major triad. It's preceded by its V7. Notice how the 3rd of V7 resolves up a half step to the root of the I chord and the ♭7 resolves down a half step to the major 3rd.

Next, play this:

V-I Resolution to Minor

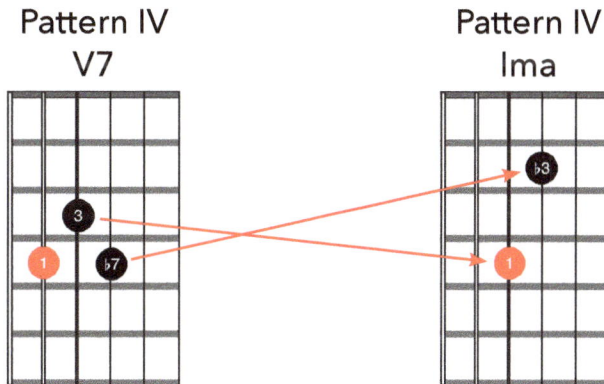

Pattern IV — V7   Pattern IV — Ima

This is example is based on the skeleton of a Pattern IV minor triad. It's preceded by its V7. Notice how the 3rd of V7 resolves up a half step to the root of the I chord and the ♭7 resolves down a whole step to the minor 3rd.

Note: For these skeleton-type illustrations, Pattern V looks just like Pattern IV so there's no reason to repeat that.

Now you have had a visual look at the V-I resolution on the fretboard and heard what it sounds like. Keep these shapes fresh in your mind. There will be many V-I resolutions in your future and these images will be a help in creating lines.

RHYTHM GUITAR

In this Module you will continue learning to comp in the Samba style. The example in this Module is used when there is no bass player. It incorporates the bass part. Remember that the Samba is normally faster than the Bossa and is felt in 2/2 (or 'cut time').

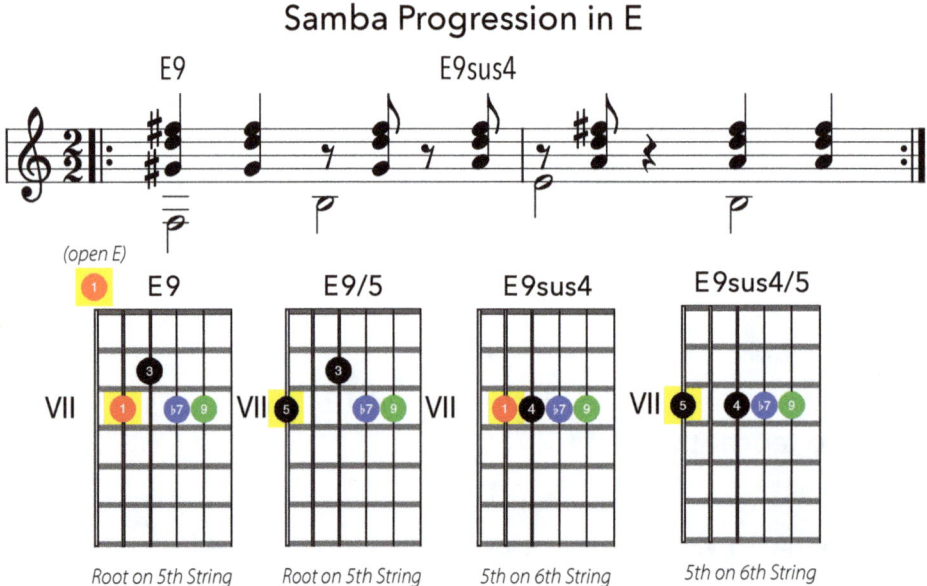

This is the same two-bar example used in the last Rhythm Guitar Module except here the bass part is played by guitar. This part is for when there is no rhythm section and therefore no bass player. It moves from E9 to E9sus and uses fingers only, no pick.

Before you work on the rhythm, learn where to place your fretting fingers and picking-hand fingers:

- Begin with your fretting hand and play E9. Notice the root is voiced on the 5th string at the 7th fret. The root can also be played with the open E; that really helps it sound like a bass part because it's the lowest note possible on guitar.
- Also note that the 5th is voiced on the adjacent string, the 6th string, at the 7th fret. These two notes, E and B, will be used to play the bass part and we'll have two options for where to play E: at the 7th fret on the 5th string or an open E.
- The bass note options are the same for E9sus.

Now with your picking hand:

- Place your thumb on the root on the 5th string.
- Then place your 1st, 2nd, and 3rd fingers in a soft-claw formation above the 2nd, 3rd, and 4th strings. Your picking hand is now in position to play the part.
- Your picking-hand thumb will alternate between the root and 5th: root on the 5th string and 5th on the 6th string.
- The root will also be played on the open E. The chord tones for the bass part are the root and 5th only.

Now that you know where to place your fretting-hand fingers and picking-hand fingers, learn the actual part. This is a two-bar phrase repeated over and over. The bass plays half notes only and the comping rhythm pattern is played on top. The challenge, like with the Bossa, is developing the independence between the thumb and the other fingers in your picking hand.

Start by just resting the claw shape on the 4th, 3rd, and 2nd strings. Just make contact with the strings and leave them in place.

- Play the bass part only: root, 5th, root, 5th. Again, the bass rhythm is half notes only.
- Root on open 6th string (could also be 5th string, 7th fret).
- 5th on the 6th string, 7th fret.
- Root on 5th string, 7th fret.
- 5th on the 6th string, 7th fret.

Next, systematically add the chord component using the claw. And remember, this is in 2/2 so there are only two beats and they're represented by half notes. There are four quarter notes: one, the 'and' of one, two, and the 'and' of two.

For the first measure:

- Begin playing the E9 played with both thumb and claw on beat one. The thumb is playing the root on the 6th string.
- On the second quarter note, which is the 'and' of one, play the claw only.
- On beat two, the 3rd quarter note, use your thumb only. Play the 5th at the 7th fret of the 6th string.
- On the 'e' of two, play the claw only.
- On the 'a' of two, play the claw only but the fretting hand has shifted to E9sus.

Review the first measure. Practice that much isolated as much as you need. The independence between your thumb and fingers is important.

For the second measure:

- Begin with the thumb of your picking hand playing the root on the 5th string at the 7th fret.
- On the 'e' of one, play the claw only, still on E9sus.
- On beat two, play both thumb and claw. The thumb is playing the 5th on the 6th string at the 7th fret.
- On the 'and' of two, play the claw only.

Review the second measure. Practice that much isolated as much as you need. The independence between your thumb and fingers is important. Then put both measures together and play the whole two-bar phrase.

Samba Progression in E

After you are feeling good about your progress, turn on the metronome very slowly. You might try half notes at 54-60 bpm but it's really up to you. Increase the tempo as you feel more in control. Once you improve your ability to play this you will see how important it is to feel this in 2 or cut time.

Again, the part played in this example is appropriate for use when there is no bass player. Don't play these bass notes when there is a bass player. You will just be in his or her way.

Regardless of the chords played in song, these picking-hand techniques are applicable. Your goal with this part, as with the Samba part for playing a rhythm section, is to have a light feel that doesn't drag or feel heavy. Be efficient with your physical movement. Move as little as possible and stay relaxed.

CHART READING

Section Markings

This Module discusses section markings in a chord chart. Keeping your place is the most important chart reading job you have. Even if you miss a chord or play the wrong one, you need to keep going. Leave your mistake in the past and keep forging ahead. Often times the mistake is minor and you're the only one who knows. Other times it's a humiliating disaster. Either way, the music can't stop.

Whatever happens, don't get lost! Human nature is to try to pause and understand what just went wrong, but you can't. Save that for later. It's important to keep your eyes moving through the chart even if you're not playing at all. There are many ways a good chart helps you stay on track. One way is to have clear markings for the sections of the song.

Rehearsal Letters

Rehearsal letters are used to mark the sections of a song. Sometimes they're called section letters or section markers. Rehearsal letters are used in alphabetical order: A, B, C, and beyond, depending on the length of the song. But there are many, many variants of rehearsal or chart section markings. Rehearsal letters are capitalized and normally written with a box around them to set them apart from chord symbols. I've seen confusing charts where it was hard to tell the rehearsal letters from the chord symbols. That's why the box around the letters is so important.

Rehearsal letters are very helpful in a rehearsal because the leader can instruct the band to go to "Letter B", for example, to work on that part of a song. Even more specifically, the leader can reference a specific location in a song that needs work. Perhaps the bass player keeps missing a part. The band leader can say something like, "check your note on the 'and of two' in the 3rd measure of Letter B." These exact coordinates can really speed up a rehearsal instead of trying to use some other way to pinpoint a trouble spot.

Sections are also set apart from each other by the use of double bars used at the beginning and ending of sections. It's subtle, but effective. Your eye will pick up these double bars and recognize structure of the song.

Other Rehearsal Markings

Other rehearsal markings for sections are common:
- 'Intro' is probably the most common non-letter rehearsal marking.
- 'Interlude' is common and usually marks a short section of a song between more substantive sections—perhaps after the first chorus and before the second verse.
- 'Solo' is also used alone without a letter but more often the solo is given a letter of its own and the word 'Solo' is written above the staff.

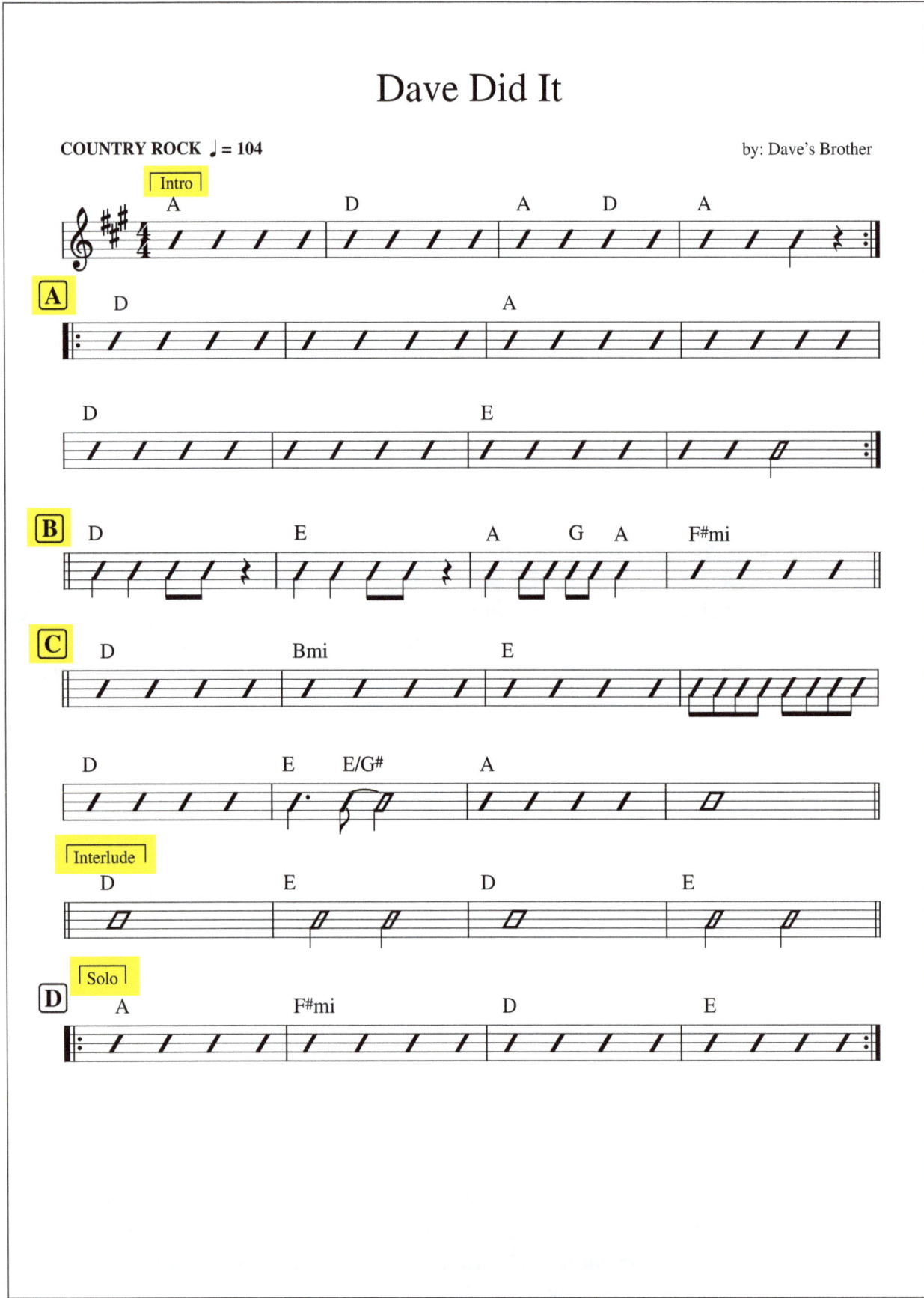

Fretboard Biology — Level 5 • Unit 4: Chart Reading

One variant of rehearsal letters is to use a small number next to the letter. For example, if the A section has to be written out three times in a chart, the first time could be marked A1, the second time A2, and the third time A3.

This works great when a section, such as 'A', has to be written multiple times because there's a slight or not-so-slight variation.

Another variant of rehearsal markings is to use words instead of letters. For example:
- Intro
- Verse
- Chorus
- Interlude
- Bridge
- Solo

You might also see these written as: Verse 1, Prechorus 1, Chorus 1, then Verse 2, and so on. If a chart has rehearsal letters, you may want to write in the words like verse and chorus on your personal copy of the chart because most singers are going to relate more to these terms than letters.

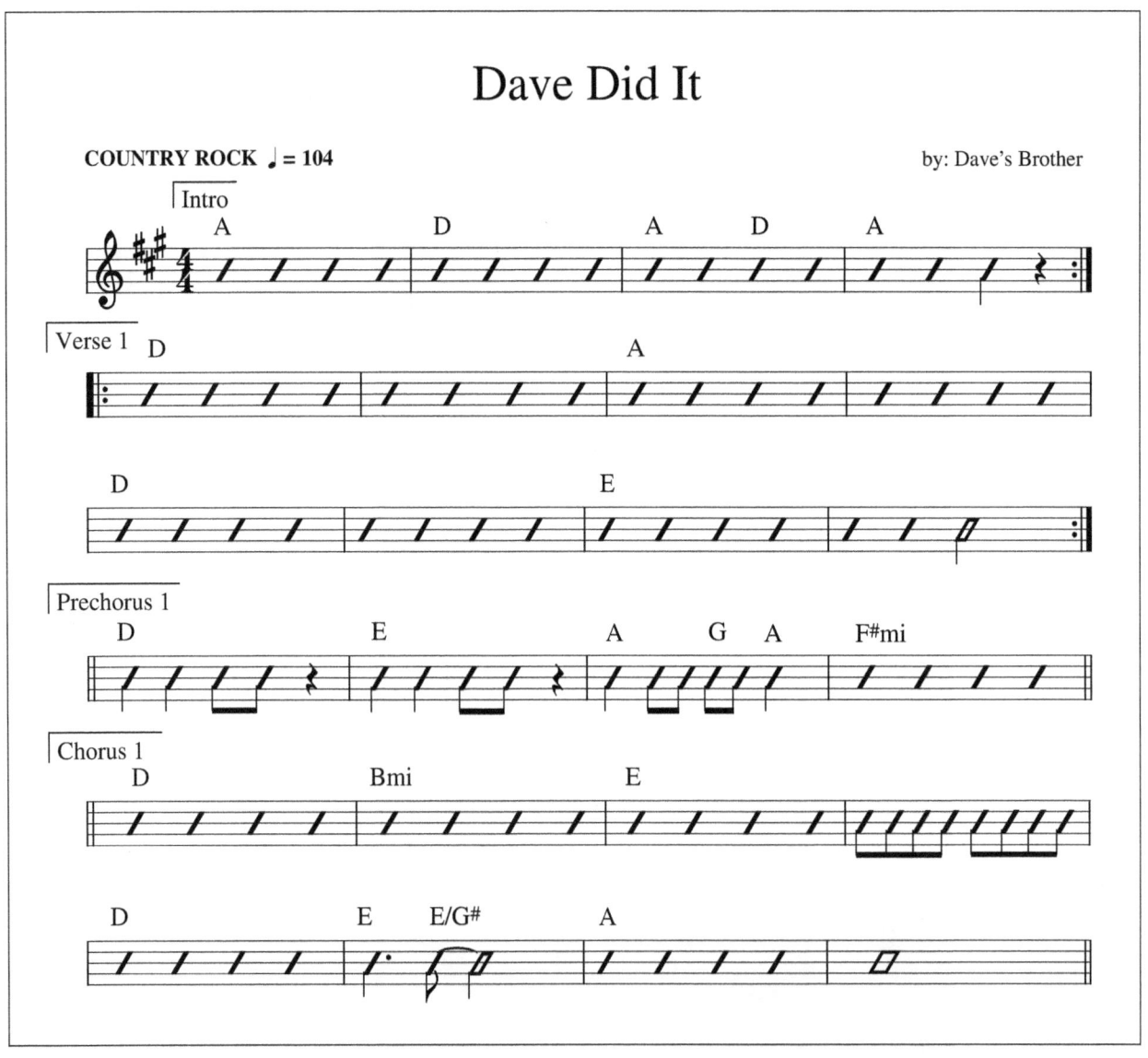

Bar Numbers

Some charts have each bar numbered. The numbers are written very small and under the barline at the beginning of each measure. This is another excellent way to pinpoint a location in a song during rehearsal.

Charts that number each bar sometimes use the number of the first bar in a new section in place of a letter like A, B, C, etc. The numbers are boxed in like the letters are.

More About Sections

There is another important point about sections. When reading a chart, your eyes are constantly shifting from the music to your fretboard—back and forth, back and forth. It's best to be able to absorb a series of measures at a glance before you shift your eyes to the guitar, and then know where you should look when you look back at the chart. So it's great when each new section on the chart begins on left margin. That helps you know where to look when your eyes return to the chart. Getting lost is no fun and it makes you feel terrible. You will feel sheer panic if you can't find your place.

One skill you learn by reading a lot of charts is to NOT look at your instrument very much. You learned root maps for playing chords by number. It's effective for reading chord charts, too. If you know your root maps, you don't need to look at the fretboard as much. You should be able to play all of your open and barre chords without looking as well.

Another important skill is to be able to absorb more than just the immediate measure or measures at a glance. Well-written charts have taken this into account and arrange measures and sections for mass-absorption, so to speak.

Remember that the Chart Reading modules in this Level are dedicated to reading charts and not to writing them properly. You will see many well-written charts, but probably even more that are poorly written. It's important for this course to present the right way to do things so you recognize when things are wrong. Don't be openly critical or judgmental about poorly-written charts, just figure out what the creator of them wants and keep your mouth shut. Criticizing charts is bad form, politically speaking.

The message is simple: Learn how a well-written chart should look as is presented here, but know that the reality is that most charts will not be 'by the book', so keep an open mind.

IMPROVISATION

The focus of the last Improvisation Module was to be intentional about the use of the Harmonic Minor Scale on specific chords. It's an approach that's a kind of 'modal interchange' within the minor world. The progression called for shifting between the parallel Natural and Harmonic Minor Scales.

We will do a similar thing in this Module using Pattern II Minor over a progression in C minor. Let's take a look at the harmonized C Natural and Harmonic Minor Scales side by side on the staff.

C Natural Minor Scale Harmonized with Triads

C Harmonic Minor Scale Harmonized with Triads

Here is the progression.

Progression in C Minor

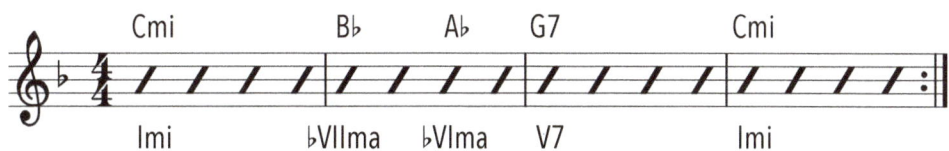

Cmi is the Imi in both the C Natural Minor and C Harmonic Minor Scale. This means that either the C Natural Minor or Harmonic Minor Scale is an appropriate source of notes for this chord. According to what you learned in the last Unit about being selective in using the Harmonic Minor Scale, consider choosing the C Natural Minor Scale.

B♭ is the ♭VIIma in the C Natural Minor Scale but does not belong to the C Harmonic Minor Scale. This means that the C Natural Minor Scale is the appropriate source of notes for this chord.

A♭ is the ♭VIma in both the C Natural Minor and C Harmonic Minor Scales. This means that either scale is an appropriate source of notes for this chord. According to what you learned in the last Unit about being selective in using the Harmonic Minor Scale, consider choosing the C Natural Minor Scale.

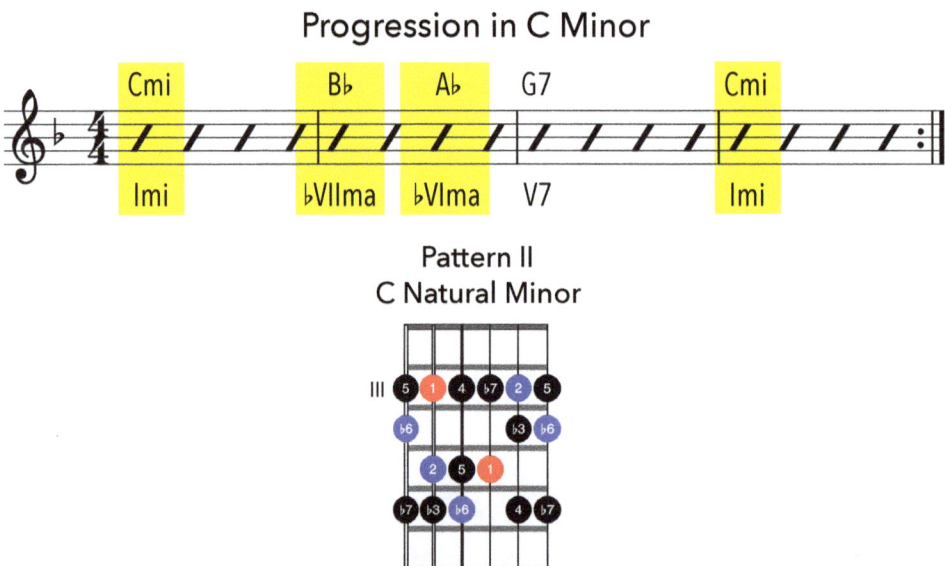

G7 is the V7 in the C Harmonic Minor Scale but does not belong to the C Natural Minor Scale. This means that C Harmonic Minor Scale is the appropriate source of notes for this chord, as is the G7 arpeggio.

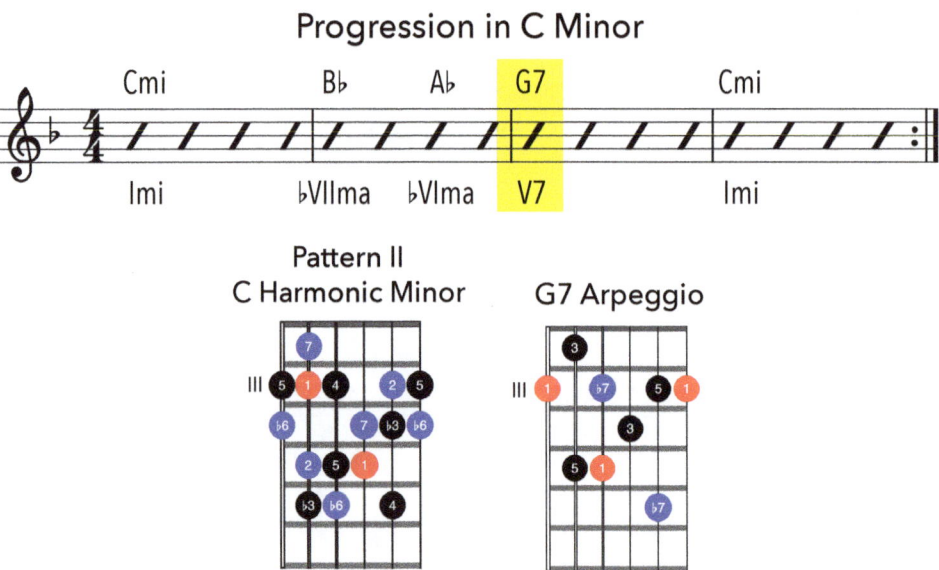

Even though both the C Natural Minor and C Harmonic Minor scales can be played on Imi and ♭VIma, I suggest using C Natural Minor for both. This saves the impact of the leading tone for the critical V7 chord. As in the last Improvisation Module, the shift is between parallel Natural Minor and Harmonic Minor. This is a relatively easy shift because it only involves one scale degree, the 7th.

- Locate the Pattern II C Natural Minor and Harmonic Minor Scale patterns in 3rd position, and the V7 arpeggio in the same vicinity. That's an Octave Shape IV G7 in 2nd position. As before, run the scale ascending and descending.
- Then create motifs and improvise using the storytelling devices you are familiar with.
- Do this again using the V7 arpeggio on G7.

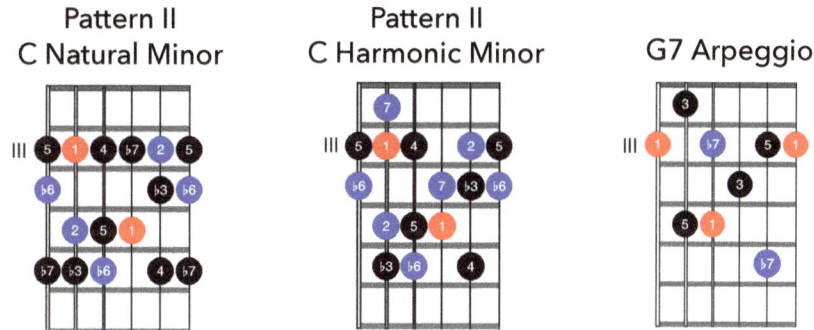

The information in this Module was presented to you in the Pattern II Octave Shape area because, like Pattern IV, it's a comfortable place for most guitarists. But know that these concepts should eventually be learned in other patterns as well.

You should add this progression to your practice routine with the others from Level 5. Your goal is to transition freely between the Natural Minor and Harmonic Minor scales and be in control of the V7 arpeggio. But as you are starting to see, the same information can be applied to all four progressions you have studied so far in Level 5.

Remember that the primary goal of combining Theory knowledge with Improvisation is to remove any mystery about what notes you can choose to solo over a single chord or group of chords.

Level 5 Unit 4 • Improv Demo

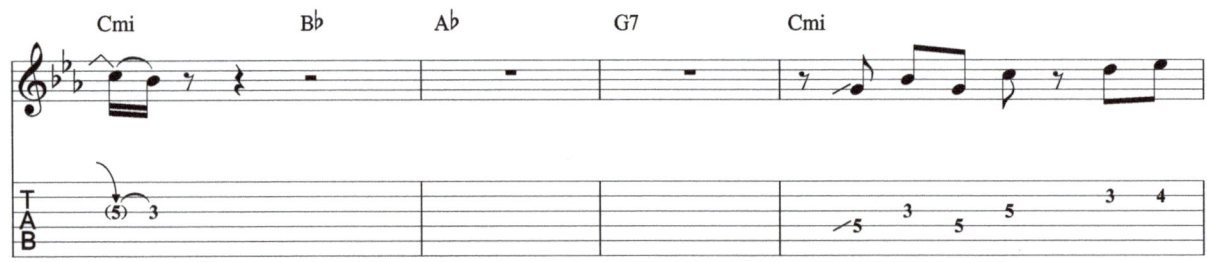

©2022 Fretboard Biology • fretboardbiology.com

Fretboard Biology — Level 5 • Unit 4: Improvisation

PRACTICE

Theory

- ☐ Go to the tabs below the Theory video on the website and complete the quiz.
- ☐ Learn the detail about the V7 chord and the concept of a tritone.

Fretboard Logic

- ☐ Understand various physical locations for a V-I resolution on the fretboard.

Rhythm Guitar

- ☐ Practice the Samba rhythm pattern over the progression in E.

Chart Reading

- ☐ Understand the use of section markings in a chart.

Improvisation

- ☐ Practice playing solos over the progression in C minor using the Pattern II C Natural Minor and Harmonic Minor Scales, and the G7 in-position arpeggio.

UNIT 5

Learning Modules

> **Theory** - The VII°7 Chord, Inversions of Diminished 7 Chords
> **Fretboard Logic** - Diminished 7 Chords and Arpeggios
> **Rhythm Guitar** - Salsa Rhythm Guitar, Montuno, Tumbao, Clave
> **Chart Reading** - Repeat Tools: One-Bar and Two-Bar Repeats, Simile, Multiple-Measure Rests
> **Improvisation** - Soloing with the Harmonic Minor Scale over the VII°7 Chord
> **Practice** - Continue Practice Routine Development

THEORY

You learned four chords of the harmonized Harmonic Minor Scale that have different qualities than the chords built on the same scale degrees in the Natural Minor Scale. They are: Imi(ma7), bIIIma7(+5), V7, and VII°7. In the last Unit we examined V7. In this Unit the focus is on VII°7.

The VII°7 Chord

The VII°7 chord from the parallel Harmonic Minor Scale is used much like V7. You're aware that songwriters often use a V7 in place of a Vmi7 to achieve the leading-tone effect in a minor tonality. You also know that the source of melody notes for a V7 chord is the Harmonic Minor Scale of the tonic. Now let's discuss the VII°7 and learn how it's used in the context of C minor.

bVII7 in Natural Minor is built on the b7 scale degree. The first thing to notice about VII°7 is that it's built on the leading tone, which is the major 7th scale degree. So in C minor, VII°7 is built on B.

The VII Chord in Natural Minor and Harmonic Minor

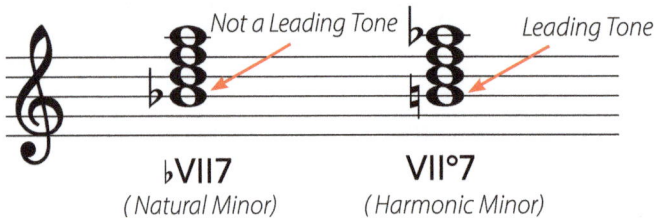

It's important to understand the similarities between V7 and VII°7. They are almost the same chord. What does B°7, which is the VII°7 in C minor, have in common with the G7, which is the V7? The leading tone, B, and the tritone between B and F.

Comparing the V7 and VII°7 Chord

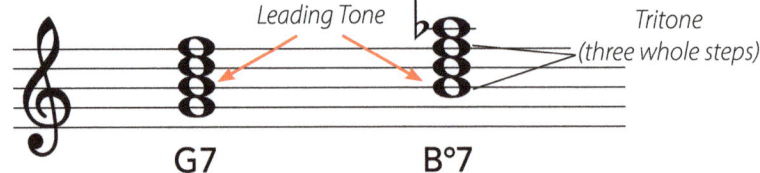

Let's take a look at the G7 and B°7 side by side. What similarities do you see?
- G7's major 3rd is the root of B°7.
- G7's perfect 5th is the 3rd of B°7.
- G7's flat 7th is the diminished 5th of B°7.

G7 and B°7 have three notes in common.

Comparing the V7 and VII°7 Chord

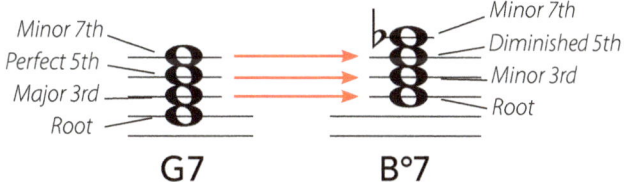

What about the A♭ of the B°7? Relative to G7, it's called a ♭9, and for now, just know it's an 'altered note', also called an 'alteration'. Alterations are discussed in great detail in later levels. They increase the tension in a dominant chord.

The next thing to notice is the tritone between the root and ♭5 in B°7. You can even argue that the VII°7 chord is like a 1st inversion of the V7. In other words, G7's 1st inversion is B°7.

The VII°7 Chord as a 1st Inversion V7 Chord

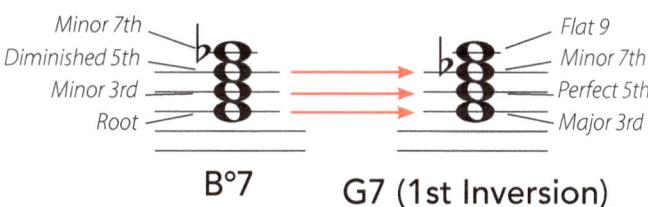

The first thing to remember about the VII°7 chord is that it functions in a true dominant chord family role. That means it evokes a strong feeling of attraction to the I chord. It shares so many characteristics with the V7 that it is essentially a twin to V7. V7 and VII°7 are often substituted for each other in both planned or spontaneous reharmonization.

Take a look at this progression.

Progression in C Minor

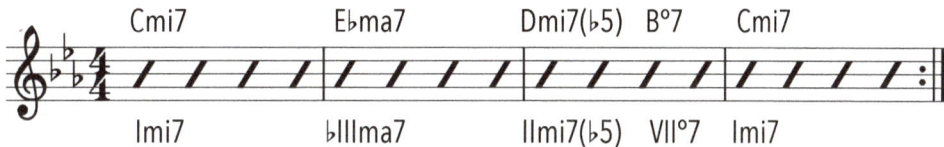

The Cmi7, E♭ma7, and Dmi7(♭5) are all diatonic to C Natural Minor and therefore the source of notes for melodies over those chords is the C Natural Minor Scale. And remember that the term 'melodies' applies to improvised lines, too.

The B°7, however, comes from the C Harmonic Minor Scale. So for the duration of the B°7 chord, the source of melody notes is the C Harmonic Minor Scale. This really isn't a radical physical difference. It's just the B leading tone of the C Harmonic Minor Scale versus the B♭ of the C Natural Minor Scale. It is only one note but it does make a harmonic difference.

Let's take another look at the relationship between the scale and the diminished 7 chord. C, in C Harmonic Minor Scale, is a half step above the root of the B°7 chord, so you would use the C Harmonic Minor Scale as your source of notes over the B°7 chord. Let's apply this same relationship to diminished 7 chords on other roots:

- If a progression is in A minor and G#°7 is present, the scale choice for the G# diminished 7 chord is A Harmonic Minor.
- If a progression is in B♭ minor and A°7 is present, the scale choice for the A diminished 7 chord is B♭ Harmonic Minor.
- If a progression is in F minor and E°7 is present, the scale choice for the E diminished 7 chord is F Harmonic Minor.

Quick Recap

To recap what you've learned so far about diminished 7 chords:

- The VII chord in Harmonic Minor is diminished 7.
- The VII°7 chord is built on the leading tone and therefore pulls the listener to the I chord.
- The diminished 7 chord in Harmonic Minor contains a tritone—the same tritone that exists in the V7 chord from the same Harmonic Minor Scale. In fact, the VII°7 chord contains the 3rd, 5th, and ♭7 of the V7 chord.
- The V7 and VII°7 chords are kind of twins and function as strong dominant family chords.
- It is common for a progression to be primarily based in Natural Minor but to have a VII°7 chord precede the I chord as a sort of V chord.
- The source of melody notes for a VII°7 chord is the Harmonic Minor Scale of the tonic.

A Deeper Dive into Diminished 7 Chords

Let's discuss another fascinating feature about diminished 7 chords. In Unit 3 you learned the construction of a diminished 7 chord. Now, let's look at the internal intervals:

- The interval between the root and minor 3rd is a minor 3rd.
- The interval between the minor 3rd and diminished 5th is a minor 3rd.
- The interval between the diminished 5th and the diminished 7th is a minor 3rd.
- The interval between the diminished 7th and the octave of the root is an augmented 2nd. However, an augmented 2nd and minor 3rd are enharmonic.

Internal Intervals of the Diminished 7 Chord

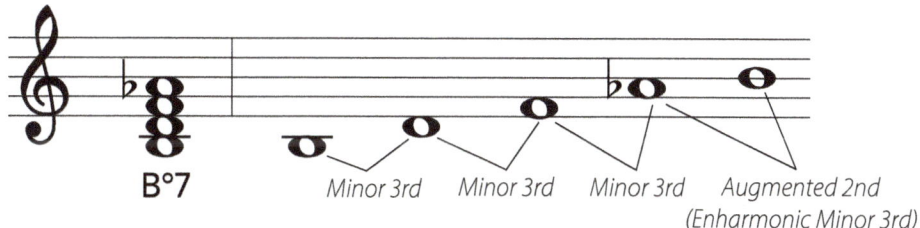

The repeating intervals within the diminished 7 chord structure are significant. This chord is often called a symmetrical chord for this reason. Because of this symmetry, the four closed-voice inversions of a diminished 7 chord maintain a minor 3rd distance between chord tones.

Inversions of the Diminished 7 Chord

For ease in illustration, it's helpful to use enharmonic equivalents.

- The 1st inversion of B°7 has D in the bass and, of course, the rest of the notes are the same.
- The 2nd inversion of B°7 has F in the bass and the rest of the notes are the same.
- The 3rd inversion of B°7 has an A♭ in the bass and the rest of the notes are the same.

Inversions of the Diminished 7 Chord

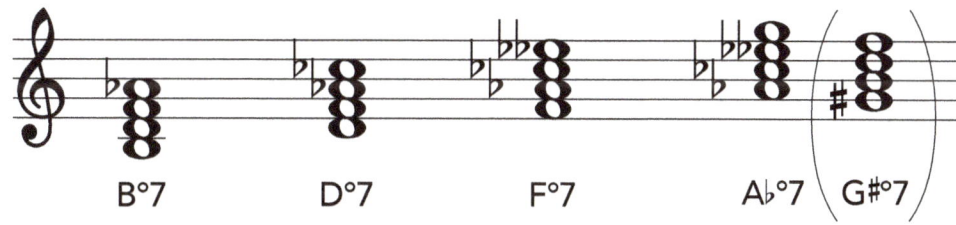

(Enharmonic equivalents: E♭♭ = D, C♭ = B, A♭ = G♯)

Another point about this symmetry is that any one of the four notes could be the root of its own diminished 7 chord and each of the four diminished 7 chords would have the same notes. B°7, D°7, F°7, and A♭°7 (G♯°7) all have the same notes:

- B°7 = B, D, F, A♭
- D°7 = D, F, A♭, C♭(B)
- F°7 = F, A♭, C♭, E♭♭(D)
- A♭°7 = G♯°7 (G♯°7 = G♯, B, D, F)

Let's take a look at a couple of progressions to illustrate the concept of inversions of Dim7 chords.

Here's a progression in C minor.

Progression in C Minor

Cmi7	Fmi7	B°7	Cmi7
Imi7	IVmi7	VII°7	Imi7

Cmi7 and Fmi7 are from C Natural Minor and B°7 is borrowed from C Harmonic Minor.

Now, compare that to these progressions:

Progressions in C Minor

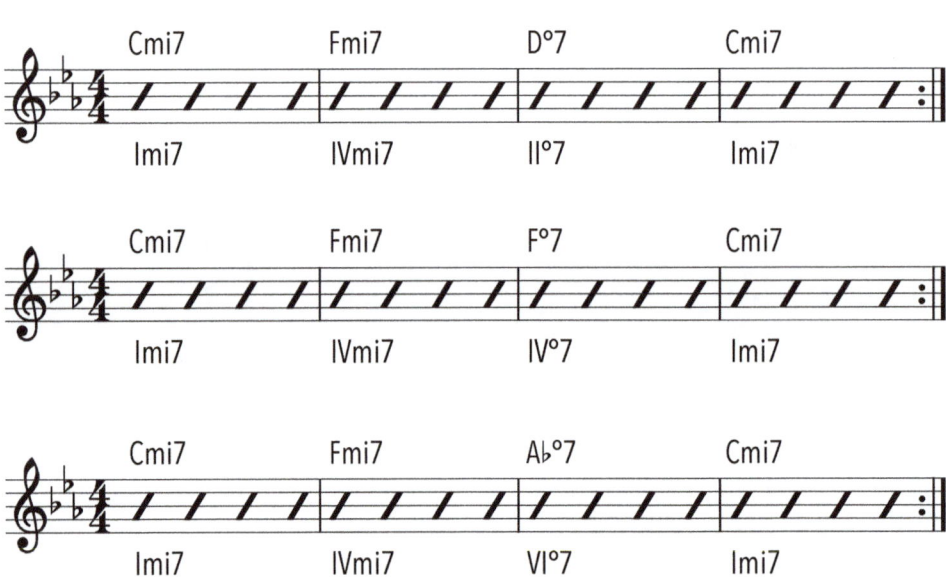

Cmi7	Fmi7	D°7	Cmi7
Imi7	IVmi7	II°7	Imi7

Cmi7	Fmi7	F°7	Cmi7
Imi7	IVmi7	IV°7	Imi7

Cmi7	Fmi7	A♭°7	Cmi7
Imi7	IVmi7	VI°7	Imi7

The third chord in each progression at first glance is different from the original progression that has B°7, but are they really different?

If you understand the symmetry presented in this Unit, you see these are all really the same chord and therefore are all functioning as dominant chords in C minor. D°7, F°7, and A♭°7 are just inversions of B°7. In a way B°7 can masquerade as one of these other chords.

You will encounter 'masquerading diminished 7 chords' from time to time and this information provides an explanation for chords that may not be recognized at first glance. By 'masquerading' I mean that what is written on the page may represent an inversion of what the chord really is. Always take care when analyzing diminished 7 chords for this reason. We'll come back to diminished 7 chords at the appropriate times in future modules and levels.

FRETBOARD LOGIC

Diminished 7 Chords and Arpeggios

In the Unit 3 Theory Module you learned to harmonize the Harmonic Minor Scale with 7th chords. This resulted in three chords that are new. One of those is the diminished 7 chord, and you learned how to construct it. It was presented as the VII chord in the Harmonic Minor Scale. In this Module you'll learn the common diminished 7 chord voicings and arpeggios.

As you learned in the Theory Module, the formula for a diminished 7 chord is: root, minor 3rd, diminished 5th, and diminished 7th.

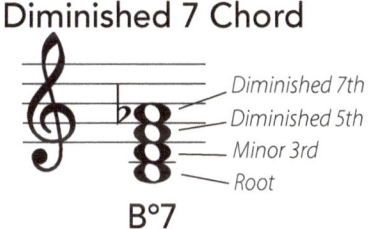

The successive minor 3rd intervals in a diminished 7 chord make closed voicings impractical on guitar. The intervals are just too close to voice on the fretboard. Because of the symmetry in the diminished 7 chord construction, any of the four chord tones can be considered the root. Also, each shape can be moved a minor third (three frets) ascending or descending while maintaining all of the same chord tones. Let's learn the three common fingerings for diminished 7 chords.

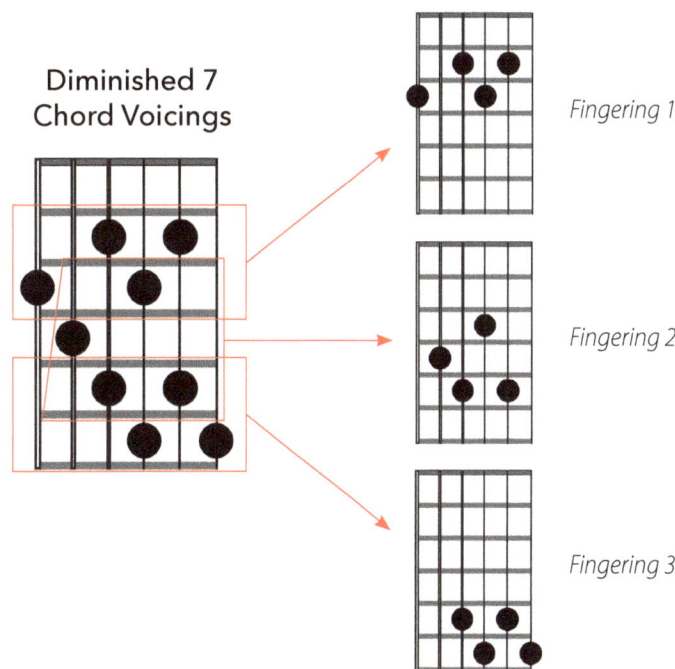

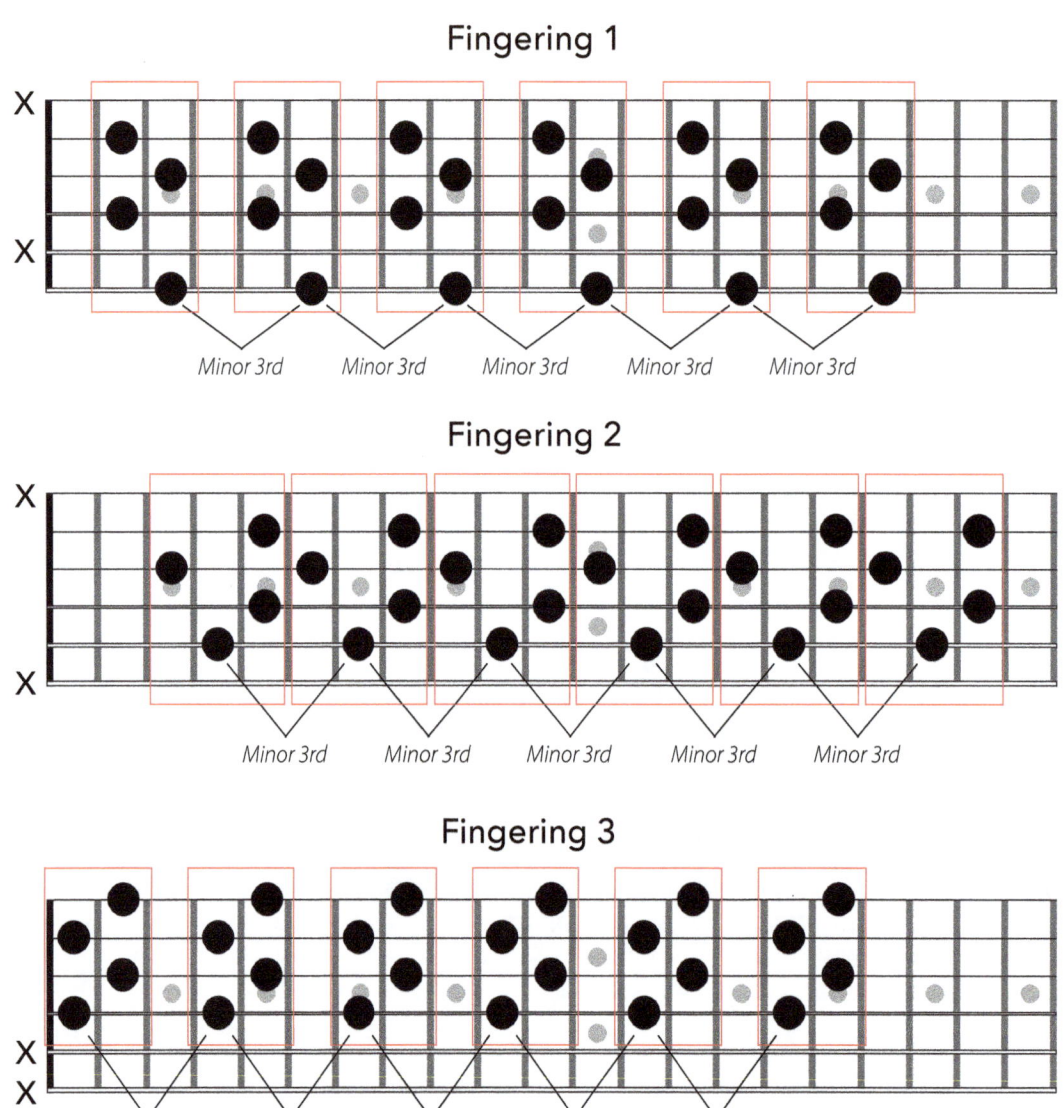

The most common way diminished 7 chords appear are as chords from the dominant family resolving up a half step to Imi in a minor key. In a minor key, the V7 and VII°7 have identical functions. They are both members of the dominant family. But there are other ways, too.

Fretboard Biology — Level 5 • Unit 5: Fretboard Logic

In the progression below, the VII°7 resolves to the Imi7. Play it three different ways using the three different diminished 7 chord voicings.

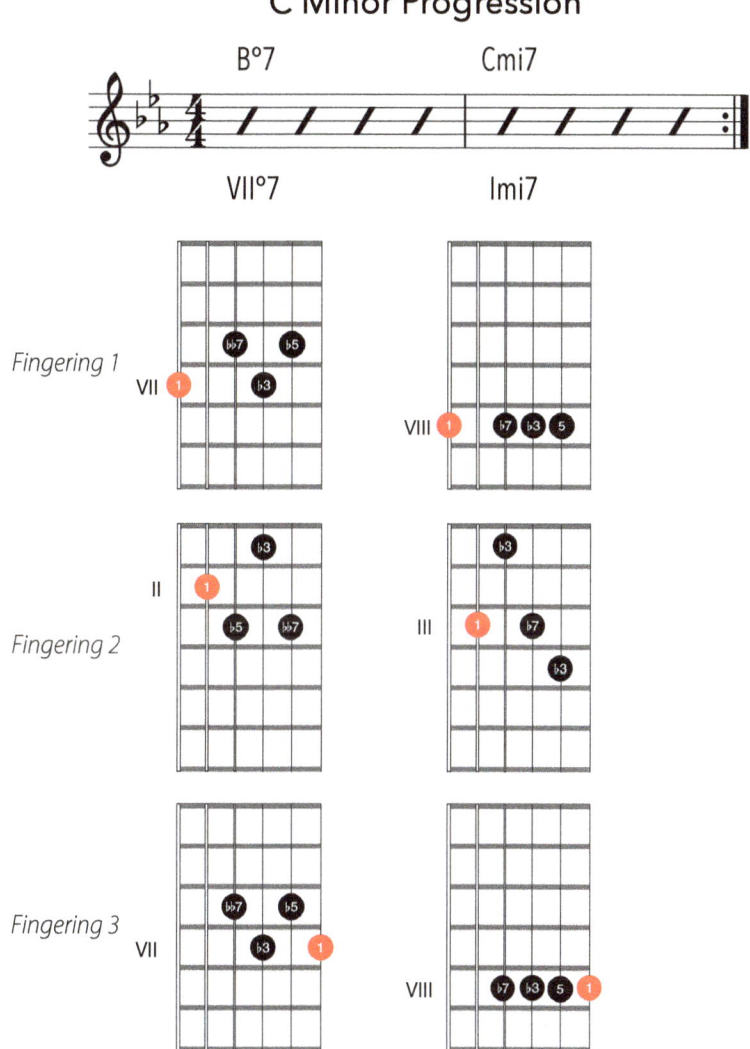

Diminished 7 chords can appear in progressions in a few different ways. Below are some progressions for you to practice.

- Practice using string set 6, 4, 3, 2 diminished voicings mixed with 6th-string and 5th-string root or shell voicings.
- Practice using string set 5, 4, 3, 2 diminished voicings mixed with 5th-string and 6th-string root or shell voicings.
- Practice using string set 4, 3, 2, 1 diminished voicings mixed with 4th-string and 5th-string string root or shell voicings.

Progression in B♭ Major

Progression in A Minor

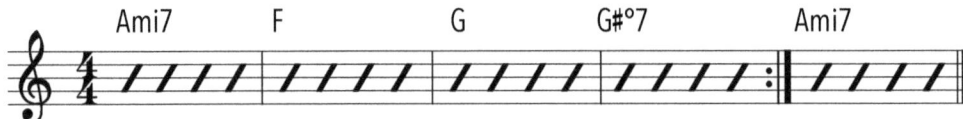

Progression in C Major

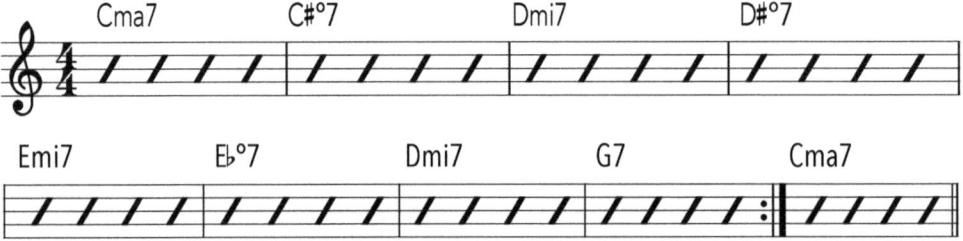

Progression in D Minor

Diminished 7 Arpeggios

There are three logical diminished 7 arpeggio fingerings. Two are confined within a five-fret span and the third one moves up the fretboard. The successive minor 3rd intervals make for shapes that are challenging to memorize. They don't fit neatly into any of the octave shapes.

These diminished 7 arpeggios, like all diminished arpeggios, are melodic devices that have several applications, the most obvious being over a diminished 7 chord. This will be addressed in the Improvisation modules.

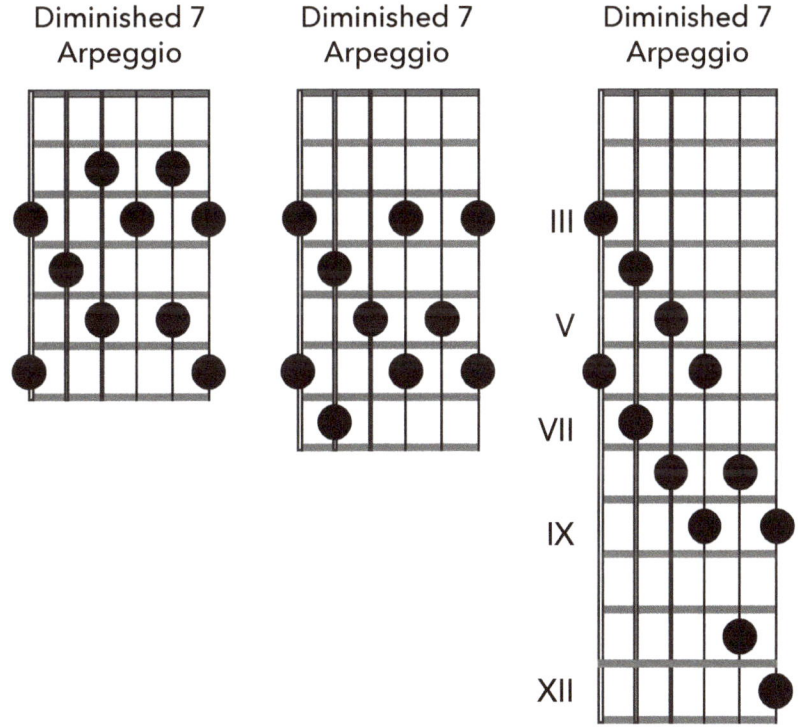

RHYTHM GUITAR

Salsa

This Module is an introduction to Afro-Caribbean music, which is sometimes labeled 'Salsa'. Salsa is popular dance music and an umbrella term for Afro-Cuban music. There are three main regional and cultural sources for Salsa: Cuba, Puerto Rico, and New York.

Salsa incorporates the genres of:
- Son
- Montuno
- Guaracha
- Cha Cha
- Mambo from Cuba
- Bomba and Plena from Puerto Rico

Son is an early folk style from which Salsa evolved. Cha Cha was developed with slower tempos so the older crowds could dance as the younger audience danced to the faster mambo.

Here are a few definitions that are important to understand before we begin:

Montuno

A montuno is a comping technique using a repetitive melodic and rhythmic pattern of notes that defines the harmony. It defines the harmony because the melodic line outlines the chords. In Son, the ancestor of Salsa, the montuno was played on Tres, which was derived from the Spanish Guitar. Montunos were later adapted for guitar and piano. The melody is placed above the montuno, whether it's sung or played by another instrument.

Tumbao

A tumbao is a melodic and rhythmic pattern played by the bass. Tumbao can also refer to the pattern played by piano.

Clave

The clave is a two-bar repetitive rhythmic pattern. It functions as a rhythmic cell around which the rhythms, melody, and harmony are built. Sometimes the pattern is actually played by a percussion instrument but often it is just implied within the other parts.

2/3 Clave

Here is the 2/3 clave. The number 2 comes first because there are two attacks in the first measure and three in the second.

2/3 Clave

3/2 Clave

Here is the 3/2 clave. The number 3 comes first because there are three attacks in the first measure and two in the second.

3/2 Clave

The guitar parts you will learn in this Module are montunos. You will learn one based on the 2/3 clave and one based on the 3/2.

Here is a montuno for a C7 using 2/3 clave. In this example, the 2/3 clave is the underlying rhythm cell around which this montuno functions. Note that there are only two places where the downbeat is played.

Montuno (2/3 Clave)

Play close attention to the rules of pick direction. The notes in this melodic line are the chord tones of C7: C, E, G, and B♭. It is a good idea to be able to play the example in more than one position, as you would any scale, arpeggio, or exercise.

Here is a montuno for C7 using 3/2 clave:

Montuno (3/2 Clave)

In this example, the 3/2 clave is the underlying rhythm cell around which this montuno functions. Note the similarities to the first example. Basically, the measures are flipped. Note again that there are only two places where the downbeat is played.

Play close attention to the rules of pick direction. The notes in this line are the chord tones of C7: C, E, G, and B♭. Again, it's good to be able to play the example in more than one position, as you would any scale, arpeggio, or exercise.

The C7 sound would be clear because the guitar montuno outlines the chord. As I mentioned before, the melody of a song will be placed above the montuno, whether it's sung or played by another instrument.

If you have an interest in learning more montunos and how they work over chords to define the harmony, there are many resources available, but the primary one is listening.

This is the last in the series of Afro-Latin Rhythm Guitar modules and what you learned is just the tip of the iceberg. This music is infectious and there is so much more to learn. I encourage you to listen to as much of this genre as you can.

CHART READING

Repeat Tools

This Unit will discuss the use of 'repeat tools' in charts. Measures, entire sections, and groups of sections of a song are often played more than once. There are a few notation tools that help save space on a chart by repeating sections in order to avoid writing the same thing again and again. These tools are best explained in a sort of hierarchical order.

Repeat tools serve several purposes. First, it's a lot easier to not have to write a figure or section over and over. Second, using repeat tools reduces the physical length of the chart. Third, and most importantly, if the exact same section or measure is written again and again, the musician has to constantly focus and read the rhythm figure as if it might be different each time. This consumes brain power that is better used to play the music.

Here is the hierarchy of repeat tools.

One-Bar Repeat

Often one measure is repeated and rather than write it out twice, a convenient device called a one-bar repeat is used. It's a diagonal line, slanting upward left to right with a dot placed on either side of the line. It means to play what was played in the previous measure.

One-Bar Repeat

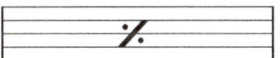

Several of these can be used in succession. They help the reader to absorb an entire section of a chart at a glance. Then the focus can be on playing musically.

One-Bar Repeats

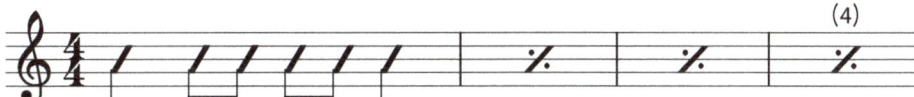

Sometimes a small number (4) is written in parentheses above the staff at the 3rd one-bar repeat sign showing that it's the fourth measure of the four-bar phrase. This is really useful for absorbing multiple measures at a glance. If the one-bar repeats continue, a small parenthesized (8) is written above the eighth bar and so on in groups of four bars throughout the section as long as the one-bar repeats keep going.

Two-Bar Repeat

Often a two-measure phrase is played again and the convenient notation tool for that is similar to the one-bar repeat. It has two parallel diagonal lines, slanting upward left to right with a dot placed on either side of the lines. There is a vertical line in the middle of the quasi-measure. The number '2' is written and centered directly above the center line. It means to play what was played in the previous two measures.

Two-Bar Repeat

Several of these can be used in succession if the same two-bar phrase is repeated multiple times. This, too, helps the reader absorb an entire section of a chart at a glance, which allows the focus to be on playing musically.

Two-Bar Repeats

Three, Four, or More Bar Repeats

Some will say that it's best not to use this kind of repeat device for three or more bars. This is often frowned upon by people who notate music for a living—that is, professional copyists. Regardless, you should be prepared to see them. They're quite common in charts prepared by people who aren't professional copyists so you need to understand them.

A three-bar repeat has three parallel diagonal lines, slanting upward left to right with a dot placed on either side of the lines. This means to play the previous three measures and several of these can be used in succession if the same three-bar phrase is played again and again. These are strange to see but not unheard of. And unusual as they may be, you need to know what they are when you see them.

A four-bar repeat has four parallel diagonal lines, slanting upward left to right with a dot placed on either side of the lines. This means to play the previous four measures, and several of these can be used in succession if the same four-bar phrase is played again and again. It's not uncommon to see this repeat because four measures of music can be represented in the physical space of one.

Three-Bar Repeat   **Four-Bar Repeat**

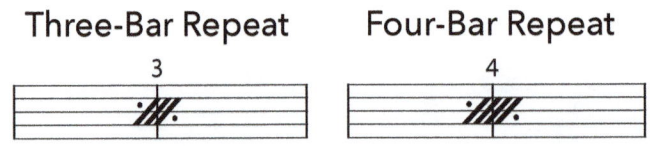

Some of the popular music-copying books set the limit the number of bars for which you can use this diagonal-line style notation to two-bar phrases. But again, don't be surprised if you see an adaptation of this notation device for a repeating three-, four-, five-, or all the way up to a 16-measure phrase and maybe even more if it's a really sloppy chart. People get creative when they write charts and are trying to save space and time. It's just a reality that people do this and you need to know what it means if you see it. In this series of Chart Reading modules, I'm not as concerned with teaching you the best way to write a chart but rather to get you prepared for what you will see, whether it's written properly or not.

In the hierarchy of repeat devices, the repeat notation tools presented here are usually used for repeating a small section of music, like one, two, or four bars, or maybe even eight bars.

Simile

Using the word 'simile' is a very useful way to keep a chart uncluttered. It's normally used when there's a rhythm figure or a rhythm figure/riff that is played multiple times. It can be used in places where a one-bar or two-bar repeat could be used, but it's not so specific to mean 'play the exact same thing'. It often does mean that, though, so I always interpret simile as 'keep playing what you just played', or 'kind of like' what you just played.

In this example, writing simile seems redundant because there's already several one-bar repeats. However, this is common and reinforces the idea that the riff should be played over each measure.

Simile

Writing simile is also useful if a riff continues over multiple successive chords. In some cases, the notes in the riff need to be adjusted to fit the successive chord or chords. Its meaning is not precise and clearly a little vague, but keep in mind that a chord chart, by definition, is not intended to be a detailed representation of the music.

In this example a riff is written in the first measure for an Emi chord. The next three measures have slash marks and different chord changes but simile is written. This usually means to adapt the same riff for the next chord and the next until something more specific is written on the chart effectively canceling the 'simile' instructions. That could be another riff or a rhythm figure.

Use of Simile for a Riff over a Progression

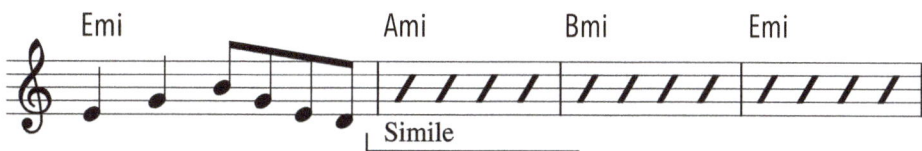

It's very common for simile to suggest that a comping rhythm pattern be used over a series of chords, an entire section, or even through the whole song.

In this example, a specific comping rhythm figure is written out in the first measure and the subsequent measures just have slash marks. Simile is written so the musician knows to use the same comping rhythm in the following measures.

Use of Simile for Comping over a Progression

The use of simile serves several purposes. First, it's a lot easier to not have to write the figure over and over. Second, and more importantly, if the exact same measure is written again and again, the musician has to constantly focus and read the rhythm figure as if it might be different in each measure. This consumes brain power that is better used to interpret and perform the music. If simile is written, the musician reads it once and knows to continue the pattern without having to read the same rhythm over and over.

Multiple-Measure Rests

So far, we have explored many ways to notate the repeat of measures and sections, but what about successive measures of rests? To keep a chart clean and concise, we need a way to notate multiple measures of rests without having to write whole rests again and again. The answer is to use a multiple-measure rest. This is written as a solid bar within a single measure with a number written above the staff indicating the number of measures to rest. This saves space on the chart and, equally importantly, allows the reader to see a lot of measures at a glance. These are commonly used for as few as two successive measures of rest up to an entire section. For example, if you are supposed to be tacit (silent) for the entire 32-bar section of a song, the chart could have a solid bar within a single measure and 32 written above the staff indicating that you should lay out for the whole section. If the section is even longer, a larger number can be used. This is no upper limit, but you normally see the maximum being the length of a section.

Multiple-Measure Rests

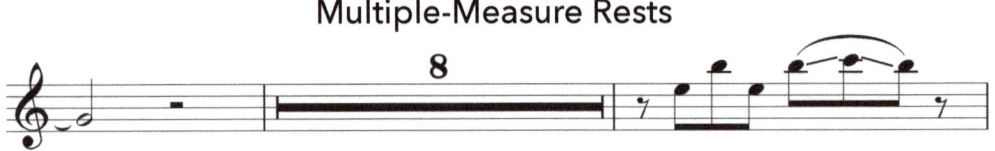

Fretboard Biology — Level 5 • Unit 5: Improvisation — 131

IMPROVISATION

In the first four Improvisation Modules you learned about soloing using the Harmonic Minor Scale as a tool for specific chords. Shifting back and forth between parallel minor scales is a kind of minor modal interchange. We've placed special focus on the V7 chord in minor key progressions as you learn to be intentional about note choices.

Harmonizing the Harmonic Minor Scale with 7th chords results in three chords that are new. One of those is the diminished 7 chord and you learned how to construct it. You learned its function as the VII chord in Harmonic Minor.

In this Module you'll learn how to play lines on the diminished 7 chord in progressions using both the Harmonic Minor Scale and diminished 7 arpeggios. Remember that the formula for a diminished 7 chord is minor 3rd, diminished 5th, and diminished 7th. By now you are very familiar with the side-by-side comparison of the parallel Natural and Harmonic Minor Scales and the chords that result from harmonizing them.

Take a look at this two-chord progression and analysis.

Progression in D Minor

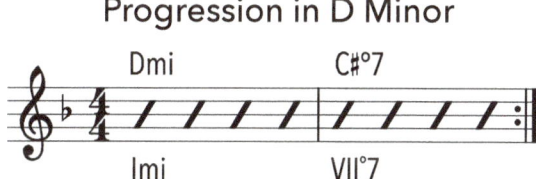

Dmi is the Imi in both the D Natural Minor and D Harmonic Minor Scales, so either scale is an appropriate source of notes. According to what you learned recently about being selective in using the Harmonic Minor Scale, consider choosing the D Natural Minor Scale. C#°7 is the VII°7 in the D Harmonic Minor Scale which means it's the appropriate source of notes, and not the D Natural Minor Scale. The shift between parallel natural minor and harmonic minor is relatively easy because it only involves one scale degree, the 7th.

Let's try this. Locate the Pattern IV D Natural Minor and Harmonic Minor Scale patterns in 10th position.

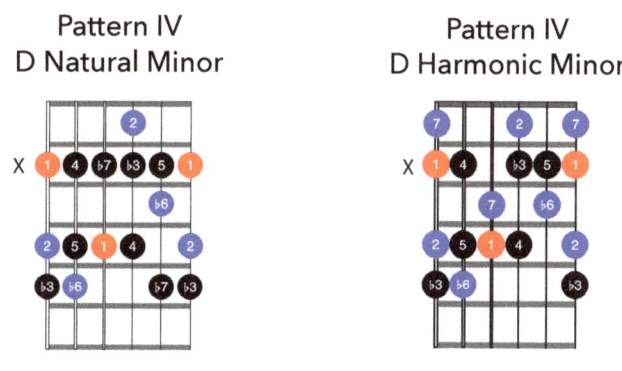

To begin, run the scale ascending and descending playing the appropriate scale for each chord so you get a feel for them. Then create motifs and improvise using the storytelling devices.

Next, stay in the same general location on the fretboard and use the Pattern IV D Natural Minor Scale pattern in 10th position. But on the C#°7, use the C#°7 arpeggio. Play the D Minor Scale over the Dmi chord, and the C#°7 arpeggio over the C#°7 chord.

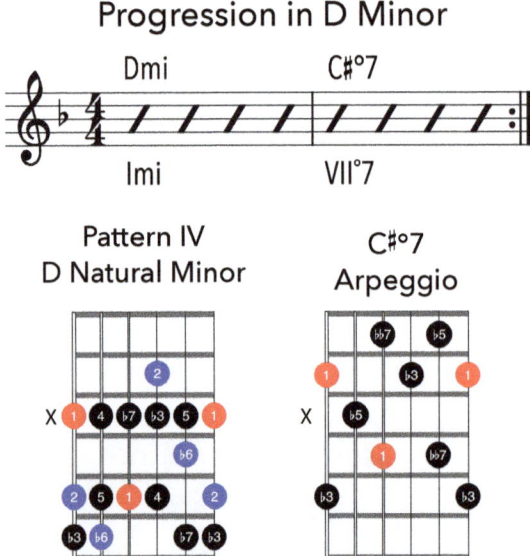

Create motifs and improvise using the storytelling devices. When creating lines and developing your lick vocabulary, it's a good idea to blend the D Harmonic Minor Scale and C#°7 arpeggio. It doesn't have to be one or the other. Besides, all the notes of the C#°7 are in the D Harmonic Minor Scale.

Because of their minor 3rd interval symmetry, diminished 7 chords offer many opportunities for repeating shapes and licks in three-fret segments. For example, any diminished 7 shape can be moved three frets, a minor 3rd, and all the notes will be the same. Your goal is to move freely between the Natural Minor and Harmonic Minor Scales and be in control of the V dominant 7 and VII°7 arpeggios.

All of the information learned in the Level 5 Improvisation modules can be applied to all five progressions you have studied so far because V7 and VII°7 are so similar. Remember that the primary goal of combining Theory knowledge with Improvisation is to remove any mystery about what notes you can choose to solo over a single chord or group of chords.

The information in this Module was presented to you in the Pattern IV Octave Shape area because it's the place that's most comfortable for most guitarists. But know that these concepts should eventually be learned in other patterns as well. Here is an example of how you could blend the D Harmonic Minor and C#°7 arpeggio when soloing over a progression.

Level 5 Unit 5 • Improv Demo

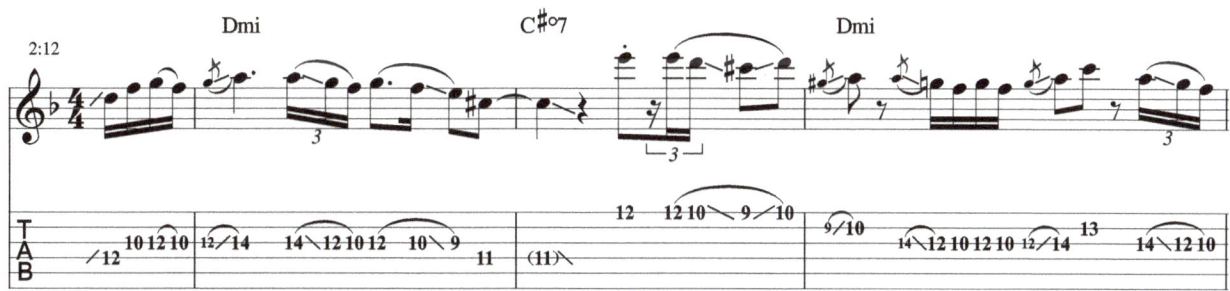

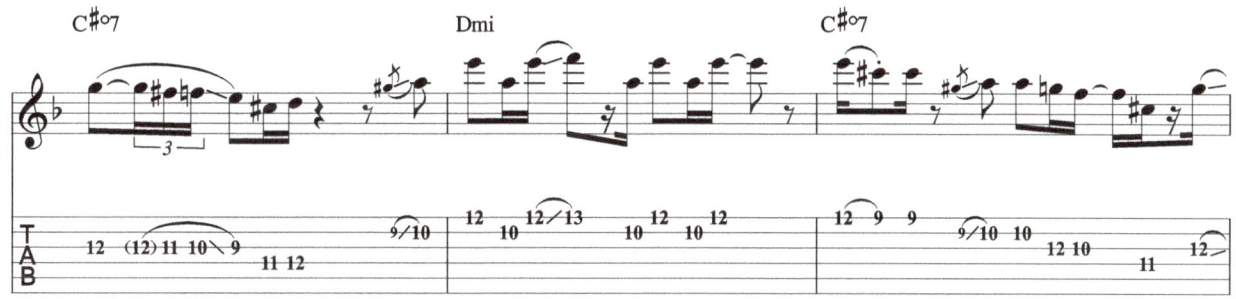

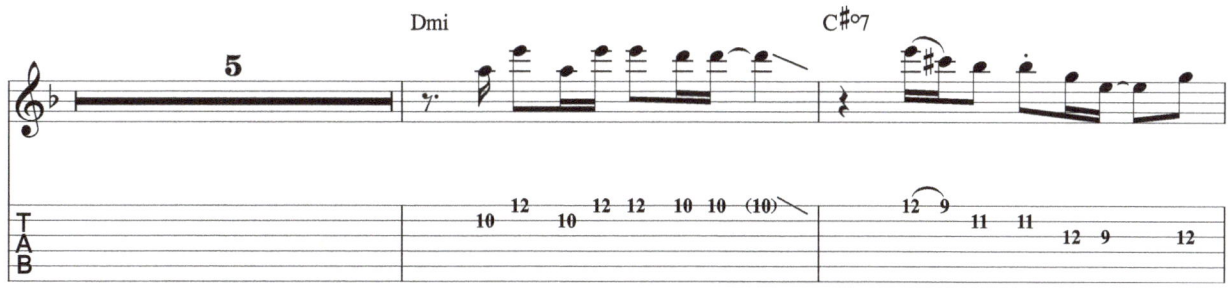

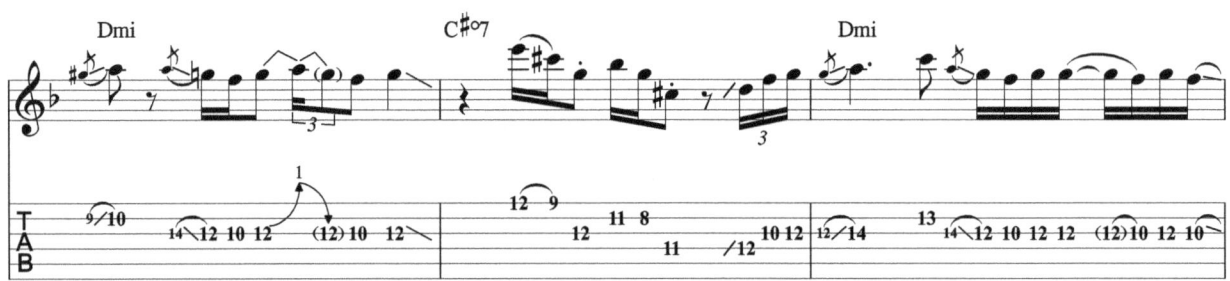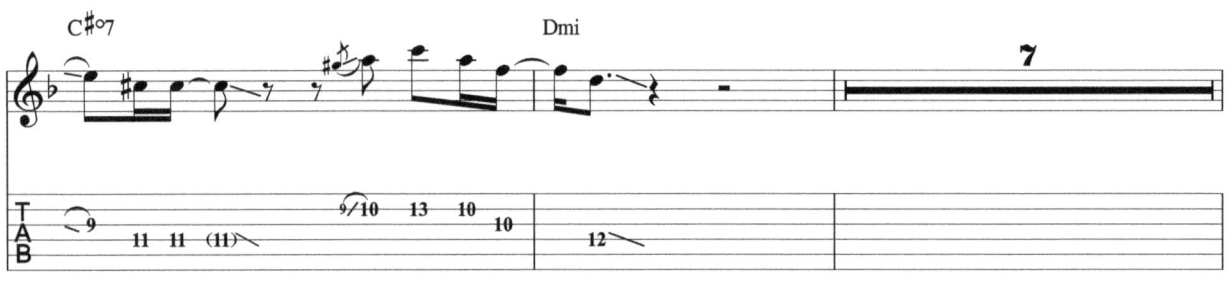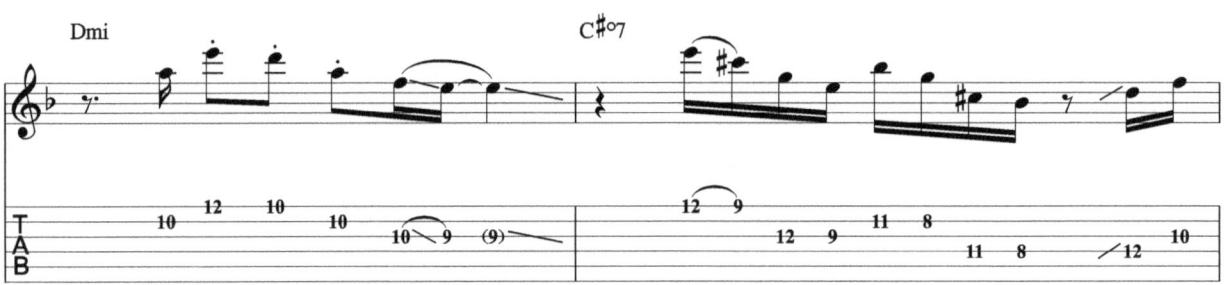

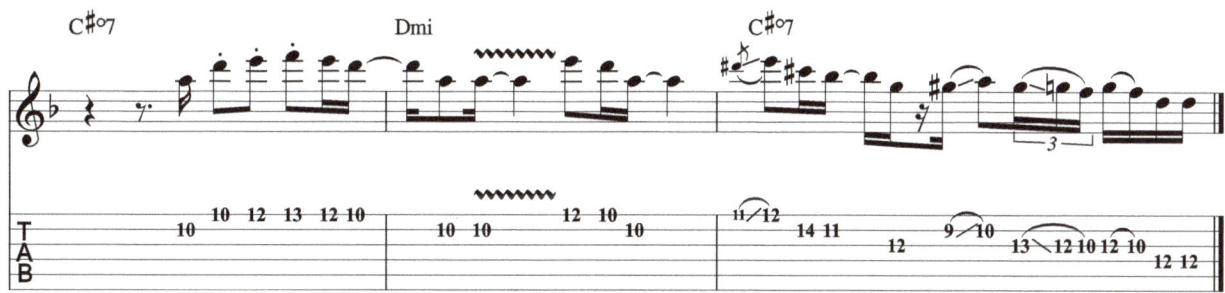

PRACTICE

Theory

- ☐ Go to the tabs below the Theory video on the website and complete the quiz.
- ☐ Learn more about the VII°7 chord and inversions of diminished 7 chords.

Fretboard Logic

- ☐ Learn the common voicings for diminished 7 chords and arpeggios.

Rhythm Guitar

- ☐ Learn and practice 2/3 and 3/2 montunos in C.
- ☐ Know the definitions of Montuno, Tumbao, and Clave.

Chart Reading

- ☐ Understand the use of repeat tools in a chart.
- ☐ Understand the hierarchy of repeat tools
- ☐ Understand the use of the term 'simile' in a chart.

Improvisation

- ☐ Practice playing solos over the progression in D minor using the Pattern IV Natural Minor and Harmonic Minor Scales, and the C#°7 in-position arpeggio.

UNIT 6

Learning Modules

> **Theory** - The Imi(ma7) Chord

> **Fretboard Logic** - Minor(Major 7) Chords and Arpeggios

> **Rhythm Guitar** - Introduction to Odd Meter

> **Chart Reading** - More Repeat Devices: Repeat Signs, Endings, Repeat Until Cue

> **Improvisation** - Soloing with the Harmonic Minor Scale over the Imi(ma7) Chord

> **Practice** - Continue Practice Routine Development

THEORY

You learned four chords of the harmonized Harmonic Minor Scale that have different qualities than the chords built on the same scale degrees in the Natural Minor Scale. They are: Imi(ma7), bIIIma7(+5), V7, and VII°7. In the last two Units we looked at V7 and VII°7. In this Unit the focus is on the Imi(ma7) chord.

The Imi(ma7) Chord

The Imi(ma7) chord has a minor 3rd, perfect 5th, and major 7th. Notice that it's a minor triad with a major 7th.

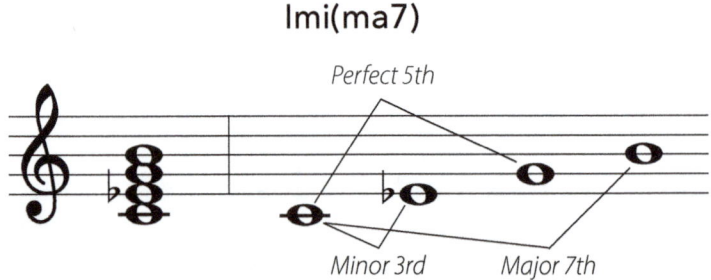

If we compare the Mi(ma7) chord to the Mi7 chord, we see that a Mi7 chord is a minor triad with a minor 7th. So the difference between a Mi(a7) and Mi7 chord is the 7th.

Comparing the Mi(ma7) and the Mi7 Chord

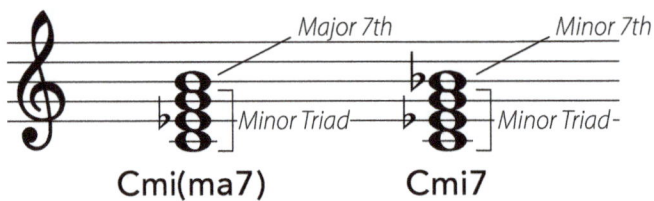

The Mi(ma7) chord is most commonly used as a transition chord between a minor triad and a minor 7 chord. It can also be used as a mysterious-sounding final chord of a song. When used to transition, it can be considered a 'passing chord'.

Let's take a look at this progression fragment.

Progression in C Minor

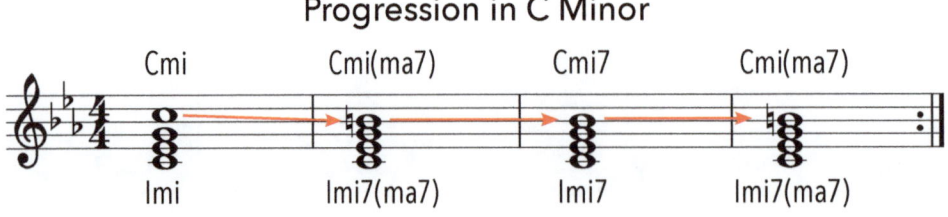

Notice how the voice of the 7th in the chord descends by half step.

- C, the root of the Cmi descends to B, the major 7th of Cmi(ma7).
- B, the major 7th of Cmi(ma7) descends to B♭, the minor 7 of the Cmi7.

There have been countless songs written with this moving line which is used to create motion over a minor chord: *Stairway to Heaven, Masquerade, My Funny Valentine, Don't You Worry 'bout a Thing*, and *Feelings*, to name just a few.

Look at this progression again.

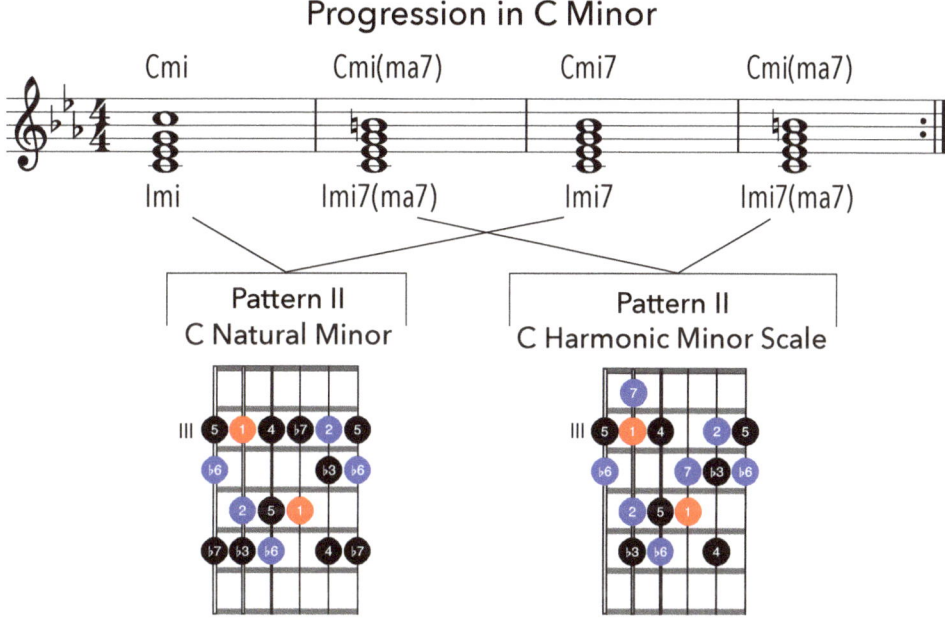

The Cmi and Cmi7 are diatonic to C Natural Minor and therefore the source of notes for melodies over them is the C Natural Minor Scale. The Cmi(ma7), however, comes from the C Harmonic Minor Scale. So for the duration of the Cmi(ma7) chord, the source of melody notes is the C Harmonic Minor Scale. This really isn't a radical physical difference. The B leading tone of the C Harmonic Minor Scale versus the B♭ of the C natural minor scale. It's only one note, but it does make a difference.

Ask yourself what the relationship is between the scale and the chord. Over any Imi(ma7) chord, the Harmonic Minor Scale built on its root is an option.

For example:

- If a progression is in A minor and there is a Ami(ma7) chord, the scale choice is A Harmonic Minor.
- If a progression is in B♭ minor and there is a B♭mi(ma7) chord, the scale choice is B♭ Harmonic Minor.
- If a progression is in F minor and there is an Fmi(ma7) chord, the scale choice is F Harmonic Minor.

It is also common for a Mi(ma7) chord to be the final chord of a song in a minor key. It has a mysterious sound and leaves the song sounding unresolved. Harmonic Minor is an appropriate choice for a Mi(ma7) chord in this situation, too.

When writing the Mi(ma7) chord symbol, be sure to parenthesize (Ma7). Parentheses are used in chord symbols to draw attention to something about the chord that is a little different than the norm.

FRETBOARD LOGIC

In the Unit 3 Theory Module you learned to harmonize the Harmonic Minor Scale with 7th chords. This resulted in three chords that are new. One of those was the Mi(Ma7) chord. It was presented as the I chord in Harmonic Minor. In this Module you will learn the common Mi(Ma7) chord voicings and arpeggios.

Minor(Major 7) Chord Voicings

The formula for a Mi(Ma7) chord or arpeggio is minor 3rd, perfect 5th, major 7th. The most efficient way to learn the common Mi(Ma7) chord voicings is to modify the existing Mi7 voicings by raising the minor 7th to a major 7th.

Take a few minutes to see whether you can figure out a voicing for each of these chord types within each of the octave shapes and then check your results with the answer key in the back of the book.

Pattern I: Minor Triad   Minor 7   Minor(Major7)

Pattern II: Minor Triad   Minor 7   Minor(Major7)

Pattern III: Minor Triad   Minor 7   Minor(Major7)

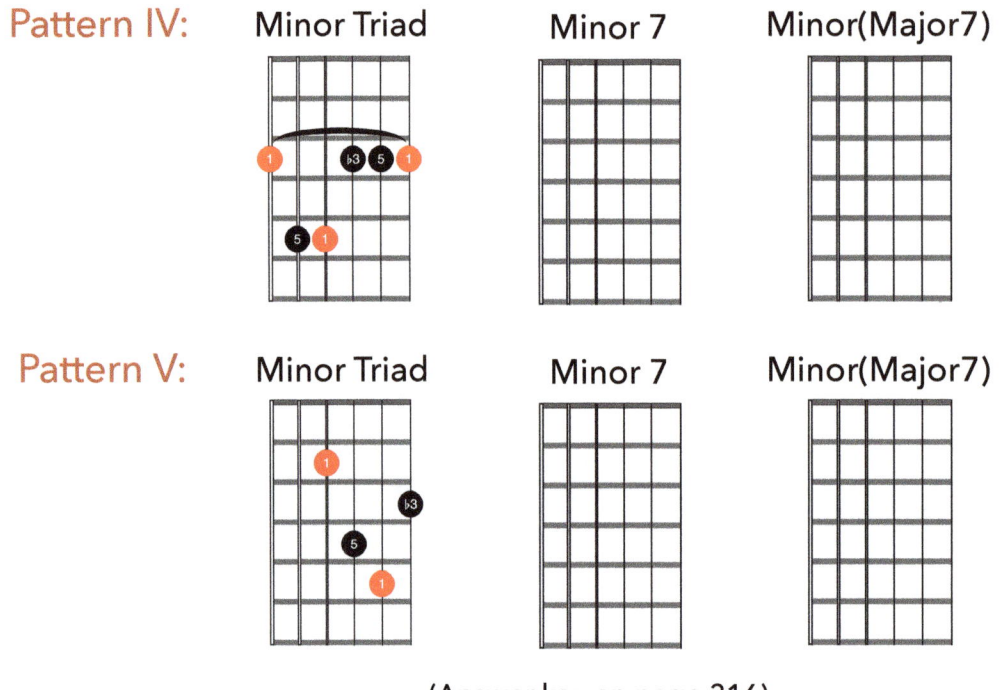

(Answer key on page 316)

Using Minor(Major 7) Chords

Mi(ma7) chords are most commonly used in transition from a minor triad to a Mi7 chord. Take a look at this progression and focus on the voice that moves from C to B natural to B♭ to A natural.

Progression in C Minor

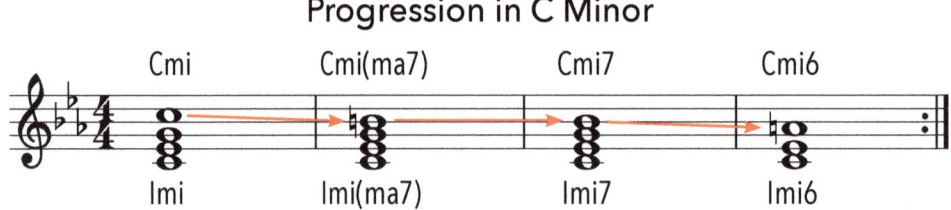

This could be reversed as well. Again, focus on the voice that moves from A natural to B♭ to B natural to C.

Progression in C Minor

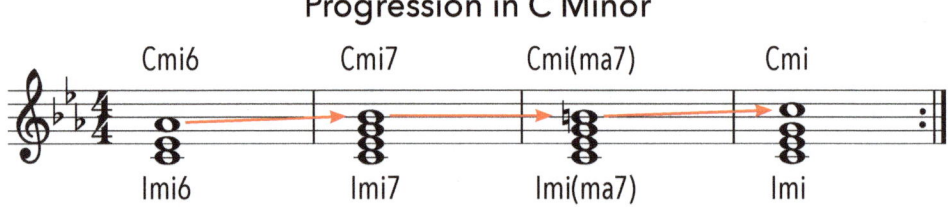

This sequence of chords is integral to many popular songs written through the years. Songs like *Stairway to Heaven*, *Masquerade*, *My Funny Valentine*, *Don't You Worry 'Bout A Thing*, *Feelings*, and many more use this sequence as the harmonic hook.

Fretboard Biology — Level 5 • Unit 6: Fretboard Logic

Often in songs that have a static minor chord for a few bars, this sequence or a segment of it can be inserted to create internal voice movement while still maintaining the basic minor chord quality. After all, these chords are all built upon a minor triad. Mi(Ma7) chords are also used as the 'last chord' in many Jazz-oriented progressions. It leaves a mysterious and unresolved feeling.

Minor(Major 7) Arpeggios

The same method we used to adapt the five Mi7 chord voicings as Mi(Ma7) voicings can be applied to arpeggios as well. The most efficient way to learn the common Mi(Ma7) arpeggios is to modify the existing Mi7 arpeggios by raising the minor 7th to a major 7th.

Like with the chord voicings, see whether you can figure out each of these arpeggios within each of the octave shapes and then check your results with voicings in the back of the book. Using these Mi(Ma7) arpeggios will be the focus of the upcoming Improvisation Module.

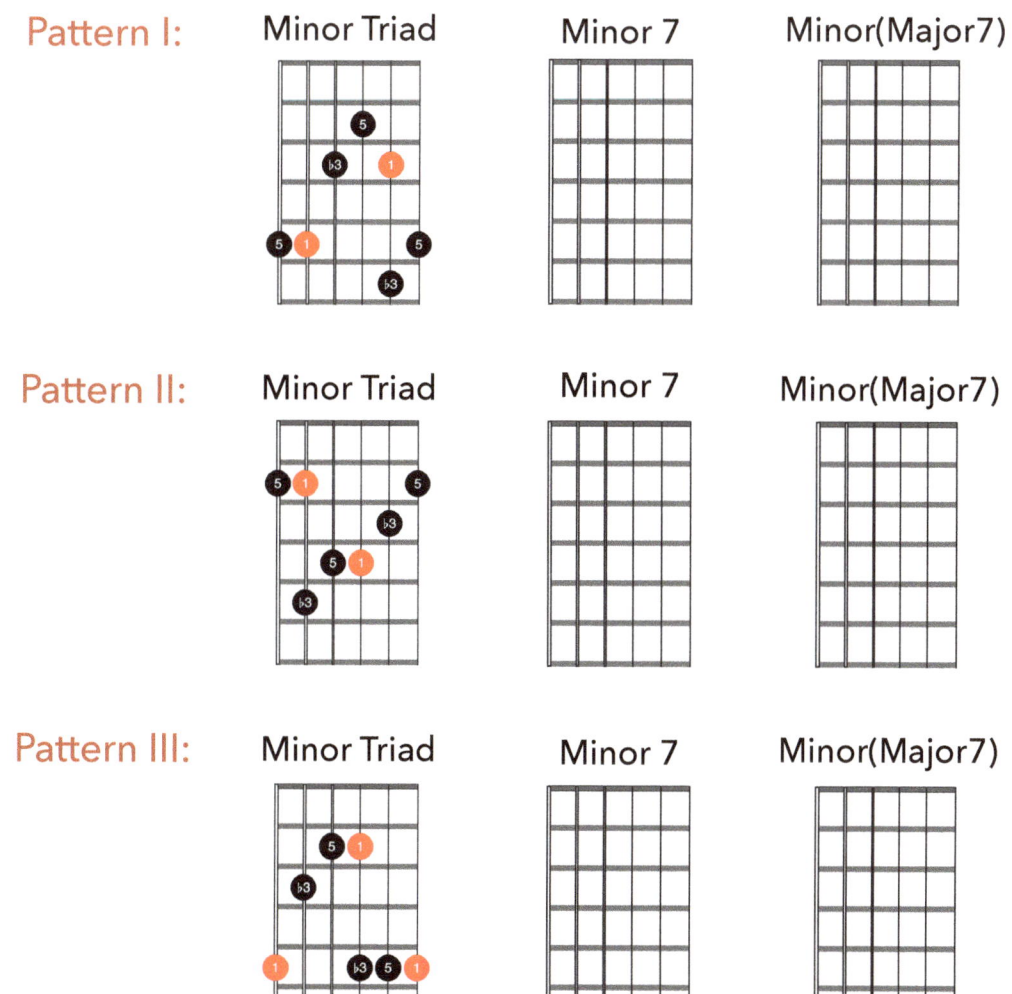

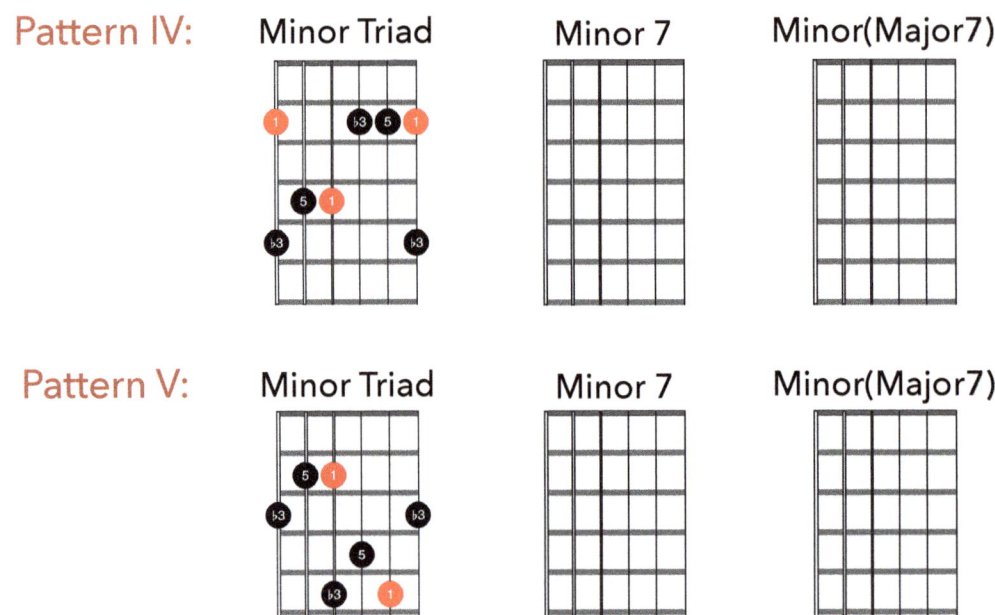

(Answer key on page 317)

RHYTHM GUITAR

Odd Meter

In the following few Rhythm Guitar modules you will learn the basics about playing in odd meters. You learned about time signatures and meter earlier in this program. To prepare, let's first go a little deeper into the world of meter with a few definitions. These definitions fall into two groups: the number of beats and the division of beats.

Number of Beats

The first group of definitions describes the number of beats in a measure: Duple, Triple, and Quadruple.

Duple

Duple means there are two beats in the measure, like 2/4 or 2/2.

Triple

Triple means there are three beats in the measure, like 3/4 or 3/8.

Quadruple

Quadruple means there are four beats in the measure, like 4/4.

Division of Beats

The second group of definitions describe how a beat is divided. These two terms are: Simple and Compound.

Simple

Simple means a beat can be divided into two notes.

Compound

Compound means a beat can be divided into three notes.

Let's look at some examples. Take this very slowly. Make sure you understand each of these. Let's start with simple. Remember, 'simple' means a beat can be divided into two notes.

2/4 Time

2/4 has two beats, therefore it is duple, and when the quarter note is divided in two, it is simple. Therefore, 2/4 time is described as simple duple.

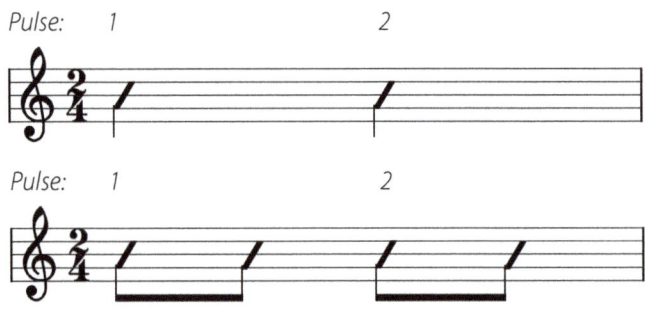

2/2 Time

2/2 is also simple duple.

3/4 Time

3/4 time has three beats, therefore it is triple, and when the quarter note is divided in two, it is simple. So 3/4 time is described as simple triple.

4/4 Time

4/4 time has four beats (quadruple) and a quarter note can be divided in two (simple). It is described as simple quadruple.

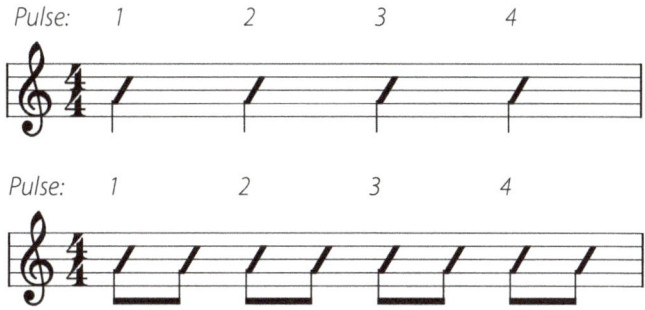

Note: Simple meter time signatures have a 2, 3, or 4 as the top number.

'Compound' means a beat can be divided into three notes. This may confuse your idea of what beats are in a measure. But in this context, think of beats as the larger pulses the listener feels. These pulses are usually subdivided.

6/8 Time

6/8 time could be explained as having six beats with each of those beats represented by an 8th note. But 6/8 is normally felt as two beats (or pulses), each divided into three parts.

So each larger pulse is represented by a three 8th notes or a dotted quarter note.

Because it is felt as two beats it is duple and because each beat is divided into three, it is compound. So 6/8 is compound duple. And again, each of the beats (pulses) can be represented by a dotted quarter note.

9/8 Time

9/8 time can be explained as having nine beats with each of those beats represented by an 8th note. But 9/8 is normally felt as three beats (or pulses) each divided into three parts.

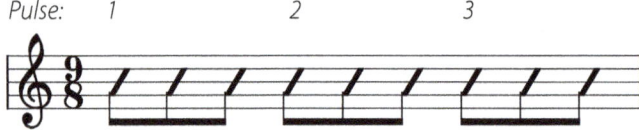

Because it is felt as three beats, it is triple, and because each beat is divided into three, it is compound. So 9/8 is compound triple. And again, each of the beats (pulses) can be represented by a dotted quarter note. Each larger pulse is represented by three 8th notes or a dotted quarter note.

12/8 Time

One way of thinking about 12/8 time is that it has twelve beats with each of those beats represented by an 8th note. But 12/8 is normally felt as four beats (or pulses), each divided into three parts.

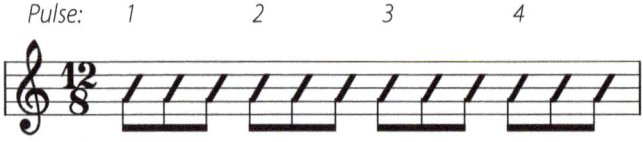

Because it is felt as four beats, it is quadruple, and because each beat is divided into three, it is compound. 12/8 is compound quadruple. And again, each of the beats (pulses) can be represented by a dotted quarter note. Each larger pulse is represented by three 8th notes or a dotted quarter note.

This can be mind boggling at first, but if you review it several times and focus on the definitions, it'll become clearer. It helps to think of the definitions in two groups.

- Duple, Triple, Quadruple: These terms refer to the number of beats (pulses) in a measure.
- Simple and Compound: These terms refer to how the pulses are divided into either two or three notes.

Odd Meter

Now you have the background to learn about odd meter. An odd meter combines both simple and compound beats. That means within the measure there is a beat or beats divided in two and a beat or beats divided in three. So, the definition of 'odd meter' is any meter that combines both simple and compound beats.

To start understanding odd meters, it is often best to think in combinations of groups of two and three 8th notes. Let's take a look at a few.

5/8 Time

5/8 is thought of as 3+2 or 2+3. The examples below have both a simple and compound beat. This creates two uneven pulses.

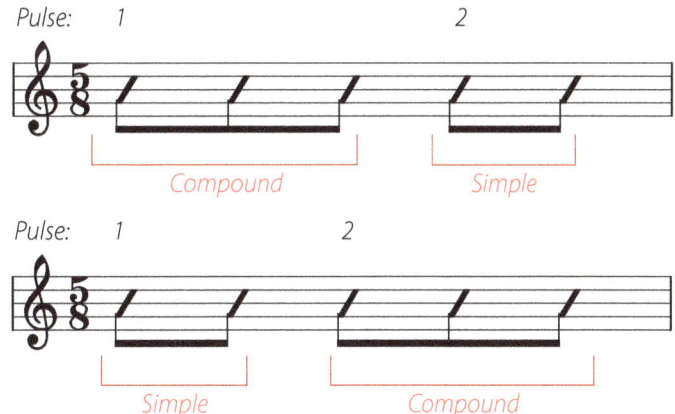

7/8 Time

7/8 can be thought of as 2+2+3 or 3+2+2 or 2+3+2. All examples below have two simple and one compound beats.

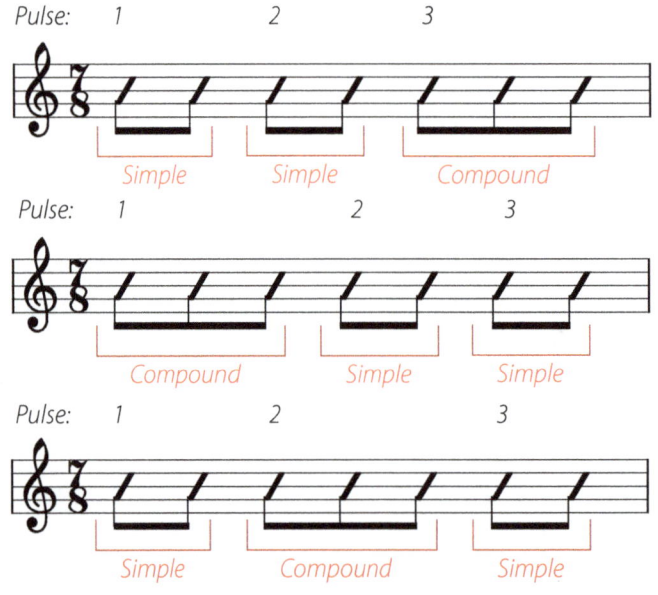

8/8 Time

8/8 can be thought of as 3+3+2 or 3+2+3 or 2+3+3. All examples below have one simple and two compound beats.

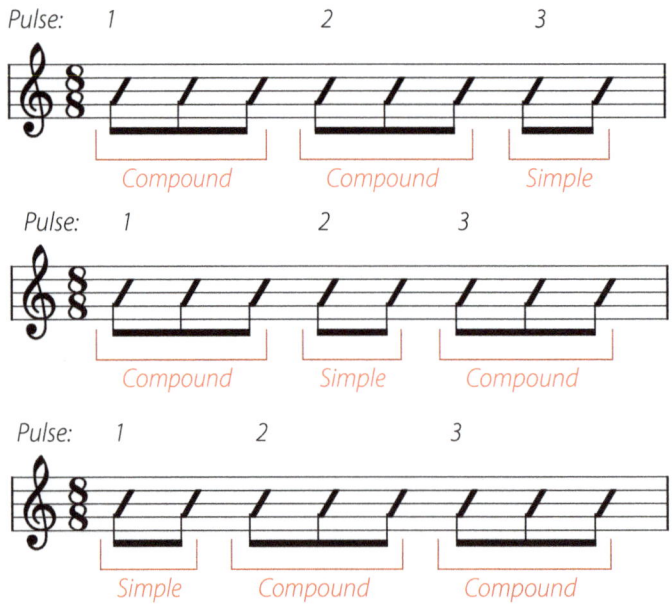

And it should be noted that theoretically 8/8 could be four groups of two 8th notes, but that is usually impractical because it would essentially be 4/4 time.

11/8 Time

11/8 can be thought of a number of ways but it is commonly seen like this: 3+3+3+2. This example has three compound beats and one simple beat. There several other groupings possible.

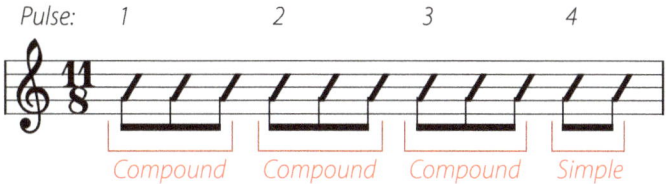

13/8 Time

13/8 can be thought of a number of ways as well. Here's one way; 3+3+3+2+2. This example has three compound beats and two simple beats. There several other groupings possible.

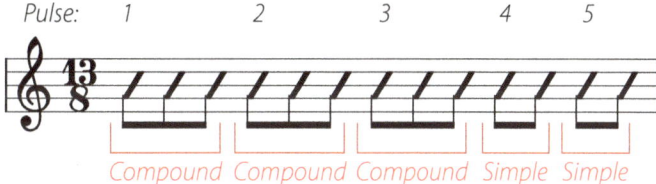

It is helpful to understand a few ways in which odd meters appear in music:

- A single odd meter as the basis for an entire composition. This means the main feel of the song is the odd meter.
- Multiple odd time signatures in a rhythmically complex composition. In complex music the time signature can switch often and mix simple and compound time.
- As a temporary accommodation for an isolated abnormal phrase. There are occasions where a phrase in the music requires more or fewer beats than a measure in the original time signature allows. As an example, a song could be in 4/4 time but a phrase may require that a 5/4 measure be inserted.

The decision about whether to use a '4' or an '8' as the bottom number is sometimes determined by the context. In cases where an odd time signature is used as a temporary accommodation for an abnormal phrase, it is always desirable to keep the note value of the beat (the bottom number) constant through any meter changes. This helps the musician keep the pulse the same as the music transitions through various meters. In most cases where 4/4 time is the norm and occasional measures with more than or less than four beats occur, it is best to use a '4' on the bottom of the time signature. Then, if you need to use a 3/4 or 6/4 or some other time signature temporarily, the '4', that is the quarter note, is constant.

The next four Rhythm Guitar Modules will focus in on how to play several odd meters: 5/8, 7/8, 11/8, and 13/8. Be sure to review the material in this Module as much as you need.

CHART READING

More Repeat Devices

This Unit discusses more repeat devices that are commonly used in chord charts. These are called repeat signs.

Repeat Signs

Repeat signs are double-lined brackets with two dots at the beginning and end of a section that is repeated.

A 'start repeat' barline is always paired with the 'end repeat' barline. The one exception is a repeat to the beginning. If a song repeats to the very beginning, only the end repeat sign is needed.

In the hierarchy of repeat devices, these are mid-level, meaning they are usually reserved for repeating a section or more but usually not major jumps back in the song. It's best to not use this kind of repeat device for repeats of less than four measures. In those cases, use one-bar or two-bar repeats introduced in the last Unit. There are exceptions.

Endings

Next, let's talk about endings. Endings are a creative way to avoid rewriting an entire section when only the last bar or two or three is different the second or third time.

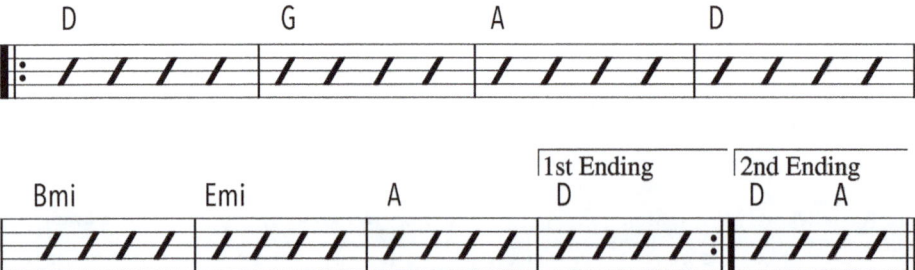

Imagine a 16-bar section of a song that repeats, but the 16th bar is different the second time. Instead of writing out the entire section again, first, second, and even third (or more) endings can be used. There will a number, the word 'ending', and a two-sided bracket over bars that are the ending.

Endings can be one, two, or more measures in length but they generally don't exceed two or three measures. Anything longer than that means the creator of the chart had some other issues trying to organize the sections.

The beginning or vertical part of the bracket should align with the beginning of the ending.

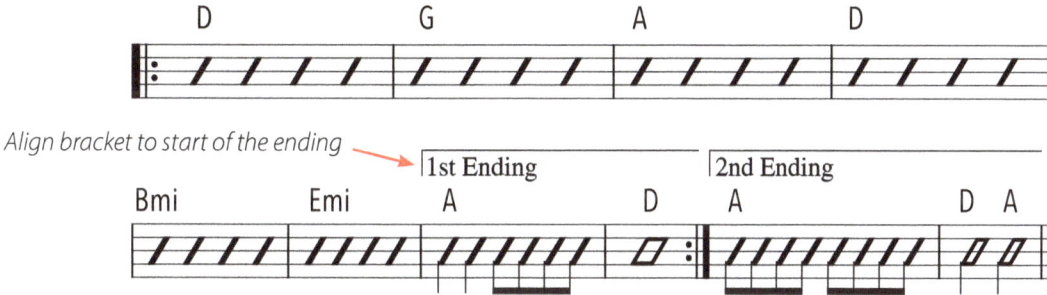

After repeating, the next time you come to the point where the first ending is, jump forward to where the bracket for the second ending begins. Second endings are common but be prepared for third, fourth, or even more endings.

If a section is to be played three times, there will also be a repeat sign at the end of the second ending. After repeating and playing the section the third time, when you come to the point where the first ending is, jump forward to where the bracket for the third ending begins. When there are no more endings, continue to the next section.

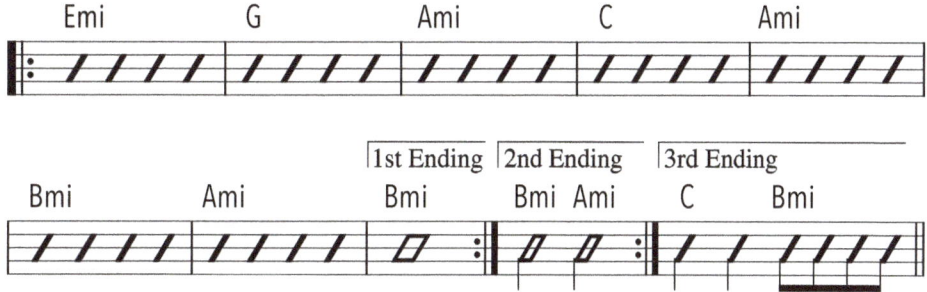

Open / Repeat Until Cue

There are also endings labeled 'open' or 'repeat until cue' with the next ending saying 'last x', which means 'last time'.

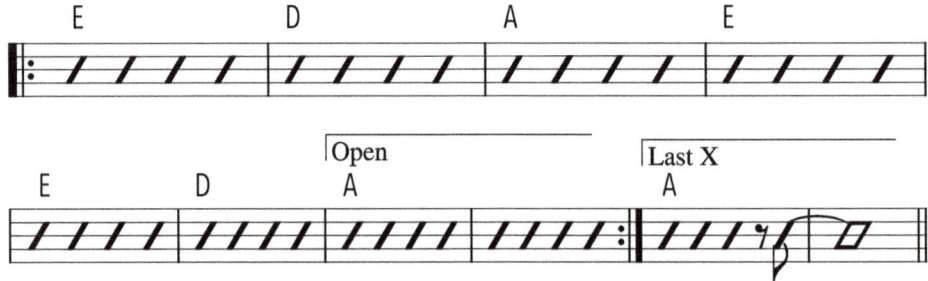

This means that the first ending labeled 'open' or 'repeat until cue' should be played again and again until the leader cues the last or final ending. This is very common.

Nested Repeats

It's important to talk about nested repeats. Nested repeats occur when a smaller section with start repeats and end repeats are placed within a larger section with start repeats and end repeats. It already sounds complicated doesn't it?

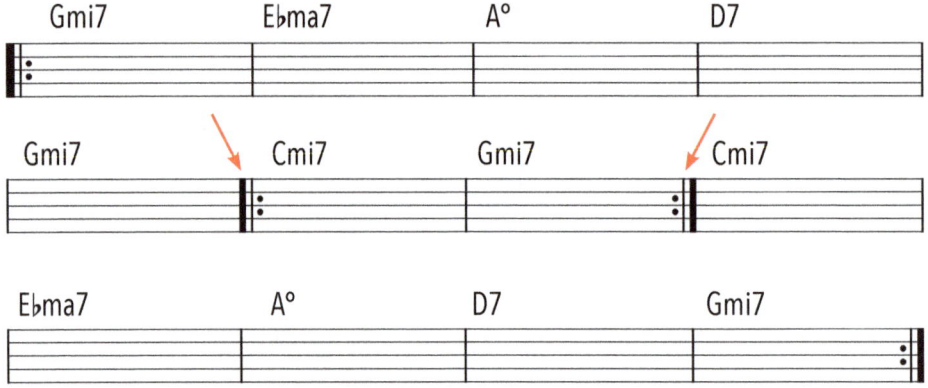

Nested repeats are bad, wrong, and confusing and you will typically only see them in poorly-written charts. It's a messy subject that's best understood by looking at examples so you can experience the confusion and possible resulting chaos and panic first-hand.

Nightmare Scenarios

There are occasions when, in the attempt to save space and time, the creator of the chart may write a pair of start and end repeats for a small number of measures within a larger section that has a pair of start and end repeats.

There is no good way to summarize how to handle each situation without seeing the specific example. But here's a nightmare scenario that you might see.

Because this is wrong, there is no universal way to interpret how to navigate through this which means you may decide to play through this one way and other musicians in the band may do it another, which, of course, spells train wreck.

The rule to remember is that only the most recent start-repeat barline applies. Don't jump back any further than the last repeat you saw. This may or may not be what the creator intended, however. They could intend for something different to happen, so that's a good question to ask at the rehearsal.

IMPROVISATION

The common thread through all of Level 5 is that the Harmonic Minor Scale can be used as a tool for specific chords. You learned how dominant V and diminished 7 chords are used in the Minor Scale and how to create lines over them. In this Module you will learn how to play lines on Mi(Ma7) chords in progressions using both the Harmonic Minor Scale and Mi(Ma7) arpeggios.

Recall that the formula for a Mi(Ma7) chord is a minor 3rd, perfect 5th, and major 7th. By now you are very familiar with the side-by-side comparison of both the scales and the arpeggios of the harmonized scales of parallel Natural Minor and Harmonic Minor. Take a look at this common progression and the analysis. This a typical progression where the Mi(Ma7) chord is used to connect a root of minor triad with the b7 of a Mi7 chord. It's the chordal hook used in countless popular songs.

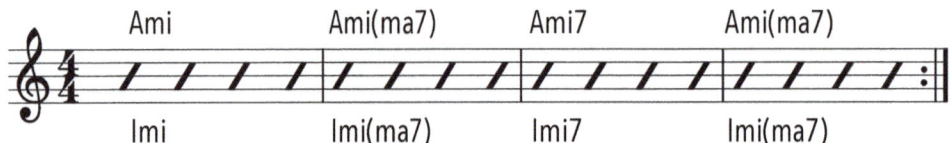

Ami is the Imi in both the A Natural Minor and A Harmonic Minor Scales, so either scale is an appropriate source of notes. According to what you learned recently about being selective in using the Harmonic Minor Scale, consider choosing the A Natural Minor Scale on the Ami and Ami7. This will preserve the uniqueness of the Harmonic Minor Scale for the Ami(ma7). But this is not a rule so experiment for yourself.

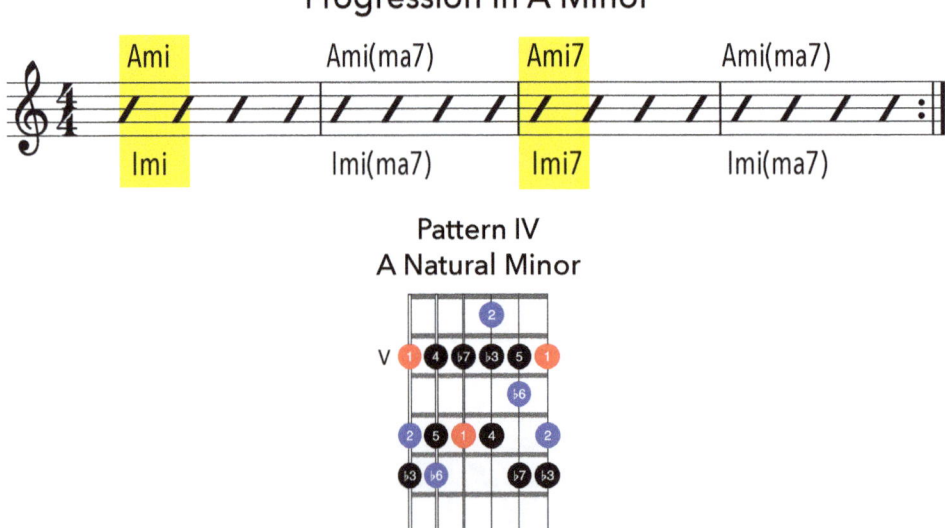

Ami(ma7) is the I chord in the A Harmonic Minor Scale, which means that the Harmonic Minor Scale is the appropriate source of notes, as is the A Mi(Ma7) arpeggio, and not the A Natural Minor scale.

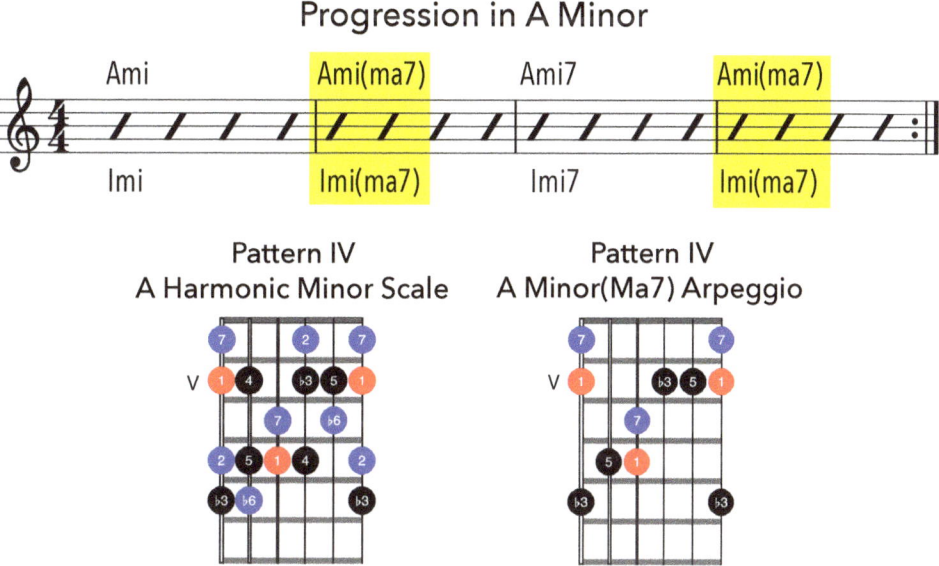

The shift between the parallel Natural Minor and Harmonic Minor Scales is relatively easy because it only involves one scale degree, the 7th.

- Locate the Pattern IV A Natural and Harmonic Minor Scale patterns in 5th position. Run the A Minor Scale over the Ami and Ami7 chords, and the A Harmonic Minor Scale and the Ami(ma7) arpeggio over the Ami(ma7) chord.
- Next, create motifs and improvise using the Pattern IV A Natural Minor Scale pattern in 5th position. But on the Ami(ma7), locate the Pattern IV Ami(ma7) arpeggio.

When creating lines and developing your lick vocabulary, it's a good idea to blend the A Harmonic Minor Scale and Ami(ma7) arpeggio. It doesn't have to be one or the other and besides, all the notes of the Ami(ma7) are in the A Harmonic Minor Scale. Your goal is to move freely between the Natural and Harmonic Minor scales and be in control of the arpeggios, too.

Remember that the primary goal of combining Theory knowledge with Improvisation is to remove any mystery about what notes you can choose to solo over a single chord or group of chords. The information in this Module was presented to you in the Pattern IV Octave Shape area because it's the place that's most comfortable for most guitarists. But know that these concepts should eventually be learned in other patterns as well.

Level 5 Unit 6 • Improv Demo

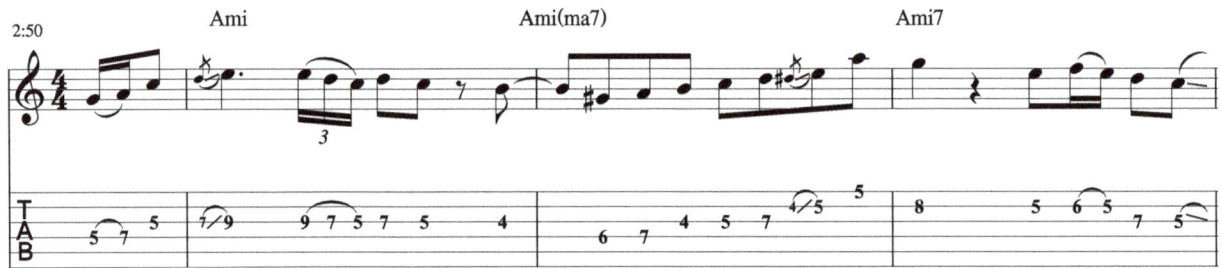

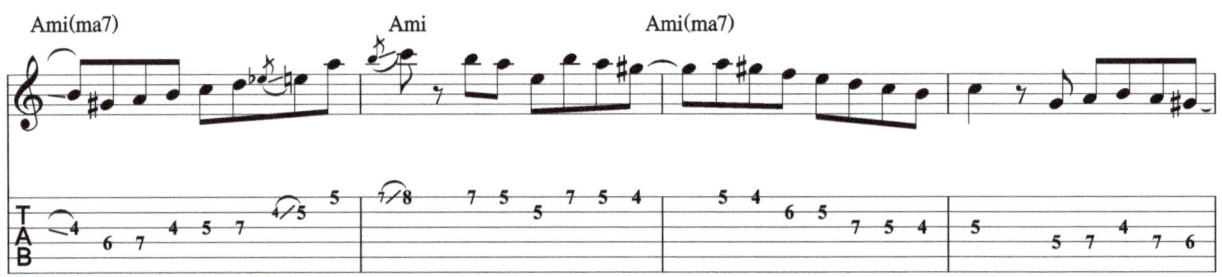

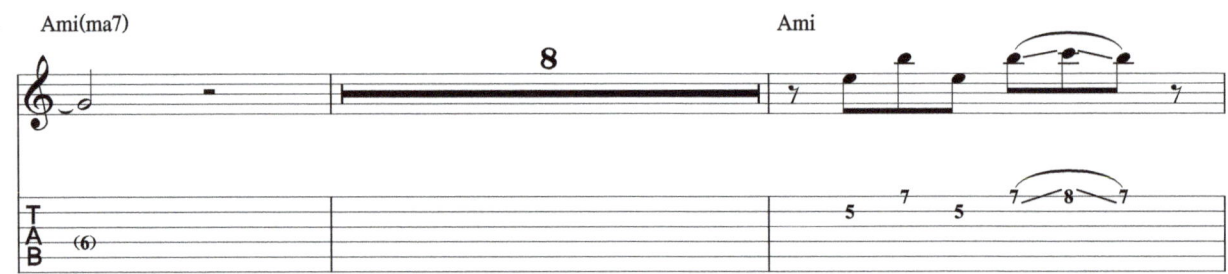

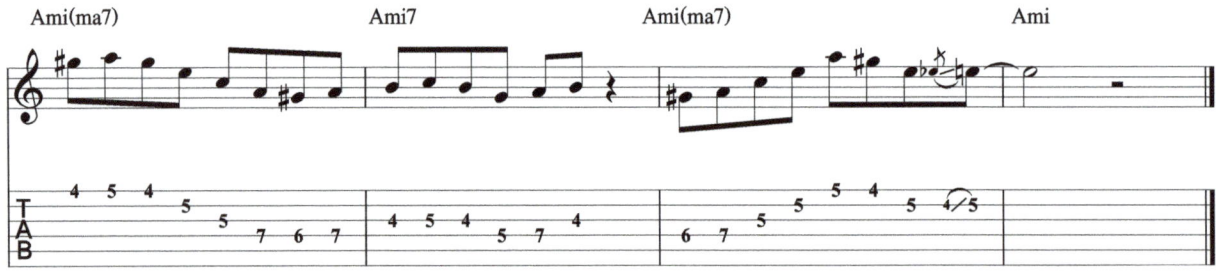

PRACTICE

Theory

- ☐ Go to the tabs below the Theory video on the website and complete the quiz.
- ☐ Learn the Imi(ma7) chord.

Fretboard Logic

- ☐ Learn the voicings for Minor(Major 7) chords and arpeggios.

Rhythm Guitar

- ☐ Understand how odd meter is built from even and odd divisions of beats.

Chart Raading

- ☐ Understand start and end repeats, multiple endings, repeat until cue, and the dangers of nested repeats.

Improvisation

- ☐ Practice playing solos over the progression in A minor using the Pattern IV Natural Minor Scale, Harmonic Minor Scale, and A mi(ma7) arpeggio.

UNIT 7

Learning Modules

> **Theory** - The ♭IIIma7(+5) Chord

> **Fretboard Logic** - Major 7(+5) Chords and Arpeggios

> **Rhythm Guitar** - Odd Meter: 5/8 Time

> **Chart Reading** - Jump Marks: D.C. and D.S

> **Improvisation** - Soloing with the Harmonic Minor Scale over the ma7(+5) Chord

> **Practice** - Continue Practice Routine Development

THEORY

You learned four chords of the harmonized Harmonic Minor Scale that have different qualities than the natural minor scale. They are: Imi(ma7), bIIIma7(+5), V7, and VII°7. In the last Unit we looked at Imi(ma7). You have learned how three of the chords are used in progressions: Imi(ma7), V7, and VII°7. In this Theory Module we will look at the last one, bIIIma7(+5).

The bIIIma7(+5) Chord

Just to review, a Ma7(+5) chord has a major 3rd, an augmented 5th, and a major 7th. I suggest you also see it as an augmented triad with a major 7th or as a Ma7 chord with a raised 5th.

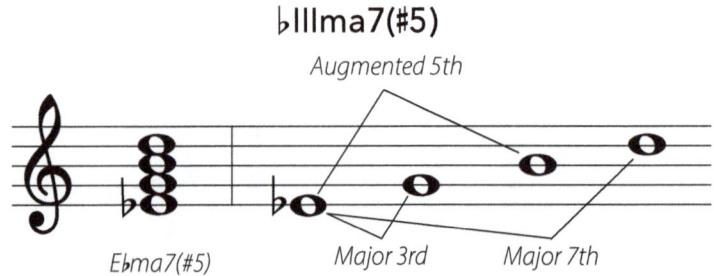

This chord sounds a little stressful when played alone but will make sense when you hear it how it is used in a song. The focus of this Module is how the Ma7(+5) chord is most commonly used, and that is as a passing chord between a major triad and a 6th chord. The use of the Ma7(+5) chord in a Jazz context will be discussed in Level 8.

First, remember the 6th chord? You learned about it in Unit 1 when you learned the 'other chord types'. The 6th chord is a major triad with a major 6th. It's probably one of the happiest sounding chords in the world. Here is a reminder about how it's constructed.

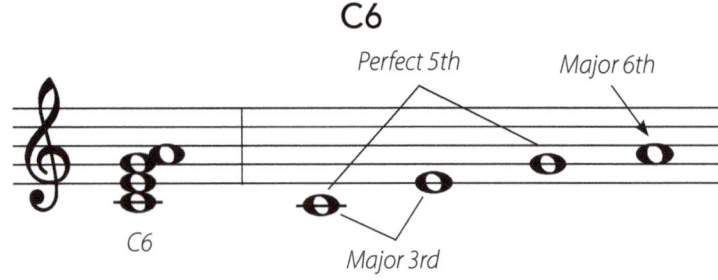

You should note that the 5th is sometimes left out of the voicing.

A C major triad and a C6 chord have a lot in common and are frequently used together. Sometimes when they are used together they are connected with a Ma7(+5) chord as a passing chord. In this case, a voice moves chromatically from chord to chord. Examine this progression fragment.

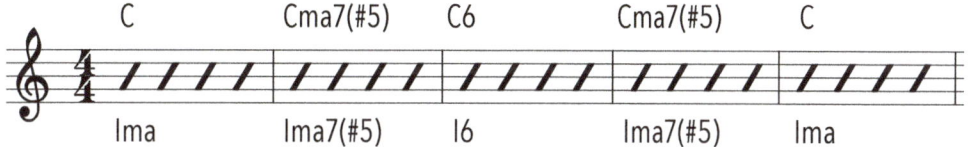

You can see the voice that starts on the 5th of the chord ascends and then descends by a half step from chord to chord.

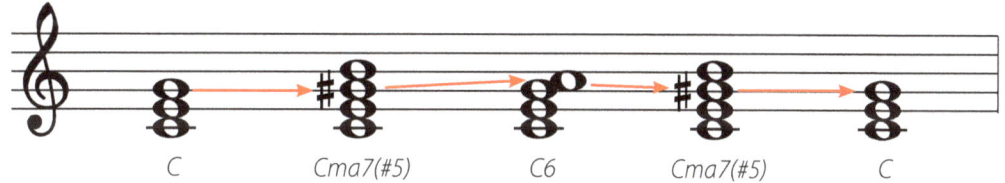

- The 5th of the C triad to the +5 of Cma7(+5)
- The +5 of Cma7(+5) to the 6th of the C6
- The 6th of the C6 to the +5 of the Cma7(+5)
- The +5 of Cma7(+5) to the 5th of the C triad

You also hear a voice move to the 7th and back to the root.

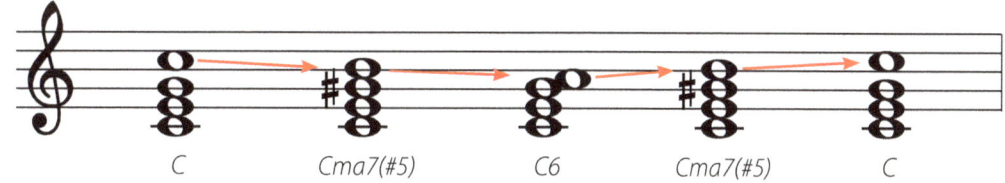

- The root of the C triad to the Ma7 of Cma7(+5)
- The Ma7 of the Cma7(+5) to the Ma6 of the C6
- The Ma6 of the C6 to the Ma7 of Cma7(+5)
- The Ma7 of the Cma7(+5) to the root of the C

This progression fragment will be a focus of this Unit's Fretboard Logic and Improvisation Modules.

Let's switch the focus to melodic note choices for Ma7(+5) chords. Before we get too far with this discussion, I need introduce a term you will hear often as we move forward in this program.

Chord Scale

A 'chord scale' is a scale that fits a specific chord. It fits the chord because the scale contains the chord tones of the chord, or at least most of them. It's common for a single chord to have several chord scales that will fit.

For example, for an A minor chord, some of the appropriate chord scales are A Minor Pentatonic, A Natural Minor, A Blues, or A Harmonic Minor. Why are they all chord scales for an Ami chord? Because all of these scales contain the chord tones of an Ami triad: A, C, and E.

You can see that idea of a chord scale is not a particularly complex concept, but there are scales that are sometimes applied to chords that, on the surface, seem unrelated. In the case of the Ma7(+5) chord, think of it as a product of Harmonic Minor. In other words, you may have never thought about a Ma7(+5) chord until Level 5. You only learned about it when you harmonized the Harmonic Minor Scale. The Ma7(+5) chord resulted from building a 7th chord on the 3rd scale degree of the Harmonic Minor Scale. A scale that sounds good when played over a Ma7(+5) is the Harmonic Minor Scale. But which Harmonic Minor Scale?

Let's reverse-engineer this. When the C Harmonic Minor Scale is harmonized, the ♭III chord is E♭ma7(+5). That means that the C Harmonic Minor Scale is the scale of choice for an E♭ma7(+5). Ask yourself what the relationship is between the scale and the chord. C, as in C Harmonic Minor Scale, is a minor 3rd below the root of the E♭ma7(+5) chord. Apply this relationship to ma7(+5) chords on other roots.

Let's look at a few examples:

- A♭ma7(+5): What note is a minor 3rd below A♭? F. Using the same logic, the scale that fits A♭ma7(+5) is F Harmonic Minor.
- Ema7(+5): What note is a minor 3rd below E? C#. Using the same idea, the scale that fits Ema7(+5) is C# Harmonic Minor.
- Gma7(+5): What note is a minor 3rd below G? E. Using the same logic, the scale that fits Gma7(+5) is E Harmonic Minor.

This is a little abstract, but once you get the hang of it, you will understand that many chord scale/chord relationships in music are similar to this. So the harmonic minor scale over a Ma7(+5) chord is a typical example of a chord scale.

To create lines on a Ma7(+5) chord, you need a scale. The scale that fits it is the Harmonic Minor Scale a minor 3rd below. You will use this chord scale in the Unit 7 Improvisation Module.

Remember from an earlier unit that there are several ways this chord name is written and spoken.

- Major7(#5), because it is a major 7 chord with a raised or sharp 5th.
- Major7(+5), because it is a major 7 chord and with a raised 5th and '+' is another way to notate '#' in a chord symbol.
- Augmented major 7. This is another way the chord is named when spoken about.

FRETBOARD LOGIC

You learned to harmonize the Harmonic Minor Scale with 7th chords in Unit 3. This resulted in three chords that are new. You have already looked at diminished 7 and Mi(Ma7). The last one to examine is the Ma7(+5) chord. It was presented as the ♭III chord in Harmonic Minor. In this Module you will learn the common Ma7(+5) chord voicings and arpeggios. As a reminder, the formula for a Ma7(+5) chord or arpeggio is major 3rd, augmented 5th, and major 7th. The root will be C for the purpose of this illustration.

Major 7(+5) Chord

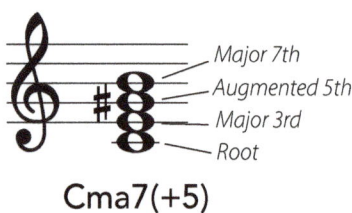

Cma7(+5)

The most efficient way to learn the common Ma7(+5) chord voicings is to modify the existing major 7 voicings by raising the perfect 5th to an augmented 5th. First see whether you can figure out a voicing for each of these chord types within each of the octave shapes and then check your results with voicings presented in the back of the book.

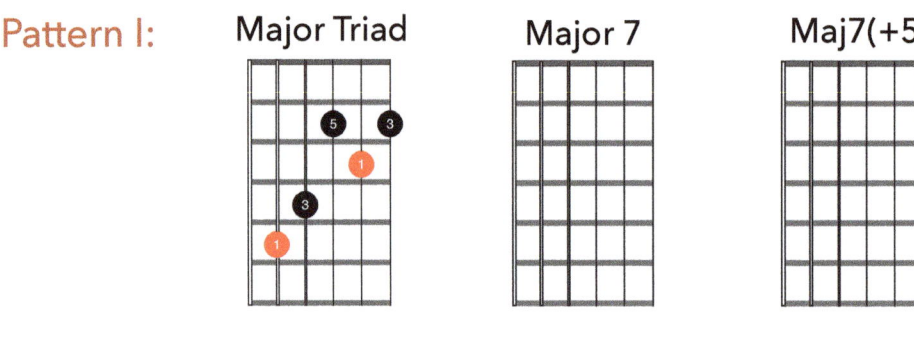

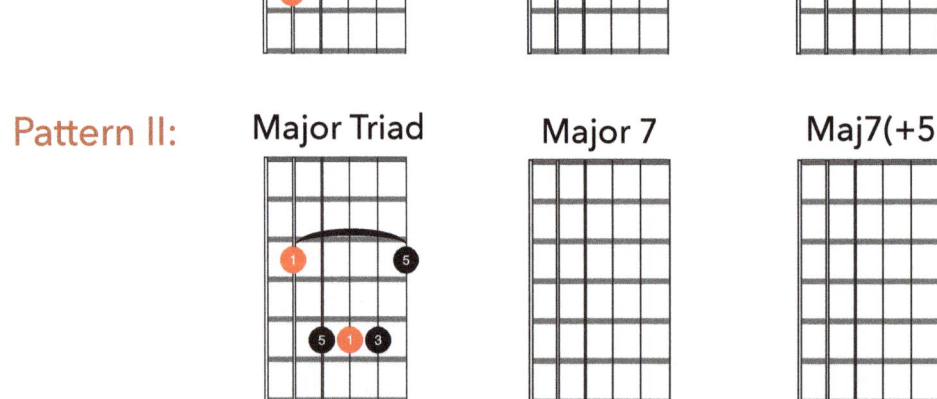

Level 5 • Unit 7: Fretboard Logic

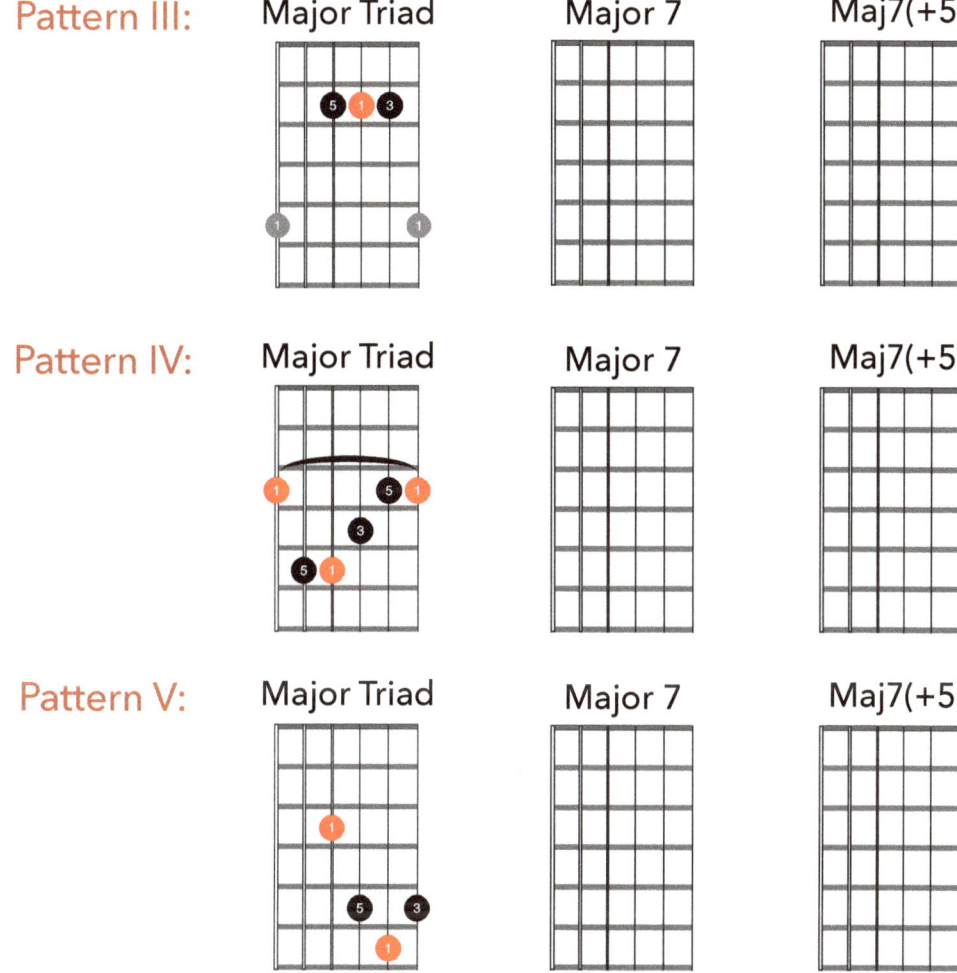

(Answer key on page 318)

There is another way to think of this chord. You could begin with an augmented triad and add a major 7. It's more important for you to know the process of how to construct these chord shapes than it is to memorize all of them.

Using Major7(#5) Chords

Ma7(+5) chords are most commonly used in transition from a major triad to a 6th chord. Play these chords and focus on the voice that moves from G to G# to A. Pay attention to how that sounds.

Progression in C Major

| C | Cma7(#5) | C6 | Cma7(#5) | C |

| Major Triad | Maj7(+5) | 6 Chord | Maj7(+5) | Major Triad |

Again, it's more important for you to know the process of how to construct these chord shapes than it is to memorize all of them.

Often times in songs with a static major chord for a few bars, this sequence, or a segment of it, can be inserted to create internal voice movement while still maintaining the basic major chord sound. After all, each of these chords have a major 3rd.

Ma7(+5) Arpeggios

The same method we used to adapt the five Ma7 chord voicings as Ma7(+5) voicings can be applied to arpeggios as well. The most efficient way to learn the common Ma7(+5) arpeggios is to modify the existing Ma7 arpeggios by raising the perfect 5th to an augmented 5th. Using Ma7(+5) arpeggios will be one focus of the Unit 7 Improvisation Module, so it is good to spend a little time getting these under your fingers.

First, see whether you can figure out each of these arpeggios within each of the octave shapes. Then check your results with voicings presented in the Appendix of the book. It's important for you to know the process of how to construct these arpeggio shapes.

Fretboard Biology — Level 5 • Unit 7: Fretboard Logic

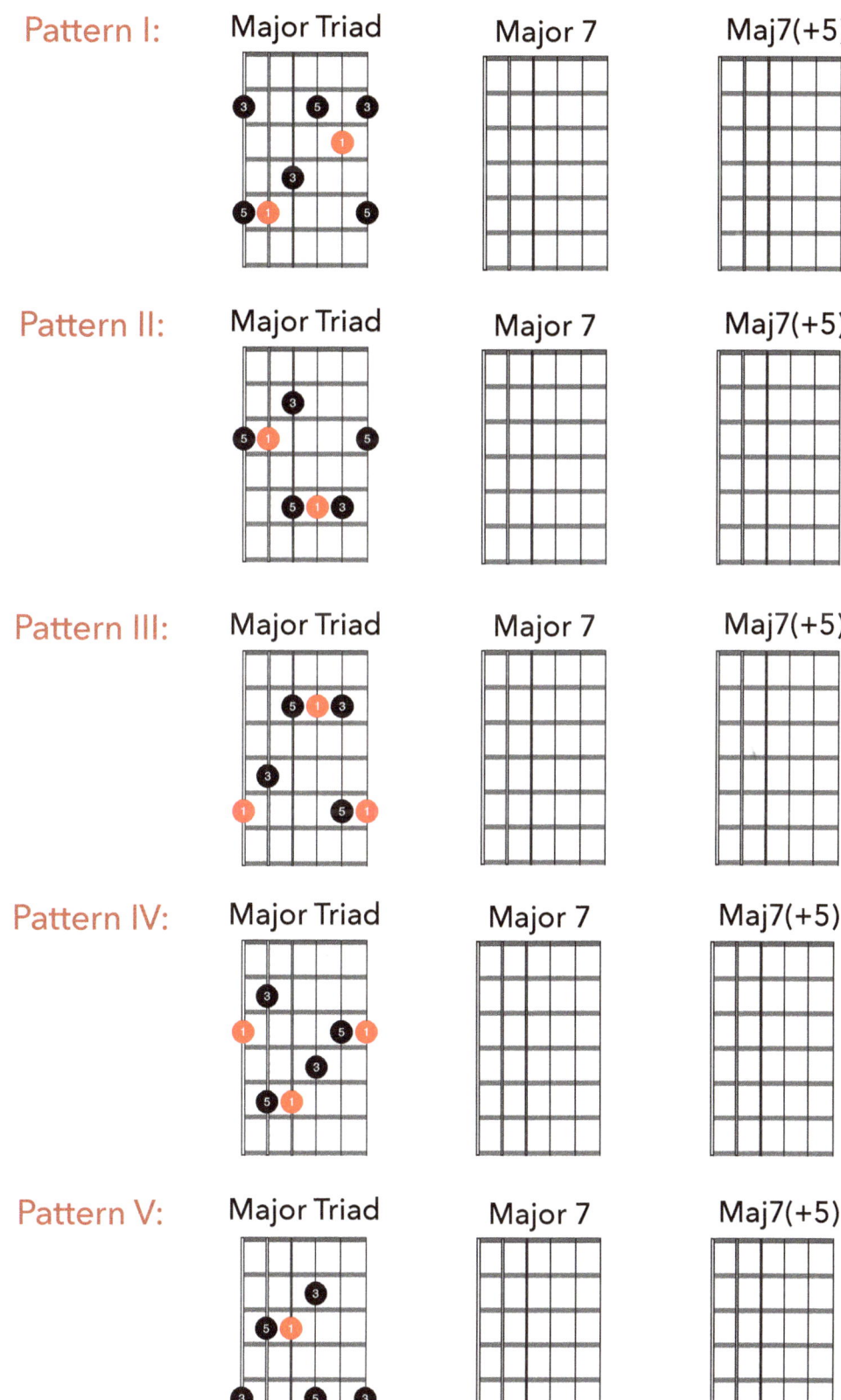

(Answer key on page 319)

RHYTHM GUITAR

In Unit 6 you learned more detail about meter. You learned that an odd meter combines both simple and compound beats. That means within the measure in odd meter there are beats divided into two and beats divided into three. This Rhythm Guitar Module examines using a single odd meter time signature as the basis for an entire composition. The Module focuses on 5/8.

5/8 Time

5/8 can be thought of as 3+2 or 2+3. Both 3+2 or 2+3 have both a simple beat and a compound beat. One effective way to conceptualize and internalize an odd meter is with a silly phrase that uses words that have two and three syllables. We tend to remember that kind of thing. I'll use that approach here.

5/8 Time

This first example is in the key of D minor. It's in 5/8, is 3+2 and has a Rock feel.

5/8 Progression in D Minor

For the compound beat, use the word 'strawberries' because it has three syllables.

For the simple beat, use the words 'with cream' because combined there are two syllables.

Say the two words back-to-back in steady rhythm: 'strawberries with cream'.

As you say the words over and over, you can feel 3+2. And notice you feel two larger pulses: the first on 'straw' of 'strawberries' and the second on 'with'. These are, of course, uneven, so some call the 5/8 feel 'uneven two'.

Let's look at the progression again and the harmonic analysis.

5/8 Progression in D Minor

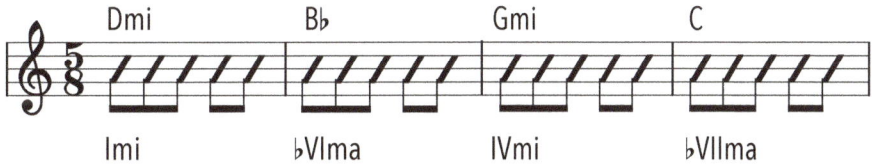

The first pulse is the group of three, or 'strawberries'. The second pulse is the group of two, or 'with cream'. This is clearly 'uneven two' because the two main pulses are of different lengths, but just the same, there are clearly two definite pulses.

The group of three 8th notes can also be represented with a dotted quarter note. The group of two 8th notes can also be represented with a single quarter note.

5/8 Progression in D Minor

You can play this example three different ways:

- First, play each of the 8th notes in the measure accenting the first of each group. That means to accent the start of the group of three, and then the start of the group of two.

- Next, play only on the start of the main two pulses per measure: the start of the group of three, and then the start of the group of two. Remember, the group of three 8th notes can be thought of as a dotted quarter note, and the group of two 8th notes can be thought of as a single quarter note.

- Last, try some variations using some dotted notes and some 8th notes or, on the group of three, a quarter note and 8th note, or 8th and quarter notes. You can create a lot of variations but it all comes back to feeling 'strawberries with cream' as the core underlying rhythm. As you go through these examples, keep the 'strawberries with cream' phrase going in your head.

Play the example until it feels natural. For this example, you can use a crunch tone if you like. Always keep the 'strawberries and cream' phrase going in your head.

Next, let's look at 5/8 as 2+3. This next example is in the key of A and is based on an A7 to A7sus. It has sort of a Blues sound. It's in 5/8, is 2+3, and has a funky feel.

5/8 Progression in A Minor

For the simple beat, use the words 'I like' because combined there are two syllables.

For the compound beat, use the word 'strawberries' because it has three syllables.

Say the two words back-to-back in steady rhythm: 'I like strawberries'.

You can feel 2+3. Notice you feel two larger pulses: the first on 'I' of 'I like' the second on 'straw' of 'strawberries'. These are, of course, uneven, and as we said before, some call the 5/8 feel 'uneven two'.

Let's look at the progression again and the harmonic analysis. There is not much to it. It is just A7 to A7sus. As before, the group of two 8th notes can also be represented with a single quarter note. The group of three 8th notes can also be represented with a dotted quarter note.

5/8 Progression in A Minor

Play this progression in time with the phrase 'I like strawberries'. Feel the two main pulses per measure. The first pulse is the group of two or 'I like'. The second pulse is the group of three which is 'strawberries'. This, again, is 'uneven two' because the two main pulses are of different lengths, but just the same, there are clearly two definite pulses.

Play this example three different ways:

- First, play each of the 8th notes in the measure accenting the first of each group. That means to accent the start of the group of two, and then the start of the group of three.

- Next, play only on the start of the main two pulses per measure: the start of the group of two, and then the start of the group of three. As before, the group of two 8th notes can be thought of as a quarter note, and the group of three 8th notes can be thought of as a dotted quarter note.

- Finally, try some variations using some dotted notes and some 8th notes or, on the group of three, a quarter note and 8th note, or 8th and quarter notes. You can create a lot of variations but it all comes back to feeling 'I like strawberries' as the core underlying rhythm. As you go through these examples, keep the 'I like strawberries' phrase going in your head.

I suggest a clean tone with this progression. Play this until it feels natural and keep the 'I like strawberries' phrase going in your head.

The goal here is to demystify odd meter. If approached in the right way, it won't be intimidating. It does require repetition and getting into the mental zone of the time signature, but that's just practice.

CHART READING

Jump Marks

We have covered several topics in the hierarchy of repeat tools. These all have to do with what we call the 'form' of the song. Form refers to the sections and in what order they're arranged. Next in the hierarchy of repeat tools are 'Jump Marks'. They are the 'DS' and 'DC' signs as well as 'Coda' signs. These are typically used to jump a greater distance in the chart than a one-bar or two-bar repeat or a standard 'start repeat/end repeat' combination. They typically appear after much of the chart has been played. That means after multiple verses, prechoruses, choruses, and solos the song returns to an earlier location in the chart.

Let's take a look at these jump marks and their definitions:

D.C.

DC stands for De Capo or 'the beginning'. When you see DC, jump back to the very beginning of the song.

D.S.

DS stands for Dal Segno or 'from the sign'. When you see D.S., you are being directed to the point in the song where 'the sign', Segno (𝄋), is located.

Coda

The Coda sign (𝄌) is another symbol that you will see. The term 'Coda' means 'ending'. When you see the Coda symbol, you are being directed to the section at the end of the song marked 'CODA'.

Let's take a look at some examples of jump marks. I suggest playing through these charts as we go through them to get some practice navigating through charts that use jump marks.

D.C.

Here is an example of the jump mark called 'DC'. Remember that DC means Da Capo, or the beginning. In this example, follow the chart until you see 'DC' written. It's normally placed below the staff, but not always.

Here's how your eyes should travel through this chart:

1. Start at the beginning, at letter A, and play through the 1st line
2. Then play through the 2nd line to the repeat.

3. At the end of the second line, the repeat directs you back to the very beginning at letter A.

4. Play through the first line again, and then the second line.

5. Continue on to the 3rd line at letter B and then the 4th line.

6. At the end of the 4th line, you encounter D.C., which instructs you to go back to the beginning of the chart (Da Capo) which is marked with letter A.

7. At that point, go back to the very beginning of the chart.

8. Play the two lines of letter A. Do not take the repeat while playing the DC.

9. Then play the two lines of letter B to the end of the chart, which is after the B section and not shown here.

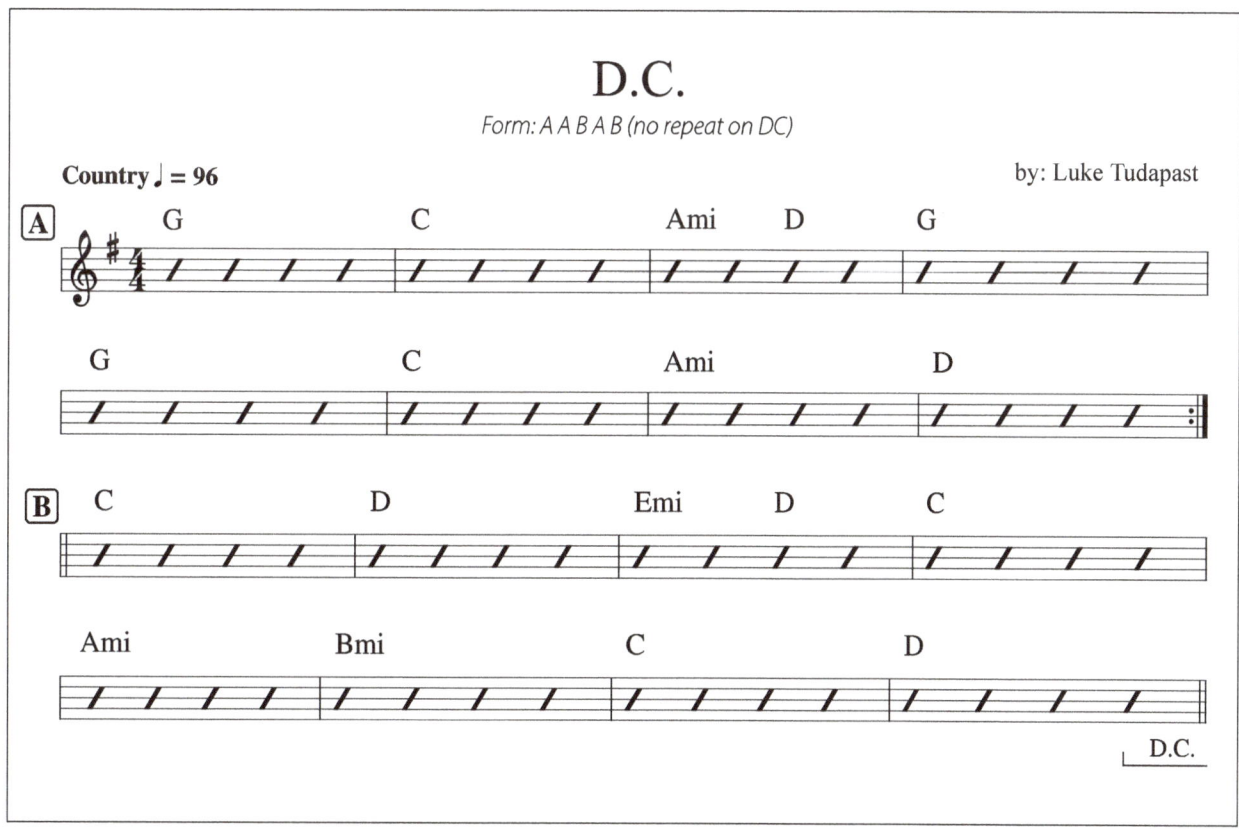

Another very common short-hand way to communicate the form of a song is to list the letters of the sections in the sequence they occur. So for example, this chart's form would be written in shorthand like this: A A B A B

If there were more sections, their letters would follow. It's common to see this sequential list of sections written on the chart at the top, bottom or even directly under the title. This is also a very helpful tool for when the form is changed in a rehearsal to accommodate some circumstance. It's common to see this list of sections written in by a previous musician.

D.S.

Here is an example of the jump mark called 'D.S'. Remember that D.S. means Dal Segno, or to the sign. In this example, follow the chart until you see 'DS' written. It's normally placed below the staff, but not always.

Here is how you would navigate through this chart:

1. Start at the beginning, which does not have a letter. Even though it isn't labeled as such, this is an Intro. Play through the 1st line.
2. Then play the 2nd line, which is letter A. Notice the start repeat and the sign.
3. Play through the 3rd line until you see the end repeat and a bracket that says "1st ending".
4. The end repeat at the 1st ending, instructs you to go back to the start repeat at letter A.
5. Play through the 2nd line again.
6. Then play through the 3rd line. But this time, skip the 1st ending and jump to and play through the 2nd ending.
7. Play through the 4th line at letter B and then the 5th line.

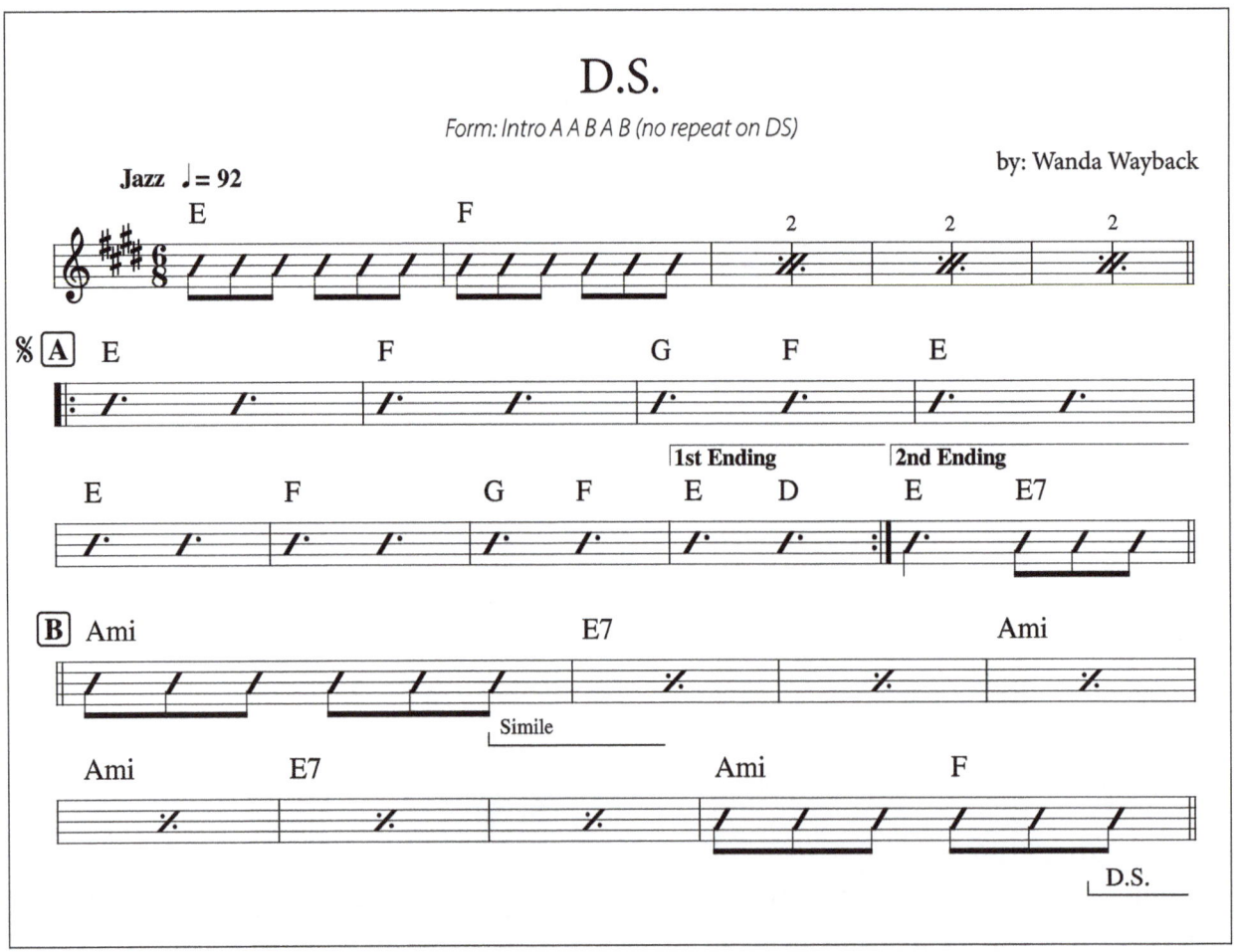

8. Notice the DS marking at the end of the 5th line. This instructs you to go back in the chart to where you see 'the sign' (Segno) at letter A.

9. At this point, play the two lines of letter A.

10. On the DS, skip the first ending and go directly to the second ending. More on this later.

11. Then play the two lines of letter B.

Like we did in the previous chart, we can write down the letters of the sections to be played to give us a shorthand for the form of the song. In this example, the form would be written: Intro A A B A B.

The path your eye is traveling on through the chart is interrupted in a significant way with a DC or DS. It's imperative that you take special note of where these signs are BEFORE you start to play. As I've mentioned before, getting lost in a chart is a terrible feeling. If you follow a short pre-game 'checklist' (where you scan the chart for specific things in a specific order), you can avoid a lot of anxiety.

What to Do after a Jump Mark

There are three different ways you will move through the chart after a DC or DS.

1. DC and on, or DS and on.
2. DC al coda, or DS al coda.
3. DC al fine, or DS al fine.

We'll discuss each of these in detail in a moment.

Repeat Signs with Jump Marks

Before we move on to explain what happens after a DC or DS, it is important to note that repeat signs are usually not 'good' on a DS or DC unless it's explicitly stated where DC or DC is written. By 'not good', I mean that the repeats are not taken during after taking the DC or DS. Sometimes charts will actually explain that and have the language 'DC al Coda (no repeats)', which is redundant but many people don't know the rule about repeats not being good after a DC or DS. Sometimes charts will have 'DC al Coda with repeats' (or 'w/rpts'), which is important whether or not you know the rule.

The common way musicians speak about repeats is to say, 'the repeat is good', meaning to follow the repeat sign. If a musician says, 'the repeat is not good', that means to not follow the repeat sign and play through to the next section.

Examples of Notating Repeat Instructions for Jump Marks

|repeats good on D.C.| D.C. (no repeats)|
|D.S. w/ repeats| D.S. (w/rpts)|

In the following examples, we will follow the rule of no repeats after the D.C. or D.S.

D.C. and On

Let's take a look at what we'll call 'D.C. and on'. D.C. is often written without the accompanying words 'al coda' or 'al fine'. You may just see D.C. In these circumstances, the jump mark only instructs you to go back to the beginning of the chart. Although we already went through a simple example of D.C. just a moment ago, let's go through a more complex chart that uses the jump mark D.C.

Here is how you should navigate through this chart:

1. Start at the top at letter A, and go through lines 1 and 2.
2. Then at the end of line 2, take the repeat back to the top, which is letter A again.
3. Play the 1st 2 lines again.
4. Then continue on to letter B.
5. Play the two lines of letter B and notice the jump mark, D.C. written at the end of the 4th line. The jump mark D.C. is telling you to go back to the beginning of the chart.
6. Go back to the very beginning at letter A, in other words, Da Capo, and play the two lines of letter A again.
7. When you reach the end of the 2nd line this time, ignore the repeat sign unless you're told otherwise. Remember that repeats are no good after a jump mark unless specified.
8. Play the two lines of letter B but this time don't take the DC. A jump mark, whether DC or DS, is only good once.
9. Play on to next section, letter C.
10. Then continue on to the next sections, C and D.

When you see just a D.C., there is no special notation that tells you to play on. That is just understood. Like in the earlier examples, let's figure out the form of the song. In other words, what is the shorthand notation that tells us the order of how the chart is to be played?

In this example, the form notation is: A A B A B C D.

D.S. and On

Let's take a look at what we'll call 'DS and on'. Like DC, DS is often written without the accompanying words 'al coda' or 'al fine'. You may just see DS.

Here is how you should navigate through this chart:

1. Start at the top and play the 1st line. Notice that this is not letter A. This is an intro that precedes letter A. Also notice the 3, 2-bar repeats, the first 2 bars plus the 3 2-bar repeats makes the 1st line 8 bars long.
2. Next go to the 2nd line which is letter A. Take note of the start repeats as well as the sign.
3. Play 2nd and 3rd lines
4. At the 4th measure of the 3rd line, take the 1st ending, which takes you back to the start repeat at letter A.
5. Play letter A again, but this time, ignore the 1s ending, and take the 2nd ending.
6. Next play letter B which are the 4th and 5th lines.
7. Notice the jump mark, DS at the end of the 5th line. The DS jump mark instructs you to go back to the sign (Segno) where letter A is.
8. Play the two lines of letter A again, but this time, ignore the repeat sign and play the 2nd ending instead of the 1st.
9. Play the two lines of letter B but this time don't take the DS. Remember, a jump mark is only good once.
10. Continue on to letter C and play the 6th and 7th lines.

Like in the last example, when you see just a D.S. jump mark, there is no special notation that tells you to play on. That is just understood. Now, let's figure out the form of the song. In other words, what is the shorthand notation that tells us the order of how the chart is to be played?

In this example, the form notation is: Intro A A B A B C .

Fretboard Biology — Level 5 • Unit 7: Chart Reading — 181

D.C. al Coda

Let's take a look DC al Coda. Here is how you would navigate through this chart:

1. Start at the top at letter A, go through lines 1 and 2.
2. Then take the repeat back to the top which is letter A again. Remember, if repeating back to the very beginning, no start repeat bracket is needed.
3. Play the first two lines again.
4. Then play the two lnes of letter B.
5. Notice the jump mark at the end of the 4th line. It says "D.C.", which means Da Capo, and it also says "al Coda" which is the important distinction here. On your way through Letter B, you might want to take note of the Coda sign as it will be important momentarily.
6. Go back to the very beginning at letter A, in other words, Da Capo, and play the two lines of letter A again.
7. When you reach the end of the 2nd line his time, ignore the repeat sign unless you're told otherwise. Remember that repeats are not good on a D.C. or D.S. unless specified.
8. Next play the first line of letter B.
9. Then play the first two measures of the 2nd line, which is where the Coda sign is. The Coda sign will be directly above the barline where you should leave the line you're on, and jump to the section somewhere below that's label 'Coda'.
10. .Next, jump to the section of the song that follows the word 'Coda' and play on through the end of the chart.

Notice how your path through this chart differed from the D.C. chart a few pages ago. Instead of just going to the beginning of the chart and playing it through to the end, the jump mark 'D.C. al Coda' includes a second set of instructions. The 'al Coda' instructs you to watch for the Coda sign in the chart, and when you reach that sign, jump to the section of the song that follows the word, Coda.

Now, let's figure out the form of the song. What is the shorthand notation that tells us the order of how the chart is to be played?

In this example, the form notation is: Intro A A B A B Coda.

D.S. al Coda

Let's take a look at a chart using the jump mark 'DS al Coda'.

1. Start at the top and play the 1st line which is an intro.
2. Then go to the 2nd line which is letter A. Play the second and 3rd lines.
3. At the end of the 3rd line, take the 1st ending, and repeat back to the start repeat bracket at letter A.
4. Play the two lines of letter A again, but this time, ignore the 1st ending, and take the 2nd ending.
5. Next play letter B, which is the 4th and 5th line. On your way through Letter B, take note of the coda sign as it will be important momentarily.
6. Notice the jump mark, DS and the end of the second line of letter B. Notice that it also says the words 'al coda' which is the important distinction here.
7. Go back to letter A where the sign is (Segno).
8. Play the two lines of letter A again, but this time, ignore the repeat sign and play the 2nd ending instead of the 1st.
9. Next play the first line of letter B.
10. Then move on to the 2nd line of letter B, notice the coda sign. It will be directly above the barline where you should leave the line you're on.
11. When you reach the Coda sign, jump to the section somewhere below that's label 'coda'. Jump to the coda and play on.

Notice how your path through this chart differed from the D.S. chart a few pages ago. Instead of just going to the sign on the chart and playing through to the end, the jump mark 'D.S. al Coda' includes a second set of instructions, al Coda. The words 'al Coda' instruct you to watch for the Coda sign in the chart, and when you reach the coda sign, jump to the section of the song that follows the word Coda.

Now, let's figure out the form of the song. What is the shorthand notation that tells us the order of how the chart is to be played?

In this example, the form notation is: Intro Intro A A B A B Coda.

Fretboard Biology — Level 5 • Unit 7: Chart Reading

D.C. al Fine

Now let's take a look DC al Fine. Here is how you would navigate through this chart:

1. Start at the top at letter A, go through lines 1 and 2.
2. Then take the repeat back to the top which is letter A again.
3. Play the 1st and 2nd lines again and continue on to letter B.
4. Play the 3 lines of letter B
5. Then play through the the 2 lines of letter C.
6. At the end of letter C, notice the jump mark labeled 'DC' and it also says 'al Fine'. This is the important distinction here. Also notice where it says 'Fine' below last bar of the 1st line of letter C. This will be important the next time you read this section.
7. The D.C. tells you to go back to the very beginning at letter A, in other words, Da Capo.
8. Play the two lines of letter A again, but this time, ignore the repeat sign unless you're told otherwise.
9. Next play the through the three lines of letter B.
10. Then play through the 1st line of letter C to where it says 'Fine'.
11. When you reach 'Fine', stop playing. This is the end of the song.

Now, let's figure out the form of the song. What is the shorthand notation that tells us the order of how the chart is to be played?

In this example, the form notation is: A A B C A B C Fine.

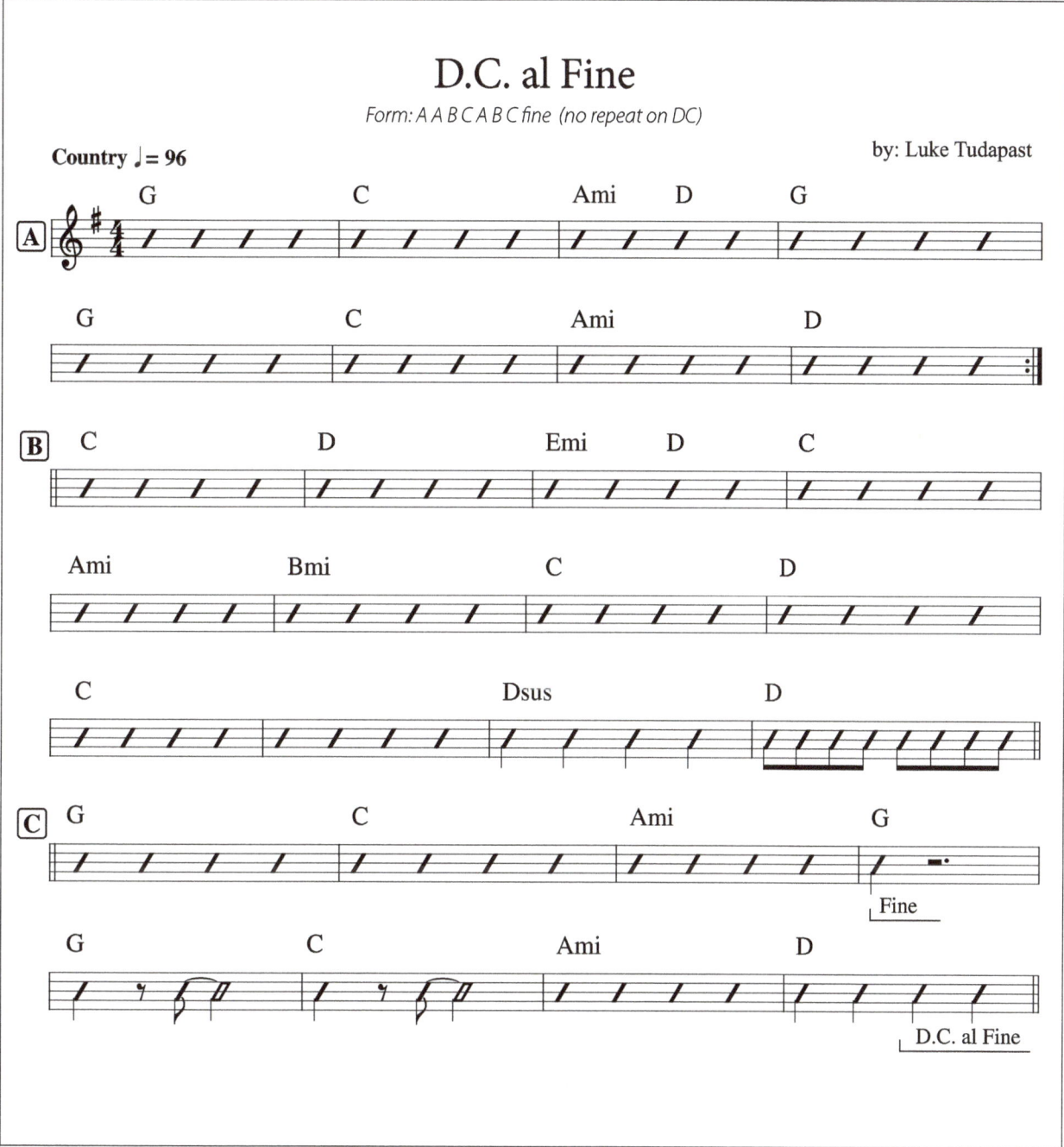

D.S. al Fine

Lastly, let's take a look DS al fine. Here is how to navigate through this chart:

1. Start at the top and play the intro that precedes letter A. This is an Intro.
2. Then continue to the 2nd line at letter A.
3. Play the 2nd and 3rd lines and take the 1st ending.
4. Repeat back to the start repeat bracket at letter A, and play letter A again.
5. At the end of the 3rd line, ignore the 1st ending, and take the 2nd ending.
6. Next play the 4th and 5th lines of letter B.
7. Then continue to letter C which is made up of the 6th, and 7th lines.
8. At the end of letter C, notice the jump mark, 'D.S.', and the words 'al Fine'. This is an important distinction here. Also notice that it says 'Fine' below the last bar of the 2nd line of letter C. This will be important the next time you read this section.
9. The D.S. instructs you to go back to the sign at letter A, in other words, dal Segno.
10. Play the two lines of letter A again, but this time, ignore the repeat sign and take the 2nd ending unless you're told otherwise.
11. Next play the through letter B
12. Then play through letter C until you reach the figure above where it says 'Fine' at the end of the 1st line of letter C.
13. When you reach Fine, stop playing. This is the end of the song

What is the shorthand notation that tells us the order of how the chart is to be played?
In this example, the form notation is: Intro A A B C A B C Fine.

Learn to recognize the jump marks D.C., and D.S., and make sure you understand how to navigate the chart when there is an 'al Coda' or 'al Fine'. Also remember that repeats are not good on a D.C. or D.S. unless specifically stated. A short pregame check list of what to scan in the seconds before you play can save you if you're methodical and quick about it. Getting lost in a chart is a horrible feeling.

IMPROVISATION

You have learned how dominant V, diminished 7, and Mi(Ma7) chords are used in minor and how to create lines over them. In this Module you'll learn how to play lines on augmented Ma7 chords in progressions using both the Harmonic Minor Scale and Ma7(+5) arpeggios. Recall that the formula for a Ma7(+5) chord is major 3rd, augmented 5th, and major 7th. The application of the Harmonic Minor Scale in this Unit will be as a chord scale.

Let's start by taking a look at the A Harmonic Minor Scale. If we harmonize it with 7th chords the result is:

A Harmonic Minor Scale Harmonized with 7th Chords

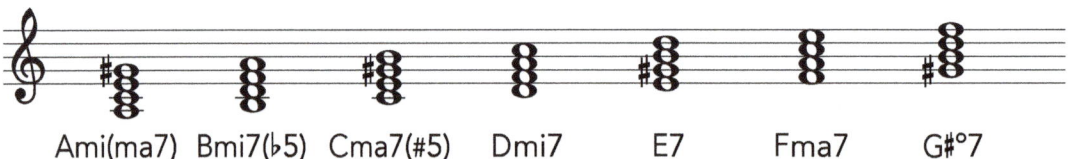

Ami(ma7) Bmi7(b5) Cma7(#5) Dmi7 E7 Fma7 G#°7

You can see that the Cma7(+5) is derived from the A Harmonic Minor Scale. So it's safe to say that the A Harmonic Minor Scale is an appropriate scale choice for Cma7(+5).

In the Theory Module, you learned about the relationship between a Ma7(+5) chord and the Harmonic Minor Scale. The scale that fits nicely over a Ma7(+5) chord is Harmonic Minor, a minor 3rd below. In other words, for a Cma7(+5) chord, the source of notes would be the A Harmonic Minor Scale—the A being a 3rd below the C. Take a minute and make sure you understand that relationship. If you need to, go back to the Theory Module and review it.

Let's use Cma7(+5) in a progression. This progression is in the key of C major.

Progression in C Major

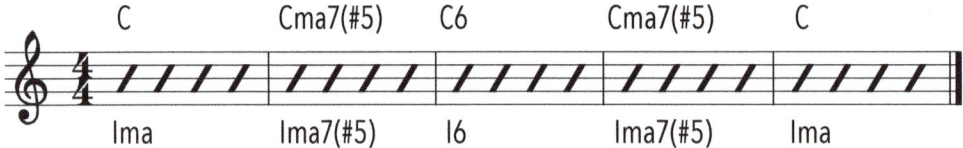

Ima   Ima7(#5)   I6   Ima7(#5)   Ima

C Major is the key and the prevailing scale. However, Cma7(+5) is not diatonic to C and therefore the C Major Scale does not align perfectly. The two sources for notes on this chord are the Cma7(+5) arpeggio and the A Harmonic Minor Scale (remember the scale that fits nicely over a Ma7(+5) chord is harmonic minor a minor 3rd below).

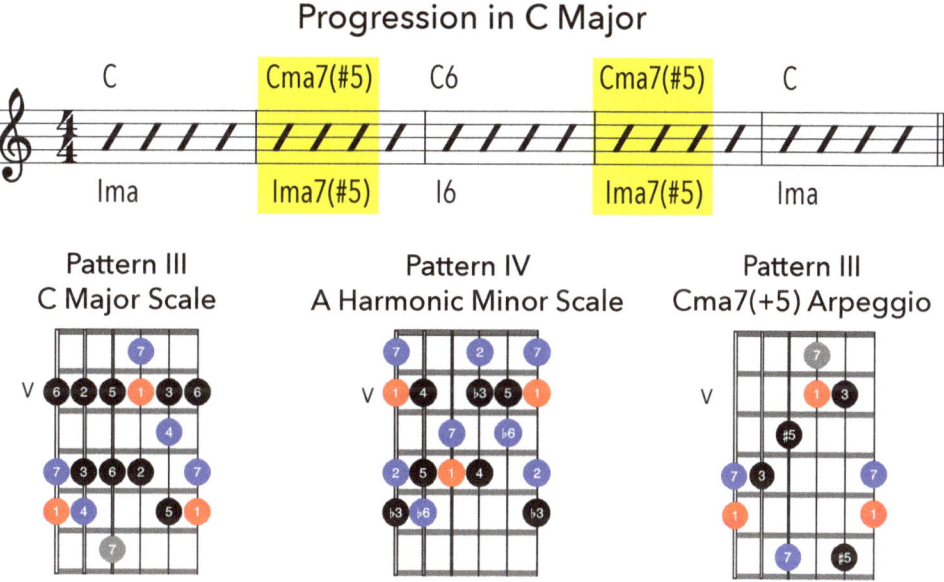

When playing this progression:
- Locate the both the Pattern III C Major Scale and Pattern IV the A Harmonic Minor Scale patterns in 5th position. You can see they occupy the same general place on the fretboard. As in the other Improvisation modules, begin by running the scales ascending and descending, playing the appropriate scale for each chord so you get a feel for it. Then, create motifs and lines.
- Next, stay in 5th position on the fretboard and again locate the Pattern III C Major Scale, and on the Cma7(+5) locate the Cma7(+5) arpeggio.

When creating lines and developing your lick vocabulary, it's a good idea to blend the scales and arpeggios on each chord. It doesn't have to be one or the other. Your goal is to move freely between these scales and arpeggios. Repetition is the answer.

Remember that the primary goal of combining Theory knowledge with Improvisation is to remove any mystery about what notes you can choose to solo over a single or group of chords. Even though information in this Module was presented to you in the Pattern III Octave Shape area, know these concepts should eventually be learned in other patterns as well.

Level 5 Unit 7 • Improv Demo

©2022 Fretboard Biology • fretboardbiology.com

PRACTICE

Theory

- ☐ Go to the tabs below the Theory video on the website and complete the quiz.
- ☐ Learn the detail about the ♭IIIma7(+5) chord.

Fretboard Logic

- ☐ Learn ma7(+5) chord and arpeggio voicings.

Rhythm Guitar

- ☐ Understand the note groupings for 5/8 time.
- ☐ Practice playing the 5/8 progressions in D minor and A.

Chart Reading

- ☐ Understand the use of the D.C., D.S., and Coda jump marks and how they direct you through the form of the song.

Improvisation

- ☐ Practice playing solos over the progression in C major using the in-position Pattern III C Major Scale, the Pattern IV A Harmonic Minor Scale, and the Cma7(+5) arpeggio.

UNIT 8

Learning Modules

> **Theory** - Primary Dominant, Functioning and Non-Functioning Dominants

> **Fretboard Logic** - In-Position Arpeggios in Harmonic Minor

> **Rhythm Guitar** - Odd Meter: 7/8 Time

> **Chart Reading** - Ensemble Rhythm Figures, Signature Riff Notation, Top Note of a Voicing Notation, Transpositional Markings

> **Improvisation** - Soloing with the Harmonic Minor Scale In-Position

> **Practice** - Continue Practice Routine Development

THEORY

In this Theory Module you will learn two important concepts:

- The primary dominant 7 chord
- Functioning and non-functioning dominants

The Primary Dominant

You have already learned that the V7 chord is the parent chord of the dominant family and pulls the listener to the I chord in both major and minor keys. Of all the chords in tonal harmony, the V7 chord is one of the most consequential. While the I chord is powerful because it is the tonal center, the V7 chord feels like a musical magnet, pulling the listener toward the tonic.

The Primary Dominant

The Primary Dominant is the V7 chord of a key. V7 chords pull the listener to the I chords. In the key of C or C minor, G7 is the V7, and the 3rd of G7 is B, the leading tone.

Here are some examples:

- In the key of C or C minor, the primary dominant is G7, because G7 is the V7 chord in the key of C or C minor.
- In the key of A or A minor the primary dominant is E7, because E7 is the V7 chord in the key of A or A minor.
- In the key of B♭ or B♭ minor the primary dominant is F7, because F7 is the V7 chord in the key of B♭ or B♭ minor.
- In the key of E or E minor the primary dominant is B7, because B7 is the V7 chord in the key of E or E minor.

The distance between the 3rd and ♭7th in a dominant 7 chord is a tritone or diminished 5th.

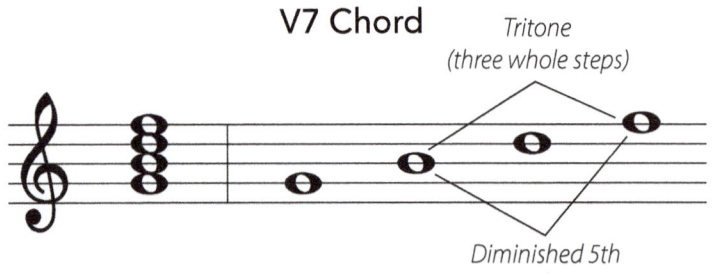

When G7 resolves to I, a C major or C minor chord, the B resolves up a half-step. And with the tritone, F, the ♭7 of the G7 chord, resolves down a half step to the E, the major 3rd of the I chord, or down to E♭, the minor 3rd of a C minor chord.

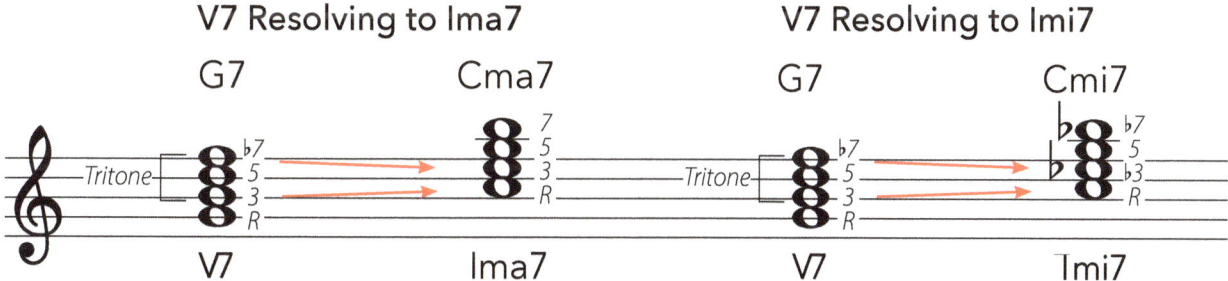

The two most important things to remember about the dominant 7 chord is that the 3rd is the leading tone and that there is a tritone between the 3rd and ♭7th. All this is to say, in the context of any key, the V7 chord feels unsettled, but when it is followed by the I chord, the progression feels resolved.

As we analyze more and more music, we see how progressions manipulate our emotions by creating stress and then relieving that stress. And with regard to the three main chord families, the listener is at rest with chords from the tonic family, pulled away from the tonic family with subdominant chords, and then pulled back toward the tonic family with dominant chords.

That 'pull' feeling is because of the dissonance within the V7 chord we just discussed. It is critical that you understand V7 chords because they play such an important role in the tension and release in so many chord progressions.

Functioning and Non-Functioning Dominants

This next subject is simple but has important implications related to note choices over dominant 7 chords. All dominant 7 chords can be divided into two groups: functioning dominants and non-functioning dominants.

Functioning Dominants

Functioning dominants resolve to 'their' I chord: They are followed immediately in a progression by their I chord. For example, if a G7 is followed by a C or Cmi, then it is considered a functioning dominant chord. This is the situation we just discussed with the leading tone resolving up a half step, and the tritone resolving the way it does.

Non-functioning Dominants

Non-functioning dominants are followed by any chord other than 'their' I chord. In these cases, the tendencies of the leading tone and tritone we discussed are not realized. For example, if G7 is followed by any chord other than C or Cmi it is considered non-functioning.

Determining whether a dominant chord is functioning or non-functioning is very simple: Just look at the chord that immediately follows. If the next chord is its I, the dominant 7 chord is said to be 'functioning'. In other words, all the resolutions we discussed happen. If the chord that follows is anything other than its I the dominant 7 chord is said to be 'non-functioning', so the resolutions discussed above don't happen. It's pretty easy to tell. The root movement from V to I is down a 5th or up a 4th.

Here are some examples of functioning dominants:
- G7-C
- A7-D
- B7-Emi
- F7-Bb
- Bb7-Ebma7
- D7-Gmi7
- C#7-F#mi7

Here are some examples of non-functioning dominants:
- G7-D
- A7-C
- B7-C#
- F7-G7
- Bb7-Dmi7
- D7-Ama7
- C#7-Bmi

Why is it important to know whether a dominant 7 is functioning or non-functioning? Because note choices for composing, arranging, or improvising can be very different for functioning dominants versus non-functioning dominants, especially in Jazz-influenced settings.

The idea of functioning and non-functioning dominants looms large as you learn about more sophisticated harmony. The study of different note choices for functioning and non-functioning dominant chords is coming in future modules.

FRETBOARD LOGIC

In Level 3 you learned about organizing arpeggios 'in-position'. This concept is important for integrating chord tones into solos. Remember that it is difficult to use chord tones in solos when you think of arpeggios as individual entities sprinkled around the fretboard. It's best to have ready access to all the arpeggios in the exact same position, in other words, 'in-position'. You already know the harmonized Major and Minor Scales organized in-position. This Module looks at the Harmonic Minor Scale and organizes the seven arpeggios within a single octave shape.

Because whole songs are rarely written entirely from the Harmonic Minor Scale, the use of the harmonized scale is different than the Major and Natural Minor Scales. Songs that are written in minor sometimes go back and forth between Natural Minor and Harmonic Minor. In these cases, generally the majority of the chords and notes are from Natural Minor while the chords and notes that are from Harmonic Minor Scale are used for effect.

Let's start with the Pattern II Harmonic Minor. This is a comfortable pattern for this demonstration. First, look at the scale and review the numbers of the scale degrees.

D Harmonic Minor Scale

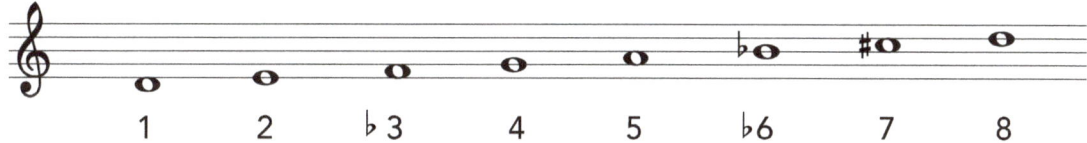

Next, review the quality of the chord built on each scale degree.

The Harmonized D Harmonic Minor Scale with 7th Chords

The goal is to be able to find and play all of the arpeggios of the harmonized Harmonic Minor Scale within the Pattern II Octave Shape. And of course this octave shape is movable to any key. And remember the source of notes for the chords or arpeggios built on each scale degree is the Harmonic Minor Scale.

Pattern II Harmonic Minor Scale

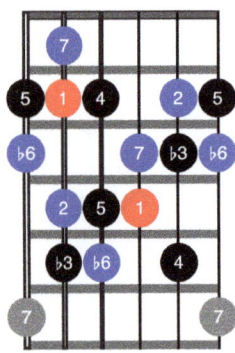

Imi(ma7) Arpeggio (In-Position)

In the Pattern II Harmonic Minor Scale, the tonic is played on the 5th string with the 1st finger. The quality of the chord built on the first scale degree is Mi(Ma7). Here is a Pattern II Mi(Ma7) arpeggio. This is the I chord shape.

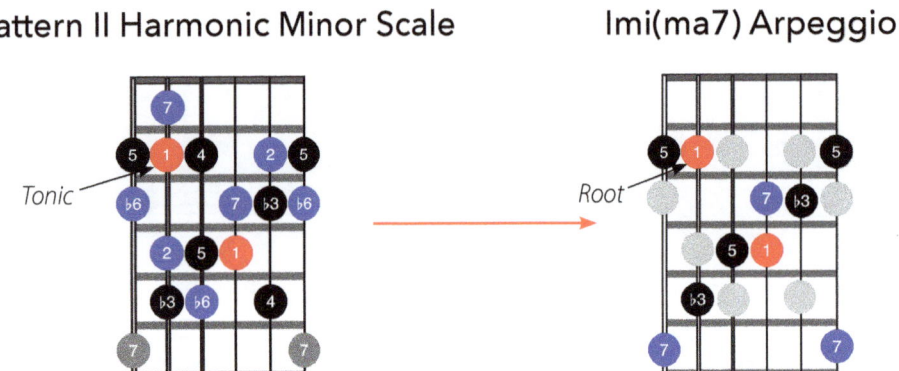

IImi7(♭5) Arpeggio (In-Position)

In the Pattern II Harmonic Minor Scale, the 2nd scale degree is played on the 5th string with the 3rd finger. The quality of the chord built on the 2nd scale degree is Mi7(♭5). Here is the Mi7(♭5) arpeggio played on the 5th string with the 3rd finger. This is the II chord shape.

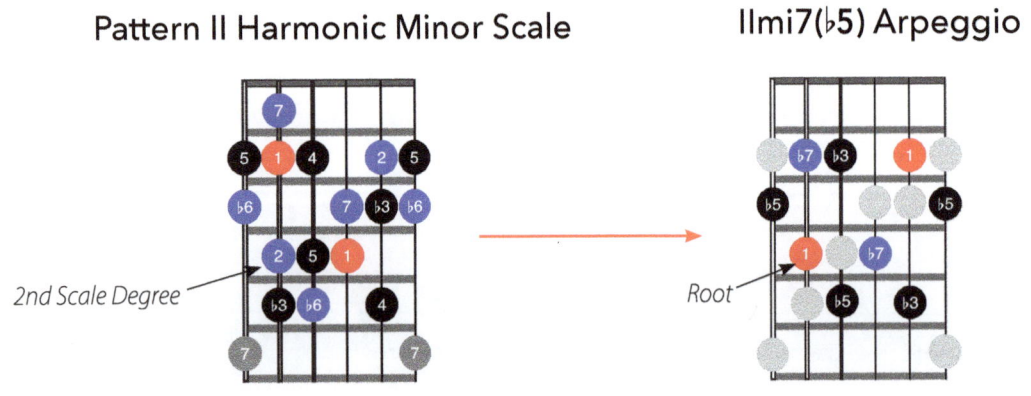

♭IIIma7(+5) Arpeggio (In-Position)

The 3rd scale degree is played on the 5th string with the 4th finger. The quality of the chord built on the 3rd scale degree is Ma7(+5). Here is the Ma7(+5) arpeggio played on the 5th string with the 4th finger. This is the III chord shape.

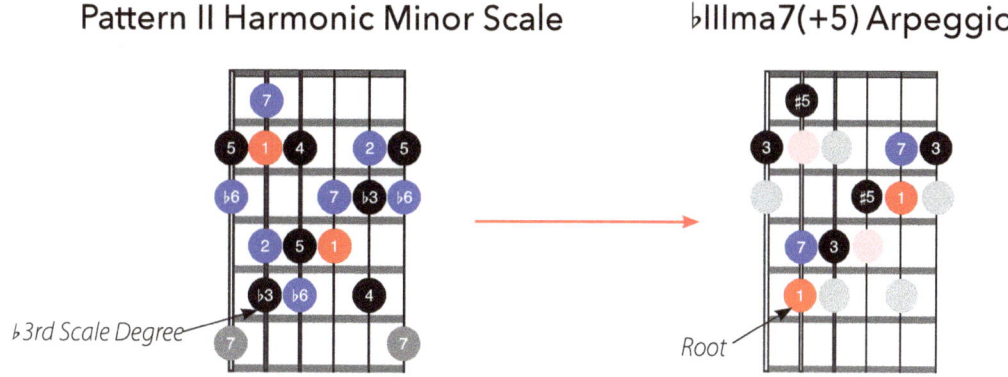

IVmi7 Arpeggio (In-Position)

The 4th scale degree is played on the 4th string with the 1st finger. The quality of the chord built on the 4th scale degree is minor 7. Here is the Mi7 arpeggio played on the 4th string with the 1st finger. This is the IV chord shape.

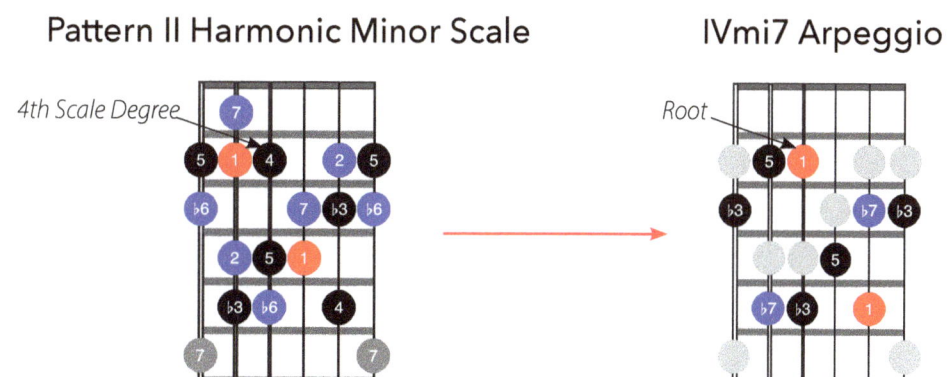

V7 Arpeggio (In-Position)

The 5th scale degree is played on the 6th string with the 1st finger but, for the dominant 7 arpeggio, use your 2nd finger. The quality of the chord built on the 5th scale degree is dominant 7. Here is the dominant 7 arpeggio played on the 6th string with the 2nd finger. This is the V chord shape.

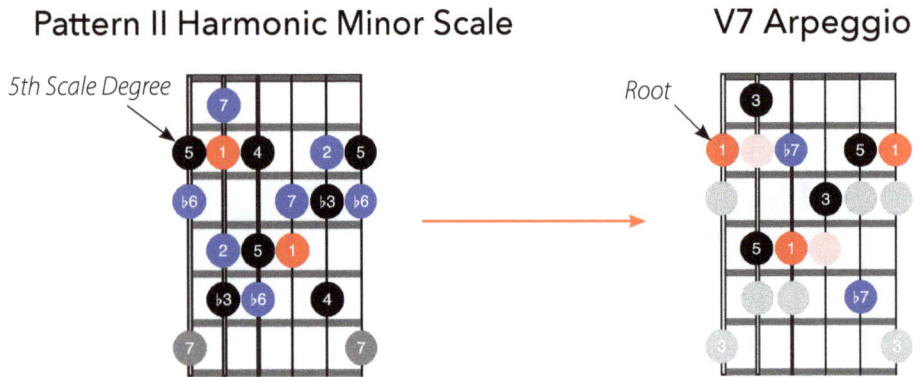

♭VIma7 Arpeggio (In-Position)

The 6th scale degree is played on the 6th string with the 2nd finger. The quality of the chord built on the 6th scale degree is Ma7. Here is the Ma7 arpeggio played on the 6th string with the 2nd finger. This is the VI chord shape.

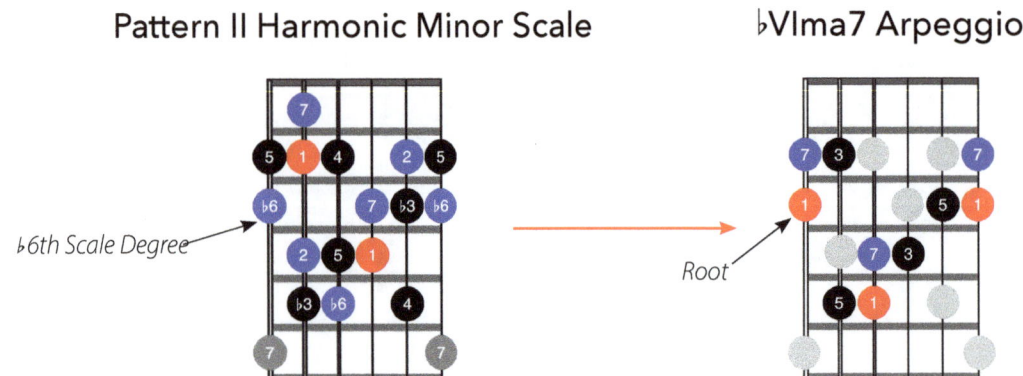

VII°7 Arpeggio (In-Position)

The 7th scale degree is played on the 5th string with the 1st finger. The quality of the chord built on the 7th scale degree is diminished 7. Here is the diminished 7 arpeggio played on the 5th string with the 1st finger. This is the VII chord shape.

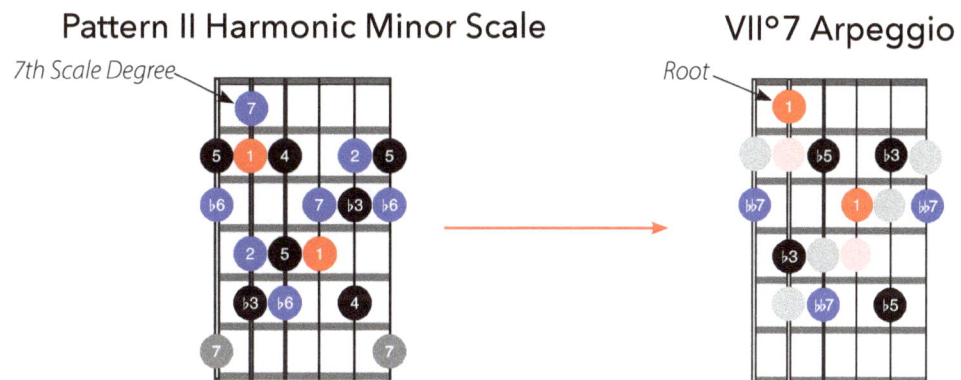

Look at how all seven arpeggios of the harmonized Harmonic Minor Scale fit inside the Harmonic Minor Scale. This is because of the source of notes for harmonizing the scale is the scale itself.

Pattern II Harmonic Minor In-Position Arpeggios

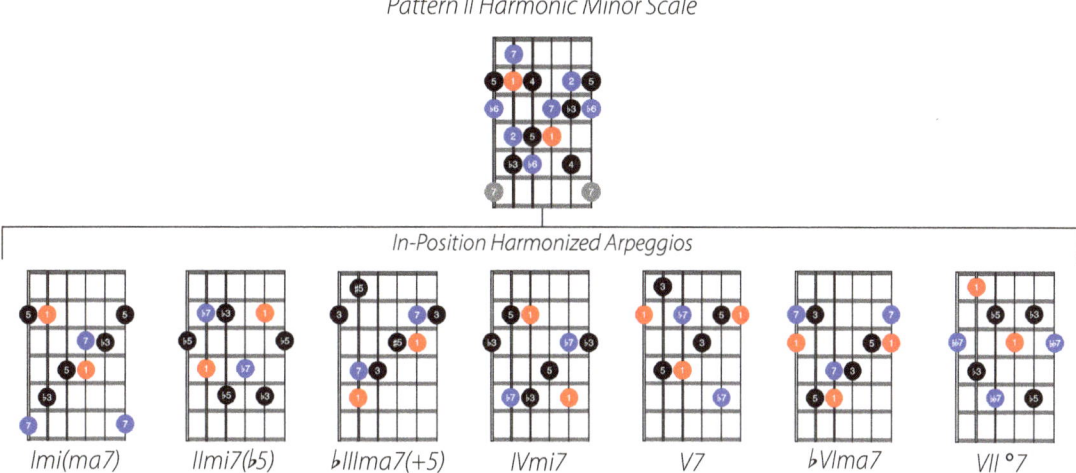

This process can be replicated in Patterns I, III, IV, and V as well.

Pattern I Harmonic Minor In-Position Arpeggios

Pattern I Harmonic Minor Scale

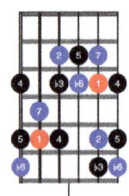

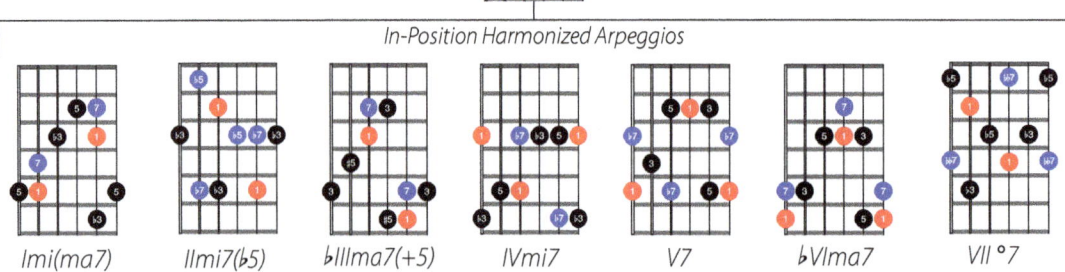

Pattern III Harmonic Minor In-Position Arpeggios

Pattern III Harmonic Minor Scale

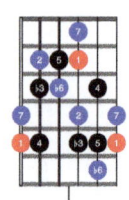

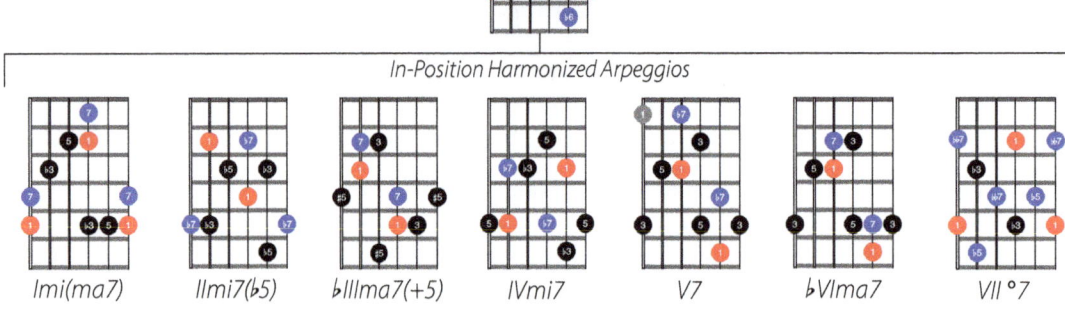

Pattern IV Harmonic Minor In-Position Arpeggios

Pattern IV Harmonic Minor Scale

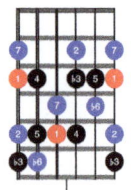

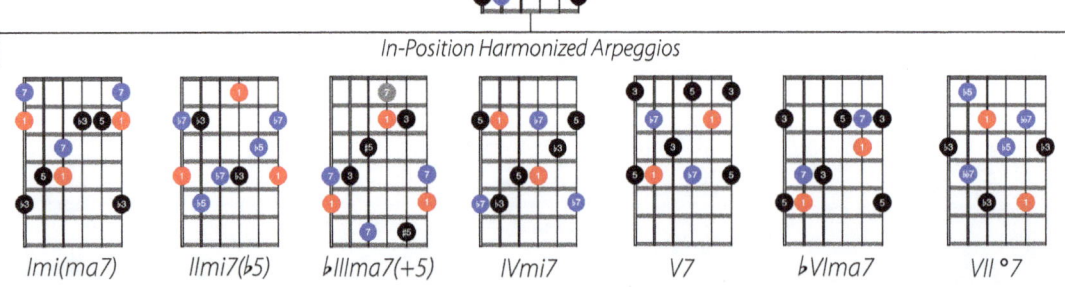

Pattern V Harmonic Minor In-Position Arpeggios

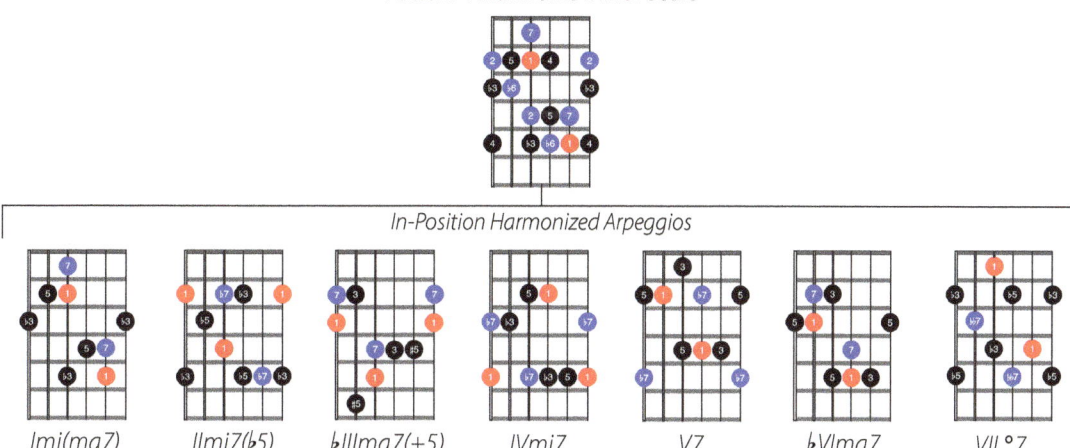

Pattern V Harmonic Minor Scale

In-Position Harmonized Arpeggios

Imi(ma7)   IImi7(♭5)   ♭IIIma7(+5)   IVmi7   V7   ♭VIma7   VII°7

Pause for a minute to take inventory of all the scales you now can harmonize with arpeggios in-position. You know all five scale patterns of Major and Natural Minor Scales harmonized with arpeggios in-position. In this Module you have seen five patterns of the Harmonic Minor Scale harmonized with arpeggios in-position.

Because whole songs are rarely written entirely from the Harmonic Minor Scale, the use of the harmonized scale will be different than the Major and Natural Minor Scale. Songs that are written in minor sometimes go back and forth between the Natural Minor and Harmonic Minor Scales. In these cases, the majority of the chords and notes are from Natural Minor and the chords and notes that are from Harmonic Minor are used for effect.

Superimposed Arpeggios

It is important to see both Natural and Harmonic Minor in the same pattern—sort of superimposed and blended—and to be able to freely move between them. That includes the chords and arpeggios that result from harmonizing these scales. Here are the Natural Minor and Harmonic Minor arpeggios presented side by side. You can see how these could be superimposed on each other on the fretboard and there would only be one note that differ between the two in the I, bIII, V and VII chords. The II, IV and bVI chords are the same in both scales.

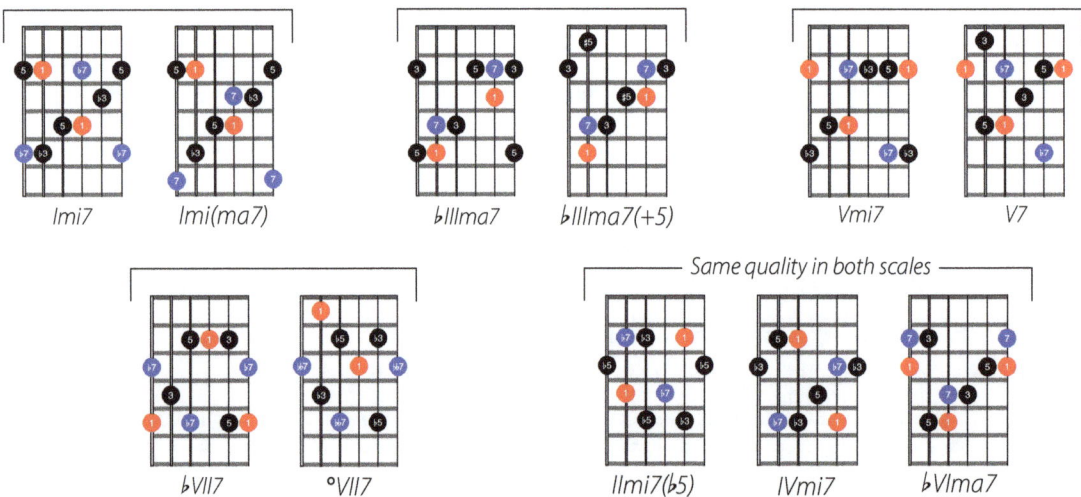

In Level 6 a concept called Composite Minor will be discussed. It relies on the ability to move freely between parallel Minor Pentatonic, Blues, Natural Minor, Harmonic Minor, Dorian Minor, and Melodic Minor Scales. It sounds harder than it is. In reality, all of these scales have a lot in common; the difference between them is subtle.

I suggest that you practice arpeggios in-position in Harmonic Minor as well. Perhaps on Mondays, Wednesdays, and Fridays you can practice the Harmonized Major Scales in Octave Shapes I through V. Then on Tuesdays, Thursdays, and Saturdays you can practice the blended Harmonized Natural Minor Scale and Harmonic Minor Scale in Octave Shapes I through V. Knowing the Harmonic Minor Scales harmonized with arpeggios is important, but I would recommend learning them as blended with the Natural Minor Scale.

Remember, it is far more important for you to understand the process of how to construct and organize these arpeggios then it is to memorize all this material.

RHYTHM GUITAR

In Unit 7 you learned about playing in 5/8. It's an odd meter, which if you recall, means that within the measure in odd meter there are beats divided into two and beats divided into three. This Module focuses on another odd meter: 7/8.

7/8 Time

7/8 can be thought of as 2+3+2, or 2+2+3, or 3+2+2. All three of these have two simple beats and one compound beat. Remember that an effective way to conceptualize and internalize an odd meter is with a silly phrase using words that have two and three syllables. That approach was used with 5/8 and it will be used here again for 7/8. Let's stay with the 'strawberry' theme.

Let's look at 7/8 as 2+3+2 first. This first example is in the key of A major. It's in 7/8, is 2+3+2, and has a Pop/Jazz sound.

For the simple beat use the words 'I like' and 'with cream', because each pair of words has two syllables.

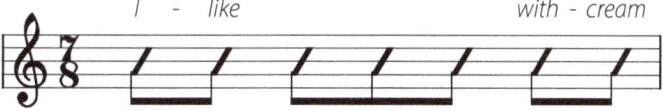

For the compound beat use the word 'strawberries' again, because it has three syllables.

Say the sequence of words back-to-back in steady rhythm: 'I like strawberries with cream.' You can feel 2+3+2.

Notice you feel three main pulses: the first on 'I', the second on the 'straw' of strawberries, and the third on 'with'. This feel is 'uneven' and is sometimes called 'uneven three'.

The first pulse is the group of two, or 'I like'. The second pulse is the group of three, or 'strawberries'. The third pulse is the group of two, or 'with cream'. This is clearly uneven three because the three pulses are of different lengths. But just the same, there are clearly three definite pulses.

7/8 Progression in A

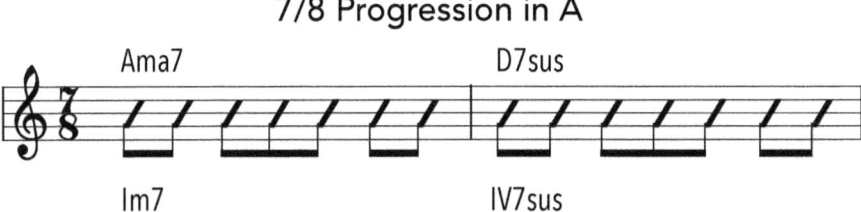

The groups of two 8th notes can also be represented with a single quarter note. The group of three 8th notes can also be represented with a dotted quarter note.

7/8 Progression in A

Play this example three different ways.

- First, play each of the 8th notes in the measure accenting the first of each group. That means to accent the start of the first group of two, then the first of the group of three, and then the first of the second group of two.

- Next, play only on the start of the main three pulses per measure. That is the start of the first group of two, the start of the group of three, and the start of the second group of two. Remember, the groups of two 8th notes can be represented with a single quarter note, and the group of three 8th notes can be represented with a dotted quarter note.

- Finally, try some variations using some dotted notes and some 8th notes or, on the group of three, a quarter note and an 8th note, or 8th and quarter notes. You can create a lot of variations but it all comes back to feeling 'I like strawberries with cream' as the core underlying rhythm.

As you work with this example, keep the 'I like strawberries with cream' phrase going in your head. I suggest a clean tone. Play this until it feels natural.

Next, look at 7/8 as 3+2+2. This next example is in the key of A minor. It's in 7/8, is 3+2+2, and has a Rock/Blues sound.

7/8 Progression in A MInor

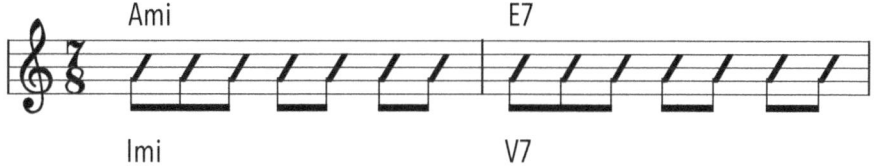

Use the words 'strawberries', 'I like', and 'with cream' again. Say the sequence of words back-to-back in steady rhythm: 'Strawberries I like with cream'. You feel 3+2+2.

Notice you feel three larger pulses: the first on 'straw', the second on 'I', and the third on 'with'. These, too, are uneven three. Again, the groups of two 8th notes can also be represented with a single quarter note. The group of three 8th notes can also be represented with a dotted quarter note.

You feel three main pulses per measure. The first pulse is the group of three, or 'strawberries'. The second pulse is the group of two, or 'I like'. The third pulse is the group of two, or 'with cream'. This is clearly uneven three because the three pulses are of different lengths. But just the same, there are clearly three definite pulses.

Like the previous example, let's play this in three ways.

- First, play each of the 8th notes in the measure accenting the first of each group. That means to accent the start of the group of three, then the start of the first group of two, and then the start of the second group of two.

- Next, play only on the start of the main three pulses per measure. That is the start of the group of three, the start of the first group of two, and the start of the second group of two.

- Then try some variations. You can create a lot of variations but it all comes back to feeling 'strawberries I like with cream' as the core underlying rhythm.

I suggest a clean tone with this progression. Play this until it feels natural. Keep the 'strawberries I like with cream' phrase going in your head.

Next, look at 7/8 as 2+2+3. This last example is also in the key of A minor. Ami is Imi and E7sus is V7sus. It's in 7/8, is 2+2+3, and has a Rock/Blues sound.

7/8 Progression in A MInor

Use the words 'with cream', 'I like', and 'strawberries' again. Say the sequence of words back to back in steady rhythm: 'with cream I like strawberries'. You can feel 2+2+3.

Notice you feel three larger pulses: the first on 'with', the second on 'I', and the third on 'straw'. These, too, are uneven three.

As before, the groups of two 8th notes can also be represented with a single quarter note. The group of three 8th notes can also be represented with a dotted quarter note.

You feel three main pulses per measure. The first pulse is the first group of two or 'with cream'. The second pulse is the second group of two, or 'I like'. The third pulse is the group of three, or 'strawberries'. This is clearly uneven three because the three pulses are of different lengths. But just the same, there are clearly three definite pulses.

Like the previous example, play this in three ways:

- First, play each of the 8th notes in the measure accenting the first of each group. That means to accent the start of the first group of two, then the start of the second group of two, and then the start of the group of three.
- Next, play only on the start of the main three pulses per measure. That is the start of the first group of two, the start of the second group of two, and the start of the group of three.
- Last, try some variations. You can create a lot of variations but it all comes back to feeling 'with cream I like strawberries' as the core underlying rhythm.

As you go through these examples, keep the 'with cream I like strawberries' phrase going in your head. Play all these examples until they feel natural.

Hopefully you're becoming more at ease with odd meter. It just requires repetition and getting into the zone of each time signature.

CHART READING

Special Details

Often chord charts have more information than the form and chords. Let's look at these now:

Ensemble Rhythm Figures

If a rhythm figure is played by the entire ensemble it's usually noted in the chart. It's typical for bands to play certain rhythm figures together and notating them on a chord chart is normal. It's a common level of detail and not considered 'extra'. Even though this module is 'special details', these ensemble rhythm figures can be considered essential.

Any rhythm played by the whole band is called an 'ensemble rhythm figure'. It could be anywhere in a song. We'll discuss two general categories: the Push and the Transition figure.

First, let's talk about the push. Often a chord is placed a quarter note, 8th note, or 16th note before beat one. That means the attack is actually in the previous measure relative to where most of it is played. Beats two, three, and four can be pushed, too.

Quarter-Note Push

If the attack is on the last quarter note of the previous measure, it's called a 'quarter-note anticipation' or sometimes people say a 'quarter-note push'. They might say the chord is pushed a quarter note.

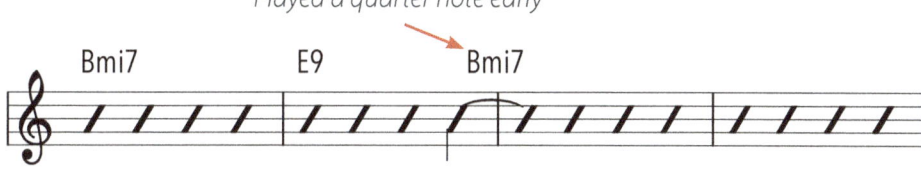

8th-Note Push

If the attack is on the last 8th note of the previous measure, it's called an '8th-note anticipation' or sometimes people say an '8th-note push'. They might say the chord is pushed an 8th note. Beats two, three, and four can be pushed, too.

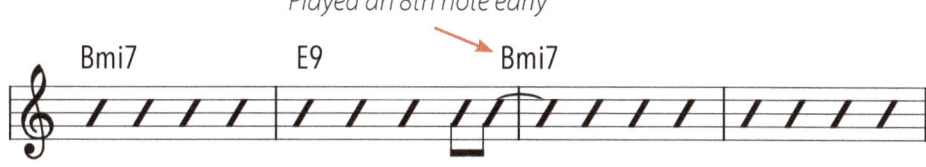

16th-Note Push

If the attack is on the last 16th-note of the previous measure, it's called a '16th-note anticipation' or sometimes people say a '16th-note push'. They might say the chord is pushed a 16th note. Beats two, three, and four can be pushed, too.

8th-note and 16th-note anticipations are very common and quarter-note anticipations are a little less common.

Sometimes slash marks are not used on a chord chart; instead just blank measures are written with chord changes placed above. In some cases, a push is the only rhythm notation you might see in a measure.

Transition Figure

Next, let's talk about the transition figure. Transition figures generally happen at the end of a section as a way to connect to the next section. Be on the lookout for them. Because they are specific rhythms, ensemble rhythm figures should have stems if they're not a whole note.

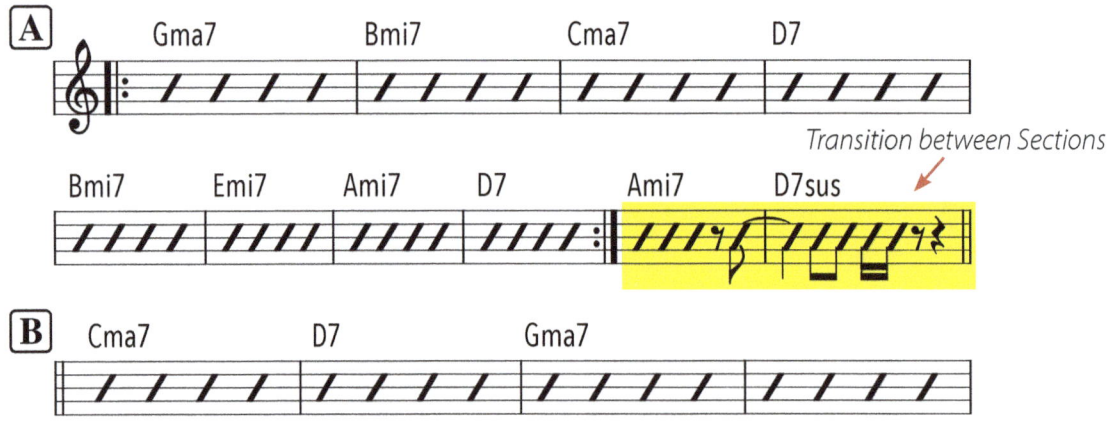

Signature Riff Notation

As mentioned earlier when discussing clef signs, many songs have signature melodic riffs that define the song. These might be riffs played by one instrument or all instruments; specific instructions can be written above or below the staff. These riffs can be considered essential to the character of the tune, meaning that if they aren't played the song won't sound like the song.

The clef sign you choose can be arbitrary or specific. If a line is played by the bass only, it's common to see a bass clef and maybe 'bass only' or 'bass' written above or below the staff.

If a line is played by the guitar only, it's common to see a treble clef and maybe 'guitar only' or 'guitar' written above or below the staff.

If a line is played by the keyboard only, it could be in either clef and maybe 'keyboard only' or 'keyboard' written above or below the staff.

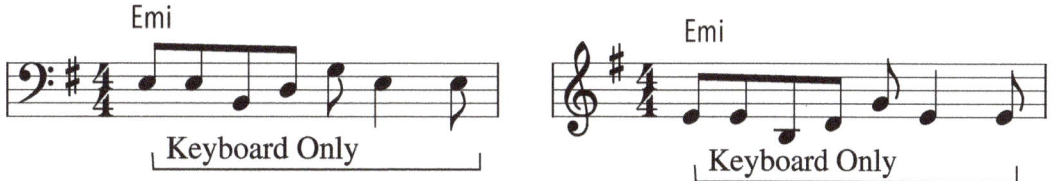

If a line is played by the most or all of the band, you could see either clef. At least one band member will need to read in a different clef than normal and perhaps transpose up or down an octave.

Simile, as you already learned, means to continue playing generally what you have just played. Simile is used a lot with riffs and lines because it's easy for the creator of the chart.

Because most signature riffs and lines are just one or two measures long, the riff just needs to be written once and then slash marks, one-bar, or two-bar repeats can be used to fill out the phrase or section until something else happens.

Top Note of a Voicing Notation

Sometimes the specific voicing of chords is critical to the sound of a song. It's rare for an entire voicing to be notated on the staff but if the top note is played, the chord has a good chance of sounding like what is on the recording. In these cases, the top note is notated with a note head and a downward stem that extends upward slightly beyond the note head, and the chord symbol is written above in its normal location. This is an effective compromise between spelling the entire voicing and only writing the chord symbol. It's amazing how playing the same note voiced on the top of the original version makes it sound 'right'. Some people follow the standard rules about stem direction and point stems up if below the middle line of the staff.

Chords normally don't change more frequently than in quarter note increments so flags are usually not an issue. But if there are 8th-note or 16th-note durations, the normal flag and beaming rules apply.

Transposition Markings

There are times the creator of a chart may write a signature bass line or riff but not place it in the correct octave. There are various reasons for this. The most common is to avoid writing groups of notes above or below the staff which requires reading many ledger lines. Ledger lines are challenging for most readers and devastating for those who barely read.

If the creator of the chart writes the line within the staff and can indicate it should be played an octave higher or lower, the use of ledger lines can be avoided. In other words, the notes are to be 'transposed' to a different octave.

Fretboard Biology — Level 5 • Unit 8: Chart Reading

8va

8va written above the staff indicates that a series of notes should be performed an octave higher than written. It is usually followed by a series of dashes that end with a downward-facing bracket marking the end of the segment that is to be transposed. 'Loco' is written above the staff where you return to reading the notes in the octave where they are written.

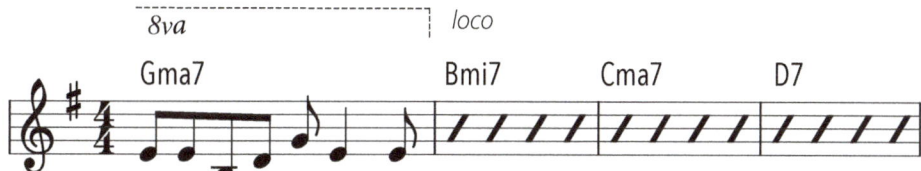

8vb

8vb written below the staff indicates that a series of notes should be performed an octave lower than written. It is usually followed by a series of dashes that end with an upward-facing bracket marking the end of the segment that is to be transposed. Where the next series of notes are to be played in the octave where they are written, 'loco' is written below the staff.

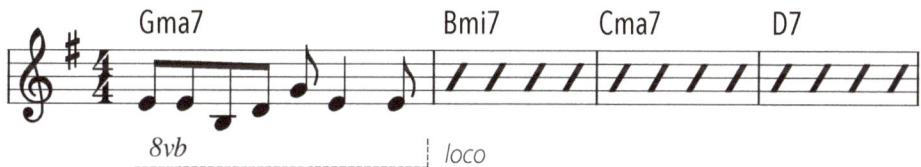

Another reason to use *8va* or *8vb* is to indicate that one instrument needs to play in a different octave. For example, on a chart that is written in treble clef, '(bass player *8vb*)' could be written in parenthesis so the bass player would know to play an octave lower.

IMPROVISATION

In the Fretboard Logic Module you learned the in-position arpeggio organization system for Harmonic Minor. Now, put the in-position system to work in a progression with four chords. This progression is in the key of G minor. Gmi7 is the Imi7 chord, the E♭ma7 is the ♭VIma7, Ami7(♭5) is the IImi7(♭5) chord, and D7 is the V7 chord.

Progression in G Minor

If you play a key-center solo you can just use the G Natural Minor Scale over the first chord, Gmi7. You have a choice between G Natural Minor and G Harmonic Minor on E♭ma7 and Ami7(♭5). G Harmonic Minor is the scale choice on D7.

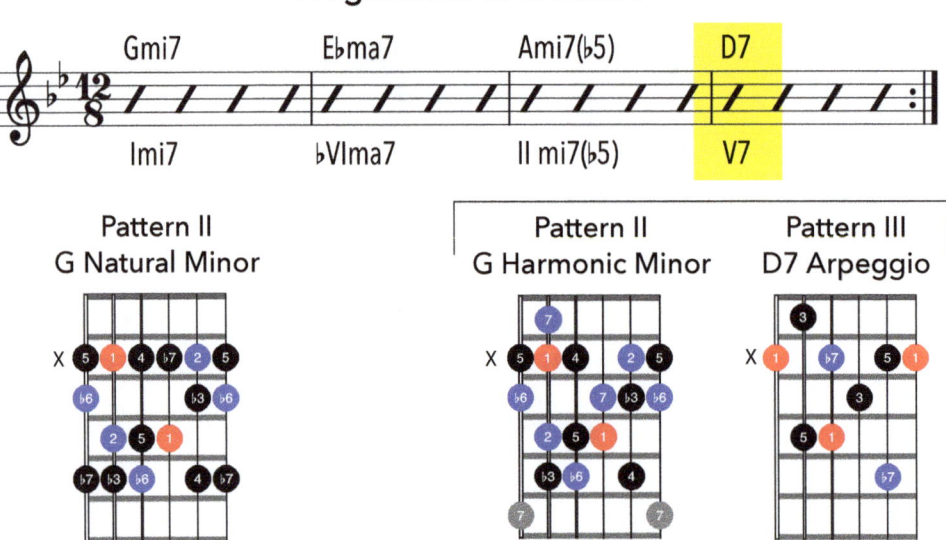

I suggest you familiarize yourself with this example by just using scales to get a feel for the changes, so start with the parallel Pattern II Natural Minor and Harmonic Minor Scales.

Next, look at the chord-tone approach with this progression using the in-position system. Let's look again at the parallel Pattern II Natural Minor and Harmonic Minor Scales harmonized in 7th chord arpeggios.

Pattern II Natural and Harmonic Minor In-Position Arpeggios

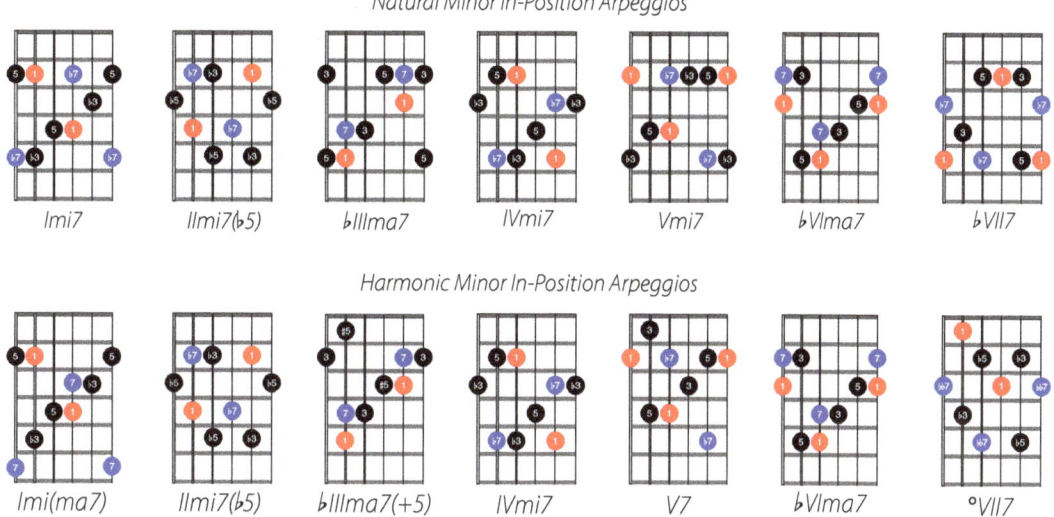

Remember that all of the arpeggios in a minor key can be played within a single scale pattern. So stay in the Pattern II G minor scale, which is in 10th position.

Gmi7 is the Imi7, and in Pattern II the Imi7 arpeggio's root is on the 5th string.

Progression in G Minor

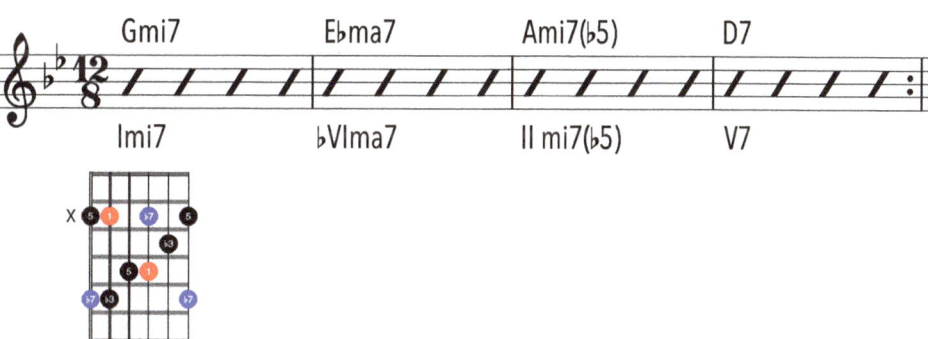

Ebma7 is the bVIma7, and in Pattern IV the bVIma7 arpeggio's root is on the 6th string.

Progression in G Minor

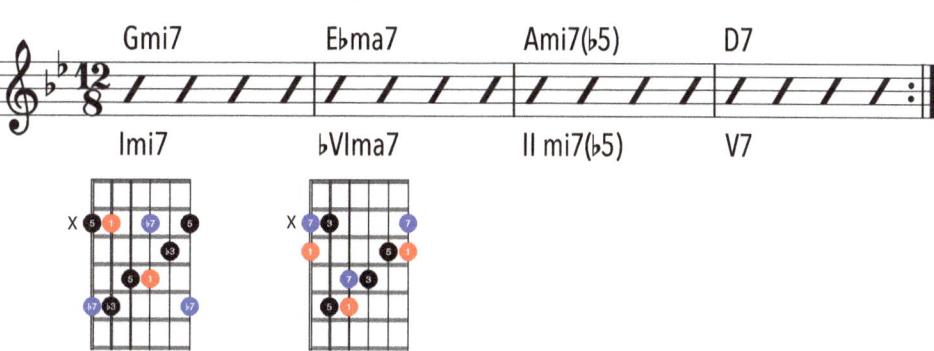

Ami7(b5) is the IImi7(b5), and in Pattern II the IImi7(b5) arpeggio's root is on the 5th string.

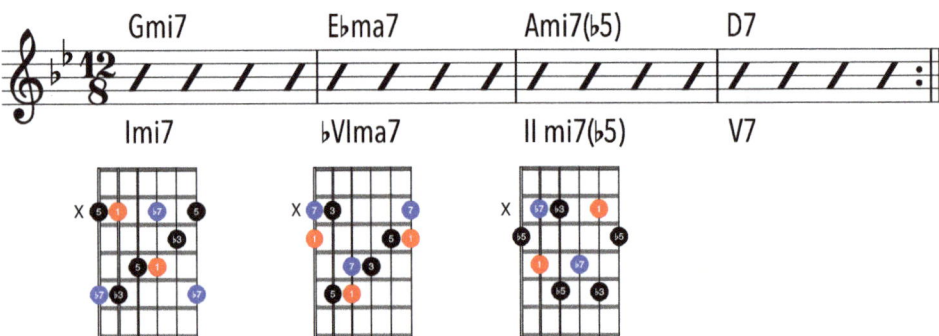

D7 is the V7, and in Pattern IV the V7 arpeggio's root is on the 6th string.

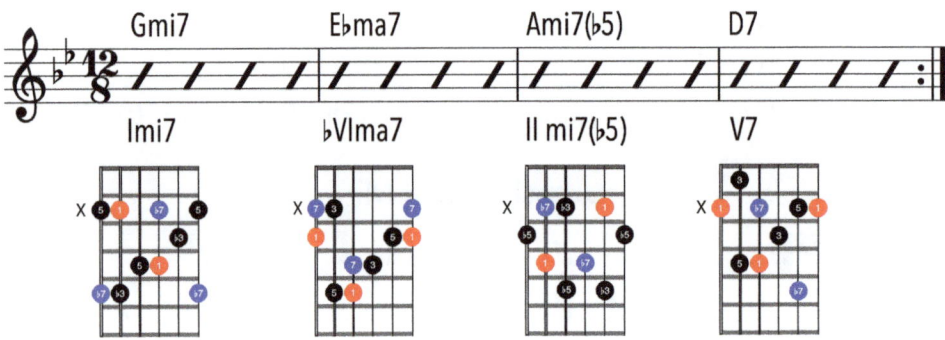

You see how convenient it is to be able to play all the arpeggios within one pattern. You are able to use arpeggios to play chord tones staying in or close to 10th position. Create short motifs that blend chord tones and scale tones. Start with arpeggios only.

When creating lines and developing your lick vocabulary, it's a good idea to blend the scales and arpeggios on each chord. It doesn't have to be one or the other. Your goal is to move freely between these arpeggios and blend them with the scales. Repetition is the only way.

Remember that the primary goal of combining Theory knowledge with Improvisation is to remove any mystery about what notes you can choose to solo over a single chord or group of chords. Even though information in this Module was presented to you in the Pattern II Octave Shape area, know that these concepts should eventually be learned in other patterns as well.

Level 5 Unit 8 • Improv Demo

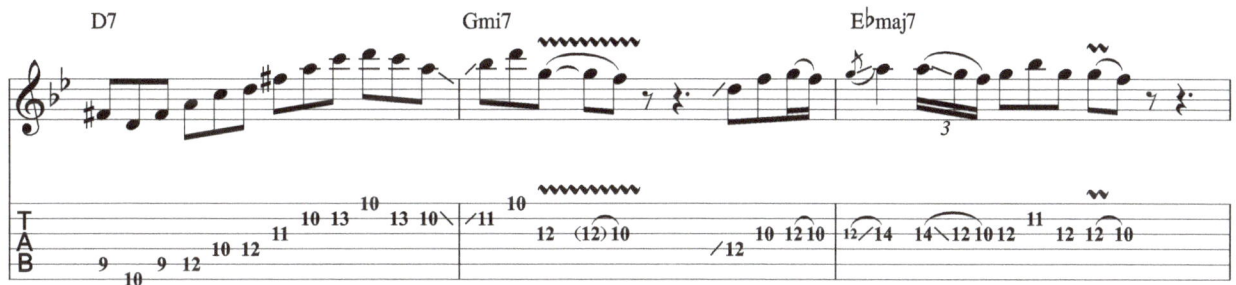
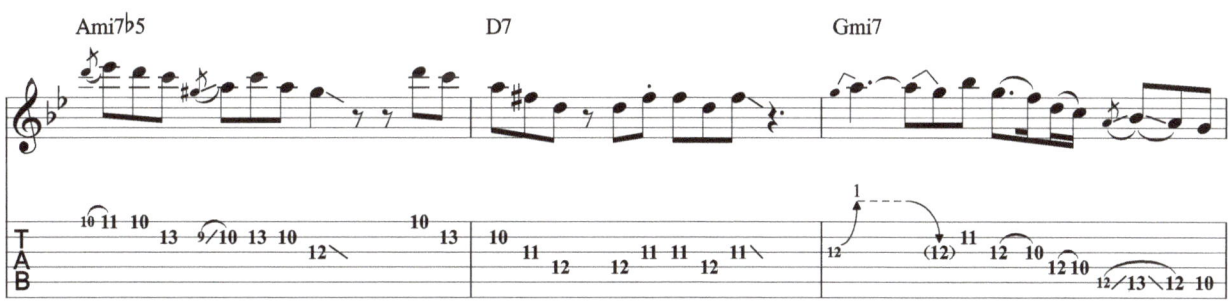
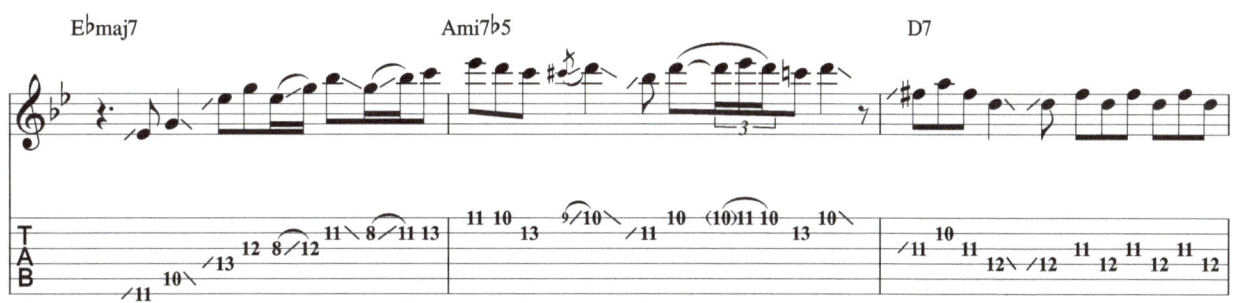

©2022 Fretboard Biology • fretboardbiology.com

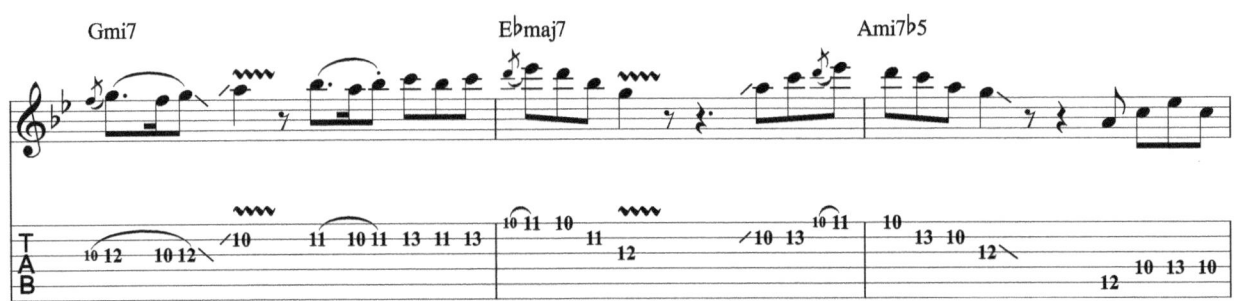

PRACTICE

Theory

- ❏ Go to the tabs below the Theory video on the website and complete the quiz.
- ❏ Learn about the primary dominant and functioning and non-functioning dominants.

Fretboard Logic

- ❏ Learn the in-position arpeggios in Harmonic Minor.

Rhythm Guitar

- ❏ Understand the note groupings for 7/8 time.
- ❏ Practice playing the 7/8 progressions.

Chart Reading

- ❏ Understand ensemble rhythm figures, signature riff notation, the top note of a voicing notation, and transposition markings.

Improvisation

- ❏ Practice playing solos over the progression in G minor using the in-position arpeggios from the harmonized Pattern II Natural and Harmonic Minor scales.

UNIT 9

Learning Modules

> **Theory** - Secondary Dominants, the Dominant ♭9 ♭13 Scale
> **Fretboard Logic** - Patterns I-V Dominant ♭9 ♭13 Scale
> **Rhythm Guitar** - Odd Meter: 11/8 Time
> **Chart Reading** - Dynamics, Accents, Markings that Affect Time
> **Improvisation** - Soloing over Secondary Dominants in Major Keys
> **Practice** - Continue Practice Routine Development

THEORY

You learned that the 3rd of the V7 chord is the leading tone and that the distance between the 3rd and ♭7 is a tritone or Dim5. You also learned that all dominant 7 chords can be divided into two groups: functioning dominants and non-functioning dominants. Functioning dominants are dominant chords that resolve to 'their' I chord. Non-functioning dominants are followed by any chord other than 'their' I chord.

Secondary Dominants

Remember in the last Unit you learned that the V7 chord is considered the primary dominant. There are other dominants that are called 'secondary dominants' and they are the next big topic. Secondary dominants are the next example of non-diatonic harmony we'll discuss in this program. You will recall the first example of non-diatonic harmony was the V7 in a minor key. Next came modal interchange. And in the previous units in this Level, you learned how the chords of Harmonic Minor are used in minor progressions.

Secondary dominants are very common, and like modal interchange, they are so common that they hardly register as sounding like they don't belong to the key. Diatonic progressions move from chord to chord within the key. For example, in the key of C, a progression might move from Ima, that's C, directly to IImi, that's Dmi, and then on to other chords within the key. That's very normal. There are progressions where instead of moving directly from C to Dmi, an A7 chord is placed right before Dmi. Here is why: Think of how the primary dominant, G7, functions when it's played before the I chord, C. G7 creates a sense of anticipation for the I chord. A7 will have the same effect for Dmi. A7 is the V7 of Dmi.

Let's look at a couple of examples to illustrate this. In this first example, there are two versions of the same progression in the key of C. In the first version, the chords are all diatonic. The progression moves from Ima to IImi to V7 and back to Ima.

Progression in C Major

| C | Dmi | G7 | C |
| Ima | IImi | V7 | Ima |

In this next version, the chords are the same with one addition: A7 is right before Dmi. A7 is the V7 of Dmi.

Progression in C Major

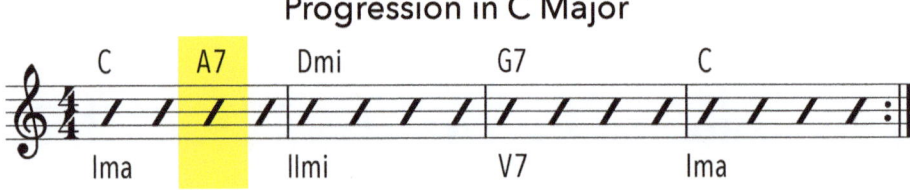

The effect of the A7 is sort of like an announcement about the arrival of the Dmi. Because it is 'set up' by the A7, Dmi sounds more important. The 3rd of A7, C#, is the leading tone of D, and it creates a greater sense of anticipation for Dmi. This extra harmonic movement makes the progression more active and interesting. A7 is called a secondary dominant because it's not the primary dominant. Remember we are in the key of C, so G7 is the primary dominant. A7 is not diatonic, either. The key of C has Ami7, not A7.

Look at these examples. Each example has two short progressions. In the first progression of each example, the tonic chord, C, moves to another diatonic chord directly. In the second progression of each example, the progression still moves from C to a diatonic chord, but that next chord is preceded by its own dominant 7 chord. These dominant chords are called secondary dominants. Play each one and compare the difference in sound between the two progressions in each example.

Progression in C Major

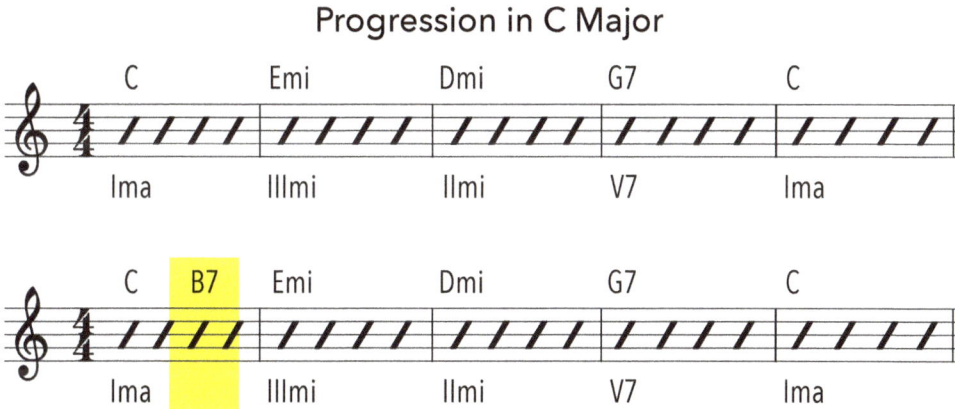

Progression in C Major

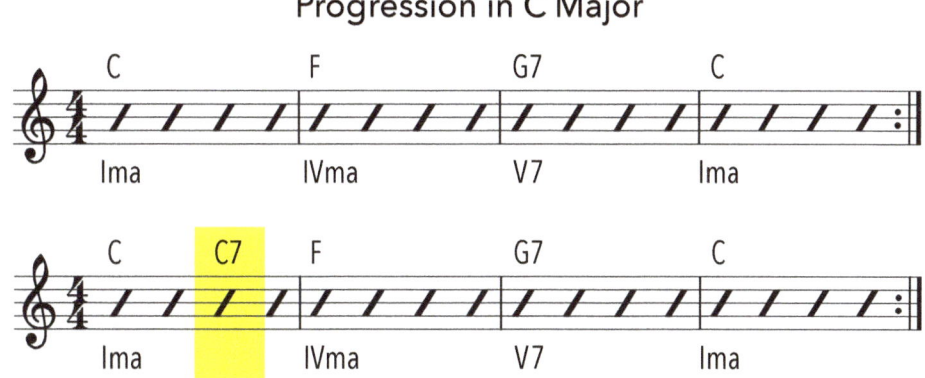

Progression in C Major

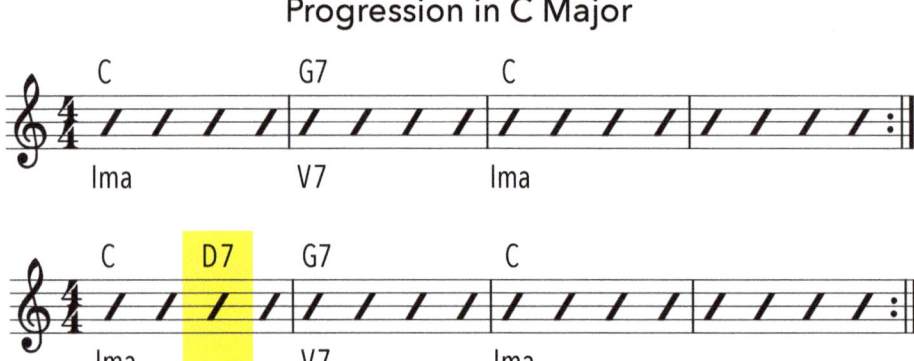

Progression in C Major

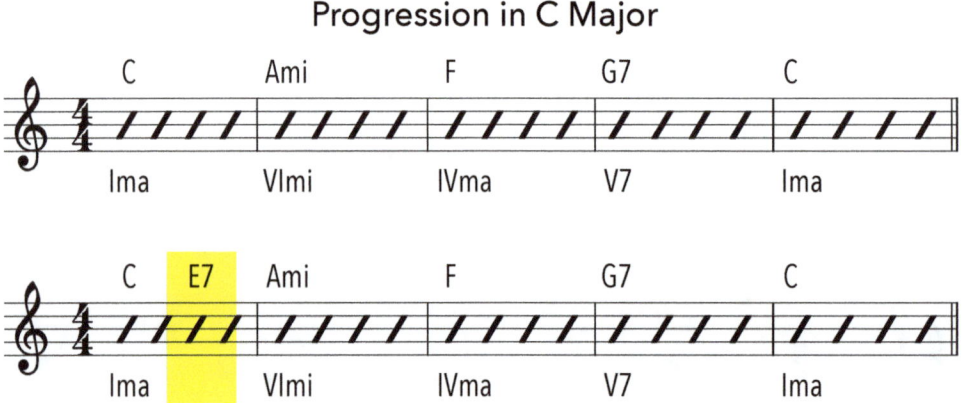

You can hear that secondary dominants create a sense of anticipation for the next chord—exactly how the primary dominant creates a sense of anticipation for the I chord. That's all due to the leading tone and tritone effects we discussed with primary dominants resolving to the I chord in previous units.

Think of it like this:

- The primary dominant pulls the listener to the tonic chord.
- Secondary dominants pull the listener toward any chord that is not the I chord in either a major or minor key.

Secondary dominants appear in many songs from all eras and you need to recognize and understand them when you see them. They each contain a non-diatonic note, so they are non-diatonic chords.

The correct way to analyze a secondary dominant is to write V7, a slash, and then the Roman numeral of the chord for which the secondary dominant is V: V7/II, V7/III, V7/IV, V7/V, and V7/VI. In speaking we say: "V7 of II", "V7 of III", "V7 of IV", "V7 of V", or "V7 of VI".

Table of Functioning Secondary Dominants in Major

HARMONIC ANALYSIS	EXAMPLE
V7 (Primary Dominant)	G7 –> C
V7/II	A7 –> Dmi
V7/III	B7 –> Emi
V7/IV	C7 –> F
V7/V	D7 –> G7
V7/VI	E7 –> Ami

So in the key of C when the II chord is preceded by its V7, A7 is labeled V7/II because A7 is the V7 of Dmi and Dmi is the II chord in the key.

Progression in C Major

In the key of C when the III chord is preceded by its V7, B7 is labeled V7/III because B7 is the V7 of Emi and Emi is the III chord in the key.

Progression in C Major

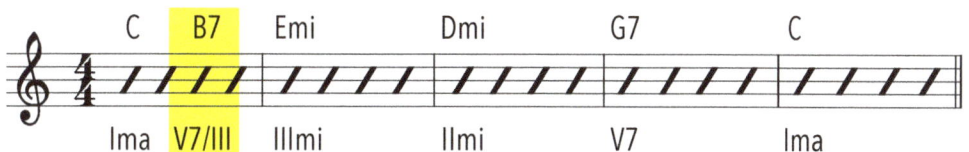

In the key of C when the IV chord is preceded by its V7, C7 is labeled V7/IV because C7 is the V7 of F and F is the IV chord in the key.

Progression in C Major

In the key of C when the V chord is preceded by its V7, D7 is labeled V7/V because D7 is the V7 of G and G is the V chord in the key.

Progression in C Major

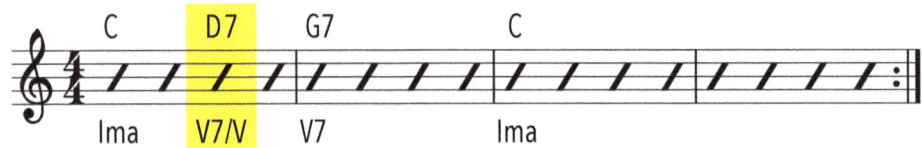

In the key of C when the VI chord is preceded by its V7, E7 is labeled V7/VI because E7 is the V7 of Ami and Ami is the VI chord in the key.

Progression in C Major

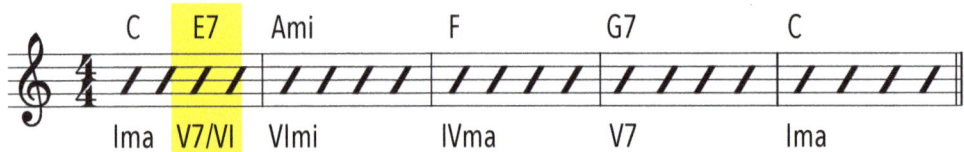

The VII chord is normally not considered capable of having a secondary dominant because it is built on a diminished triad, and a diminished triad is not stable enough to have the sort of temporary tonic status of the other chords of the key.

Take a look at these same progressions again. Notice that in each of these examples, the secondary dominants are functioning. Remember what that means: A functioning dominant is one that resolves to its I chord. Take another look at the table to verify. You will see that in each case the secondary dominant is followed by the chord it is V of. For example, if Ami were the I chord, E7 would be it's V chord, so, E7 is a functioning secondary dominant when it precedes that Ami chord in the key of C.

Because secondary dominants have non-diatonic notes they are non-diatonic chords, and therefore the tonic scale doesn't fit in most cases. So we will need to use a chord scale. The chord-scale solutions are pretty simple. Over secondary dominants that are the V7 of chords that are normally minor, the Harmonic Minor Scale of the minor chord is the inside-sounding scale choice.

For example, on V7 of II, if II is normally minor, play the Harmonic Minor Scale of the II chord. On the II chord you're back to the tonic scale, which is C major.

Progression in C Major

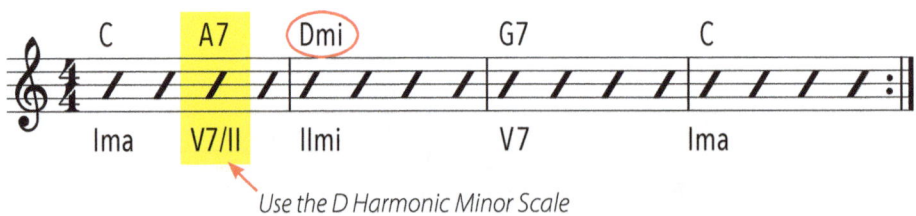

Use the D Harmonic Minor Scale

On V7 of III, if III is normally minor, play the Harmonic Minor Scale of the III chord. On the III chord you're back to the tonic scale.

Progression in C Major

C	B7	Emi	Dmi	G7	C
Ima	V7/III	IIImi	IImi	V7	Ima

Use the E Harmonic Minor Scale (under V7/III)

On V7 of VI, if VI is normally minor, play the Harmonic Minor Scale of the VI chord. On the VI chord you're back to the tonic scale, which is C major.

Progression in C Major

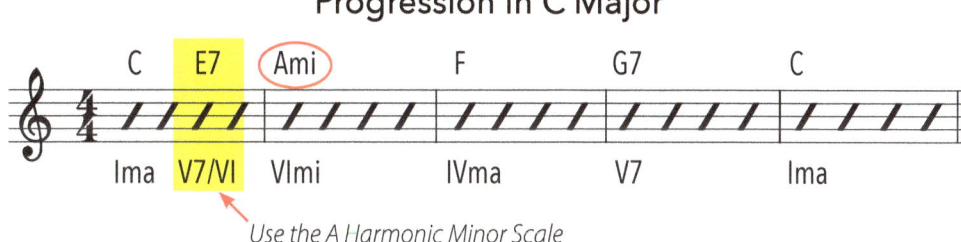

C	E7	Ami	F	G7	C
Ima	V7/VI	VImi	IVma	V7	Ima

Use the A Harmonic Minor Scale (under V7/VI)

Over secondary dominants that are V7 of chords that are normally major, the Major Scale of the major chord is the inside-sounding scale choice. For example, on V7 of IV, if IV is normally major, play the Major Scale of the IV chord. On the IV chord you're back to the tonic scale, which is C major.

Progression in C Major

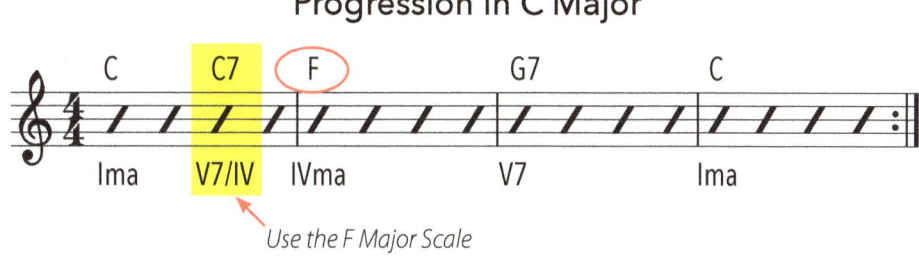

C	C7	F	G7	C
Ima	V7/IV	IVma	V7	Ima

Use the F Major Scale (under V7/IV)

On V7 of V, if V is normally major, play the Major Scale of the V chord. On the V chord you're back to the tonic scale, which is C major.

Progression in C Major

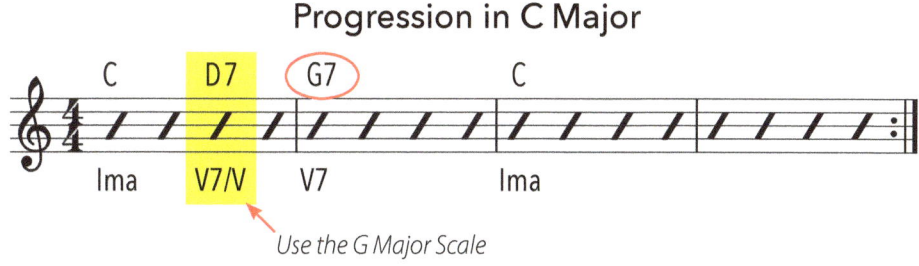

C	D7	G7	C
Ima	V7/V	V7	Ima

Use the G Major Scale (under V7/V)

We need to look at another way secondary dominants appear in songs. There are many examples of non-functioning secondary dominants. These would be Dom7 chords that are V of a chord in the key, but they are not followed by that chord. In these cases, the normal resolutions of the dominant 7 chord's 3rd and ♭7 don't happen.

Here are some common examples of non-functioning secondary dominant 7 chords. The same chord scales apply whether the secondary dominant is functioning or not.

Progression in C Major

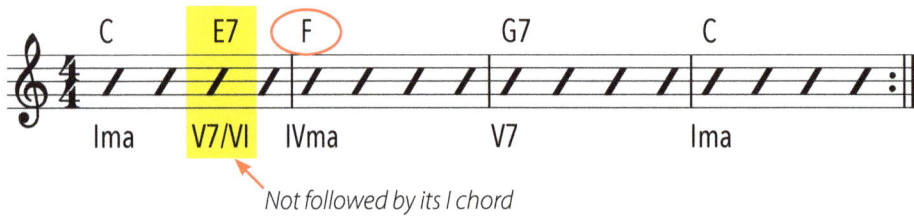

Not followed by its I chord

Progression in C Major

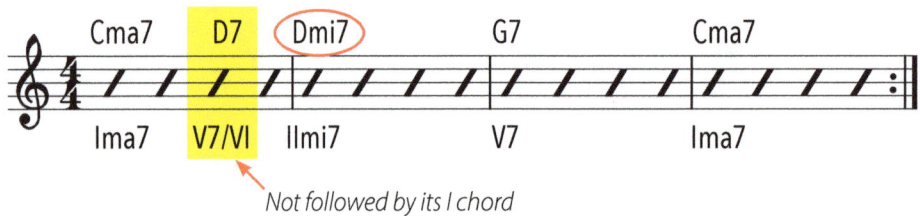

Not followed by its I chord

Progression in C Major

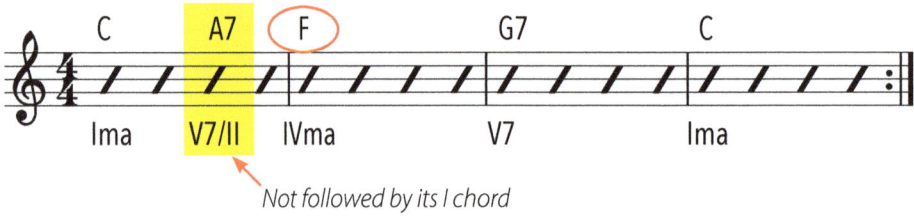

Not followed by its I chord

Secondary dominants, both functioning and non-functioning, can occur in minor keys as well. Look at the examples below. Each example has two short progressions. In the first progression of each example, the tonic chord, Cmi, moves to another diatonic chord directly. In the second progression of each example, the progression moves from Cmi to a diatonic chord but that chord is preceded by its own dominant 7 chord, the 'secondary dominant'. Play each of these, and compare the difference in sound between the two progressions in each example.

Progression in C Minor

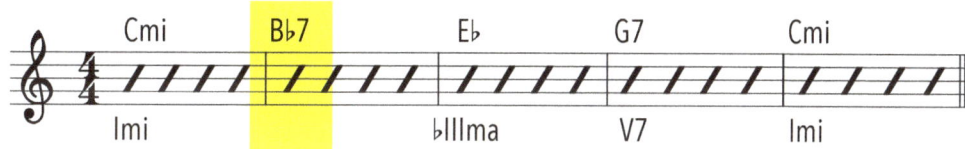

Progression in C Minor

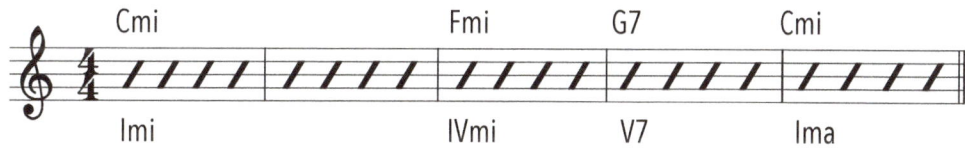

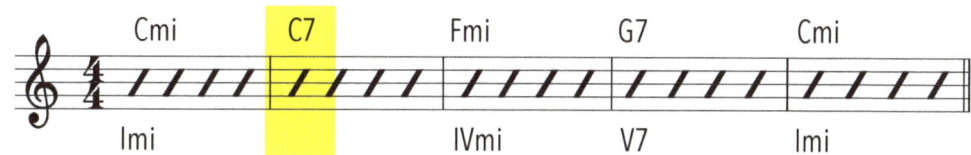

Progression in C Major

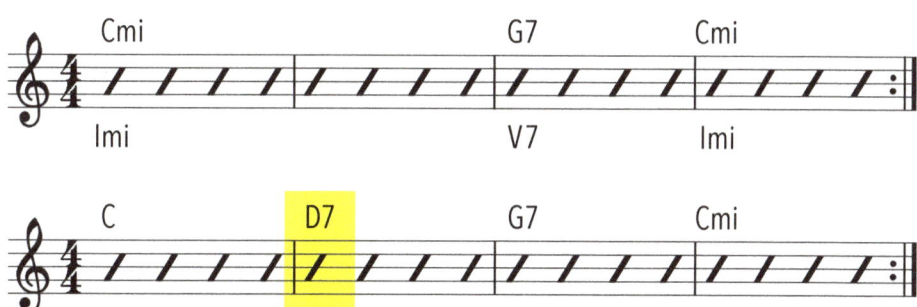

Progression in C Minor

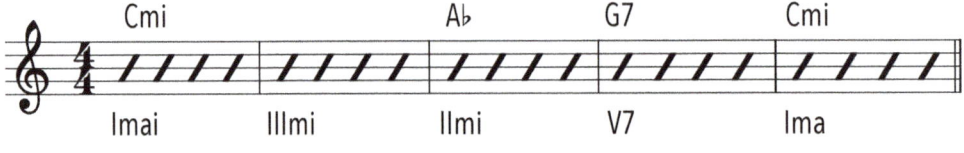

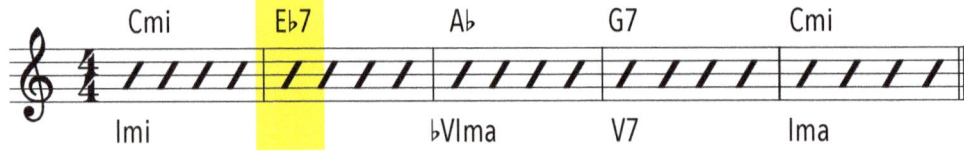

Progression in C Minor

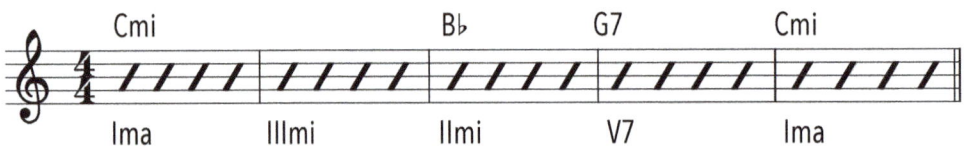

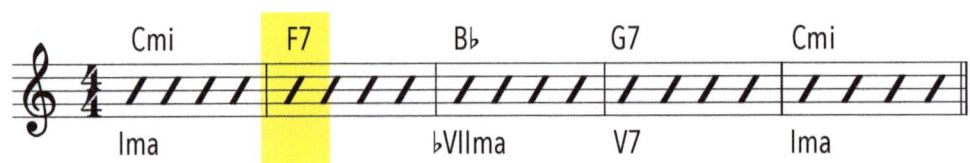

The correct notation for a secondary dominant in a minor key is the same as major but adapted for minor. Write V7, a slash and then the Roman numeral of the chord for which the secondary dominant is V. In speaking we say: "V7 of ♭III", "V7 of IV", "V7 of V", "V7 of ♭VI", and "V7 of ♭VII".

Table of Functioning Secondary Dominants in Natural Minor

HARMONIC ANALYSIS	EXAMPLE
V7 (Primary Dominant)	G7 –> Cmi
V7/♭III	B♭7 –> E♭
V7/IV	C7 –> Fmi
V7/V	D7 –> G7
V7/♭VI	E♭7 –> A♭
V7/♭VII	F7 –> B♭

In the key of Cmi when the ♭III chord is preceded by its V7, B♭7 is labeled V7/♭III because B♭7 is V7 of E♭ and E♭ is ♭III in the key. It should be noted in this example that B♭7 is also the diatonic ♭VII7 chord but because it is functioning as a secondary dominant, we analyze it as V7/♭III. If it was non-functioning, we would analyze it as ♭VII7. This is the only secondary dominant chord that has no non-diatonic notes.

Progression in C Minor

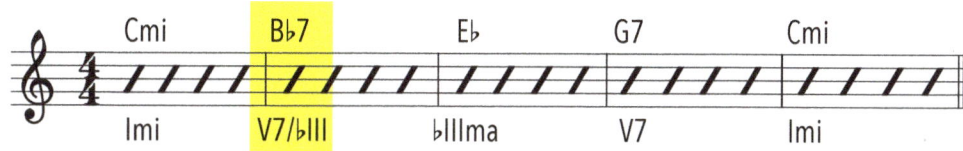

In the key of Cmi when the IV chord is preceded by its V7, C7 is labeled V7/IV because C7 is V7 of Fmi and Fmi is the IV chord in the key.

Progression in C Minor

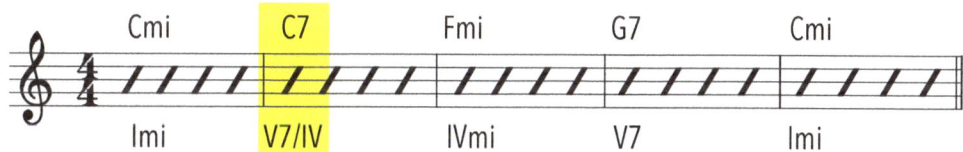

In the key of Cmi when the V chord is preceded by its V7, D7 is labeled V7/V because D7 is V7 of G and G is the V chord in the key.

Progression in C Major

In the key of Cmi when the ♭VI chord is preceded by its V7, E♭7 is labeled V7/♭VI because E♭7 is V7 of A♭ and A♭ is the ♭VI chord in the key.

Progression in C Minor

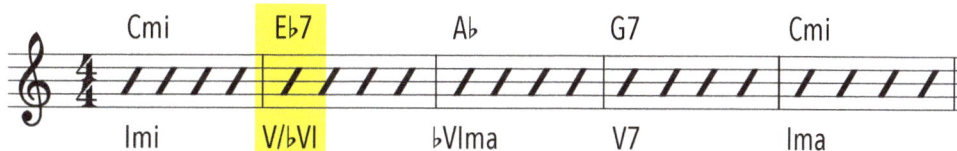

In the key of Cmi when the ♭VII chord is preceded by its V7, F7 is labeled V7/♭VII because F7 is V7 of B♭ and B♭ is the ♭VII chord in the key.

Progression in C Minor

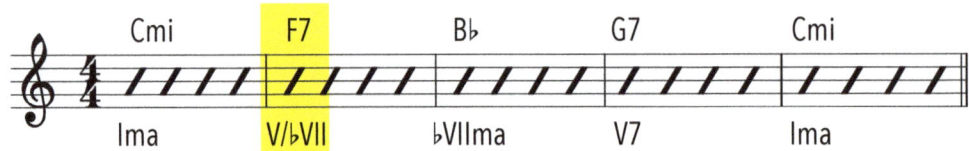

It should be noted in this example that F7 is also the common IV7 chord from the Dorian Scale which will be studied in Level 6, but because it is functioning as a secondary dominant, we analyze it as V7/♭VII.

The II chord in minor is normally not considered capable of having a secondary dominant because it is built on a diminished triad, and a diminished triad is not stable enough to have the sort of temporary tonic status of the other chords of the key.

In each of these examples, the secondary dominants are functioning. Remember what that means: A functioning dominant is one that resolves to its I chord. Take another look to verify. In each case, the secondary dominant is followed by the chord it is V of.

The chord-scale solutions in minor follow the same logic as we saw with major. Over secondary dominants that are V7 of chords that are normally minor, the Harmonic Minor Scale of the minor chord is the inside-sounding scale choice.

For example on V7 of IV, if IV is normally minor, play the Harmonic Minor Scale of the IV chord. On the IV chord you're back to the tonic scale, which is C minor.

Progression in C Minor

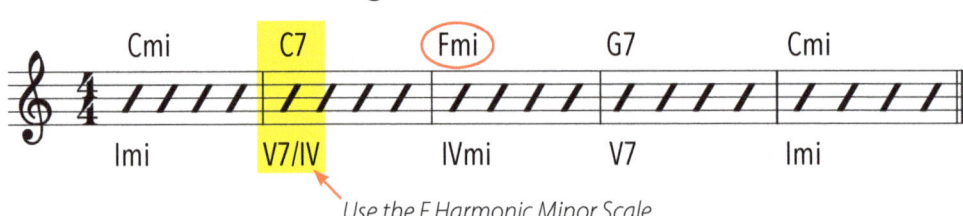

Use the F Harmonic Minor Scale

On V7 of V, where V is normally minor, play the Harmonic Minor Scale of the V chord. On the V chord, use the tonic Harmonic Minor tonic scale, which is C Harmonic Minor

Progression in C Major

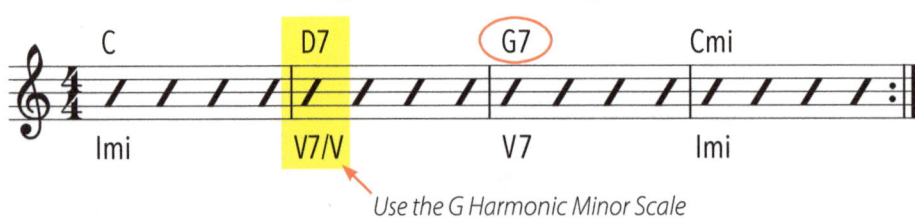

Use the G Harmonic Minor Scale

Over secondary dominants that are V7 of chords that are normally major, the Major Scale of the major chord is the inside-sounding scale choice. On V7 of ♭III, if ♭III is normally major, play the Major Scale of the ♭III chord. But you'll notice this is the same as the tonic scale.

Progression in C Minor

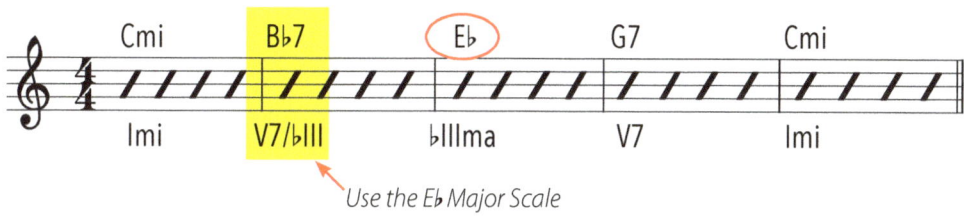

Use the E♭ Major Scale

On V7 of ♭VI, if ♭VI is normally major, play the Major Scale of the ♭VI chord. On the ♭VI chord you're back to the tonic scale, which is C minor.

Progression in C Minor

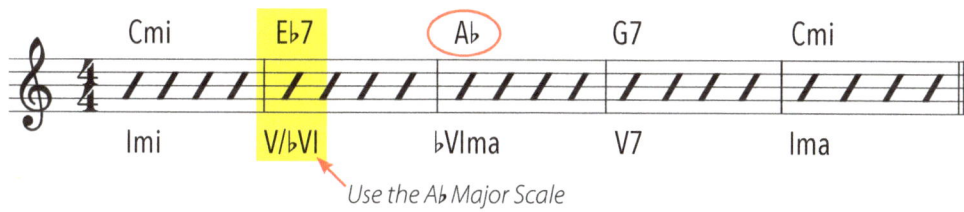

Use the A♭ Major Scale

On V7 of ♭VII, if ♭VII is normally major, play the Major Scale of the ♭VII chord. On the ♭VII chord you're back to the tonic scale, which is C minor.

Progression in C Minor

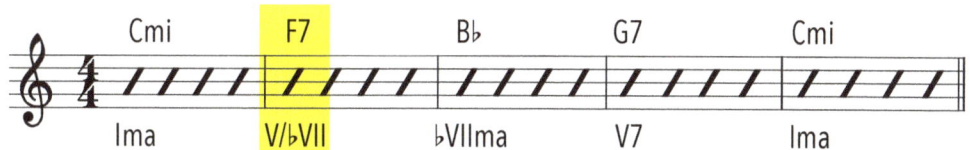

Labeling a secondary dominant as 'V7 of' another chord is correct for accurate harmonic analysis but impractical for quick and easy communication on stage or in a rehearsal. It's normal to refer to a secondary dominant by its 'shortcut name'. This is determined by the number of the scale degree the secondary dominant is built on plus '7'.

Table of Shortcut Names for Secondary Dominants in Major

HARMONIC ANALYSIS	SHORTCUT NAME
V7 (Primary Dominant)	V7
V7/II	VI7
V7/III	VII7
V7/IV	I7
V7/V	II7
V7/VI	III7

Table of Shortcut Names for Secondary Dominants in Natural Minor

HARMONIC ANALYSIS	SHORTCUT NAME
V7 (Primary Dominant)	V7
V7/♭III	♭VII7
V7/IV	I7
V7/V	II7
V7/♭VI	♭III7
V7/♭VII	IV7

It's also important to note that non-functioning dominants can occur in minor keys as well as in major keys.

Alternate Approach

There's an alternative chord-scale approach for a secondary dominant that is V7 of a minor chord. In the long-term, you can consider this alternative approach as just another way to explain using the Harmonic Minor Scale of the chord the secondary dominant is V of, or you can adopt this as the primary way you want to think about it. Whether you decide to approach it using the Harmonic Minor Scale or this alternative way is entirely up to you. But I would be remiss if I didn't at least offer to explain the alternative.

The approach uses a chord scale that goes by several names:

- Dominant ♭9 ♭13 Scale
- Mixolydian ♭9 ♭13
- Phrygian Major

Back in Unit 7 you learned that a 'chord scale' is a scale that fits a specific chord. It fits because it contains all or most of the chord tones of the chord. It's common for chords to have several chord scales that fit over them. Much of Level 6 is dedicated to learning Diatonic modes. Here in Level 5 we will start thinking in terms of modes. This is in the context of a scale that is a derivative of the Harmonic Minor Scale. What you're about to learn is actually a mode of Harmonic Minor.

You have already learned that over a secondary dominant that is V7 of a chord that is normally minor, the Harmonic Minor Scale of the minor chord is the inside-sounding scale choice. Make sure you feel solid about that before we go on. We could leave it right there and be fine, but the Dominant ♭9 ♭13 chord Scale I mentioned above is another way to explain the exact same thing. Let's take a look.

Look at the C Harmonic Minor Scale written over two octaves with the interval formula and the scale degrees numbered.

The Harmonic Minor Scale

What if we extracted a segment of the interval formula and called it a new scale?

The Harmonic Minor Scale

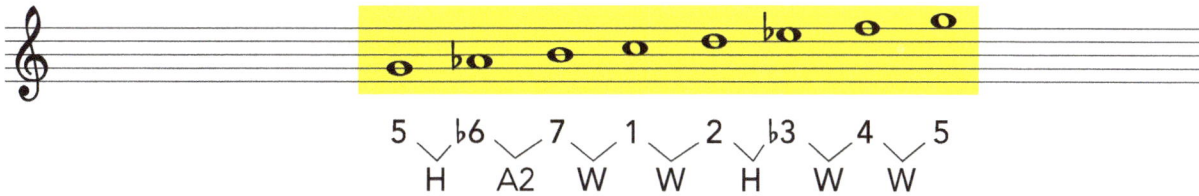

If we extracted the segment from G to G, this would be the resulting scale and the interval formula would be: H A2 W W H W W

The name of this scale is G Dominant ♭9 ♭13.

The G Dominant ♭9 ♭13 Scale

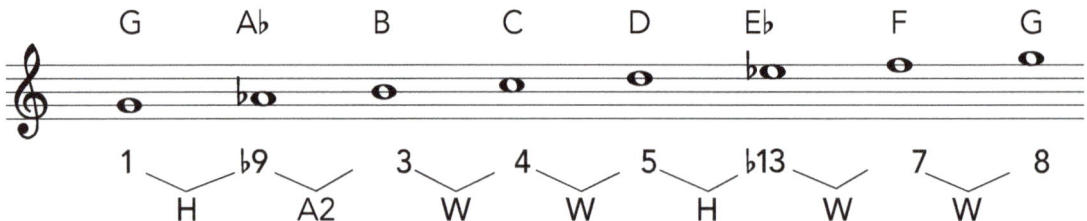

Does this scale contain the same notes as the C Harmonic Minor Scale? Yes. Examine them side by side.

So the C Harmonic Minor and G Dominant ♭9 ♭13 Scales have the same notes:

The C Harmonic Minor Scale

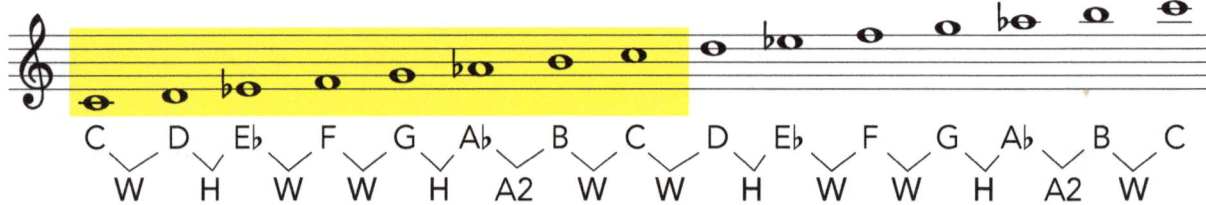

The G Dominant ♭9 ♭13 Scale

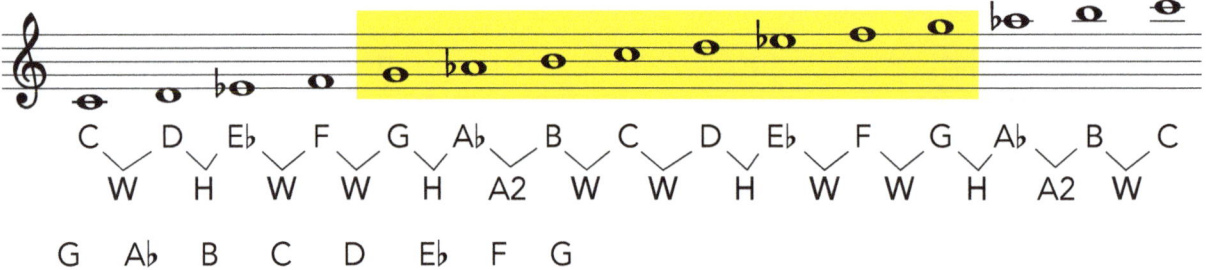

G A♭ B C D E♭ F G

Let's number the scale degrees and discuss each one.

- G is the foundational note for which the scale is named so it is 1.
- A♭ is the 2nd scale degree and we name it ♭2. In popular language, it's sometimes named ♭9. The 9 is used because it is the octave of 2.
  Much more on that in a later module. For now, think of ♭2 and ♭9 as the same.

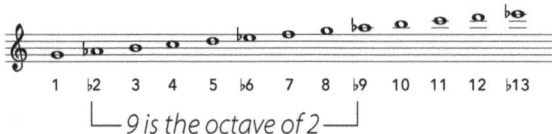

- B is the 3rd and it's a major 3rd.

- C is the 4th and it's a perfect 4th.
- D is the 5th and it's a perfect 5th.
- E♭ is the 6th, and we will name it ♭6 or, in popular language, ♭13. 13 is used because it is the octave of 6. More on that in a later module. For now, think of ♭6 and ♭13 as the same.
- F is the 7th, a flatted 7th or minor 7th if you prefer that term.

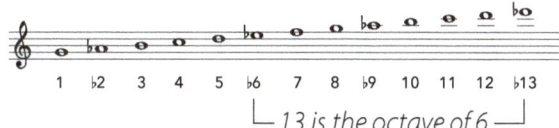

Scales like G Dominant ♭9 ♭13 that share the same notes with a sort of parent scale as in this case, C Harmonic Minor, are sometimes called modes. Because G Dominant ♭9 ♭13 is like playing the C Harmonic Minor Scale starting on the 5th, it's called the 5th mode of C Harmonic Minor. And as for what chord it's used, look to the chord built on the 5th scale degree of the C Harmonic Minor Scale. That is G7.

And now notice this connection: the name of this scale is Dominant ♭9 ♭13. 'Dominant' implies that it has an application for a dominant 7 chord. Look at how and why this works.

In the G Dominant ♭9 ♭13 Scale, the G, B, D, and F spell a G7 chord.

Let's bring this all together.

The G7 Chord

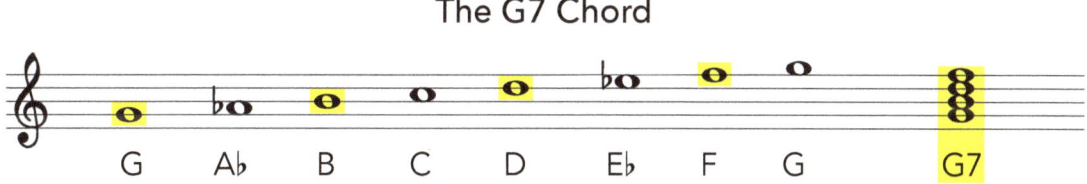

The word 'dominant' in the name Dominant ♭9 ♭13 implies that this is a chord scale for a dominant 7 chord. We proved it by highlighting the G, B, D, and F—that is the root, major third, perfect 5th, and minor 7th. G, B, D, and F are the chord tones of a G7. Dominant ♭9 ♭13 also tells you that it has a ♭9 and ♭13. A♭ is ♭9, and E♭ is ♭13.

The application of the chord scale named Dominant ♭9 ♭13 is for a dominant 7 chord, but specifically a dominant 7 chord that is followed by a minor chord. We know this because Dominant ♭9 ♭13 is the 5th mode of the Harmonic Minor Scale. After all, it was born out of the Harmonic Minor Scale: It was created by playing the Harmonic Minor Scale from the 5th scale degree. The chord built of the 5th scale degree of the Harmonic Minor Scale is dominant 7.

So the conclusion is that the Dominant ♭9 ♭13 Scale is a chord scale that fits over the V7 of a minor chord. Remember that the Dominant ♭9 ♭13 Scale is a chord scale that contains the chord tones of the V7.

Let's look at a few examples.

In this example, A7 is V7 of Dmi7. The A Dominant ♭9 ♭13 Scale is a chord scale that fits over A7. And remember this important correlation: A Dominant ♭9 ♭13 is derived from D Harmonic Minor. On Dmi7, return to the D Minor Scale or whatever the parent scale is.

In this progression. E7 is V7 of Ami7. The E Dominant ♭9 ♭13 Scale is a chord scale that

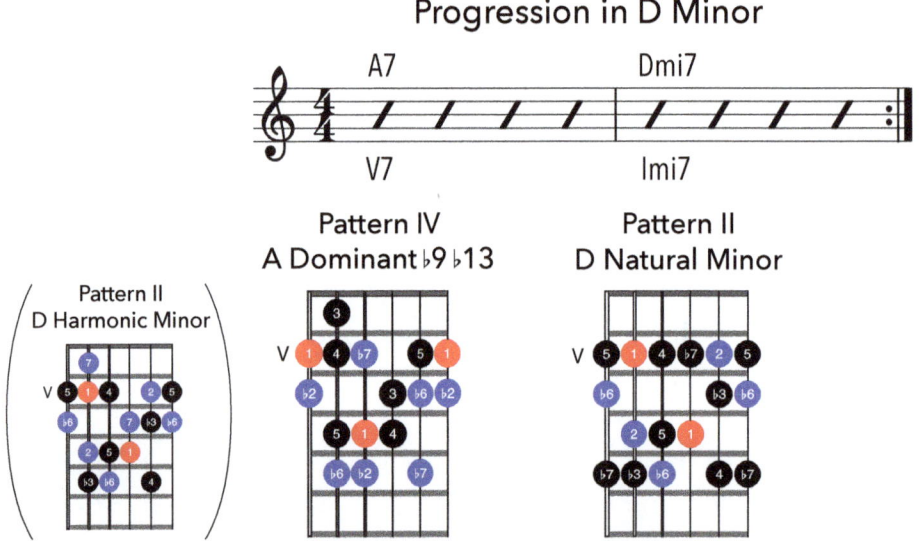

fits over E7. And remember this important correlation: E Dominant ♭9 ♭13 is derived from A Harmonic Minor. On Ami7, return to the A Minor Scale or whatever the parent scale is.

In this progression, F7 is V7 of B♭mi7. The F Dominant ♭9 ♭13 Scale is a chord scale

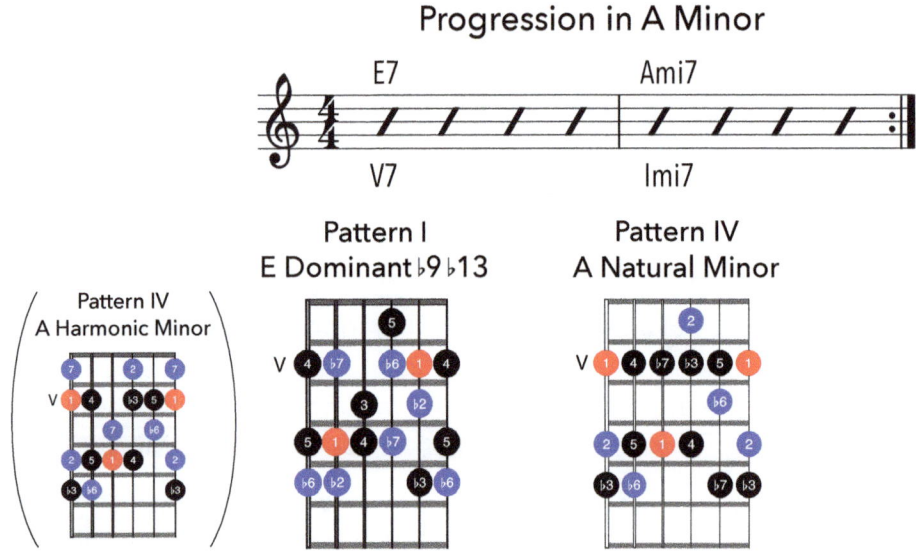

that fits over F7. Remember this important correlation: F Dominant ♭9 ♭13 is derived from B♭ Harmonic Minor. On B♭mi7, return to the B♭ Minor Scale or whatever the parent scale is.

Let's review and wrap this up. There are many occasions in progressions where a

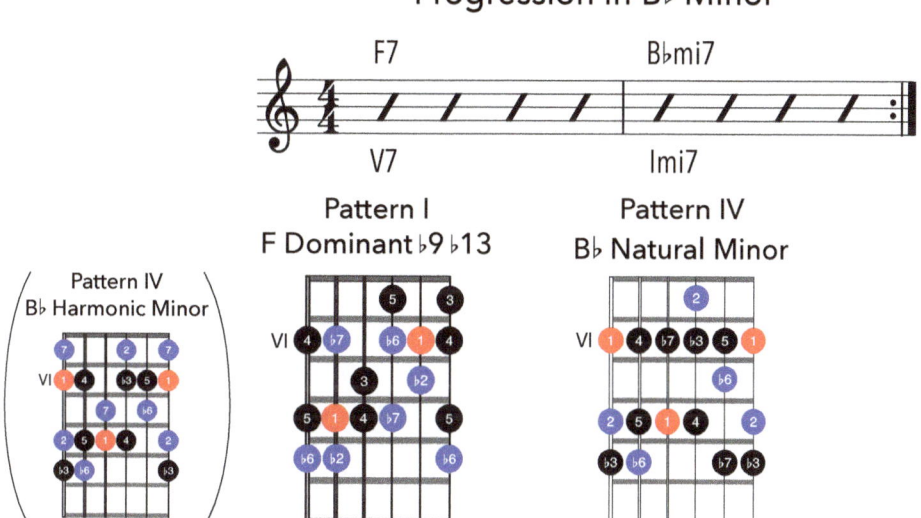

minor or Mi7 chord is preceded by its V7 chord. In these cases, the Dominant ♭9 ♭13 Scale of the V7 chord is the chord scale that fits over that dominant 7 chord.

But know that the Dominant ♭9 ♭13 Scale is the same as the Harmonic Minor Scale of the minor chord it precedes.

I mentioned this scale is known by several other names:

- Phrygian Major: You have not learned about modes yet but know that Phrygian is a minor mode. The name Phrygian Major refers to the similarity to the Phrygian Minor Scale, but with a major 3rd.

- Mixolydian ♭9 ♭13: Again, you have not learned about modes yet but know that Mixolydian is a major mode with a flat 7. The name Mixolydian ♭9 ♭13 refers to the Mixolydian Scale with a ♭9 and ♭13.

FRETBOARD LOGIC

The Dominant ♭9 ♭13 Scale

You learned about the Dominant ♭9 ♭13 Scale in the Theory Module. It is derived from the Harmonic Minor Scale by playing from the 5th scale degree. It can also be thought of as the fifth mode of Harmonic Minor. There are many occasions in progressions where a minor or Mi7 chord is preceded by its V7 chord. In these cases, the Dominant ♭9 ♭13 Scale of the V7 chord is one chord scale choice for the dominant 7 chord that is V7 of a minor chord.

Because the Dominant ♭9 ♭13 Scale is derived from Harmonic Minor, there is no reason to physically practice it separately as part of your Fretboard Logic routine. You will effectively be practicing it when you practice the Harmonic Minor patterns. From a Fretboard Logic standpoint, it is more important for you to associate the Dominant ♭9 ♭13 Scale patterns with those of the the Harmonic Minor Scale from which they are derived.

Take a look at the figures below. To the left you see the Pattern I Harmonic Minor Scale with the 5th scale degree highlighted. Why is it highlighted? Because the Dominant ♭9 ♭13 Scale is the same as Harmonic Minor from the 5th scale degree. In the center is the Pattern III Dominant ♭9 ♭13 Scale. To the right is the dominant chord on which the Scale is played.

Pattern I Harmonic Minor Scale

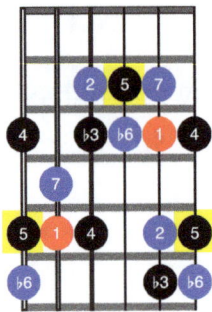

Pattern III Dominant ♭9 ♭13 Scale

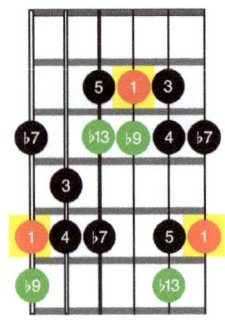

Pattern III Dominant 7 Chord

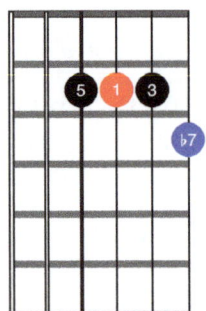

Let's look at another. On the opposite page is the Pattern II Harmonic Minor Scale with the 5th scale degree highlighted. This is because the Dominant ♭9 ♭13 Scale is the same as Harmonic Minor from the 5th scale degree. Next is the Dominant ♭9 ♭13 Scale and if you focus on the starting note for this, it is Octave Shape IV. To the right is the dominant chord on which the Scale is played.

Fretboard Biology — Level 5 • Unit 9: Fretboard Logic

Pattern II
Harmonic Minor Scale

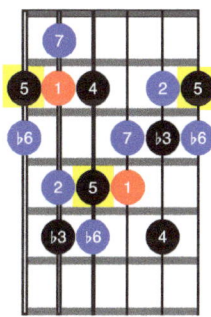

Pattern IV
Dominant ♭9 ♭13 Scale

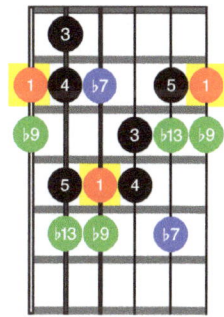

Pattern IV
Dominant 7 Chord

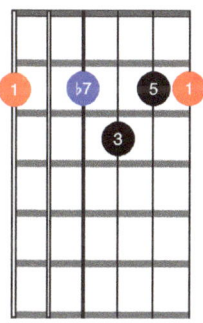

Next, let's look at Pattern III. On the left is the Pattern III Harmonic Minor Scale with the 5th scale degree highlighted. Again, this is because the Dominant ♭9 ♭13 Scale is the same as Harmonic Minor from the 5th scale degree. In the center is the Pattern V Dominant ♭9 ♭13 Scale and to the right is the dominant chord on which the Scale is played.

Pattern III
Harmonic Minor Scale

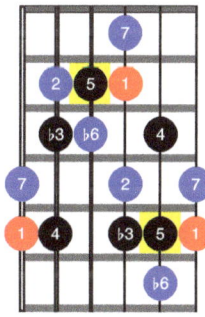

Pattern V
Dominant ♭9 ♭13 Scale

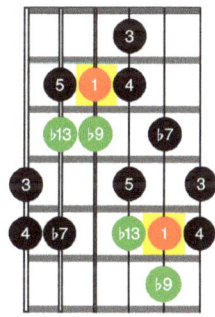

Pattern V
Dominant 7 Chord

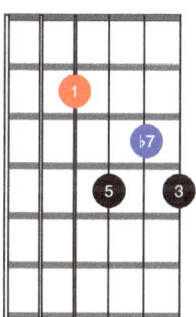

Let's move on to Pattern IV. Here is the Pattern IV Harmonic Minor Scale with the 5th scale degree highlighted because, as we have discussed, the Dominant ♭9 ♭13 Scale is the same as Harmonic Minor from the 5th scale degree. In the center is the Pattern I Dominant ♭9 ♭13 Scale, and on the right is the dominant chord on which the Scale is played.

Pattern IV
Harmonic Minor Scale

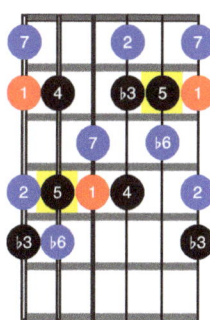

Pattern I
Dominant ♭9 ♭13 Scale

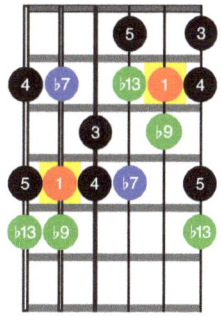

Pattern I
Dominant 7 Chord

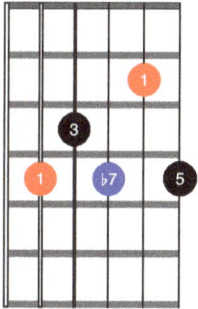

Let's do one more. To the left is the Pattern V Harmonic Minor Scale with the 5th scale degree highlighted, because, again, the Dominant ♭9 ♭13 Scale is the same as Harmonic Minor from the 5th scale degree. In the center is the Pattern II Dominant ♭9 ♭13 Scale and on the right is the dominant chord on which the Scale is played.

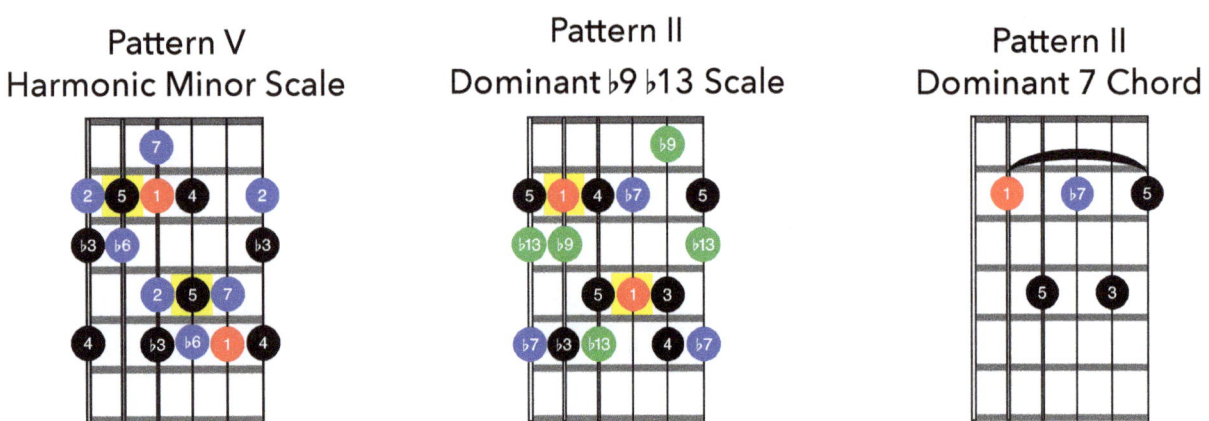

As mentioned earlier, learning these scales as brand new shapes is unnecessary. What is important is practicing the application in the Improvisation modules. It is important to see the correlation between the dominant 7 chord, the arpeggio, and the scale.

RHYTHM GUITAR

11/8 Time

This Module focuses on 11/8. The 8th notes in 11/8 can be grouped a number of ways but the focus here will be on the most common way: 3+3+3+2. I suggest that you continue internalizing odd meter phrases by using the silly-phrase method.

Because this has three compound and one simple beats, we need three three-syllable words and one two-syllable word. Use 'strawberries, strawberries, strawberries with cream'.

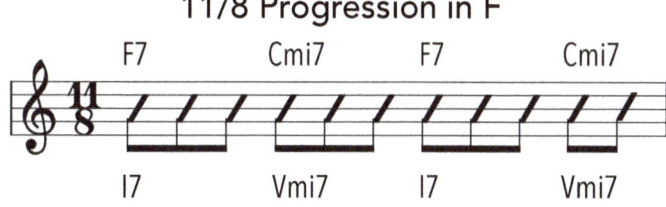

This example is in the key of F. It's in 11/8, is 3+3+3+2 and has a Latin Jazz sound. F7 is I7, Cmi7 is Vmi7, F7 again is the I7, and Cmi7 again is the Vmi7.

There are four main pulses per measure. The first three pulses are groups of three, or 'strawberries', 'strawberries', 'strawberries'. The fourth pulse is the group of two, or 'with cream'. This is clearly 'uneven four' because not all four pulses are the same length, but just the same, there are clearly four strong pulses.

As you play this progression, say the phrase, 'strawberries, strawberries, strawberries with cream'. Notice the feel of 3+3+3+2 when you say that. Notice you feel four larger pulses: The first, second, and third on the 'straw' of each 'strawberries', and the fourth on 'with'. This almost feels like 12/8 that's been cut short at the end.

The groups of three 8th notes can also be represented by a dotted quarter note, and the group of two 8th notes can be represented by a single quarter note.

As in the other Rhythm Guitar modules, play this three ways.

- First, play each of the 8th notes in the measure accenting the first of each group. That means to accent the first of each group of three, then the first of the group of two.
- Next, play only on the start of the main four pulses per measure. That would be the start of each group of three, and the start of the last group of two. Remember, the groups of three 8th notes can be represented with a dotted quarter note, and the group of two 8th notes can be represented with a single quarter note.
- Finally, try some variations using some dotted notes and some 8th notes or on the group of three, a quarter note and 8th note, or 8th and quarter notes. You can create a lot of variations but it all comes back to feeling 'strawberries, strawberries, strawberries with cream' as the core underlying rhythm.

As you go through these examples, keep the 'strawberries, strawberries, strawberries with cream' phrase going in your head. Play this until it feels natural.

If you find 11/8 or other odd meters interesting, experiment with other ways to group simple and compound beats.

CHART READING

More Detail

There is even more musical information that can be included on a chord chart than we have discussed thus far, but the further we go in this series of Chart Reading modules, the less common it is. This in no way means that this information isn't important and doesn't affect the sound of the song, but rather it's just that the chord chart is really an elaborate cheat sheet and often just shows the minimum.

Let's go over the minimum components again:
- Title
- Tempo
- Style
- Clef
- Key signature
- Time signature
- Form
- Chord changes
- Any rhythm figures played by the whole band
- Any signature bass, guitar, or keyboard riffs

There are also ways a musician can be instructed to interpret and perform the song. These include:
- Dynamics: Dynamics tell the musician how loud or soft to play.
- Accents: Accents tell the musician where and how to place emphasis.
- Phrase Markings: Phrase markings tell the musician how groups of notes or chords can be linked together musically for emotional impact.
- Markings that affect the time.

There are other ways charts instruct musicians which affect the horizontal axis of music. In other words, how music happens over time. These include:
- Fermata
- Railroad Tracks (Caesura)
- Ritard

Dynamics

Dynamics refer to how loud or soft musicians should play and are usually only notated on chord charts when the creator of the chart is fairly experienced. Dynamics can change from section to section, phrase to phrase, or bar to bar, and can have a profound effect on how dramatic a band can sound. Just think of the difference between shouting and whispering in conversation. How dynamics are interpreted is relative to the environment. They are generally written below the staff.

There are a many symbols that communicate dynamics, but the two basic dynamic markings are:

- *p* = soft. The word associated with this symbol is 'piano'.
- *f* = loud. The word associated with this symbol is 'forte'.

Degrees of softness or loudness can be notated with multiple p's or f's. For example:

- '*pp*' (double piano) is softer than '*p*' (piano) and '*ppp*' (triple piano) is even softer.
- '*ff*' (double forte) is louder than '*f*' (forte) and '*fff*' (triple forte) is even louder.

In many cases in chord charts the words 'soft', 'very soft', 'loud', or 'very loud' are used instead, or something very direct in English. Plain English is often used in place of the traditional musical terms, which are Italian words.

There are other markings used to notate subtle degrees of soft or loud. An '*m*' along with *p* or *f* means, moderately softer or louder. The word associated with '*m*' is 'mezzo'.

- '*mp*' is 'mezzo piano' and means moderately soft.
- '*mf*' is 'mezzo forte' and means moderately loud.

Table of Dynamic Symbols

SYMBOL	NAME	MEANING
ppp	pianississimo	very, very soft
pp	pianissimo	very soft
p	piano	soft
mp	mezzo piano	moderately soft
mf	mezzo forte	moderately loud
f	forte	loud
ff	fortissimo	very loud
fff	fortississimo	very, very loud

Crescendo

Dynamic changes can be sudden or gradual. If a song changes from soft to loud or loud to soft suddenly and dramatically, one of the markings will be written where the change is to happen. If a song gradually changes from soft to loud, that's called a crescendo. It is notated below the staff with two diverging lines that begin at a point where the crescendo begins. There are often dynamic markings at the beginning and end to inform you about how soft to start and how loud to get by the end.

Crescendos can be very short within a few notes or long over several or many bars. In many cases in chord charts the words 'get louder', or something very direct in English, are used instead.

Decrescendo

If a song gradually changes from loud to soft, that's called a decrescendo. It's notated below the staff with two separate lines that end at a point where the decrescendo ends. There are often dynamic markings at the beginning and end to inform you about how loud to start and how soft to get by the end. Decrescendos can be very short within a few notes or long over several or many bars.

In many cases in chord charts the words 'get softer', or something very direct in English are used instead.

Fade Out

Sometimes 'Fade' or 'Fade Out' is written at the end of a song on a repeating section. This means to gradually play softer until you are completely silent. It's often on a repeating segment of two or four bars. It could be a static chord or a loop of two or more chords.

Accents

Accents instruct the musician to play a single note or chord stronger and often louder. Just as with speech, we emphasize certain words at times to make our point. The same happens with music. Accents are written above the staff.

Three of the marks are commonly used in chord charts:

- Horizontal wedge
- Vertical wedge
- Dot (but not like a dotted quarter note—this is different)

Horizontal Wedge

The horizontal wedge is the most commonly used on a chord chart. It instructs the musician to emphasize the note or chord above which it's written.

Vertical Wedge

The vertical wedge is less common on a chord chart. It instructs the musician to emphasize the note or chord above which it's written and play short.

Dot

A dot means the note is to be played staccato. 'Staccato' means 'short', meaning there's separation between the notes written with staccato markings above them. A general rule of thumb is to play staccato notes at half of their written value.

Dots (Stacatto)

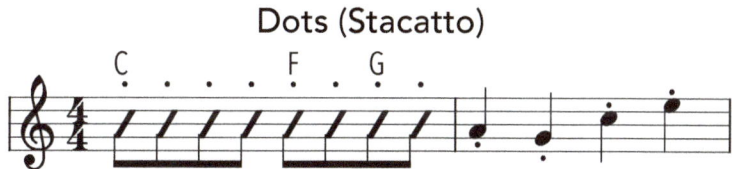

Phrase or Slur

A phrase marking tells the musicians how groups of notes or chords can be linked together musically for emotional impact. It's also called 'slur'. It's generally used for melodic passages so it doesn't appear on a lot of chord charts unless a riff is notated. It's a curved line written above or below the staff. It means to play the notes associated with it 'legato' and as a single phrase. Legato means 'smooth and connected'.

Phrase or Slur (Legato)

When you play a series of notes legato, there is no space between them. A note's duration is over when the next note begins.

Markings that Affect Time

In addition to the time signature and tempo markings, there are markings that instruct musicians how music happens over time. The ones we will discuss here are:

- Fermata
- Railroad Tracks (Caesura)
- Ritard

Fermata

A fermata instructs the musician to pause or hold a note or chord longer than is written. On a chord chart it's most often used on the last note or chord, but it could be at the end of a phrase in the interior of the song. Just know that it interrupts the normal time of the song.

Whether it's used in the middle of a song, which is rare with bands, or on the last note or chord, it's common for someone on stage to cut it off.

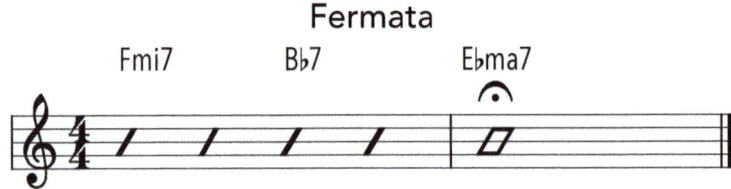

In rock bands the classic cut off is the guitarist who jumps in the air. The note is cut off when he or she lands on the stage. A fermata is also called a 'bird's eye' because it looks like an eye.

Railroad Tracks (Caesura)

Railroad tracks (Caesura) are a notation to cut off a phrase. 'Caesura' means 'to break'. The marking is two parallel lines that slant right from the 4th line on the staff to approximately where the 1st ledger line would be. 'Railroad tracks' is a slang term that comes from the appearance of two parallel lines. This symbol can be written to mark the end of a fermata.

Ritard

Ritard or 'rit' written on a chart means to slow down. In popular music this is a normal marking for the very end of the song where the tempo slows down for dramatic effect. It can be written above or below the staff. It's wise to watch the leader when you see ritard written.

Because ritard instructs the band to slow down, the normal tempo marking is now null and void and it's easy for band to become rhytmically disconnected. The singer, leader, or drummer may direct the ritard with an exaggerated gesture.

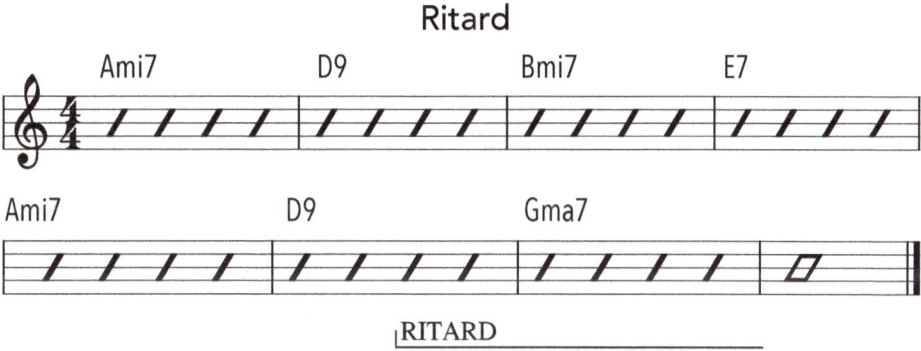

IMPROVISATION

You learned about secondary dominants in the Theory Module of this Unit. Here is a little review. Progressions move from chord to chord within the key, but a stronger sense of anticipation for the next chord in a progression can be achieved by preceding it with its own sort of 'personal' dominant 7 chord. The 'personal dominant chord' is a secondary dominant. If you don't fully understand secondary dominants, go back and review the Theory Module.

Soloing over secondary dominants is baffling for most guitarists, but it's very possible if you understand what is happening musically. Nearly every secondary dominant chord has at least one note that is not diatonic to the key. This means key-center soloing doesn't really work over secondary dominant chords. That's a problem that needs a solution.

In progressions that are all diatonic, guitarists can usually fall back on key-center soloing if they can't 'make the changes'. But you can't do that with secondary dominants because they have non-diatonic notes. Unless you learn what notes sound right on secondary dominants, you'll probably stumble and regret not learning what to play on them.

In this Module you'll learn to play over secondary dominants in a major-key context. In Unit 10 you'll learn to play over secondary dominants in a minor-key context. It's important to break down the issues for each secondary dominant.

Review what the secondary dominants are. We'll use the key of C for this explanation:

- In the key of C, V7/II is A7. The C# in A7 is not in the key of C.
- In the key of C, V7/III is B7. The D# in B7 is not in the key of C.
- In the key of C, V7/IV is C7. The B♭ in C7 is not in the key of C.
- In the key of C, V7/V is D7. The F# in D7 is not in the key of C.
- In the key of C, V7/VI is E7. The G# in E7 is not in the key of C.

Let's get back to the main goal: determining the good notes to play on a secondary dominant when soloing. You can always play the arpeggio because the arpeggio is an exact reflection of the chord: The arpeggio is made up of the chord tones.

The focus of this Module is on what chord scales can be played on each of the secondary dominants. Remember that a 'chord scale' is called a chord scale because it contains the notes of the chord—the chord tones. So the chord scale applications you learn here will contain the chord tones of the secondary dominant.

The 'normal-sounding' scale choices to play over secondary dominants can be made simple:

- Over secondary dominants that are V7 of chords that are normally minor, the Harmonic Minor Scale of the minor chord it's V of is the inside-sounding scale choice. That's V/II, V/III, and V/VI. That's because II is normally minor, III is normally minor, and VI is normally minor. And you also learned in the Alternate Approach section of the Theory Module that you can play the Dominant ♭9 ♭13 Scale of the dominant chord. Remember the close relationship between Harmonic Minor and the Dominant ♭9 ♭13 Scales.

- Over secondary dominants that are V of major chords, the Major Scale of the next chord is an appropriate choice. That's V/IV and V/V. That's because IV is normally major and V is normally major.

This, by the way, is the same as the Mixolydian Scale of the secondary dominant. The Mixolydian mode will be studied in depth in Level 6.

For now, know that the Mixolydian Scale is a major scale with a minor 7th.

C Mixolydian Scale

| 1 | ma2 | ma3 | P4 | P5 | ma6 | mi7 | P8 |

Notice it has the chord tones of a dominant 7 chord: R, Ma3, P5, Mi7.

The logistical challenge is to find the chord scale for the secondary dominant in the same location on the fretboard where you find the notes to play over the other chords. In other words, you need to locate and play the secondary dominant chord scale generally in-position with the diatonic scale.

Use these secondary dominant chord scales over each of the five secondary dominants. To make this as manageable as possible, these progressions are all written in the key of C. To begin, use Octave Shape III where you are already very comfortable.

Don't think too hard on the diatonic chords. For now, key center is fine. Your focus is on the secondary dominant.

Progression 1 - V7/II

Here is Progression 1. Locate the Pattern III C Octave Shape in 5th position. This will be home base. Use the Pattern III Major Pentatonic Scale or Major Scale for the diatonic chords.

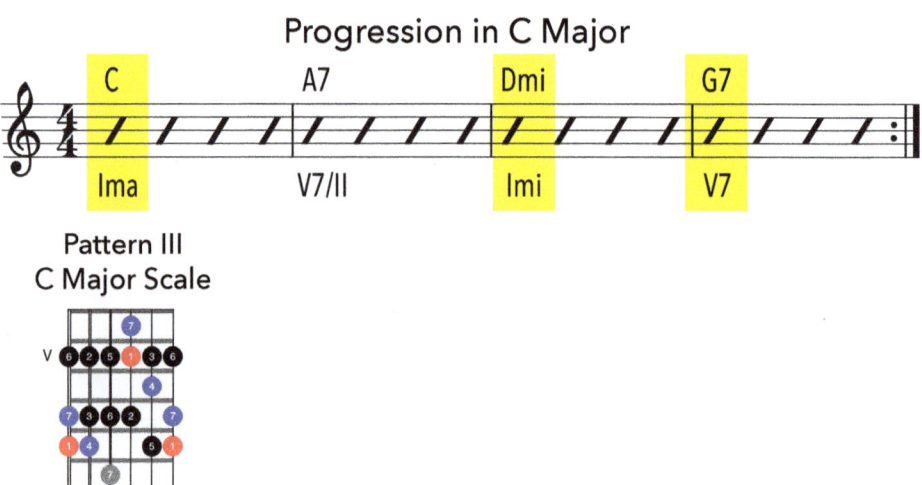

But what about A7? Because A7 is V7/II, and II is minor, D minor, D harmonic minor is the inside-sounding chord scale. So locate the D Harmonic Minor Scale in or around 5th position. This could also be A Dominant ♭9 ♭13, too. Remember, they're the same.

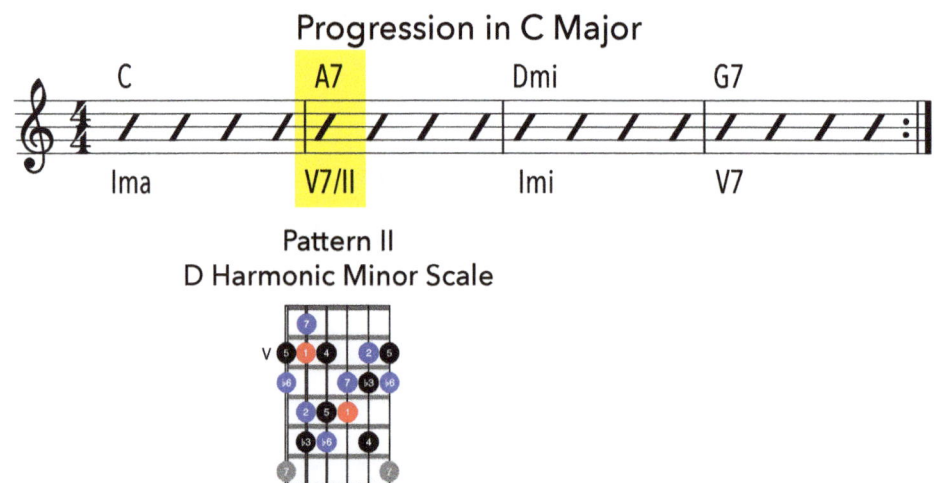

Experiment with this. The secondary dominant chord scale is played only for the duration of the chord. It's important to return the diatonic scale or a chord tone of the next chord on the next chord.

Level 5 Unit 9 • Improv Demo #1

Progression 2 - V7/III

Progression in C Major

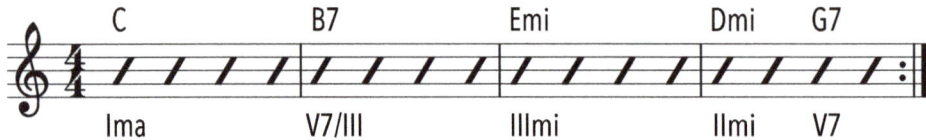

For Progression 2, stay with the Pattern III C Octave Shape. Again, you can play all of your diatonic options in-position.

Progression in C Major

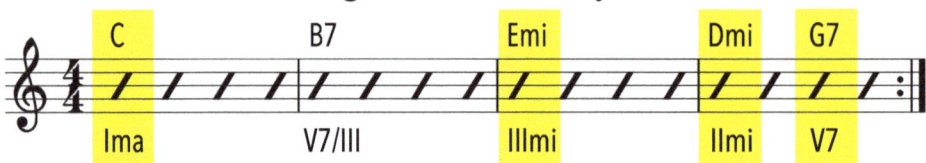

**Pattern III
C Major Scale**

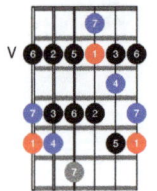

But, B7, the secondary dominant, has a non-diatonic note. Since B7 is V7 of Emi, play the E Harmonic Minor Scale on B7. Find an E Harmonic Minor Scale pattern in or around 5th position. This could be B Dominant ♭9 ♭13, too. Remember, they're the same.

Progression in C Major

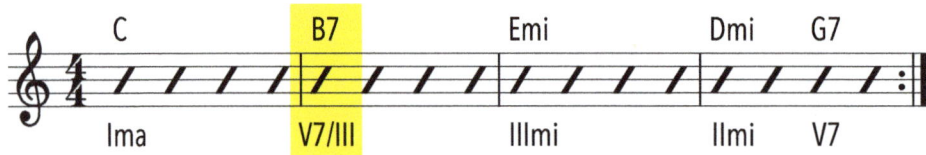

**Pattern I
E Harmonic Minor Scale**

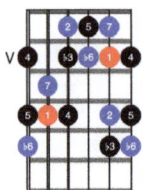

Experiment with this very slowly and deliberately. And again, the secondary dominant chord scale is played only for the duration of the chord. Return to the diatonic scale or a chord tone of the next chord on the next chord.

Level 5 Unit 9 • Improv Demo #2

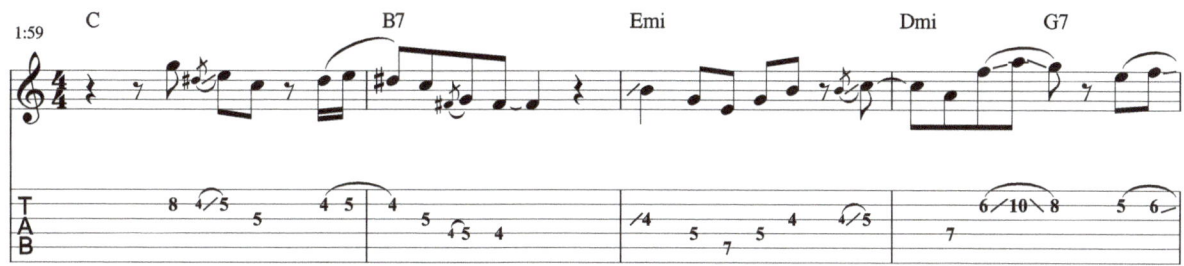

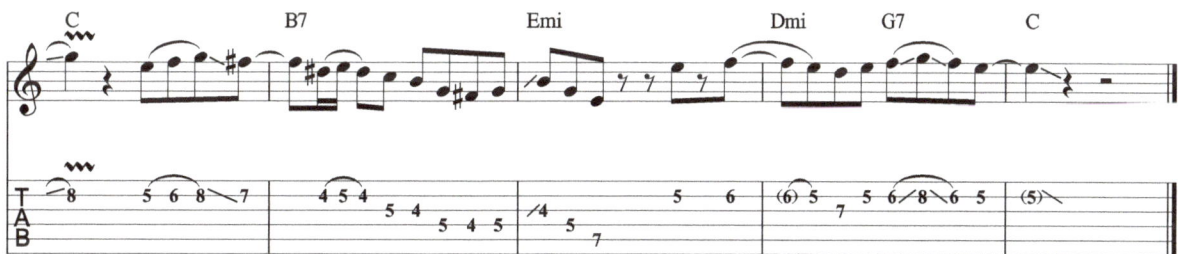

Progression 3 - V7/IV

Progression in C Major

C	C7	F	G7
Ima	V7/IV	IVma	V7

For Progression 3, stay in the Pattern III C Octave Shape. Again, you can play all of your diatonic options in-position with the C Major Pentatonic or C Major Scale.

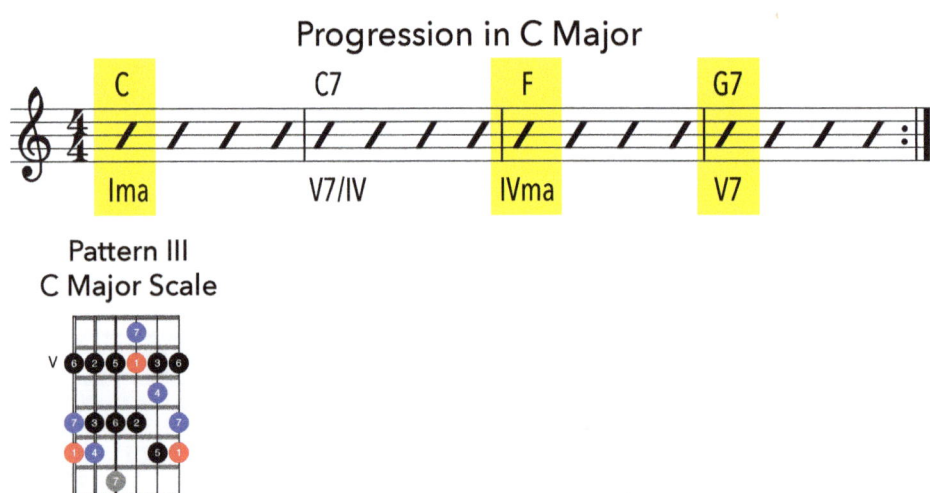

But, C7 is a secondary dominant. It's non-diatonic so we have to make some accommodation. Since C7 is V/IV, which is major, we have to play the major scale of the chord it approaches. That would be F major. Now the task is to locate the F Major Scale, which is in the same as C Mixolydian at the same spot of the fretboard, 5th position.

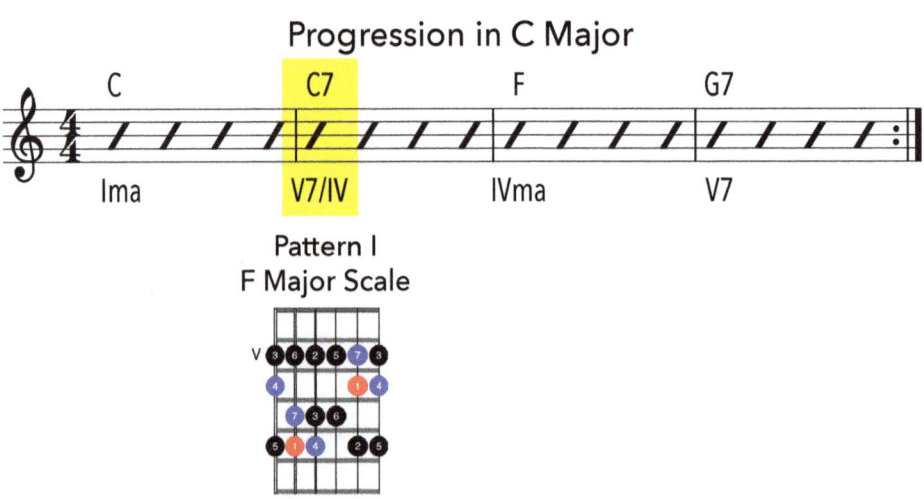

Experiment with this very deliberately and remember that the secondary dominant chord scale is played only for the duration of the secondary dominant chord.

Level 5 Unit 9 • Improv Demo #3

Progression 4 – V7/V

Progression in C Major

For Progression 4, stay in the Pattern III C Octave Shape. Again, play all of your diatonic options in-position.

Progression in C Major

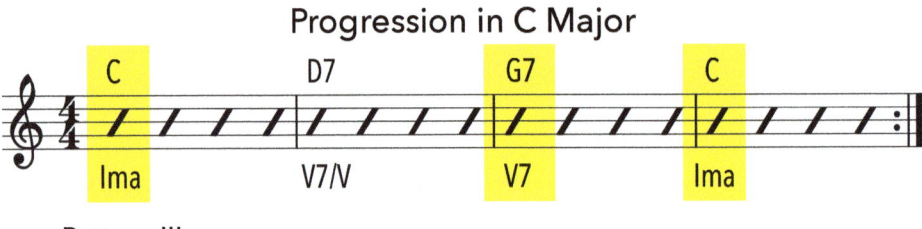

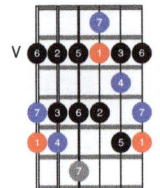

Pattern III
C Major Scale

D7, however, is not diatonic. D7 is a secondary dominant. So, over D7, the inside-sounding scale choice is G major. Now the task is to locate the G Major Scale, which is in the same as D Mixolydian at the same spot of the fretboard, 5th position.

Progression in C Major

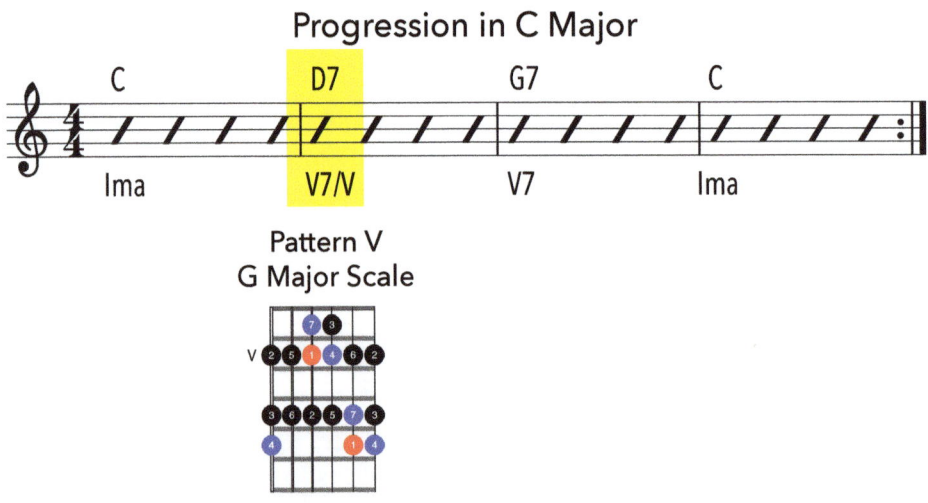

Pattern V
G Major Scale

Again, experiment with this very slowly. The secondary dominant chord scale is played only for the duration of the secondary dominant.

Level 5 Unit 9 • Improv Demo #4

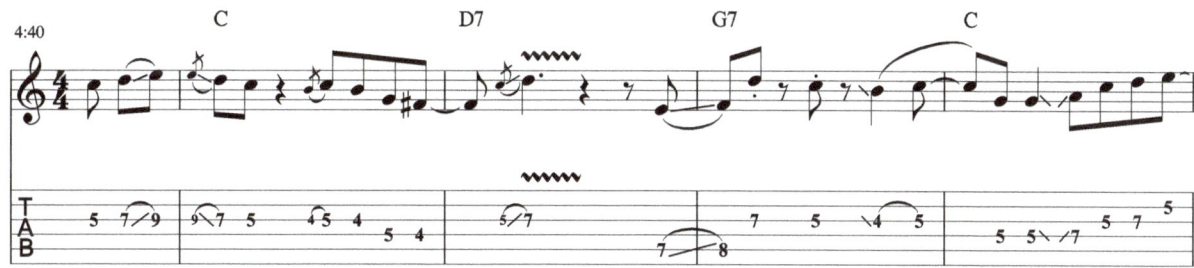

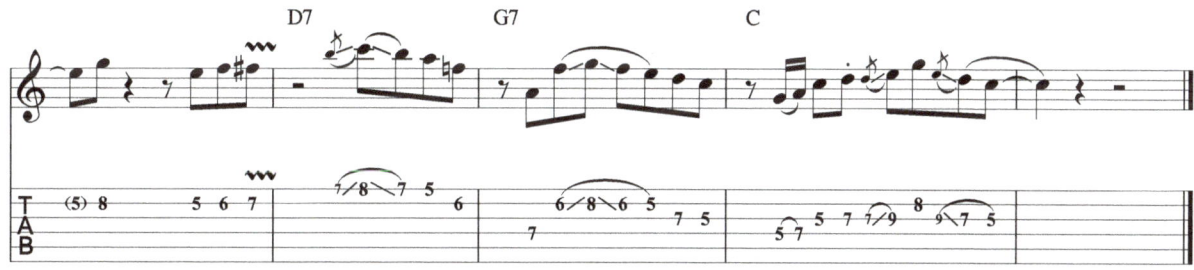

Progression 5 - V7/VI

Progression in C Major

For Progression 5, stay in the Pattern III C Octave Shape with all of your diatonic options in-position.

Progression in C Major

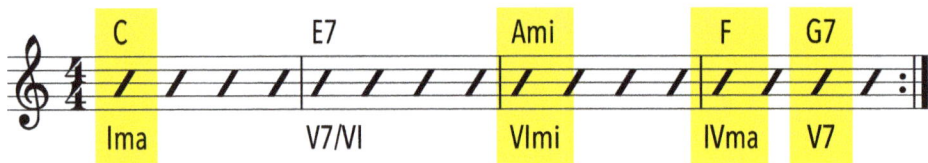

Pattern III
C Major Scale

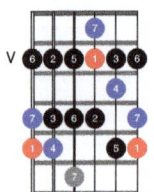

E7, however, is not diatonic to C. It is a secondary dominant. It is V7 of A minor, and since A minor is the VI chord, E7 is V7/VI. The inside-sounding scale for E7 is the A Harmonic Minor Scale. Now the task is to locate the A Harmonic Minor Scale in the same area of the fretboard. This is in 5th position. This could be E Dominant ♭9 ♭13, too. Remember, they're the same.

Progression in C Major

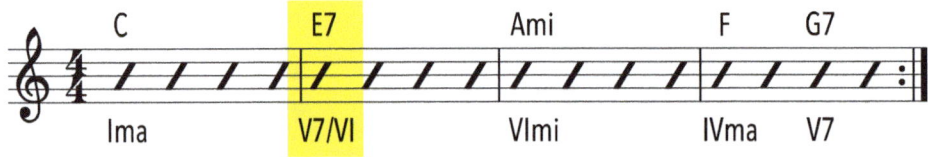

Pattern IV
A Harmonic Minor Scale

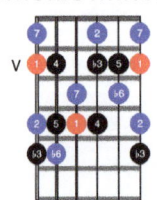

Again, experiment with this very slowly and deliberately. Play the secondary dominant chord scale only for the duration of the secondary dominant chord.

Level 5 Unit 9 • Improv Demo #5

This is a lot to remember, and it takes time to develop the understanding and skill to solo over secondary dominants. Consider it more important to understand the reasoning behind how to find the chord scales needed for each secondary dominant. If you understand the 'why', you can always find what to play on the fretboard. All of this information can be applied in all of the five octave shapes. Don't expect to learn how to do this in all octave shapes quickly. It is wise to go through the steps we just followed for each of the octave shapes to test your comprehension.

Here is the short list of how to reason your way to a chord-scale solution for secondary dominants. The 'normal-sounding' scale choices to play over secondary dominants can be made simple:

- Over secondary dominants that are V7 of chords that are normally minor, the Harmonic Minor Scale of the minor chord it's V of is the inside-sounding scale choice. And you learned that it's the same as the Dominant ♭9 ♭13 Scale of the dominant chord. For secondary dominants that are V of major chords, the Major Scale of the next chord is an appropriate choice. And this the same as the Mixolydian Scale of the secondary dominant.
- Next determine the octave shape where you will play the diatonic notes.
- Next determine the correct chord scale for the secondary dominant in the progression.
- Finally find the chord-scale pattern in-position with the diatonic scale or as close as possible.

If you remember this short list, you can reason your way to the solution every time. That's really the goal of the whole Fretboard Biology program—to make you self-reliant with respect to theory and the fretboard matrix.

In this Module you learned to play over secondary dominants in a major-key context. In Unit 10 you'll learn to play over secondary dominants in a minor-key context.

PRACTICE

Theory

- ❑ Go to the tabs below the Theory video on the website and complete the quiz.
- ❑ Learn the concept of secondary dominants and how to identify them in a progression.
- ❑ Learn the Dominant ♭9 ♭13 Scale.

Fretboard Logic

- ❑ Learn and practice the Patterns I-V Dominant ♭9 ♭13 Scale.

Rhythm Guitar

- ❑ Understand the note groupings for 11/8 time.
- ❑ Practice playing the 11/8 progression in F major.

Chart Reading

- ❑ Understand notation of dynamics, accents, and markings that affect time.

Improvisation

- ❑ Practice playing solos over progressions in C major using the appropriate chord scale over the secondary dominant chord in each progression.

UNIT 10

Learning Modules

> **Theory** - Harmonic Analysis of Secondary Dominants
> **Fretboard Logic** - In-Position 7th Chord Voicings for the Harmonized Harmonic Minor Scale
> **Rhythm Guitar** - Odd Meter: 13/8 Time
> **Chart Reading** - The Chart Checklist, Analyzing Charts, Memorization
> **Improvisation** - Soloing over Secondary Dominants in Minor Keys
> **Practice** - Continue Practice Routine Development

THEORY

In the last Unit, you learned about secondary dominants. In this Theory Module, we will put all this information to work and do some harmonic analysis of progressions with secondary dominants. Let's review this checklist for how to analyze a progression:

1. Look at the key signature to determine the key.
2. If there is no key signature, look at the last chord and assume, at least until some other evidence in the progressions makes you think otherwise, that it's the tonic chord.
3. Go through the progression chord by chord and analyze and label the easy ones, that is, the diatonic root position chords.
4. If there are inversions, analyze and label them.
5. Look for modal interchange chords; analyze and label them.
6. Look for dominant chords that are not the primary dominant. They might be secondary dominants.

Progression Analysis - Group 1

Let's analyze two groups of progressions. This first group has diatonic chords and secondary dominants in both major and minor keys. Keep in mind that not all secondary dominants are functioning. Secondary dominants should be analyzed and labeled the same way whether they are functioning or non-functioning. Go through and analyze these progressions and then check your answers with the Answer Key in the Appendix.

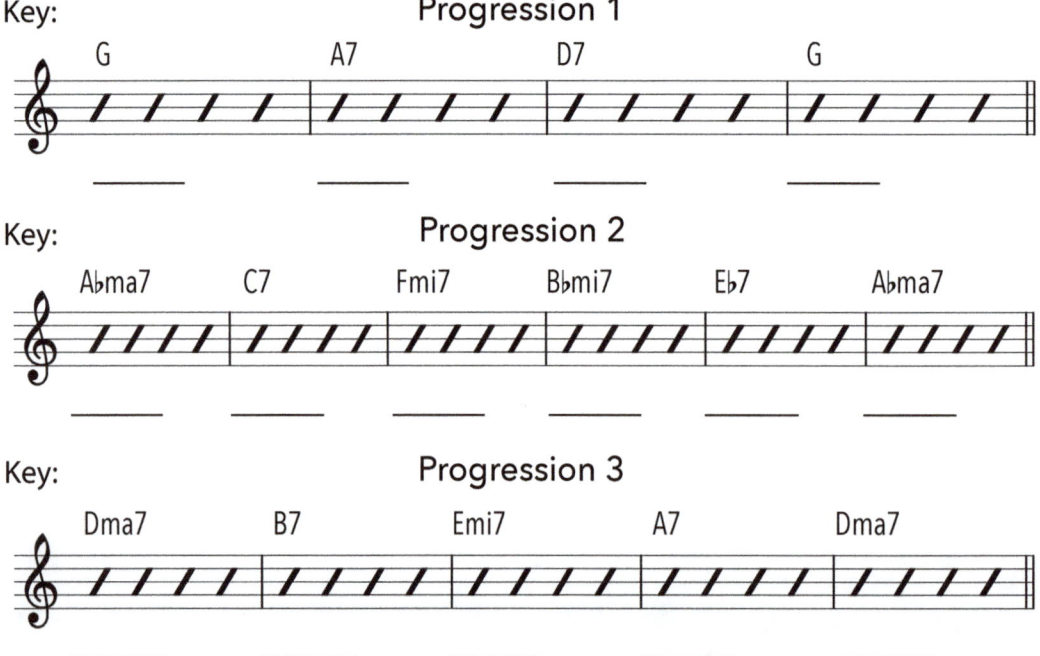

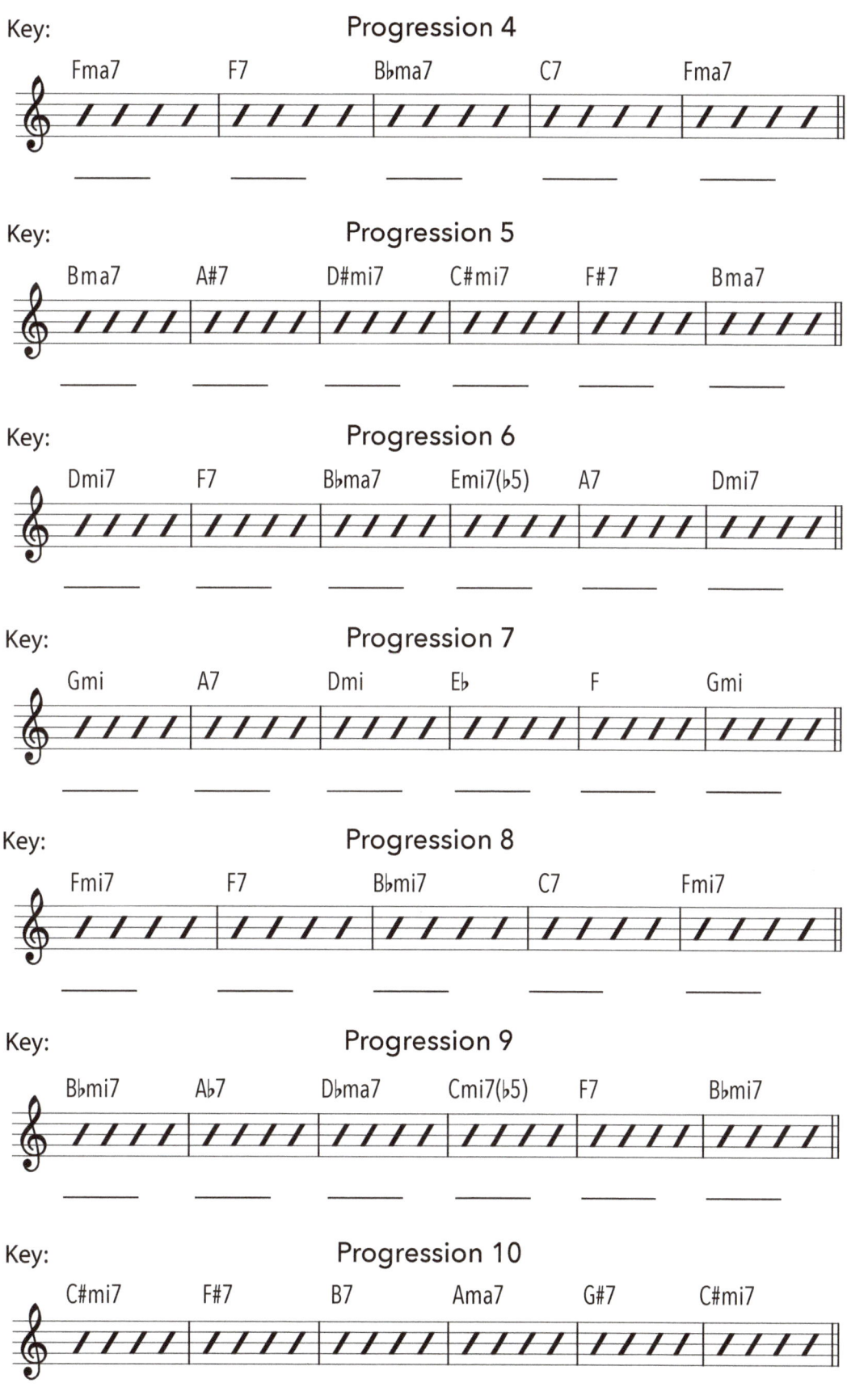

Progression Analysis - Group 2

This second group of progression may include diatonic chords, chords with modal interchange, inversions, and secondary dominants in both major and minor keys. Analyze each of these progressions and check your answers with the Answer Key in the Appendix.

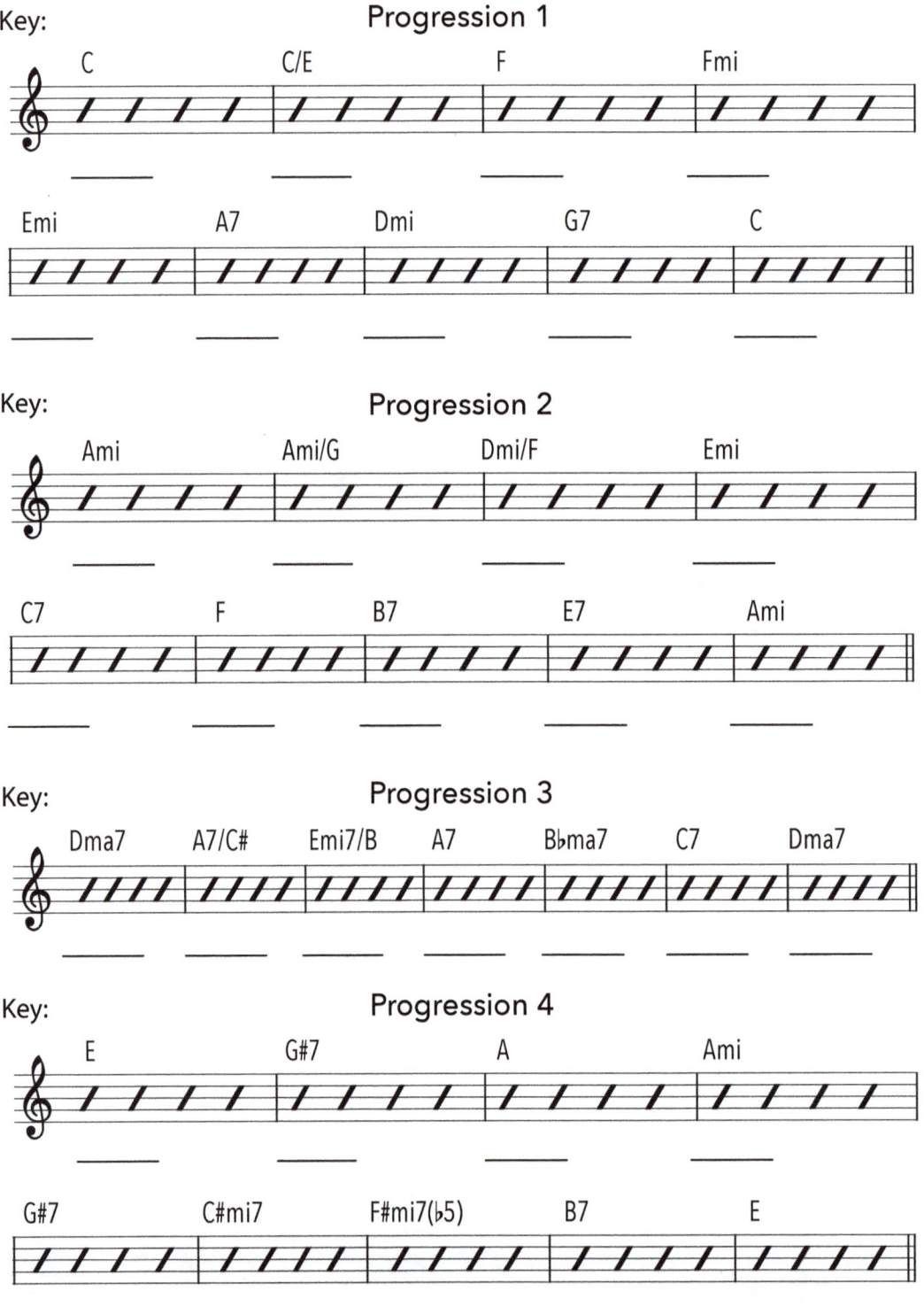

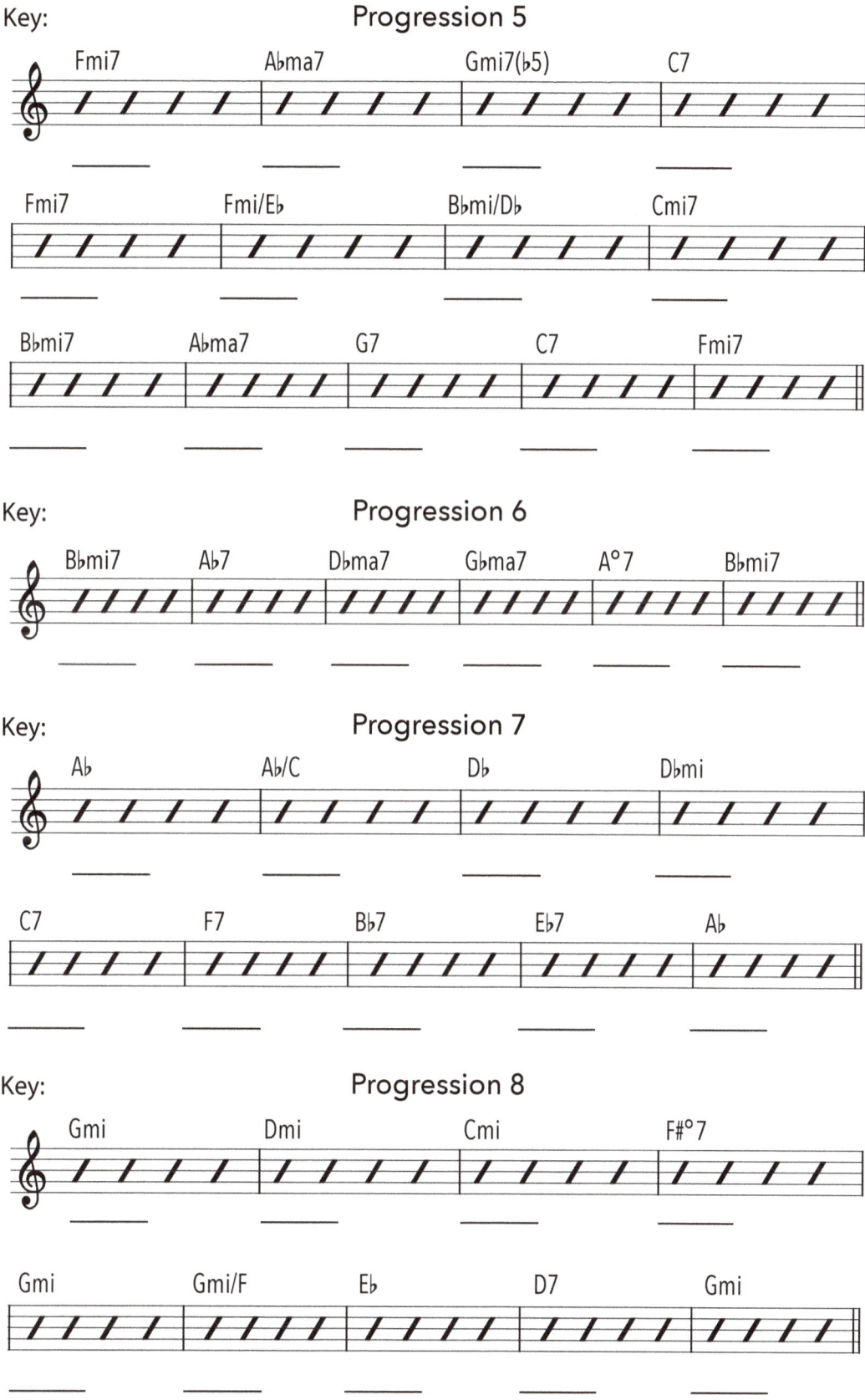

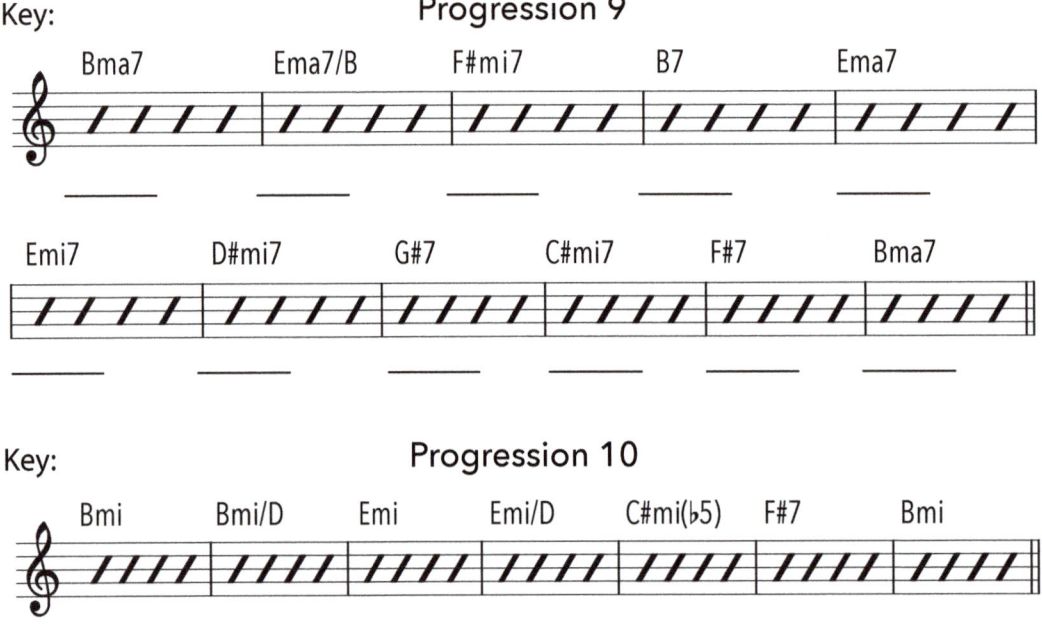

Make sure you pay special attention to the steps of harmonic analysis. The method will serve you well. In each progression, work from the easiest chords to hardest.

Wrap-Up

This is the end of Level 5 Theory. You learned how to construct and harmonize the Harmonic Minor Scale. It's important to know that the Harmonic Minor Scale is usually not the basis for an entire progression. Instead, a sort of minor modal interchange occurs where the Natural Minor Scale is the primary basis for a song, and chords and melody notes from Harmonic Minor are borrowed for emotional effect.

You learned about Mi(Ma7), Ma7(+5), and Dim7 chords and how they are used in progressions. You learned how dominant 7 chords work and the difference between functioning and non-functioning dominant 7 chords. You learned about secondary dominants, how they function, and how to analyze them.

Be sure to keep the step-by-step checklist for analyzing progressions front of mind. It's effective.

Fretboard Biology Level 5 • Unit 10: Fretboard Logic

FRETBOARD LOGIC

In-Position Chord Voicings

You have learned how to organize the arpeggios of harmonized scales in-position. You have now learned or at least been exposed to this organizational system in five patterns of Major, Natural Minor, and Harmonic Minor Scales. In this Module, you will learn how to also organize the chords of harmonized scales in-position. The system is essentially the same as organizing the arpeggios of harmonized scales in-position.

The same notes that make up the chords make up the arpeggios. Essentially chords equal arpeggios and arpeggios equal chords. We just play them differently. The only difference is that with arpeggios, you can play two notes on one string since you play them melodically, one note at a time. With chords, you can only play and hear one note on a string at a time.

Let's organize the practical chord voicings built on each scale degree in-position on the fretboard just like we did with arpeggios. This can be done in each of the five patterns for each scale we've studied: Major, Minor and Harmonic Minor, but we'll demonstrate with just one. We will start with Major.

Follow the same process that was used way back when the Major Scale was harmonized with arpeggios. You already know all of the chord voicings used here. You can play all the notes of a scale within one octave shape, therefore you can play all of the seven chords that result from harmonizing the scale within the octave shape.

Pattern I Major Chord Voicings

The Ima7 Chord

In Pattern I of the Major Scale the tonic is played on the 5th string with the 4th finger. The I chord is Ma7. Here is a practical Ma7 chord voicing played with your 4th finger playing its root on the 5th string. It's all within the Pattern I Octave Shape.

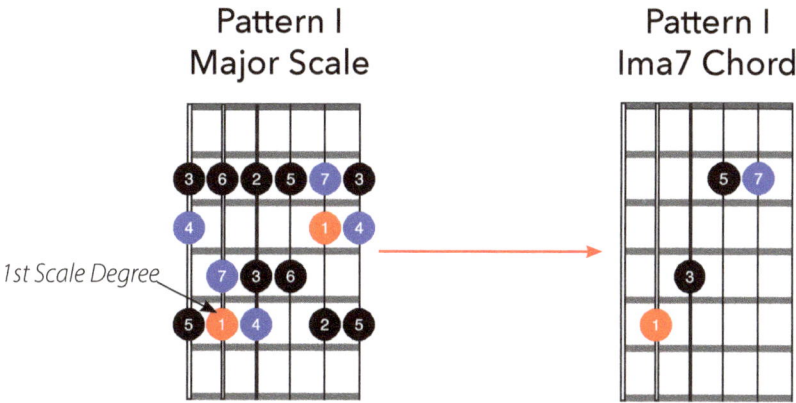

The IImi7 Chord

In Pattern I of the Major Scale the 2nd scale degree is played on the 4th string with the 1st finger. The II chord is Mi7. Here is a practical Mi7 voicing with your 1st finger playing its root on the 4th string. This is all within the Pattern I Octave Shape.

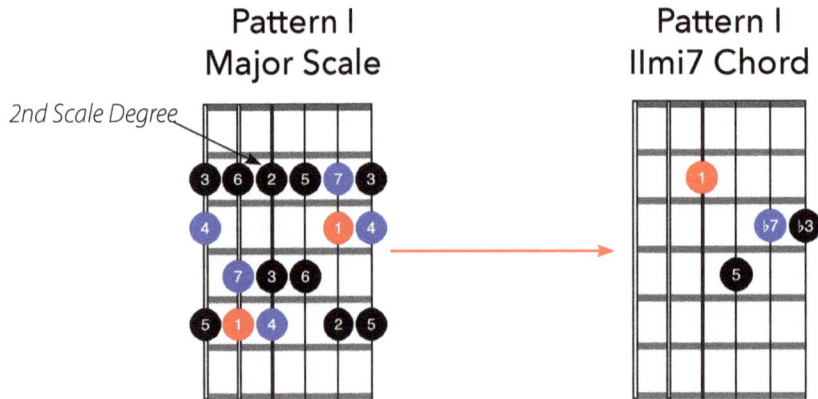

The IIImi7 Chord

The 3rd scale degree is played on the 4th string with the 3rd finger. But it can be played an octave lower on the 6th string with your 1st finger. The III chord is Mi7. Here is a practical Mi7 chord voicing played with your 1st finger playing its root on the 6th string, and it fits within the Pattern I Octave Shape.

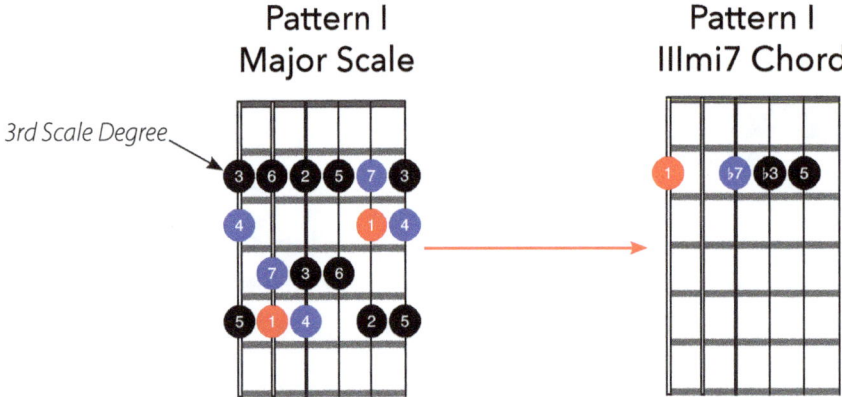

The IVma7 Chord

The 4th scale degree is played on the 6th string with the 2nd finger. The IV chord is Ma7. Here is a practical Ma7 chord voicing with your 2nd finger playing the root on the 6th string within the Pattern I Octave Shape.

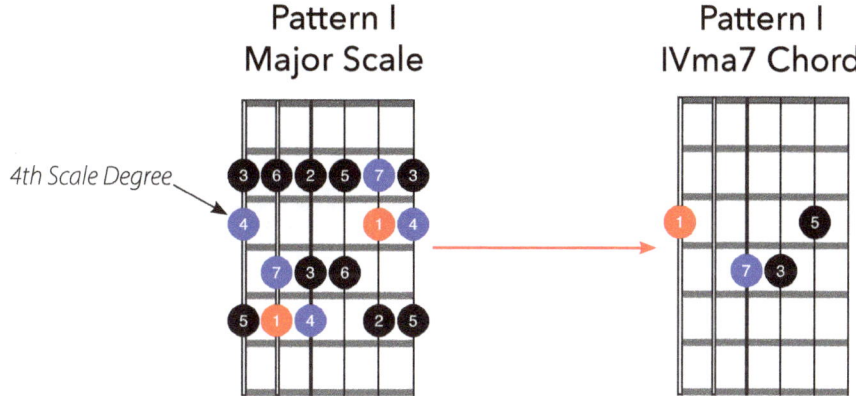

The V7 Chord

The 5th scale degree is played on the 6th string with the 4th finger. The V chord is dominant 7. Here is a practical dominant 7 chord voicing played with your 3rd finger on the 6th string, or your 1st finger on the 4th string. It, too, is within the Pattern I Octave Shape.

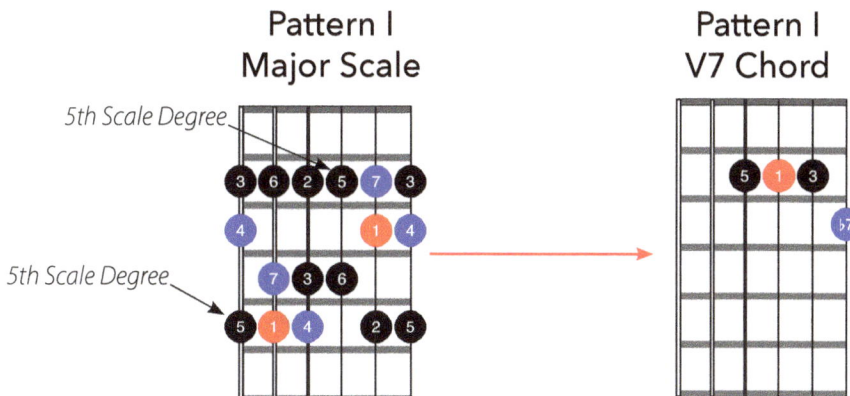

The VImi7 Chord

The 6th scale degree is played on the 5th string with the 1st finger. The VI chord is Mi7. Here is a practical Mi7 chord voicing played with your 1st finger on the 5th string within the Pattern I Octave Shape.

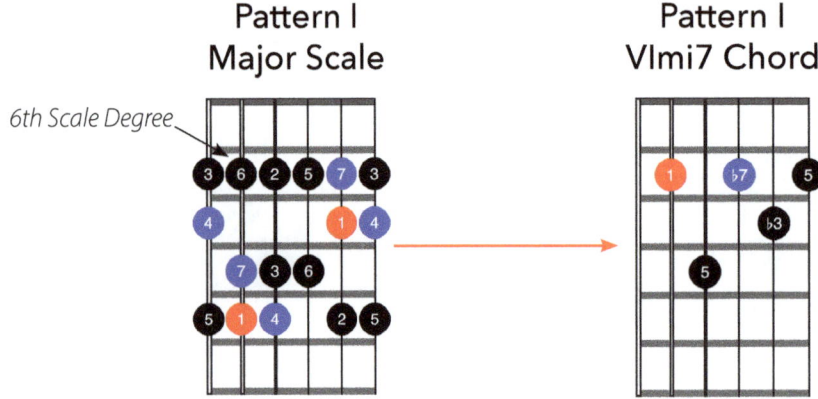

The VIImi7(b5) Chord

Finally, the 7th scale degree is played on the 5th string with the 3rd finger. The VII chord is Mi7(b5). Here is a practical Mi7(b5) chord voicing played with your 1st finger on the 5th string. This, too, is within the Pattern I Octave Shape.

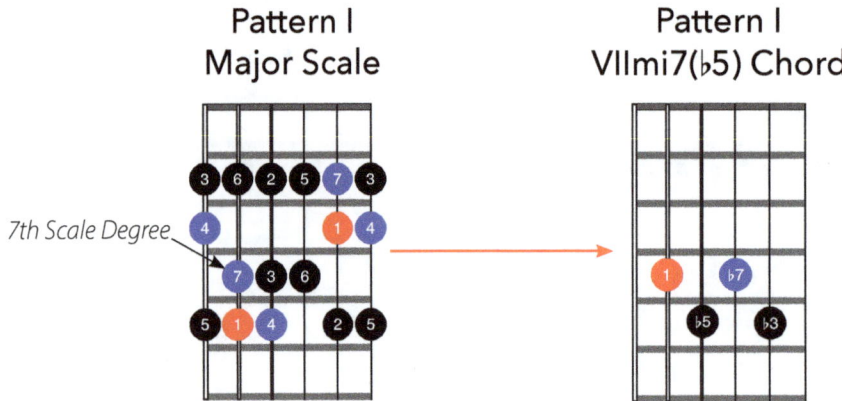

Pattern I Major Chord Voicings

Look at how all seven of these chord voicings of the Harmonized Scale fit precisely inside the major scale. Again, this is because of the source of notes for harmonizing the Major Scale IS the Major Scale itself.

Pattern I Major In-Position Chord Voicings

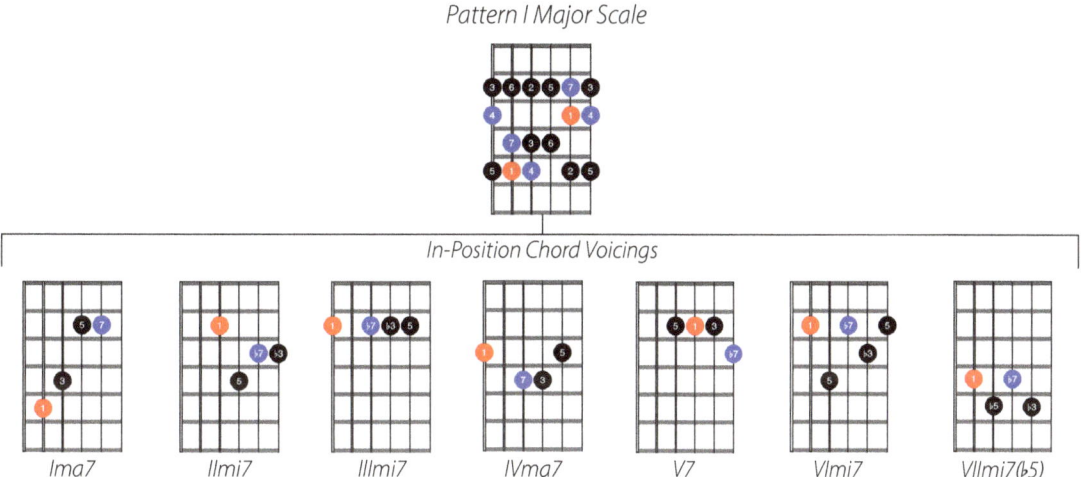

This can be replicated with the other Major Scale patterns in Octave Shapes II, III, IV, and V. For the most part you can use chord shapes you already know to fill out each the remaining patterns. There are a couple here and there are that are not in common use but with your knowledge from Theory and Fretboard Logic, you have the ability now to reason your way through all of the Major Scale patterns. This process can also be replicated in all five Natural Minor Scale patterns, and now that you have learned the Harmonized Harmonic Minor Scale, you can replicate this with all five Harmonized Minor Scale patterns, too.

The goal is to have the skill and knowledge to find and play all of the practical chord voicings of the Harmonized Major, Minor, and Harmonic Minor Scales within each octave shape. I wouldn't spend a high percentage of your practice time running through all the chords of five Major, five Minor, and five Harmonic Minor Scale patterns harmonized with chords. You can condense this into a five-minute-or-less drill with one repetition per pattern each practice day. Remember that with many practice items, the consistency of playing something for a very short time each day over many days yields better results and better long-term retention than spending a lot of time in one day.

Here is the complete picture of practical in-position chord voicings for major. You can find alternative voicings for some of these; feel free to be creative and find what works for you.

Pattern II Major In-Position Chord Voicings

Pattern II Major Scale

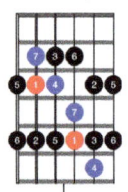

In-Position Chord Voicings

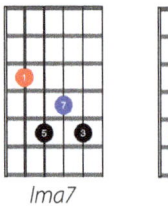 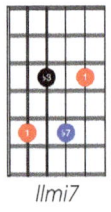 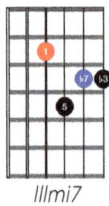 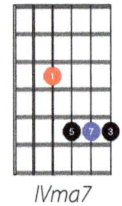 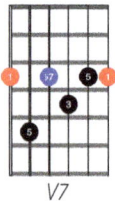 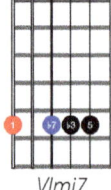 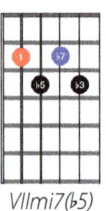

Ima7   IImi7   IIImi7   IVma7   V7   VImi7   VIImi7(♭5)

Pattern III Major In-Position Chord Voicings

Pattern III Major Scale

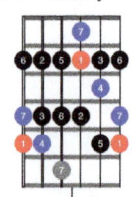

In-Position Chord Voicings

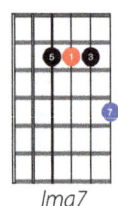 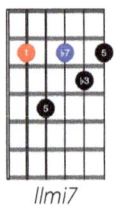  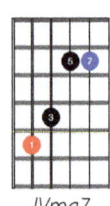 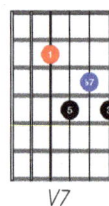 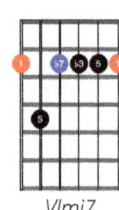 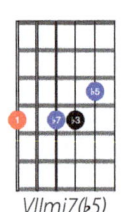

Ima7   IImi7   IIImi7   IVma7   V7   VImi7   VIImi7(♭5)

Pattern IV Major In-Position Chord Voicings

Pattern IV Major Scale

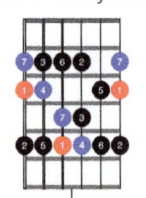

In-Position Chord Voicings

  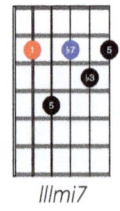 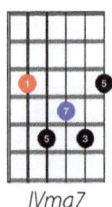 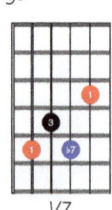 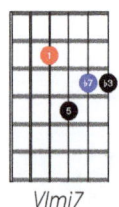 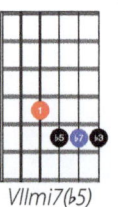

Ima7   IImi7   IIImi7   IVma7   V7   VImi7   VIImi7(♭5)

Pattern V Major In-Position Chord Voicings

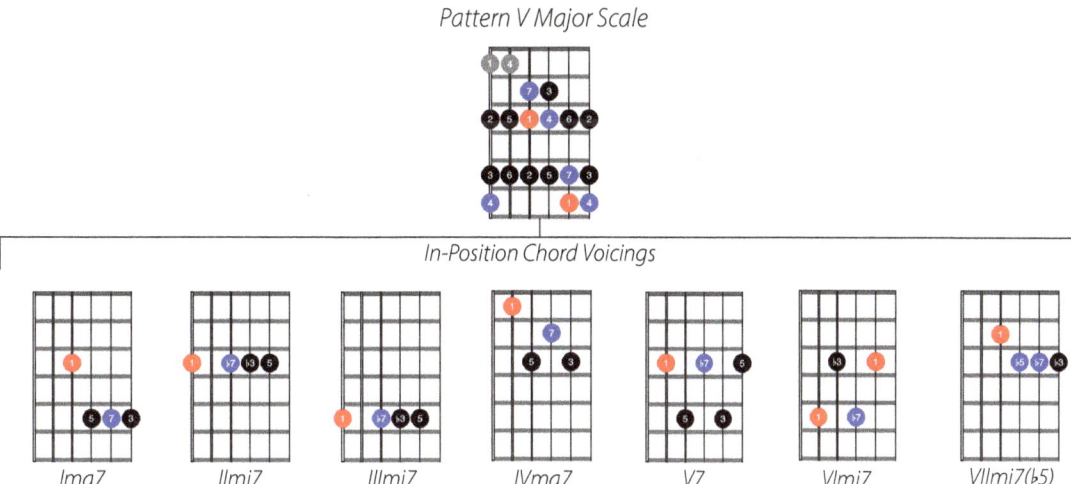

Natural Minor Chord Voicings

Now, let's repeat the same process for Natural Minor. Here are the in-position 7th chord voicings for natural minor.

Pattern I Natural Minor In-Position Chord Voicings

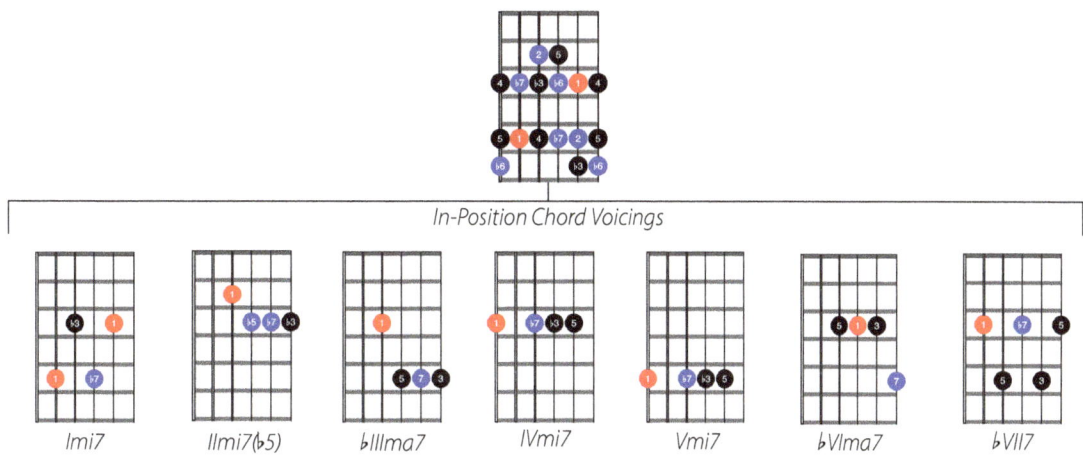

Pattern II Natural Minor In-Position Chord Voicings

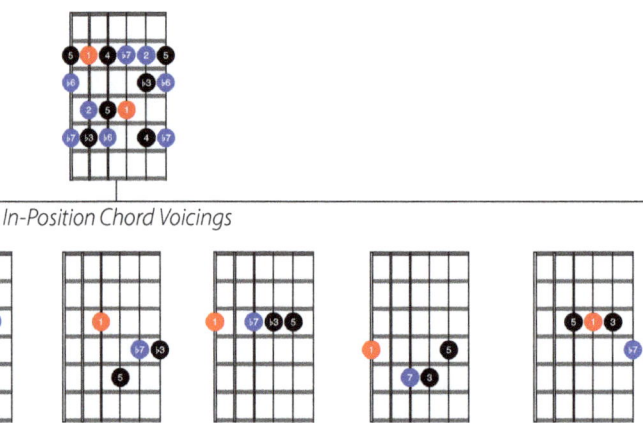

Pattern III Natural Minor In-Position Chord Voicings

Pattern III Natural Minor Scale

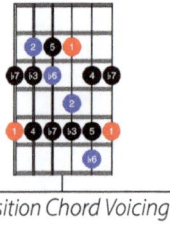

In-Position Chord Voicings

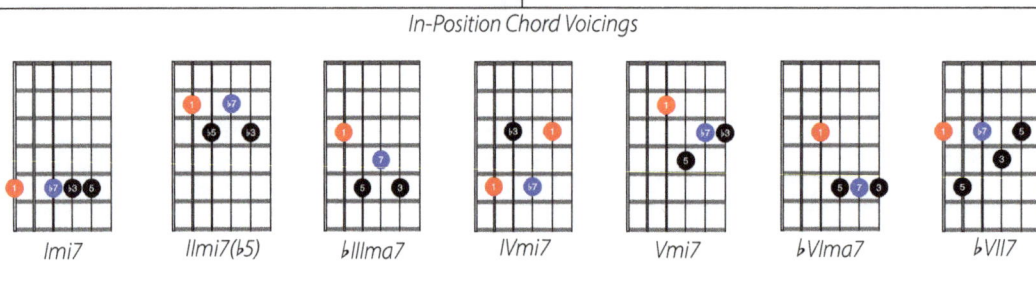

Imi7 　 IImi7(b5) 　 bIIIma7 　 IVmi7 　 Vmi7 　 bVIma7 　 bVII7

Pattern IV Natural Minor In-Position Chord Voicings

Pattern IV Natural Minor Scale

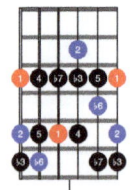

In-Position Chord Voicings

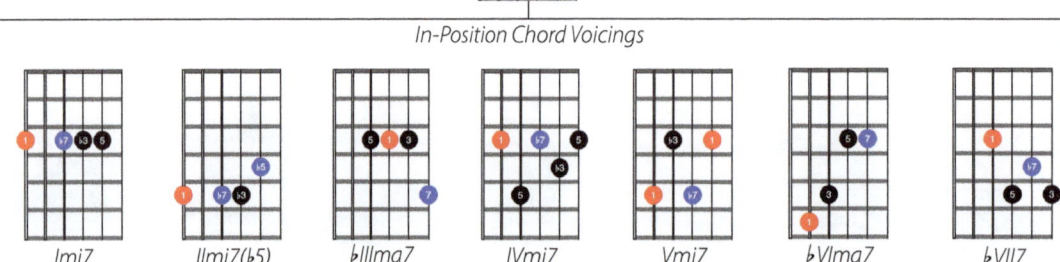

Imi7 　 IImi7(b5) 　 bIIIma7 　 IVmi7 　 Vmi7 　 bVIma7 　 bVII7

Pattern V Natural Minor In-Position Chord Voicings

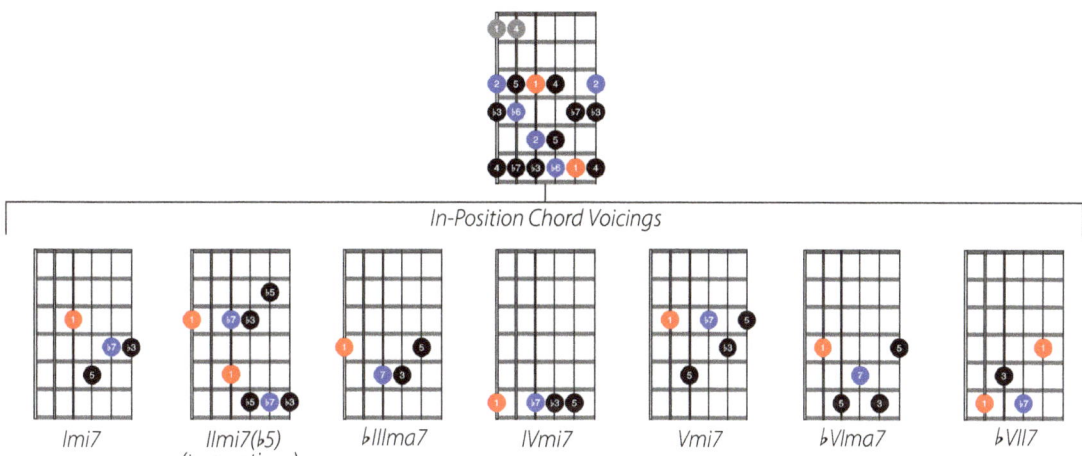

Harmonic Minor Chord Voicings

Now, let's repeat the same process for Harmonic Minor. Here are the in-position 7th chord voicings for harmonic minor.

Pattern I Harmonic Minor In-Position Chord Voicings

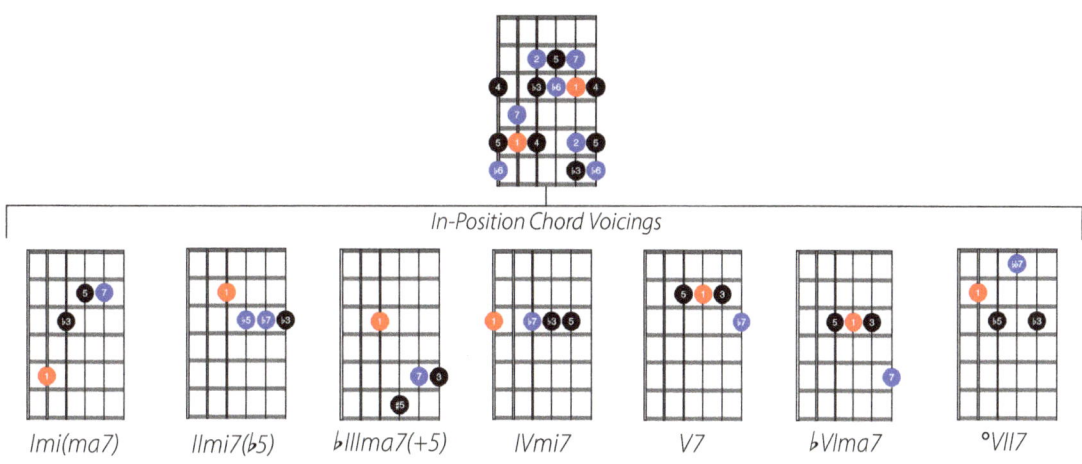

Pattern II Harmonic Minor In-Position Chord Voicings

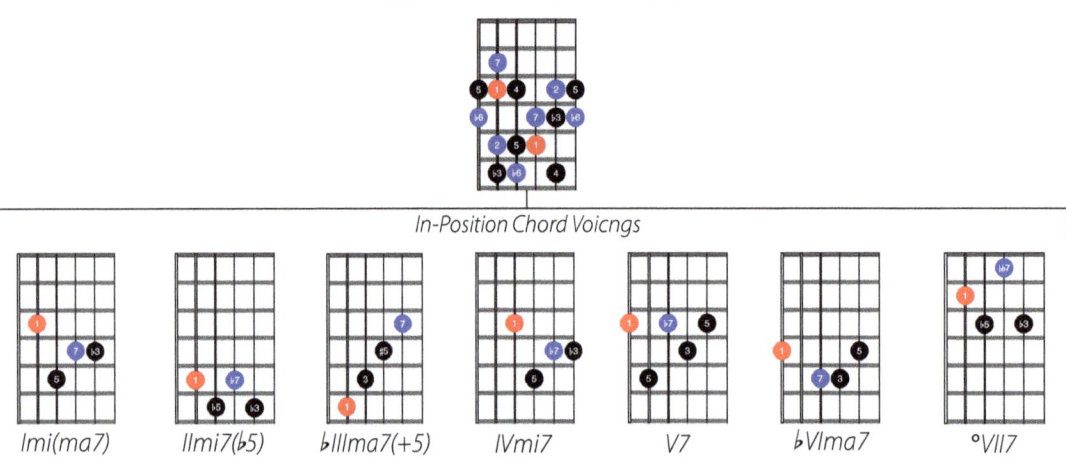

Pattern III Harmonic Minor In-Position Chord Voicings

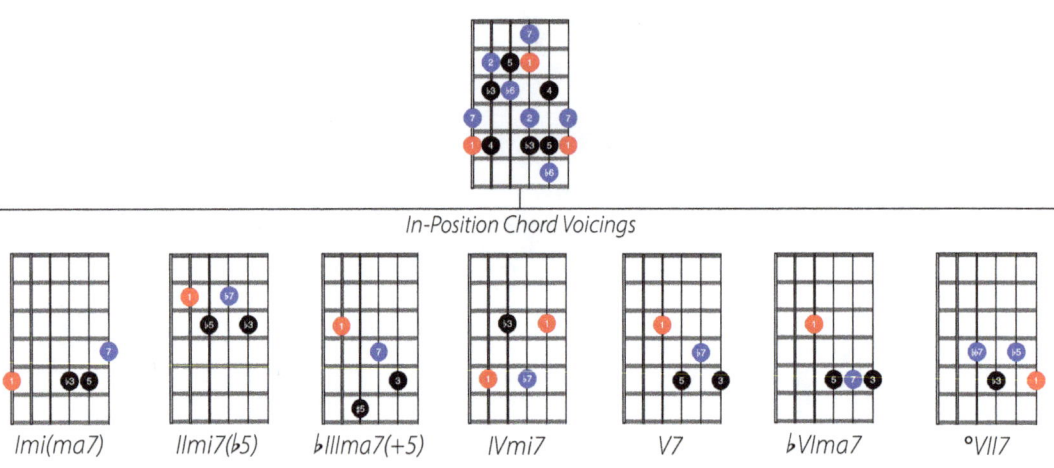

Pattern IV Harmonic Minor In-Position Chord Voicings

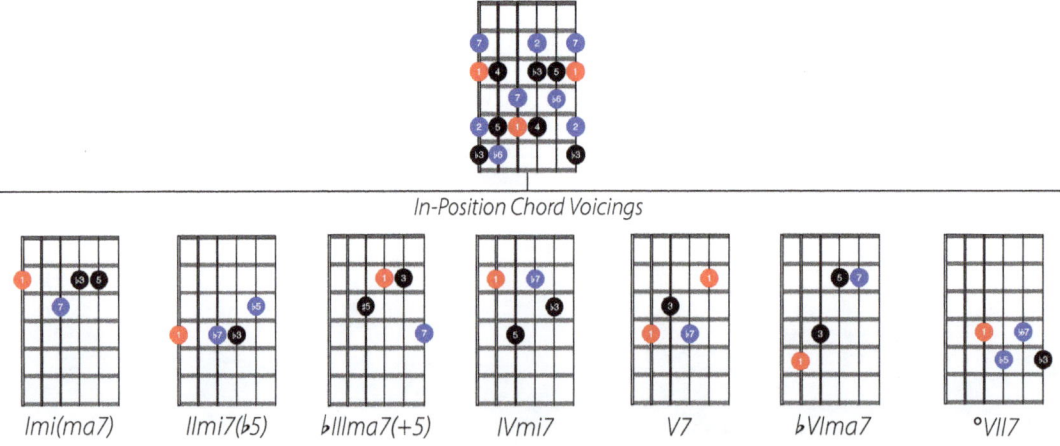

Pattern V Harmonic Minor In-Position Chord Voicings

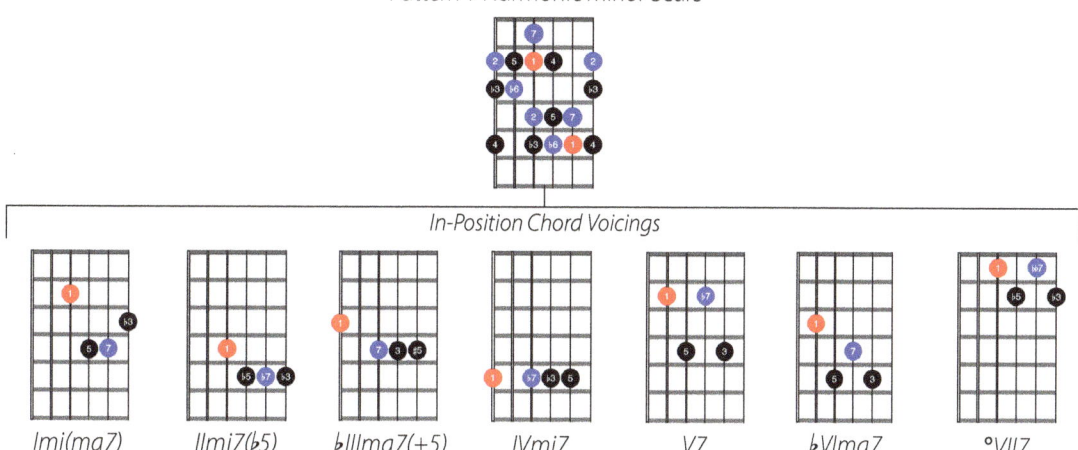

Knowing the all of the scales harmonized with chords is interesting but not as important as knowing the scales harmonized in arpeggios. Always remember that chords and arpeggios are really the same thing. Perhaps when practicing the arpeggios, play the chord first and then the arpeggio. That's another way to cover a massive amount of information in your practice routine while being efficient.

This concludes the Level 5 Fretboard Logic modules. The most important takeaways should be clear:

- You learned five Harmonic Minor Scale patterns.
- You learned about chord scales.
- You learned augmented and diminished triad arpeggios and chord voicings.
- You learned Dim7, Mi(Ma7), and Ma7(+5) arpeggios and chord voicings.
- You learned the in-position organization system for the arpeggios of the harmonized Harmonic Minor Scale patterns.
- You learned the side-by-side comparison of the Natural Minor and Harmonic Minor Scales harmonized with arpeggios.
- You learned the construction of a group of chords we called 'other chords': Suspended Chords, Add 2 chords (sometimes called Add 9 or even just 2 chords), 6 Chords, 6/9 Chords, and power chords.
- You learned the concept of organizing chords of a scale in-position.

See you in the next Level where the focus will be on the modes.

RHYTHM GUITAR

13/8 Time

You have learned about the most common odd meters: 5/8, 7/8, and 11/8. This Module focuses on 13/8. The 8th notes in 13/8 can be grouped a number of ways but in this Module we will look at the most common way: 3+3+3+2+2. Continue internalizing odd meter phrases using a silly phrase.

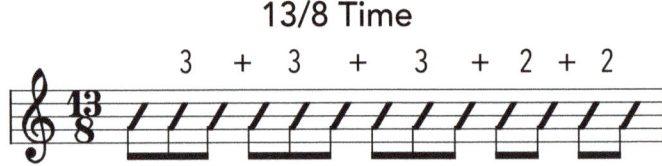

Because this has three compound beats and two simple beats, we need three three-syllable words and two two-syllable words. Use: 'strawberries, strawberries, strawberries with cream I like'.

This example is in the key of G. It is in 13/8, is 3+3+3+2+2, and has a contemporary Jazz sound. Gma7 is Ima7, C7sus is IV7, D7sus is V7, C7sus is IV7, and D7sus is V7.

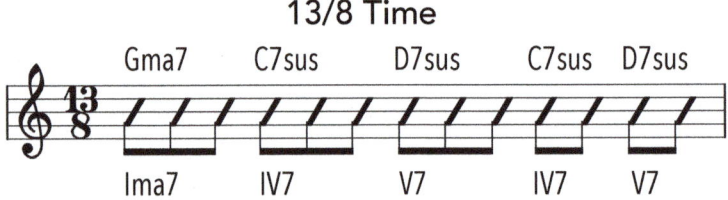

You feel five main pulses per measure. The first three pulses are groups of three, or 'strawberries', 'strawberries', 'strawberries'. The fourth pulse is the first group of two, or 'with cream'. The fifth pulse is the second group of two, or 'I like'.

Like in the other examples, say the sequence of words back-to-back in steady rhythm as you play the progression: 'strawberries, strawberries, strawberries with cream I like'. Notice the feel of 3+3+3+2+2. Notice you feel five larger pulses: The first, second, and third on the 'straw' of each 'strawberries', the fourth on 'with', and the fifth on 'I'.

The groups of three 8th notes can also be represented by a dotted quarter note, and the group of two 8th notes can be represented by a single quarter note.

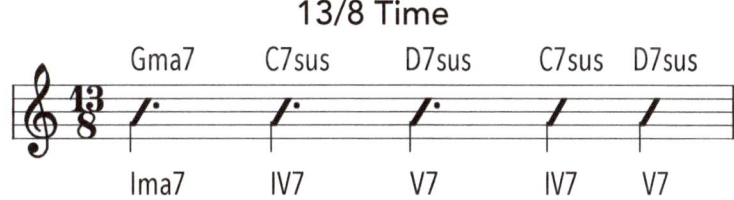

As in the previous Rhythm Guitar modules, play this three ways.

- First, play each of the 8th notes in the measure accenting the first of each group. That means to accent the first of each group of three, then the first each group of two.

- Next, play only on the start of the main five pulses per measure. That would be the start of each group of three, and the start of each group of two. Just a reminder, the groups of three 8th notes can be represented with a dotted quarter note, and the groups of two 8th notes can be represented with a single quarter note.

- Finally, try some variations using some dotted notes and some 8th notes or on the group of three, a quarter note and 8th note, or 8th and quarter notes. You can create a lot of variations but it all comes back to feeling 'strawberries, strawberries, strawberries with cream I like' as the core underlying rhythm.

As you go through these examples, keep the 'strawberries, strawberries, strawberries with cream I like' phrase going in your head. I would use a clean tone. Play this until it feels natural.

If you find 13/8 or other odd meters interesting, experiment with other ways to group simple and compound beats.

I mentioned back in Unit 6 that it is helpful to understand the three ways that odd meters appear in music:

- As a single odd meter as the basis for an entire composition.
- Multiple odd time signatures in a rhythmically complex composition.
- As a temporary accommodation for an isolated abnormal phrase.

In Units 7 through 10, you have learned the first of these ways that odd meters appear in music: as a single odd meter as the basis for an entire composition. The program won't delve deep in to the second of the ways, where multiple odd time signatures are used in a rhythmically complex composition.

Here's a random example of one possibility of how multiple odd-time signatures might appear, but there are an infinite number of possibilities.

Multiple Odd-Meter Example

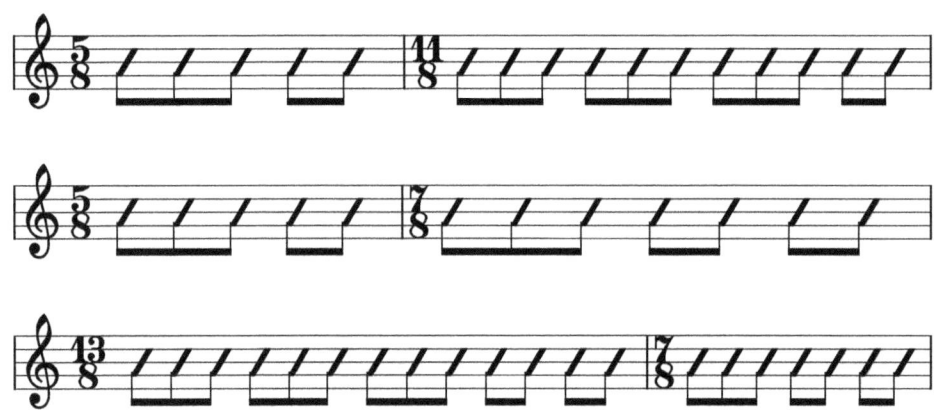

There are examples of progressive Rock and Jazz and other art music that move through multiple time signatures. This example is all odd meter but there could be simple time signatures mixed in as well.

The third one of the ways is perhaps the most common way odd meter might appear in more mainstream music, and that is as a temporary accommodation for an isolated abnormal phrase. This isn't really under the heading of 'odd meter', but it is important to note that there are plenty of instances where the meter shifts just to accommodate a shorter or longer phrase, perhaps for the lyrics and melody, or sometimes for a dramatic pause.

This concludes the units dedicated to odd meter. You should now have a grasp on the fundamentals of counting and, more importantly, feeling odd meters. It's all about two things:

- Feeling the larger pulses.
- How the smaller notes are grouped in those larger pulses.

CHART READING

How to Approach a Chart

In this Chart Reading Module, let's talk about how to approach a chart when you see it for the first time. You will see charts in these environments.

- On a gig where you are sight reading.
- At a rehearsal where you see the chart for the very first time and are sight reading.
- At home preparing for a rehearsal or gig.

Regardless of the situation, use a pre-game checklist. If you're on a gig, this needs to be swift and efficient, and the same is true for a rehearsal. If you're at home, you have more time. The pre-game checklist is basically the same regardless of which environment; what's different is how much time you have to go through the list. You can customize the checklist for your personal comfort, but I suggest you consider my suggestion and use it as a starting point as you develop your own checklist.

Chart Checklist

Here is a typical way to look at a chart. It can be done, to some degree, in a few seconds. Obviously, any extra seconds or even minutes that you can spend on this will make you feel more secure.

Take a look at this six-item Chart Checklist.

1. Look at the top left corner where all the preliminary information is:
    a. Key signature: At the very minimum you need to know the key.
    b. Time signature: At the very minimum you need to know the feel.
    c. Style: At the very minimum you need to know the style. This determines the kind of part you play and the tone you use.

    With this information you can at least fake it.

2. Tempo: The drummer will count off the song, but it's important to prepare yourself for the 'tempo attitude' of the song.

3. Scan the form: Form refers to the various sections and in what order they're arranged. I suggest you do this before looking at chords or rhythm figures. Avoid getting lost by scanning the road map. If you're lost, nothing else matters unless it's a really easy song and you can hear the chord changes. Scan the form in reverse hierarchical order. Look for jump marks (DS, DC) first. Then look for start and end repeat signs with endings. And last, look for two-bar and one-bar repeats and simile markings.

4. Seek out any figures that need to be played. These could be rhythm hits the whole band plays together or a riff that you play alone or with other band members. In particular, look at the first and last figures written. The audience will notice the first thing played and the last thing played. You don't want to stumble out of the blocks or crash land at the end.

5. Scan the chords for the ones that are new or difficult for you. The temptation is always to look at the chords first. As your skill with chords develops you will have more confidence that if you see a chord, you can play it. Style determines a lot about the voicings you use. If there are challenging chords, quickly determine a 'Plan B' if necessary. That might include playing just the triad of a tough chord or perhaps playing just the root. Just don't play a wrong chord. You will develop survival 'fake it' skills. Everyone does. Use what you learned in the Rhythm Guitar modules to create an appropriate part 'in the style of'.

6. Seek out more detailed instructions like dynamics, accents, and expression markings.

One of the best phrases you can keep in mind is: *"When in doubt, lay out."* This means that if you are unsure of what to play in a particular passage, *don't play anything*! This is so important. If you play wrong notes and rhythms, it'll probably be heard by someone in the band or audience. If you are silent for a second, at least the wrong stuff won't be played and therefore won't be heard!

Other Markings

There are other tricks of the trade that can be adapted for either physical paper charts or in digital form. These Include things like:

- Personal markings: It's common for each musician to write notes to themselves. These can remind you about a specific fingering or voicing, or they could be alerts about something slightly unusual that could trip you up. If you are reading a from a professional book of charts, it's smart to ask before writing on a chart that belongs to the leader. There could be a lot of cost involved in creating what you're reading and you don't want to be the one who marked it up. In cases where you download the chart or are viewing in digital format, that's not an issue. Personal notes to yourself are commonplace and can make a huge difference.

- Color coding: A special approach to personal markings is color coding. Because colors stand out on a stark white page, highlighting can make a difference. Markings like section markings, repeat signs, endings, DCs, DSs, codas, and other markings tend to blend into the sea of black and white on lengthier and more-involved chord charts. It's helpful to use a highlighter to assist your eyes in navigating the road map. Again, if it's a paper chart, it's always best to ask the leader if it's OK.

Let's practice following the road maps with two charts. This will take some time, but it's worth it to walk through a couple of realistic examples. Keep in mind that many charts you will read in your life will be substandard—and that's being gentle. Just be on your toes for all the 'bad notation' you will certainly face.

In the charts you're about to read you will find most of the topics discussed in this Level's Chart Reading modules. You will see:

- Title
- Indication of Style
- Tempo
- Clef sign
- Key Signature
- Time Signature
- The Form
- Chord changes
- Rhythm figures
- Riffs or ensemble lines

In more detail, you'll also see examples of the following:

- Slash marks
- Slash marks with stems and flags
- Slash marks with stems and beams
- Slash marks that are tied to other slash marks
- Slash marks that represent 8th notes, quarter notes, half notes, and whole notes
- Measures with a combination of slash marks without stems and with stems

You'll also see the various repeat devices like:

- One-bar repeats
- Two-bar repeats
- Simile
- Start and end repeat barlines
- 1st and 2nd endings

You'll also see jump marks like DSs and DCs:

- DS al Coda
- DS al Fine
- DS where you just play on
- DC al Coda
- DC al Fine
- DC where you just play on

You will see notation showing the top note of a voicing as well as transposition markings. There are examples of notation that affect the time like the fermata, railroad tracks, and ritard. There are also examples of accents and dynamics. In other words, these charts have a lot of information in them to help you know how the song should be performed.

Tune #1

Let's discuss Tune #1. There are three versions of this song. Each version has a slightly different form and therefore uses different jump markings. The three versions use the DS marking three ways:

1. DS al Coda
2. DS al Fine
3. DS, where you just play on the second time you come to the place where the DS was

It's important for you to go through each one to make sure you can follow the road map on your own. If you can't follow the repeat notation and jump marks, you'll certainly get lost. Remember, #3 on your checklist says to scan the form.

Your Assignment

Your assignment is to look at each chart and follow all of the repeat and jump mark notation so your eyes will travel through the chart correctly.

1. First, find your way through each chart without looking at the answer key.
2. Next, write down the order of the sections (i.e., Intro, A, A, B, C, A, etc.)
3. Lastly, check the way you think the chart should be read with the matching answer in the Appendix.

(Answer key on page 320)

Fretboard Biology — Level 5 • Unit 10: Chart Reading

What is the order of the sections you would play in this chart?

Tune #1 - DS al Coda

What is the order of the sections you would play in this chart?

Tune #1 - DS al Fine

Fretboard Biology — Level 5 • Unit 10: Chart Reading

What is the order of the sections you would play in this chart?

Tune #1 - DS

Tune #2

Let's move to Tune #2.

Make sure that you understand DC al Coda, DC al Fine, and DC when you just play on. If any of that doesn't make sense, go back and review it again. There are three versions of this song. Each version has a slightly different form and therefore uses different jump markings. The three versions use the DC marking three ways:

1. DC al Coda
2. DC al Fine
3. DC, where you just play on the second time you come to the place where the DC was

It's important for you to go through each one to make sure you can follow the road map on your own. If you can't follow the repeat notation and jump marks, you'll certainly get lost. Remember, #3 on your checklist says to scan the form.

Your Assignment

Your assignment is to look at each chart and follow all of the repeat and jump mark notation so your eyes will travel through the chart correctly.

1. First, find your way through each chart without looking at the answer key.
2. Next, write down the order of the sections (i.e., Intro, A, A, B, C, A, etc.).
3. Lastly, check the way you think the chart should be read with the matching answer in the Appendix.

(Answer key on page 320)

Fretboard Biology — Level 5 • Unit 10: Chart Reading

What is the order of the sections you would play in this chart?

Tune #2 - DC al Coda

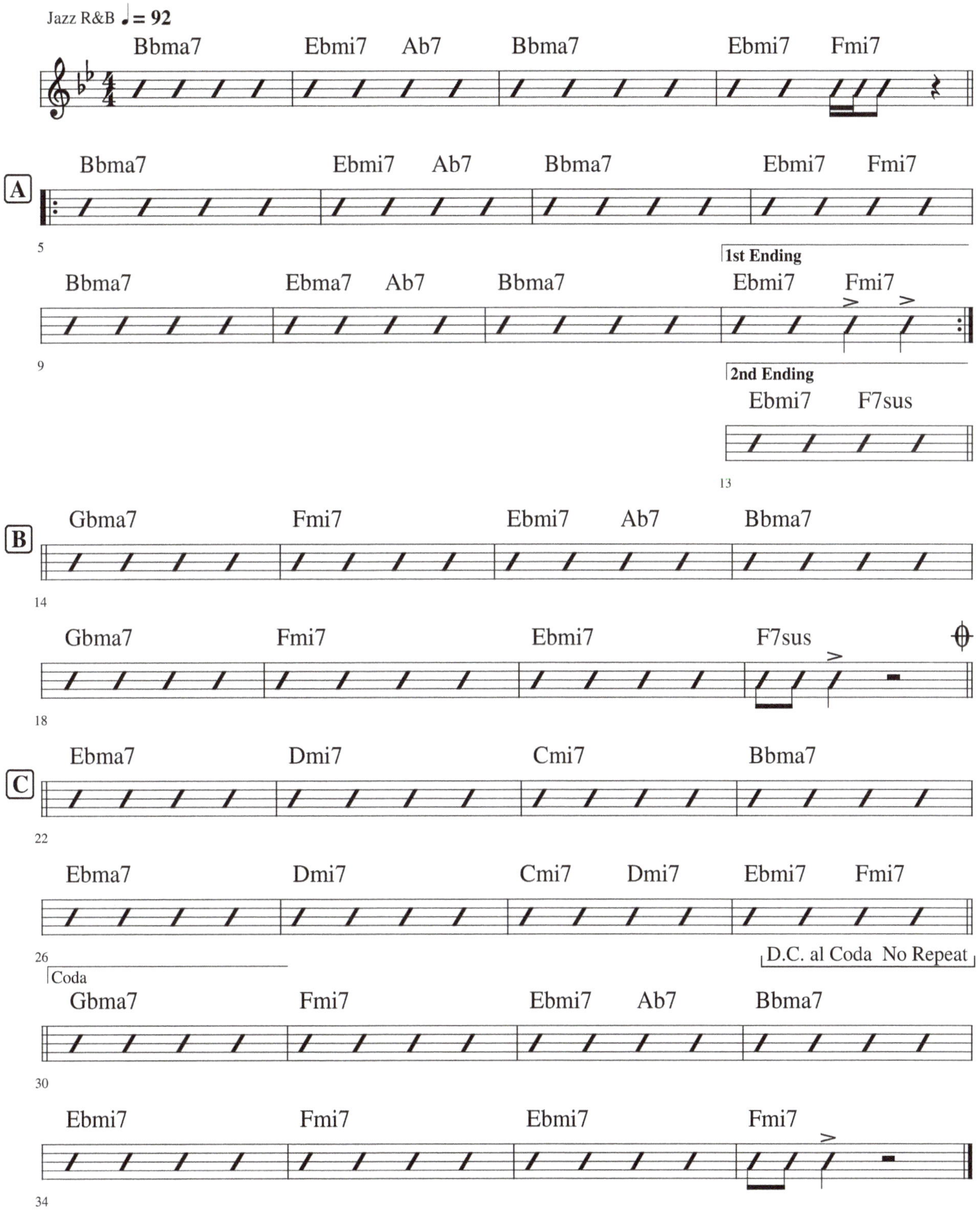

298 Level 5 • Unit 10: Chart Reading — Fretboard Biology

What is the order of the sections you would play in this chart?

Tune #2 - DC al Fine

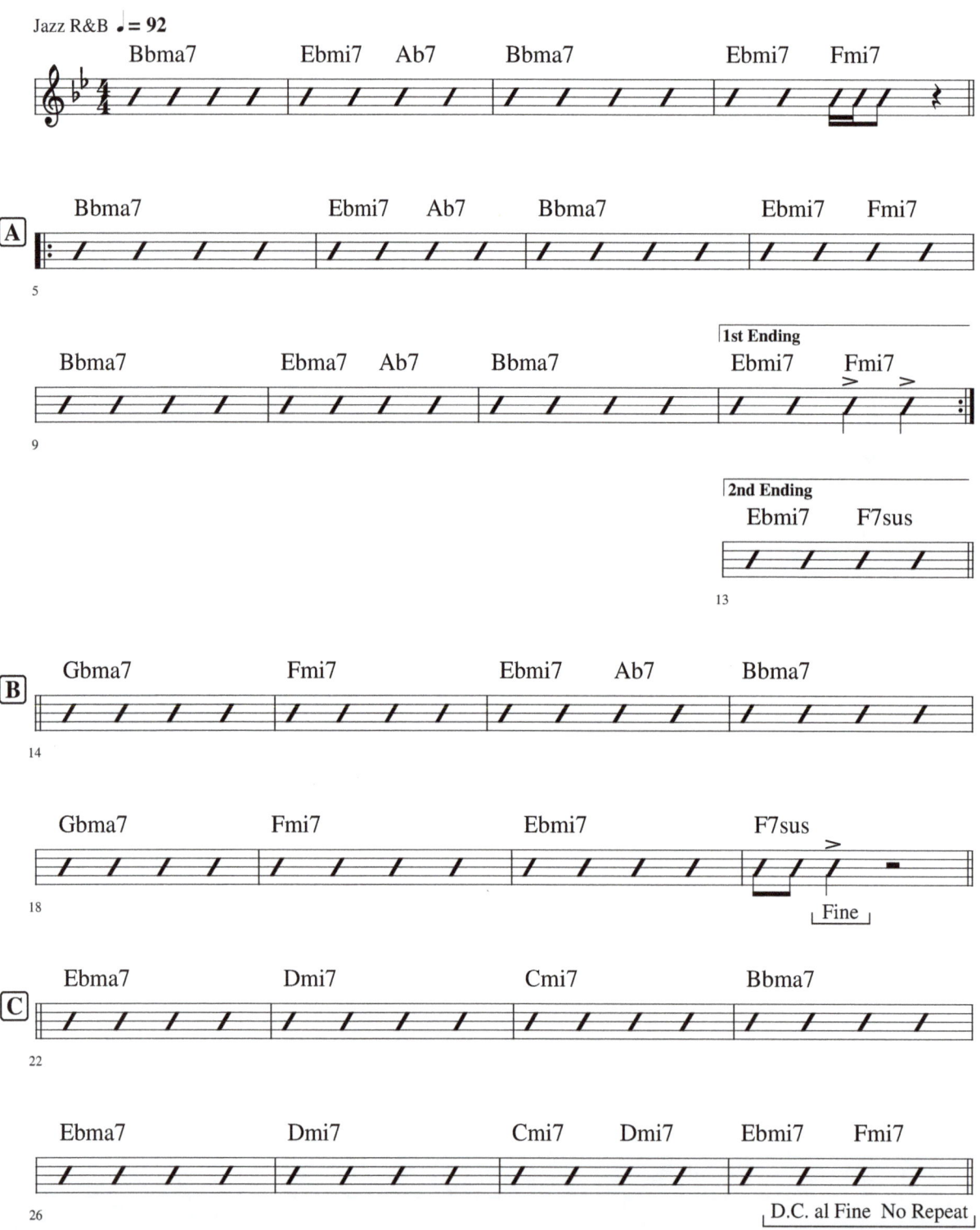

Fretboard Biology — Level 5 • Unit 10: Chart Reading

What is the order of the sections you would play in this chart?

Tune #2 - DC

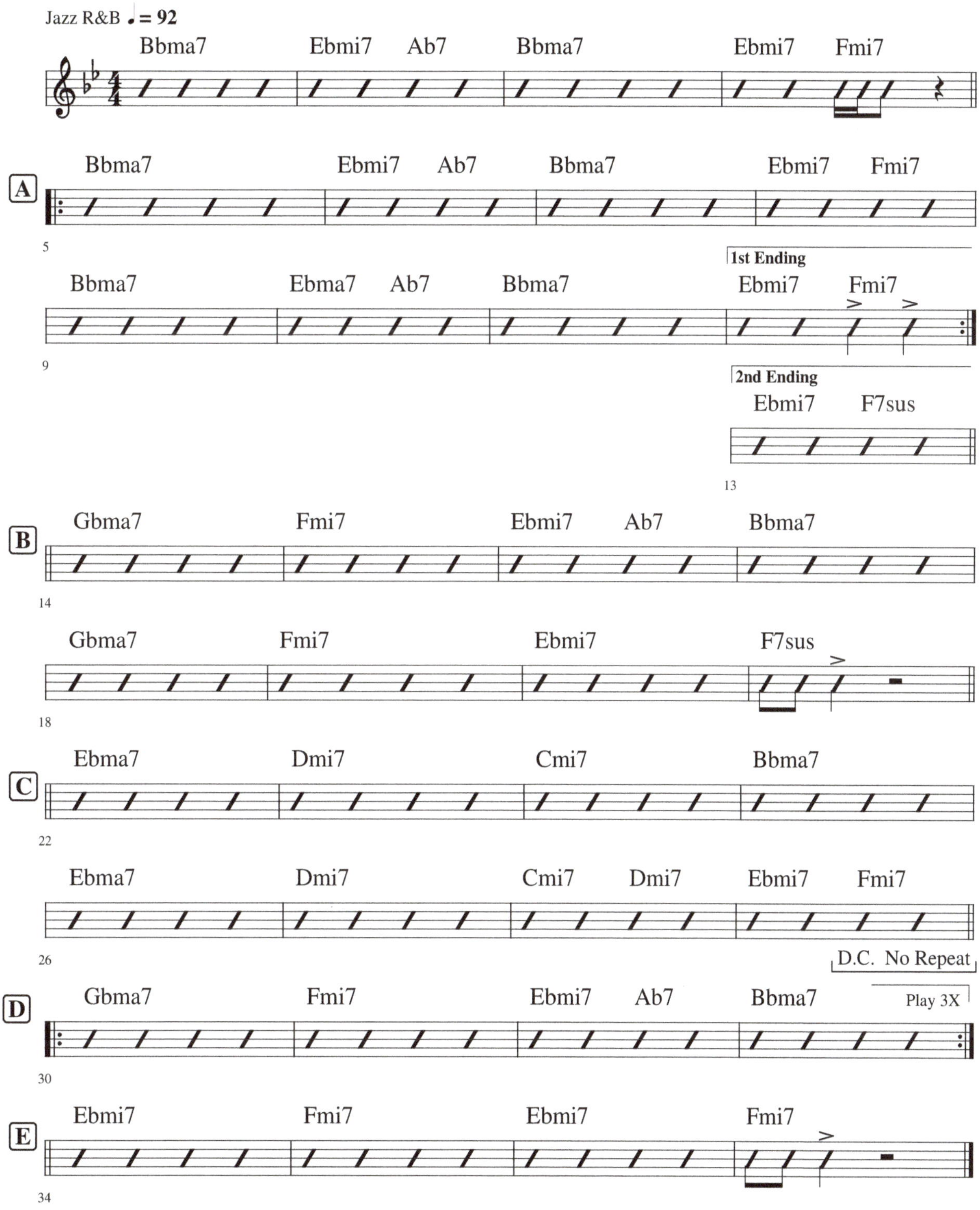

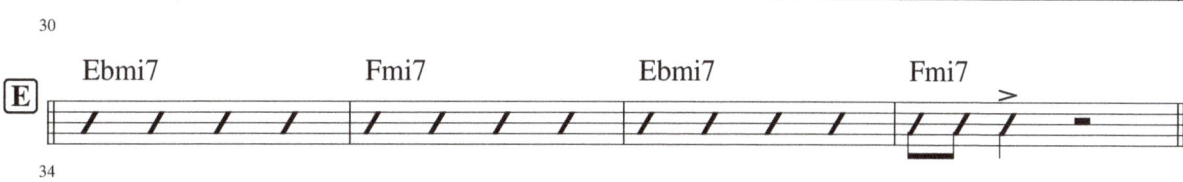

These six charts are basically different versions of two different songs. They're here to show you how to follow a common road map. You need practice reading charts—lots of practice—and some of that will come in Level 6 where the Rhythm Guitar modules focus on chart reading for the various styles you've learned in all the Rhythm Guitar modules going back to Level 1.

Remember that the term 'reading music' can mean a couple of different things. Let's review the two variations of the term that need some clarification: Reading and Sight Reading. These are related but different skills.

'Reading' music means that you are able to decipher notated music and transfer that information to your instrument. You may not be fast at it but you are able associate written music with your instrument. Having this skill opens many doors. You are able to learn notated music whether you have heard it or not. If a leader asks if you can read a chord chart, you can say yes.

'Sight reading' music means you can read and perform music simultaneously. This skill requires a lot of practice. Very few guitarists are skilled sight readers; it's just not the way most guitarists learn. But in larger cities where there are show gigs, theatre gigs, and certain types of session work, there is demand for guitarists who can sight read.

There is another differentiation of terms that is important. Reading a chord chart is one part of reading. Reading single notes or lines on guitar is another part of reading. Far more guitarists learn to read chord charts than single-note lines.

Memorization

There are many performance environments where charts aren't allowed on stage or where reading a chart just looks out of place. So, while you may learn the song by using a chart, you need may need to memorize it. You need a way to get the song off the page and into your head. Sometimes you have ample time to do this but often you need to memorize the music in a hurry.

Here's a tip for memorizing a song. If you count the total number of bars played in a song it might seem overwhelming to memorize but there's a way that makes it easier. Let's look at the last version of Tune #2 and look at the sequence of sections by letter. This form is: *Intro A A B C Intro A B C D D D E*

Fretboard Biology
Level 5 • Unit 10: Chart Reading

Tune #2 - DC

Now look at the number of bars by section:

Section	Bars	Section	Bars
Intro	4	B	8 - that's 66
A	8 - that's 12	C	8 - that's 74
A	8 - that's 20	D	4 - that's 78
B	8 - that's 28	D	4 - that's 82
C	8 - that's 36	D	4 - that's 86
Intro	4 - that's 40	E	4 - that's 90
A	8 - that's 58		

The total number of bars is 90. But do you really have to memorize 90 measures? No You only need memorize:

- The Intro's four bars, which happen twice
- The A section's eight bars, which happen three times
- The B section's eight bars, which happen twice
- The C section's eight bars, which happen twice
- The D section's four bars, which happen three times
- And the E section's four bars, which happen once

That's a total of 36 bars. Plus, the D sections are the first half of the B sections. If you memorize each section and then the order of the sections, you can memorize a lot of music more efficiently. In this example: *Intro A A B C Intro A B C D D D E*

I highly recommend you start to see songs this way whether you're reading or memorizing. Think of the song as a sequence of sections. That way you understand the structure, and memorization is so much easier. It also helps you if you get lost.

This concludes the Level 5 Chart Reading modules. As I mentioned, in the Level 6 Rhythm Guitar modules you'll get more practice reading chord charts. Level 6 also has 10 modules dedicated to creating chord charts. This will prove very useful to you if you lead a group.

We'll see you in the next Level.

IMPROVISATION

In the last Unit you learned to play over secondary dominants in a major-key context. In this Unit you'll learn to play over secondary dominants in a minor-key context. Secondary dominant chords in minor have at least one note that is not diatonic to the key, that is, except for V7/bIII. This means 'key-center soloing' over secondary dominant chords doesn't work. It's important to learn what notes to play on each secondary dominant.

Let's review the secondary dominants in a minor-key context using the key of C minor for this explanation.

- In the key of C minor, V7/bIII is Bb7. All the notes of Bb7 are in the key of C minor.
- In the key of C minor, V7/IV is C7. The E natural in C7 is not in the key of C minor.
- In the key of C minor, V7/V is D7. The F# in D7 is not in the key of C minor.
- In the key of C minor, V7/bVI is Eb7. The Db in Eb7 is not in the key of C minor.
- In the key of C minor, V7/bVII is F7. The A natural in F7 is not in the key of C minor.

Let's return to the main goal: To know what to play on a secondary dominant when soloing in a minor key. Remember, you can always play the arpeggio because the arpeggio is an exact reflection of the chord: The arpeggio is made up of the chord tones.

The focus of this Module is to know the appropriate chord scales for each of the secondary dominants, but now in a minor context. The same 'normal-sounding' scale choices you learned in a major context apply in minor.

What to play over secondary dominants can be made simple:

- Over secondary dominants that are V7 of chords that are normally minor, the Harmonic Minor Scale of the minor chord it's V of, is the inside-sounding scale choice. That's V/IV and V/V. And you learned you can play the Dominant b9 b13 Scale of the dominant chord. Remember the close relationship between Harmonic Minor and the Dominant b9 b13 Scales.
- For secondary dominants that are V of major chords, the Major Scale of the next is an appropriate choice. That's V/bIII, V/bVI, and V/bVII.

The logistical challenge is to find the chord scale for the secondary dominant in the same area of the fretboard where you find the notes to play over the other chords. You need to locate and play the secondary dominant chord scale in-position with the diatonic scale as you are playing over the other chords. So let's use these secondary dominant chord scales over each of the five secondary dominants. To make this as manageable as possible, these progressions are all in the key of C minor and we'll use Octave Shape IV where we are already very comfortable. Don't think too hard on the diatonic chords. For now, key center is fine. Your focus is on the secondary dominant.

Progression 1 - V7/♭III

Progression in C Minor

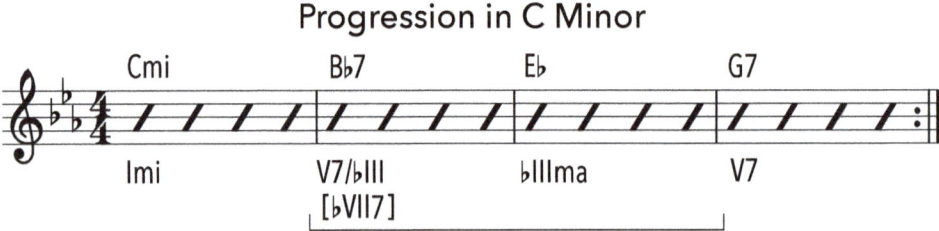

For Progression 1, locate the Pattern IV C Minor Scale in 8th position. You are comfortable playing the Minor Pentatonic Scale, the Minor Scale, and all the diatonic chords in-position. And, of course, play the C Harmonic Minor Scale on the V7 chord, the G7.

Progression in C Minor

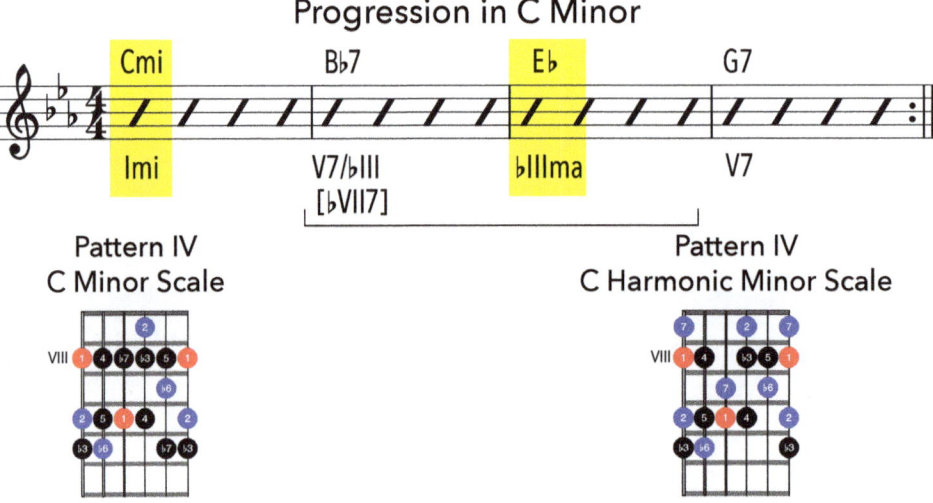

But what about B♭7? Because B♭7 is V7/♭III, and ♭III is major, the E♭ Major Scale is the inside-sounding scale choice. So locate the E♭ Major Scale in the same area of the fretboard.

Progression in C Minor

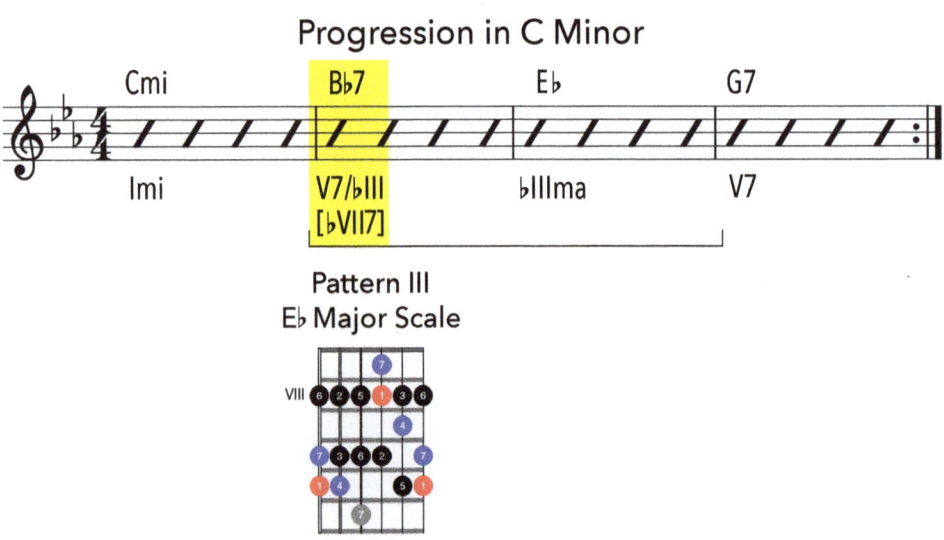

Fretboard Biology — Level 5 • Unit 10: Improvisation

This is in 8th position. You know an E♭ Major Scale in 8th position. This could be B♭ Mixolydian, too. Remember, they're the same notes. It happens to be that these are the same notes as C Minor. E♭ Major or B♭ Mixolydian both have the same notes as C Minor, so no movement is necessary.

This particular chord movement, from ♭VII to ♭III in a minor tonality, is naturally strong. It resembles a modulation (change of key) to the key of the ♭III chord. And consider this: the ♭III chord is the relative major of the key. E♭ major and C minor are relative keys. So when ♭VII moves to ♭III in a minor key, it feels like a temporary modulation to the relative major.

Level 5 Unit 10 • Improv Demo #1

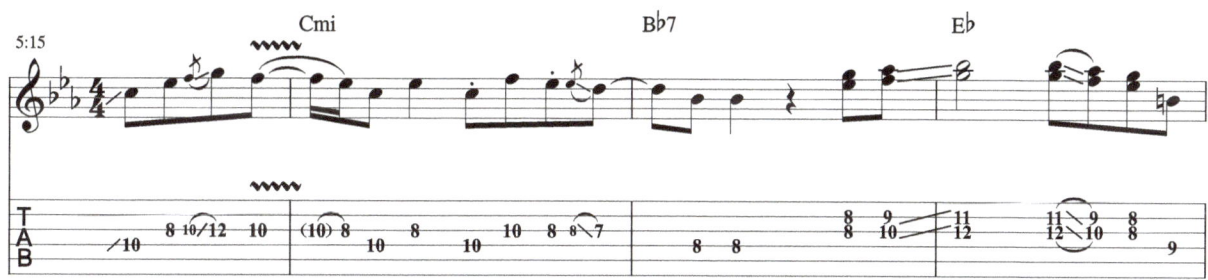

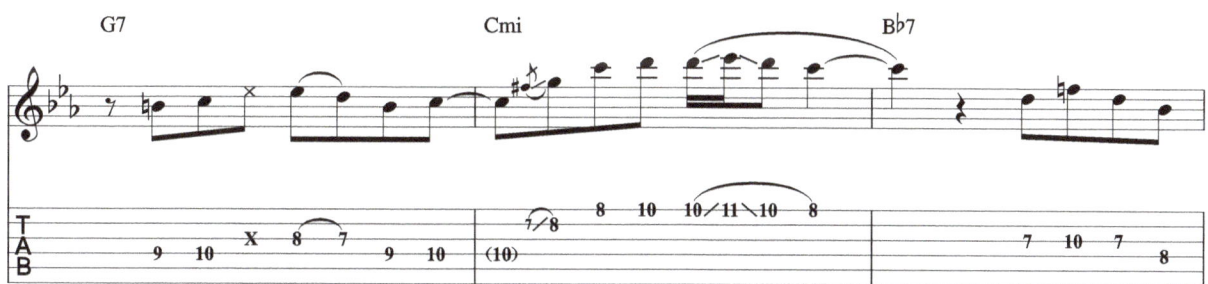

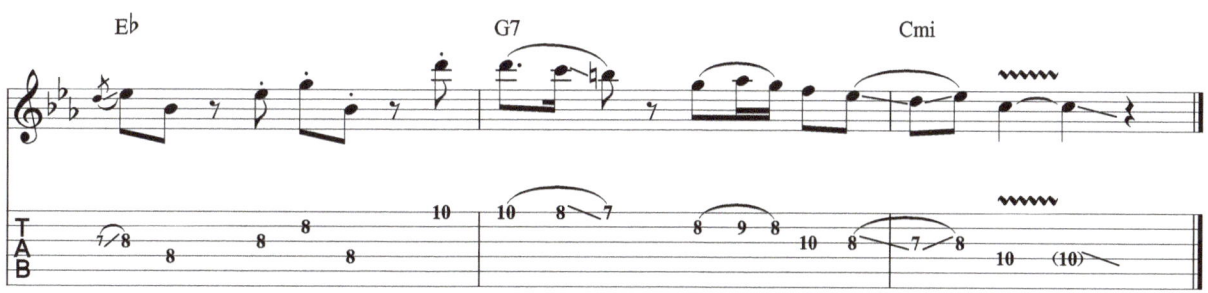

Progression 2 - V7/IV

Progression in C Minor

For Progression 2, stay with the Pattern IV C Minor Octave Shape. Again, you can play all of your diatonic options in-position.

Progression in C Minor

**Pattern IV
C Minor Scale**

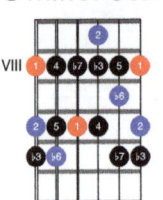

But what about C7? Because C7 is V7/IV, and IV is minor, F minor, the F Harmonic Minor Scale is the inside-sounding chord scale. So locate the F Harmonic Minor Scale in the same area of the fretboard. This is in 8th position. Remember that this could be C Dominant ♭9 ♭13, too; they're the same notes.

Progression in C Minor

**Pattern II
F Harmonic Minor Scale**

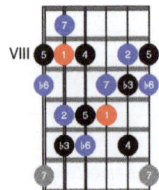

Play this very slowly and deliberately. Remember, the secondary dominant chord scale is played only for the duration of the chord. Return to the diatonic scale or a chord tone of the next chord on the next chord.

Level 5 Unit 10 • Improv Demo #2

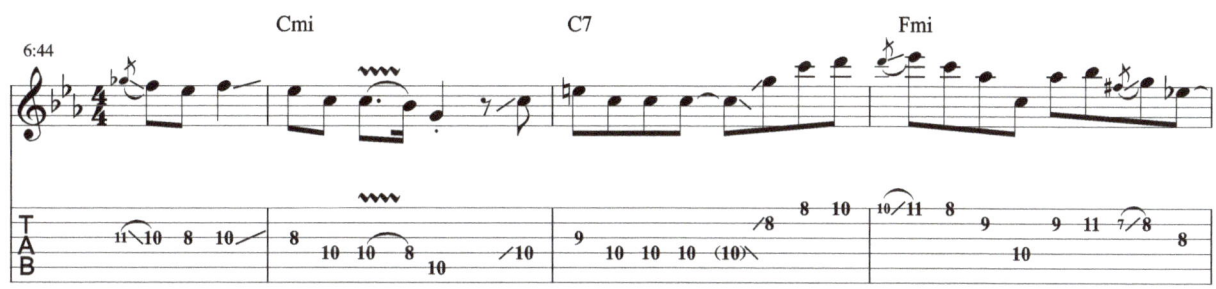

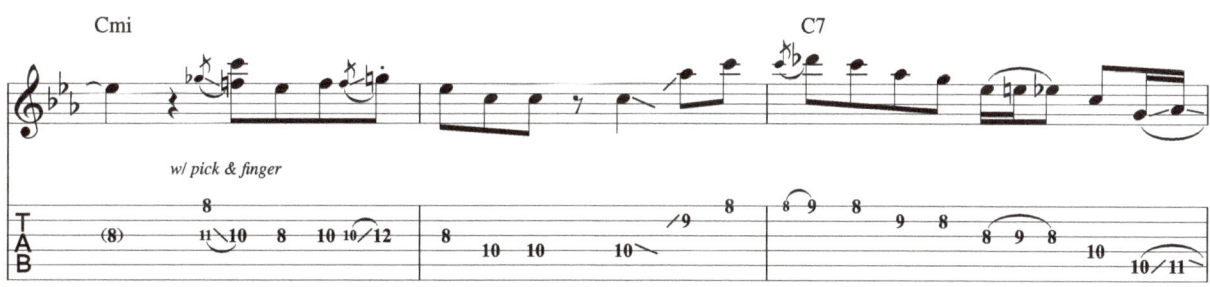

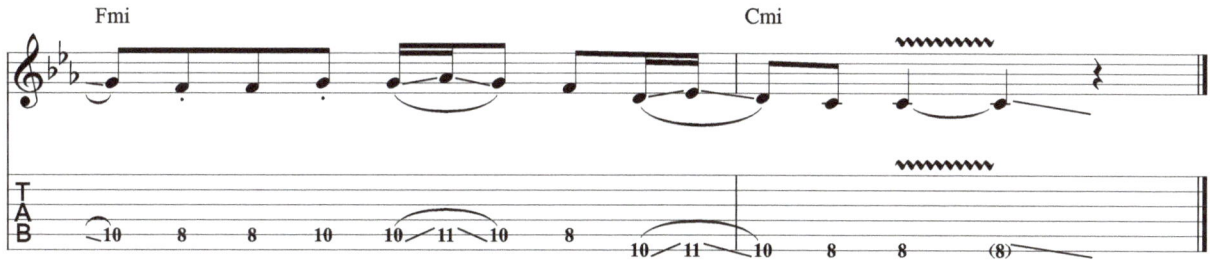

Progression 3 - V7/V

Progression in C Minor

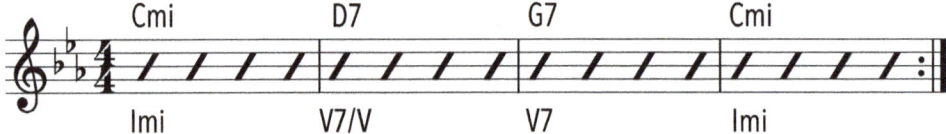

For Progression 3, stay in the Pattern IV C Minor Octave Shape. Again, you can play all of your diatonic options in-position with the C Natural Minor Scale. Play the C Harmonic Minor Scale on the V7 chord, the G7

Progression in C Minor

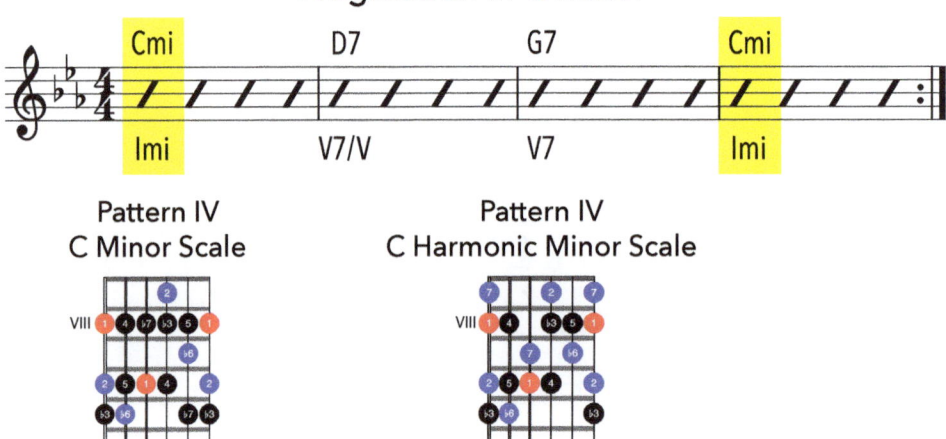

But, D7 is a secondary dominant and has a non-diatonic note. So since D7 is V7 of G7, the G Harmonic Minor Scale is the chord scale of choice. Locate the G Harmonic Minor Scale in the same area of the fretboard. This is in 8th position. This could be D Dominant ♭9 ♭13, too; they're the same notes.

Progression in C Minor

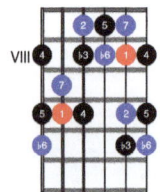

Practice this very slowly and remember the secondary dominant chord scale and the primary dominant sound is played only for the duration of the chord.

Level 5 Unit 10 • Improv Demo #3

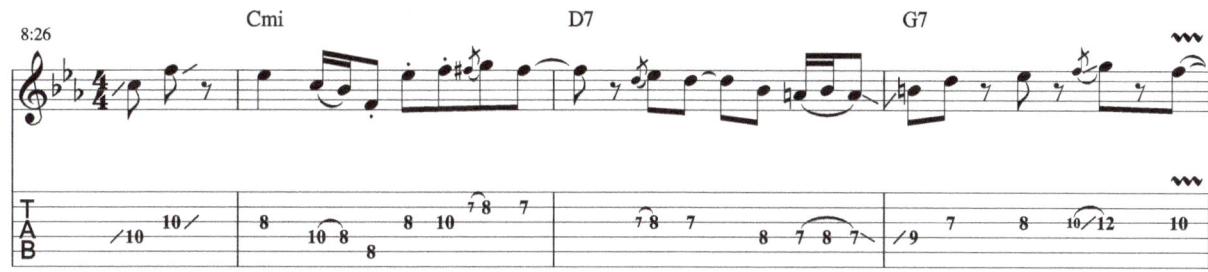

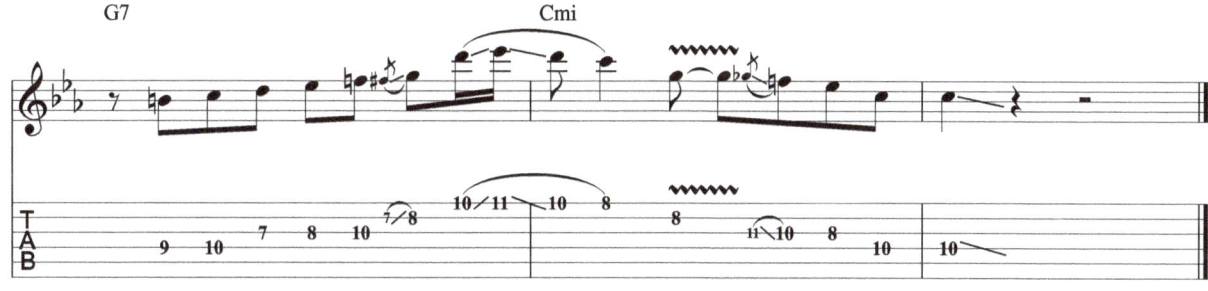

Progression 4 - V7/♭VI

Progression in C Minor

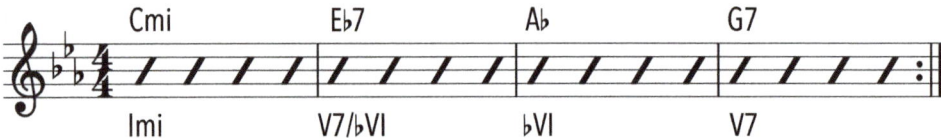

For Progression 4, again, stay in the pattern IV C Minor Octave Shape. As in the other examples, play all of your diatonic options in-position. Like in the other progressions, play the C Harmonic Minor Scale on the V7 chord, the G7

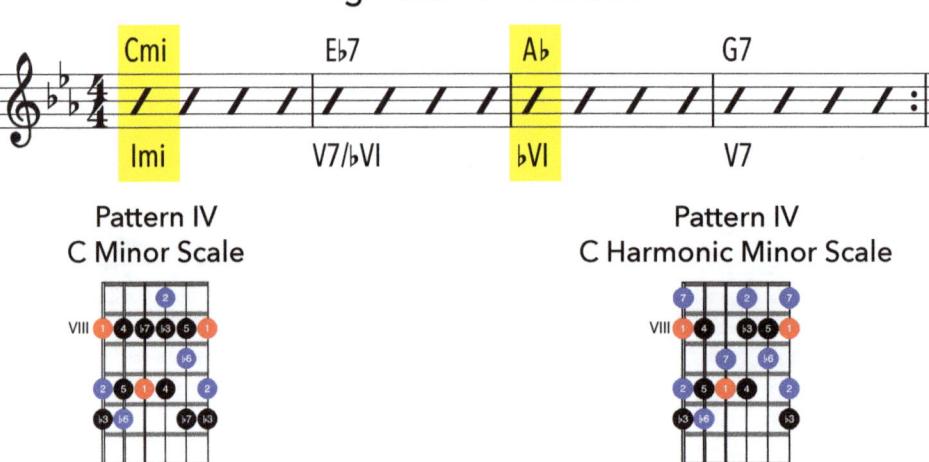

But what about the E♭7? Since E♭7 is V7/♭VI, and ♭VI is major, the A♭ Major Scale is the inside-sounding scale choice. This could be E♭ Mixolydian, too; they're the same.

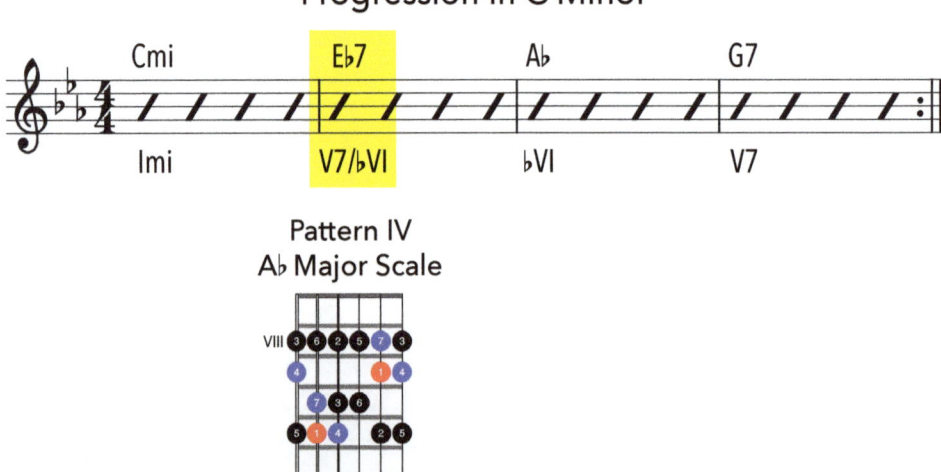

As always, remember the secondary dominant chord scale and the primary dominant sound is played only for the duration of the chord.

Level 5 Unit 10 • Improv Demo #4

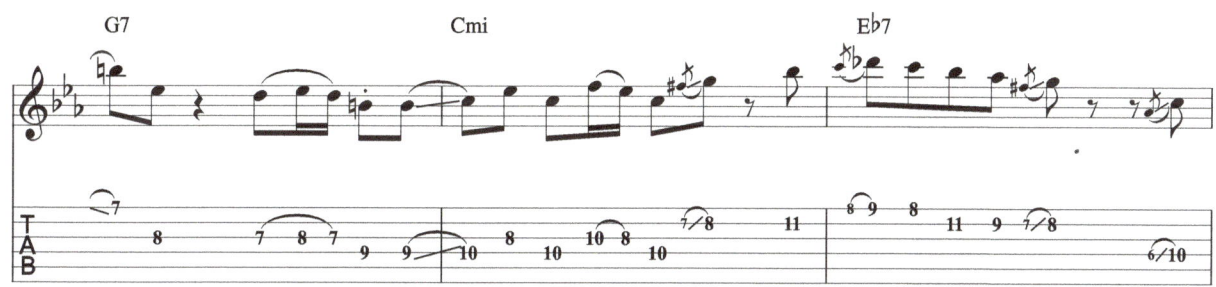

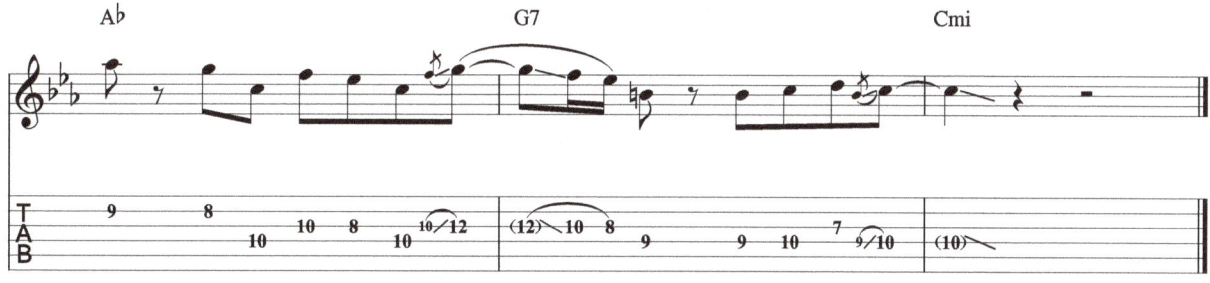

Progression 5 - V7/♭VII

Progression in C Minor

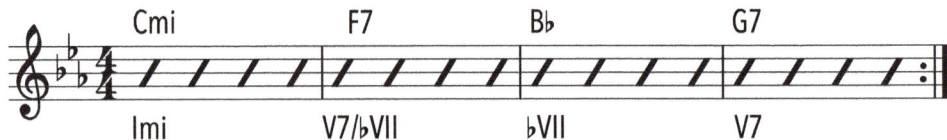

Here is Progression 5. Again, stay in the Pattern IV C Minor Octave Shape with all of your diatonic options in-position. And, of course, play the C Harmonic Minor Scale on the V7 chord, the G7

Progression in C Minor

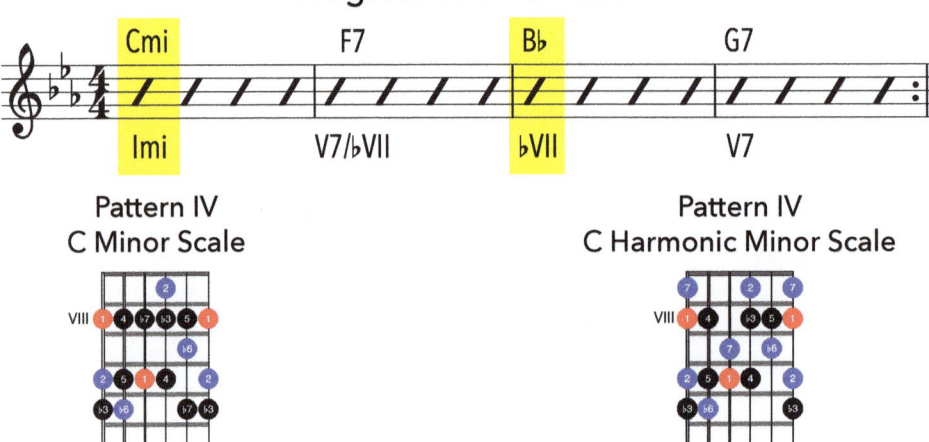

What about F7? Since F7 is V7/♭VII, and ♭VII is major, the appropriate scale choice would be the B♭ Major Scale. Do you know a B♭ Major Scale in 8th position? Yes, you do. Remember, this could be F Mixolydian, too; they're the same notes.

Progression in C Minor

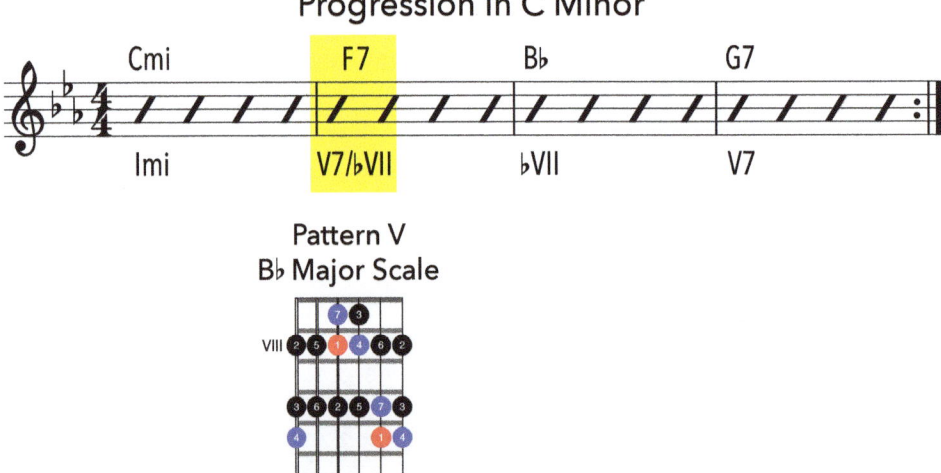

As before, practice this very slowly and deliberately, and remember to play the secondary dominant chord scale only for the duration of the chord.

Level 5 Unit 10 • Improv Demo #5

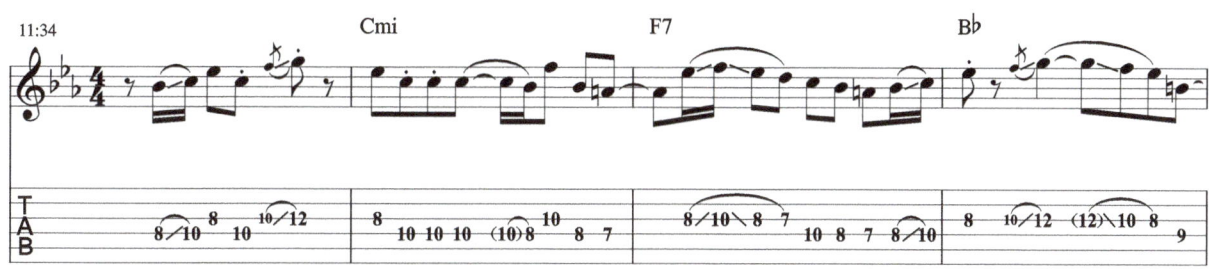

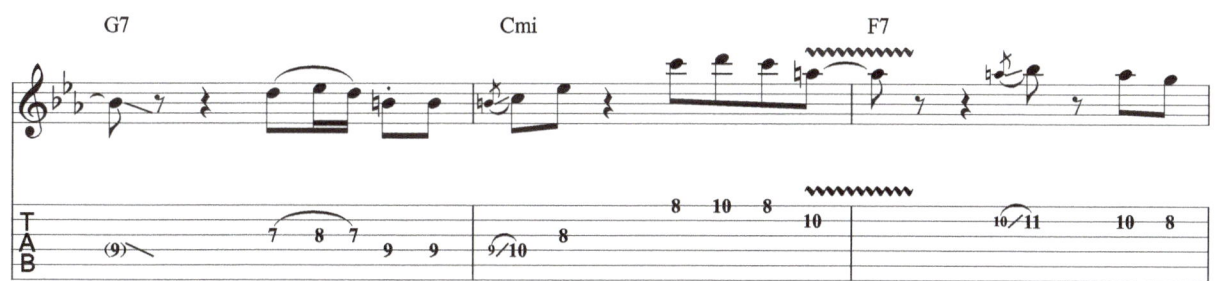

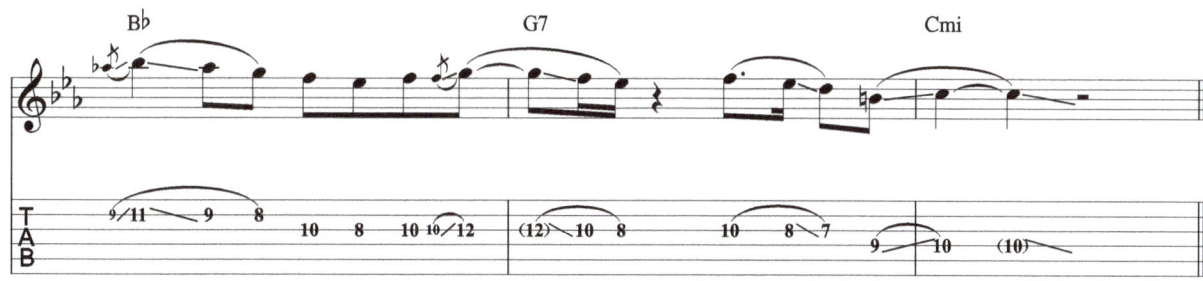

This is a lot to remember. As I said in Unit 9, it's more important to understand the reasoning behind how we find the chord scales needed for each secondary dominant. This can be done in all of the five minor scale octave shapes. Don't expect to learn all of this in all octave shapes quickly, but it is a good idea to go through the steps of reasoning we just followed in every octave shape to test your understanding.

Here is the short list of how to reason your way to a chord-scale solution for secondary dominants again:

- Over secondary dominants that are V7 of chords that are normally minor, the Harmonic Minor Scale of the minor chord it's V of, is the inside-sounding scale choice. And you learned that's the same as the Dominant ♭9 ♭13 scale of the dominant chord.
- For secondary dominants that are V7 of major chords, the Major Scale of the next chord is an appropriate choice. And these are the same notes as the Mixolydian Scale of the secondary dominant.
- Next determine the octave shape where you will play the diatonic notes.
- Next determine the correct chord scale for the secondary dominant in the progression.
- Last find the chord scale pattern in-position with the diatonic scale or as close as possible.

Remember this short list and you will be able to reason your way to the solution every time. That's really the goal of the whole Fretboard Biology program: To make you self-reliant.

This concludes the Level 5 Improvisation modules. You learned a lot about the Harmonic Minor Scale and its use, more than is practical to summarize here. As you travel deeper and deeper into the program, your intellectual knowledge will outpace your ability to actually do all the things you learn.

That's normal. That's OK.

Strive to be self-reliant with respect to theory and the fretboard matrix, and with a well-planned practice routine you will work to gradually gain control of the knowledge.

PRACTICE

Theory

- ☐ Go through the harmonic analysis exercise for each of the progressions and check your answers in the back of the book.

Fretboard Logic

- ☐ Learn the in-position 7th-chord voicings for the harmonized Harmonic Minor Scale.

Rhythm Guitar

- ☐ Understand the note groupings for 13/8 time.
- ☐ Practice playing the 13/8 progression in G major.

Chart Reading

- ☐ Understand how to approach a chart and use the Chart Checklist.
- ☐ Go through each chart and write down the order of the sections (the form), then check your answers in the back of the book.

Improvisation

- ☐ Practice playing solos over the progressions in C minor using the appropriate chord scale over the secondary dominant chord in each progression.

Appendices

- > **Appendix 1** - Exercise Answer Keys
- > **Appendix 2** - Table of Inverted Intervals
- > **Appendix 3** - Shell Voicings
- > **Appendix 4** - Root Maps
- > **Appendix 5** - Chord Charts

Unit 1 Theory - Chord Identification Answer Key

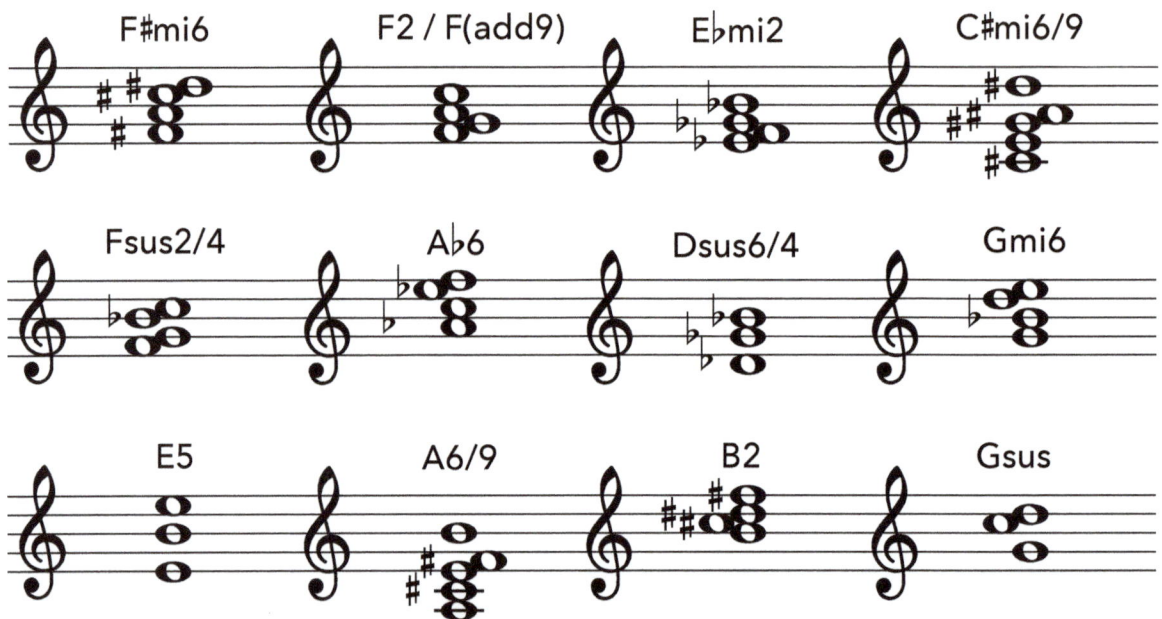

Unit 1 Theory - Chord Construction Answer Key

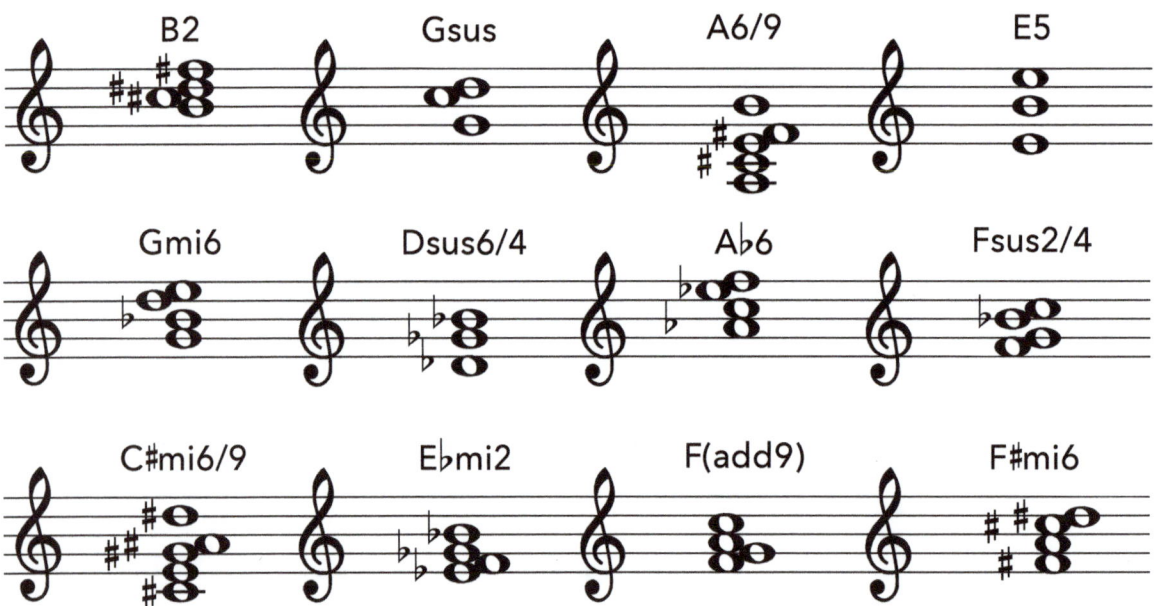

Unit 1 Fretboard Logic - Sus4 Chord Answer Key

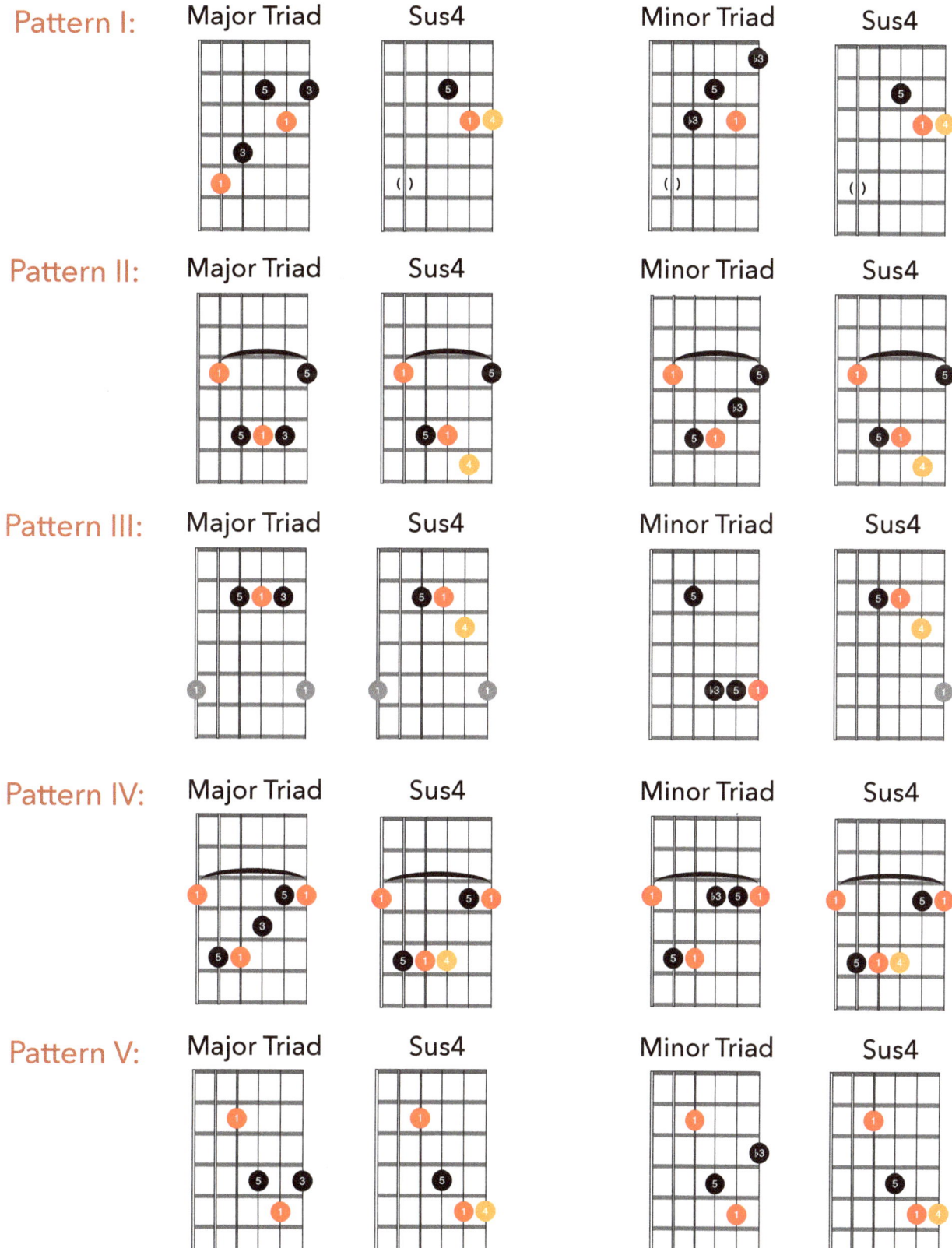

320 Appendix 1: Answer Keys — Fretboard Biology

Unit 1 Fretboard Logic - 7sus4 Chord Answer Key

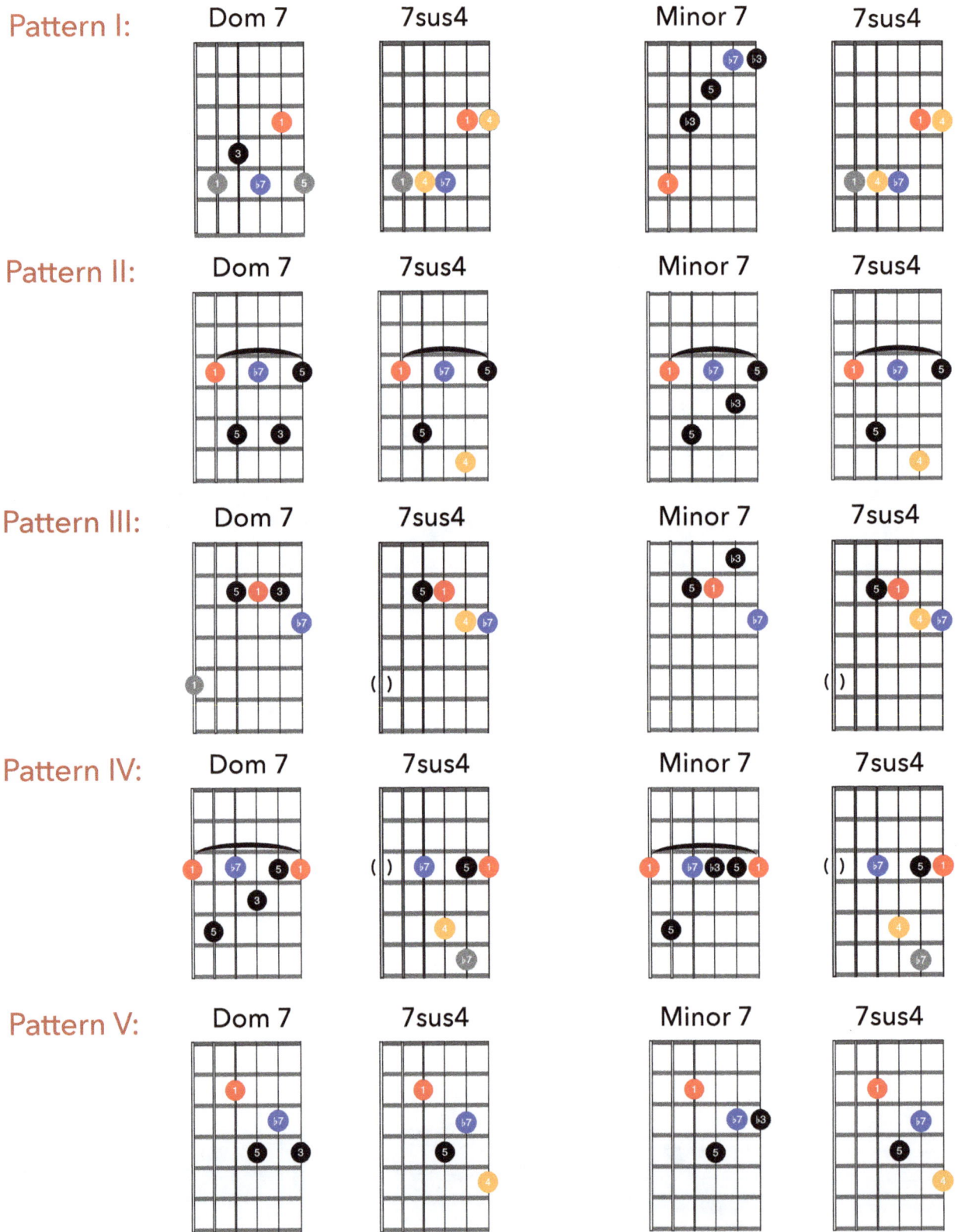

Unit 1 Fretboard Logic - Sus2 Chord Answer Key

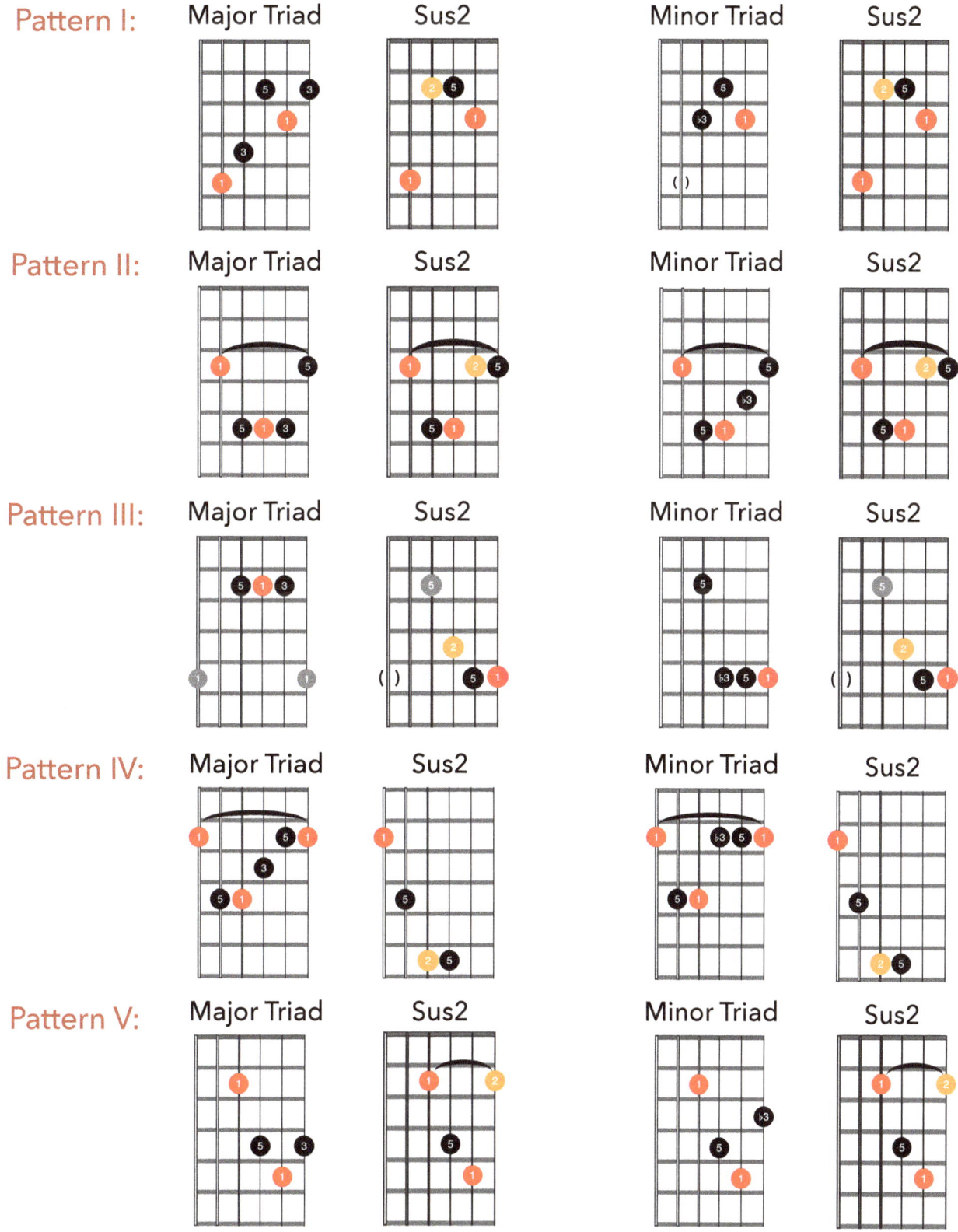

322 Appendix 1: Answer Keys — Fretboard Biology

Unit 1 Fretboard Logic - Sus6/4 Chord Answer Key

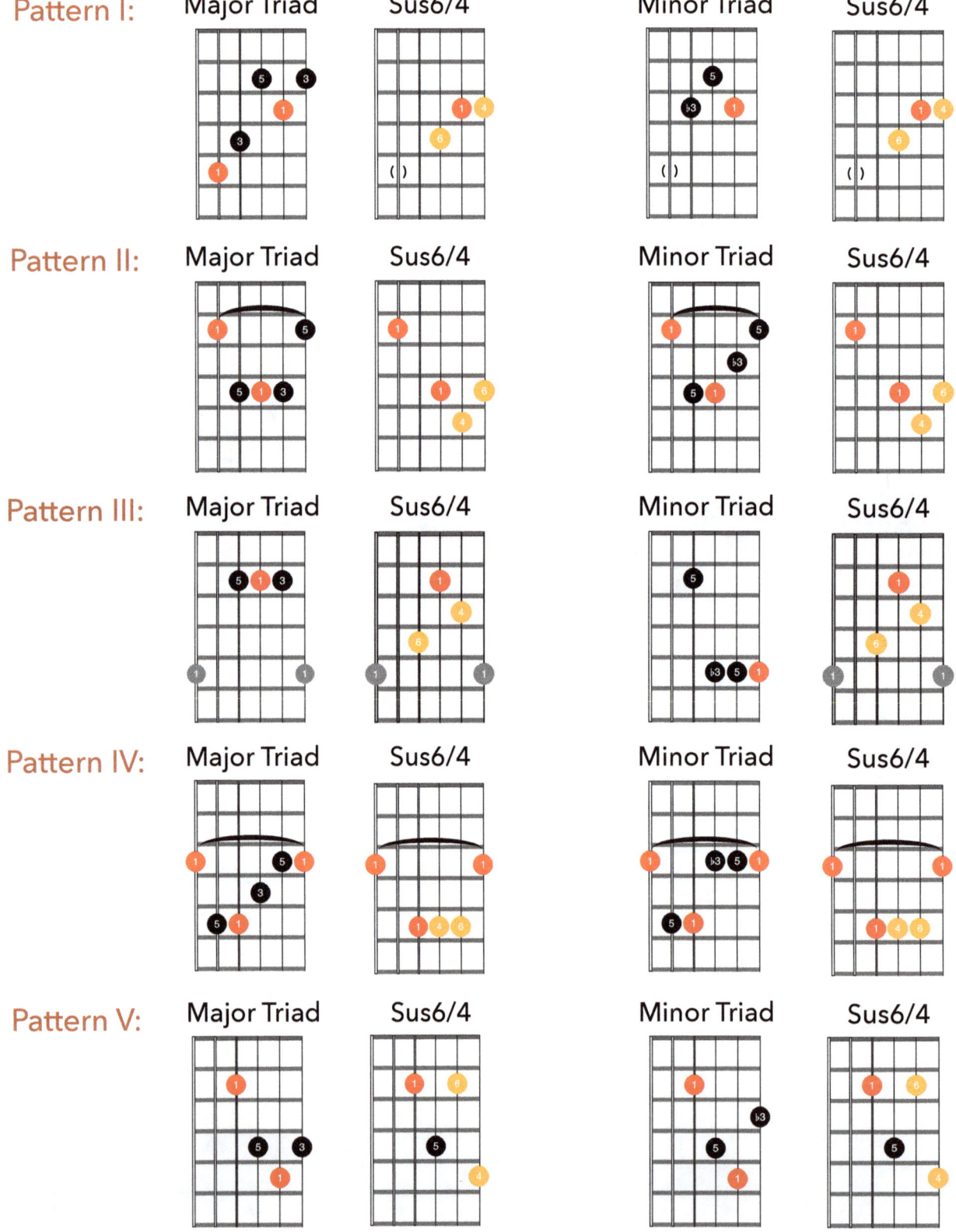

Fretboard Biology — Appendix 1: Answer Keys

Unit 1 Fretboard Logic - Sus2/4 Chord Answer Key

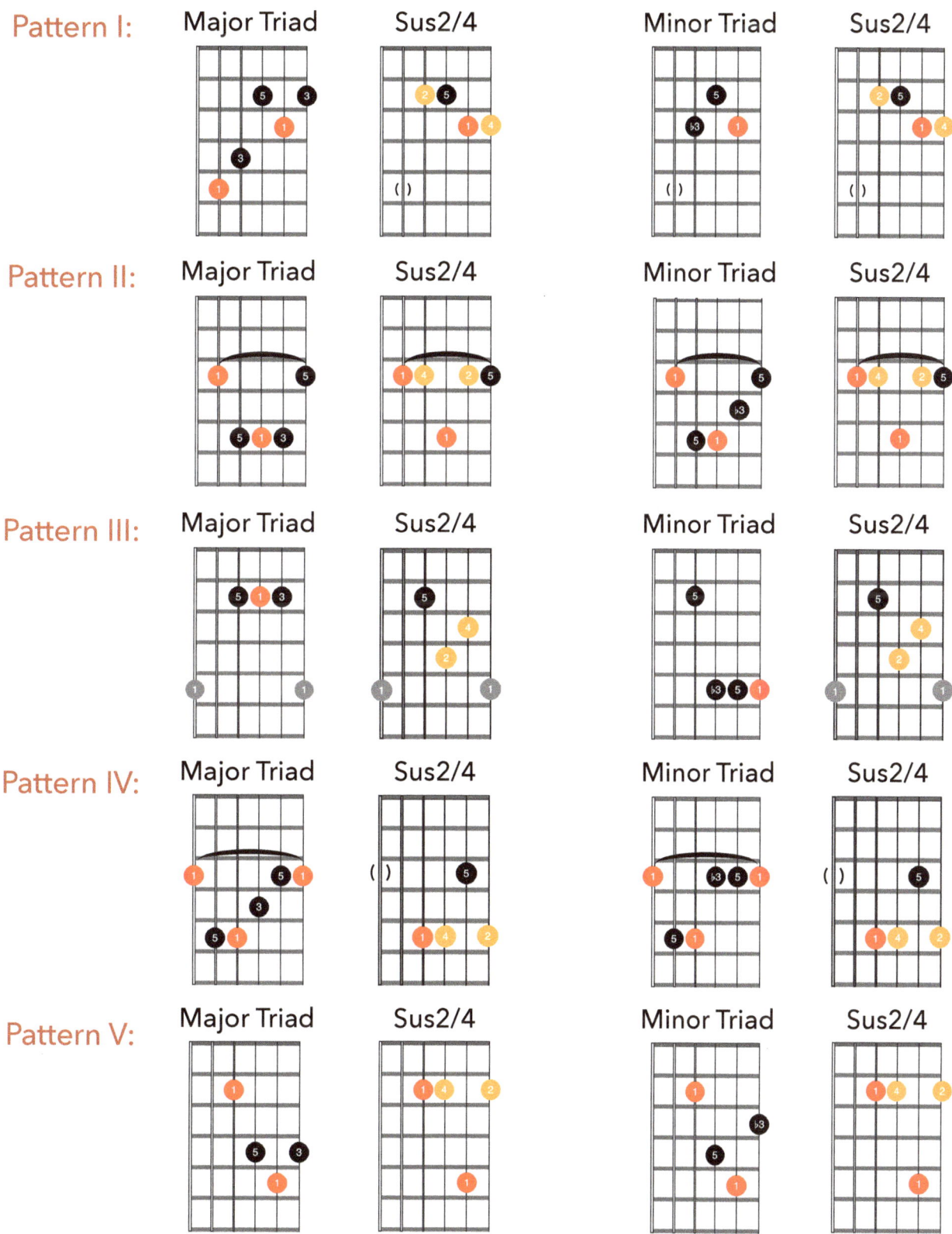

Unit 1 Fretboard Logic - 2 Chord Answer Key

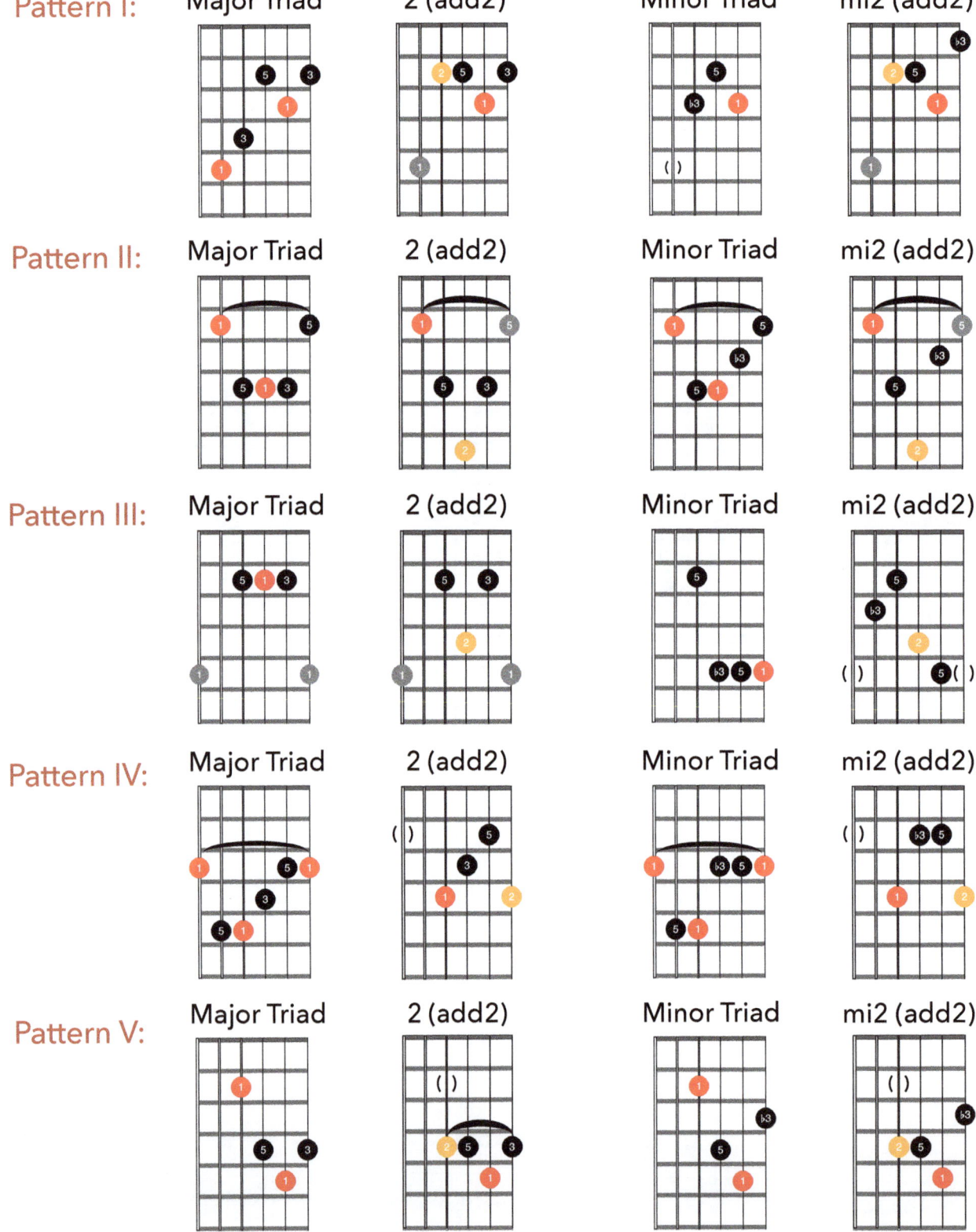

Unit 1 Fretboard Logic - 6 Chord Answer Key

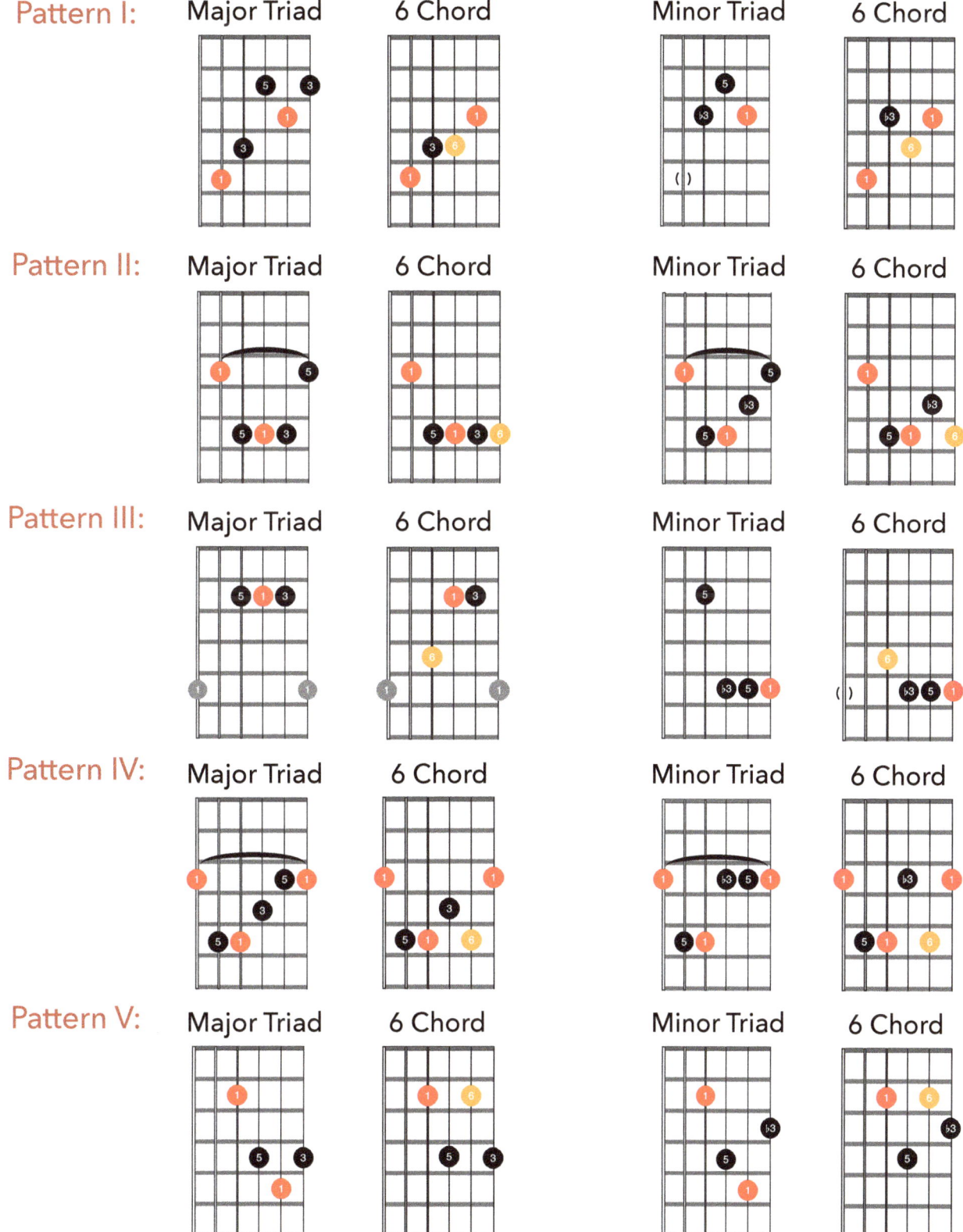

Unit 1 Fretboard Logic - 6/9 Chord Answer Key

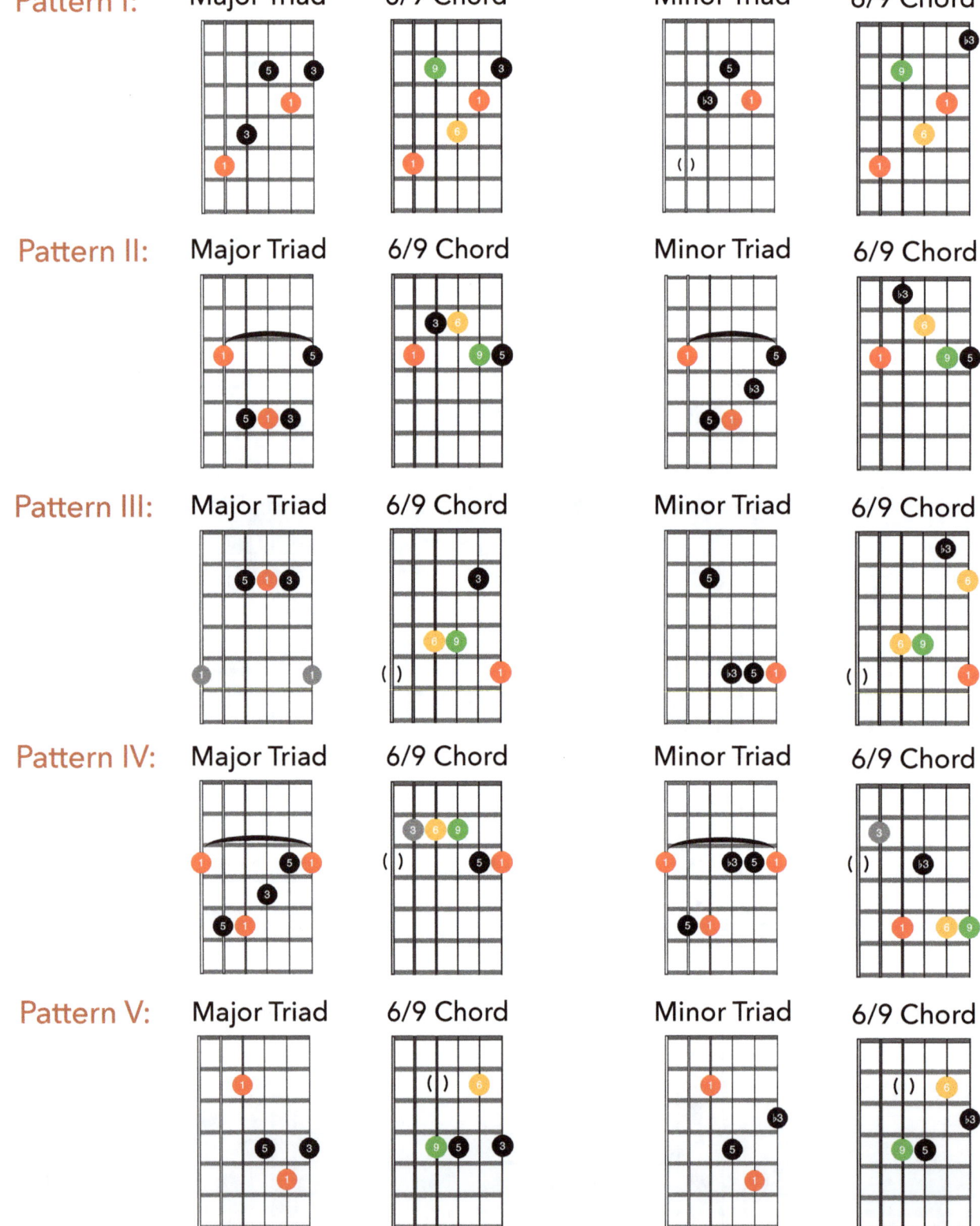

Unit 1 Fretboard Logic - 5 Chord (Power Chord) Answer Key

Pattern II: Major Triad | 5 Chord | Minor Triad | 5 Chord

Pattern IV: Major Triad | 5 Chord | Minor Triad | 5 Chord

Pattern V: Major Triad | 5 Chord | Minor Triad | 5 Chord

Unit 6 Fretboard Logic - Chord Voicing Answer Key

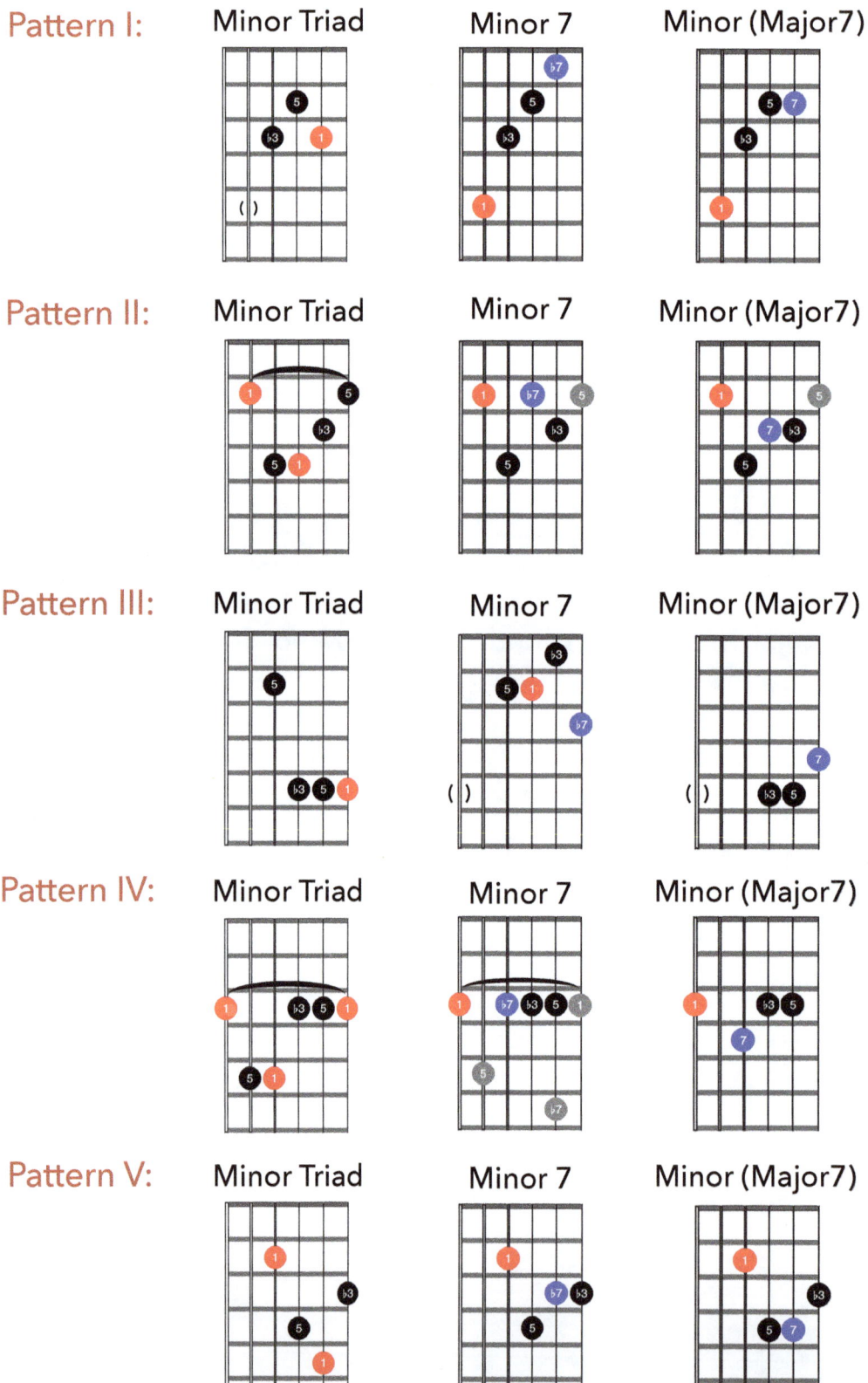

Unit 6 Fretboard Logic - Arpeggio Voicing Answer Key

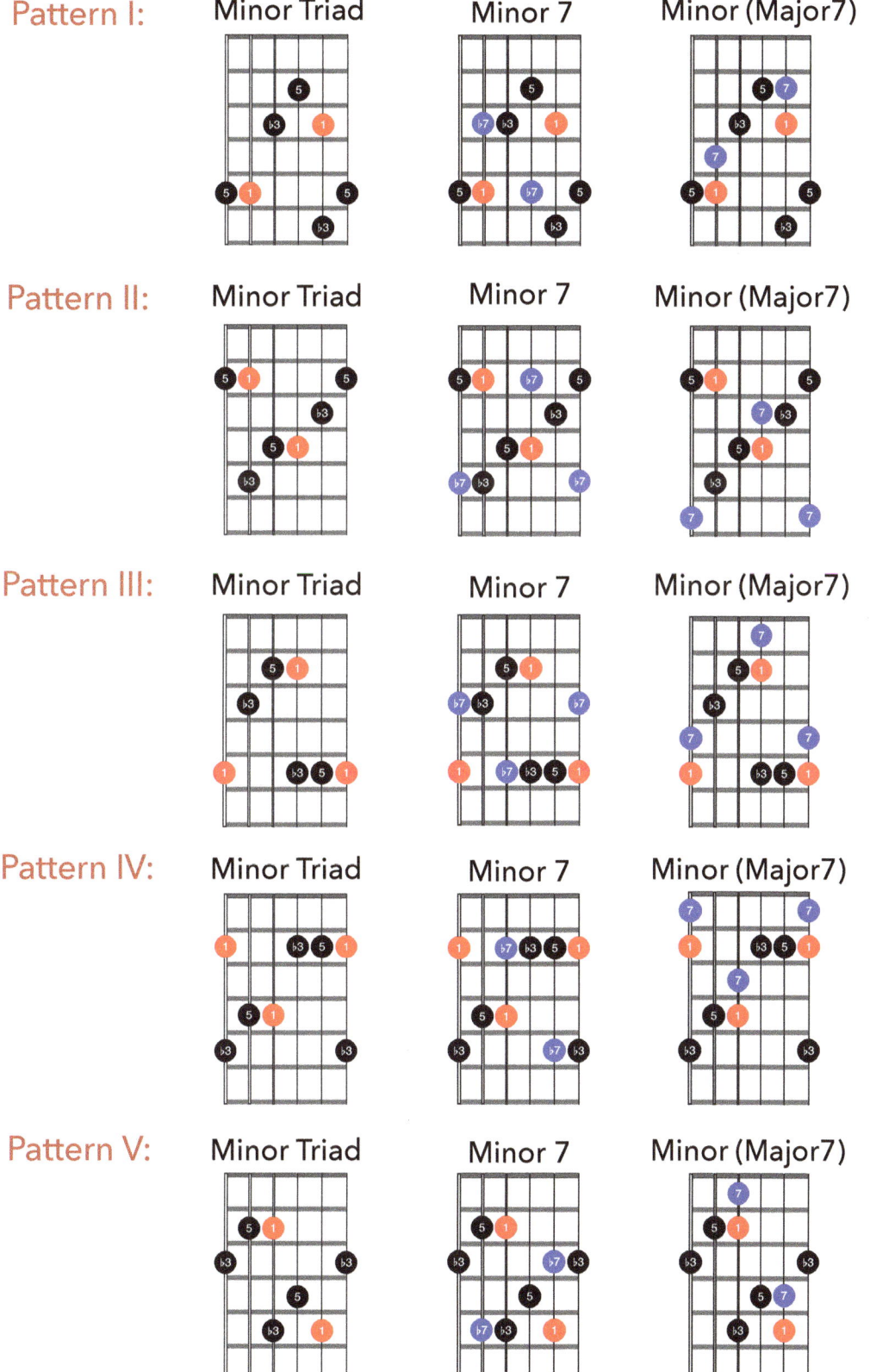

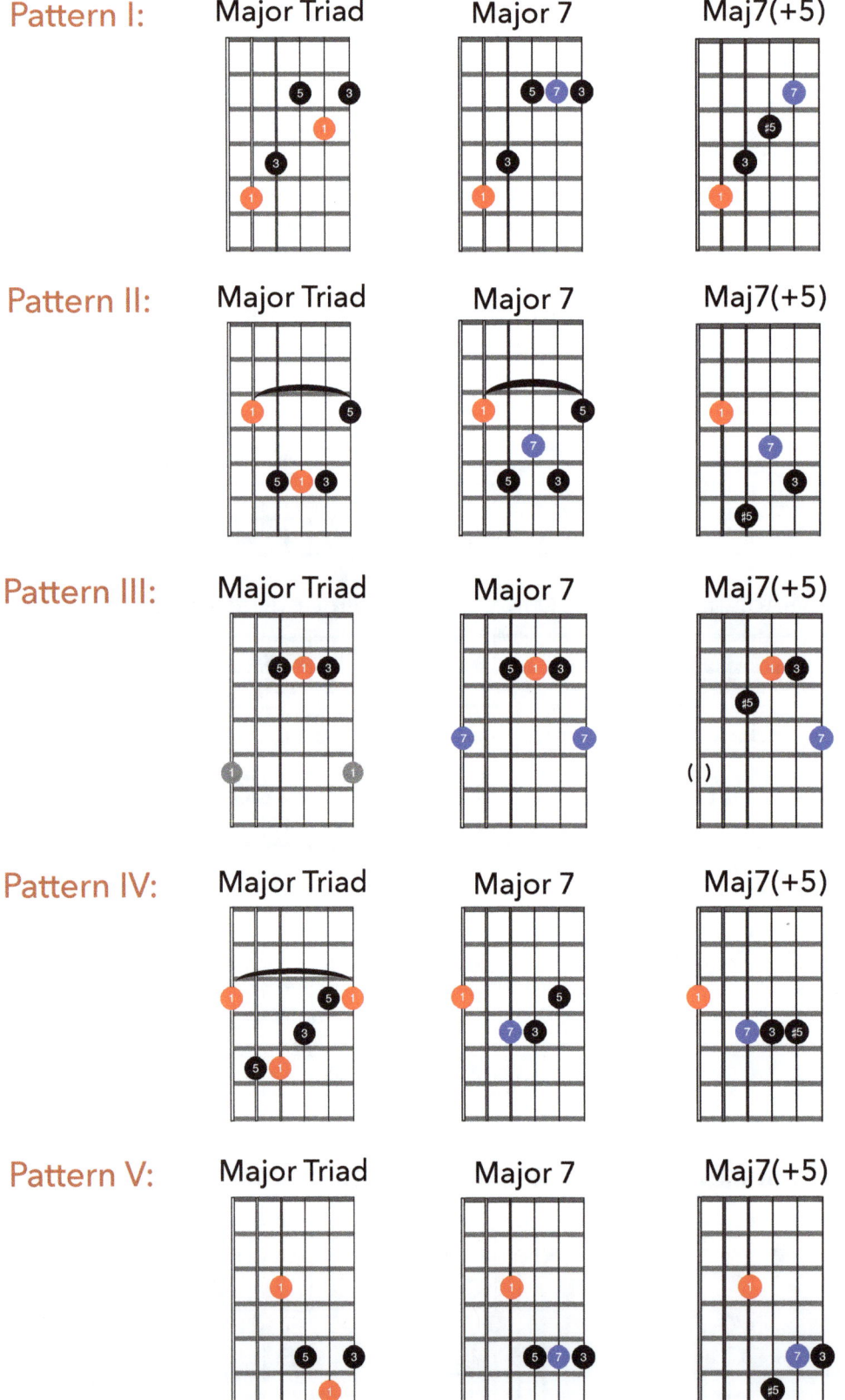

Unit 7 Fretboard Logic - Arpeggio Voicing Answer Key

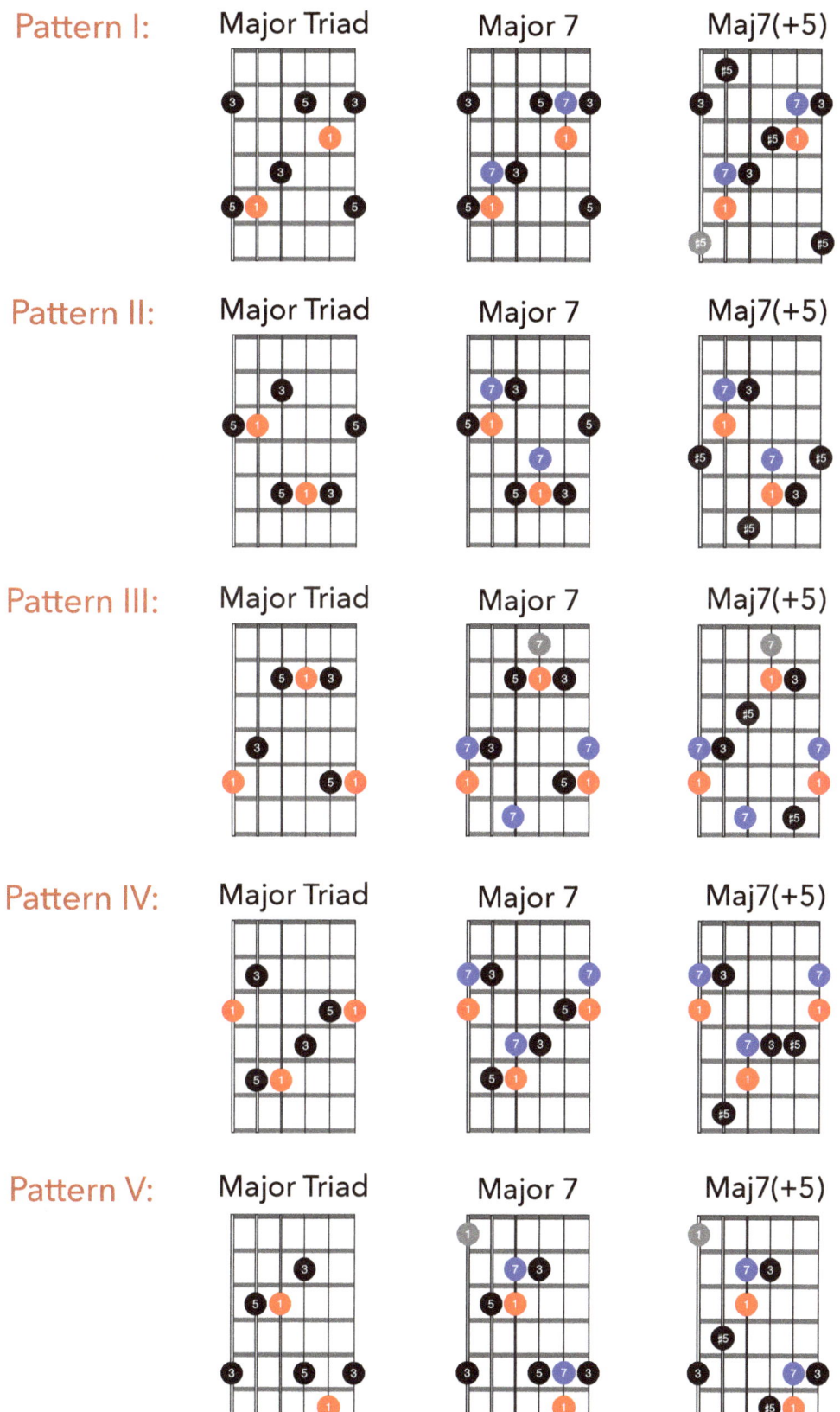

Unit 10 Theory - Progression Analysis - Group 1

Progression 1 - G Major

Progression 2 - A♭ Major

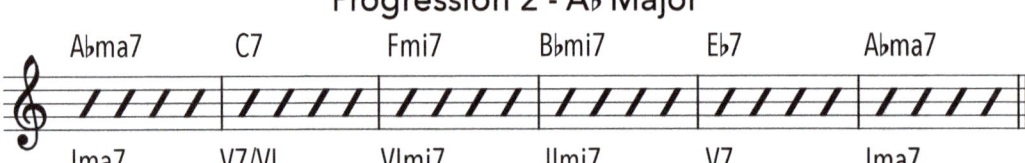

Progression 3 - D Major

Progression 4 - F Major

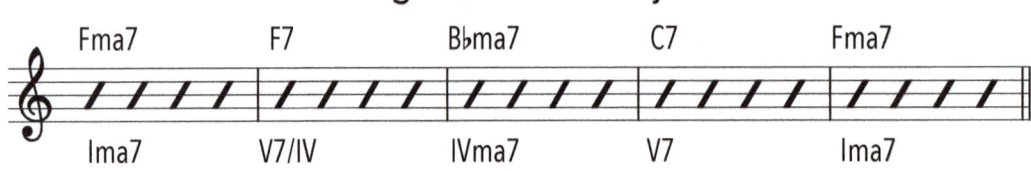

Progression 5 - B Major

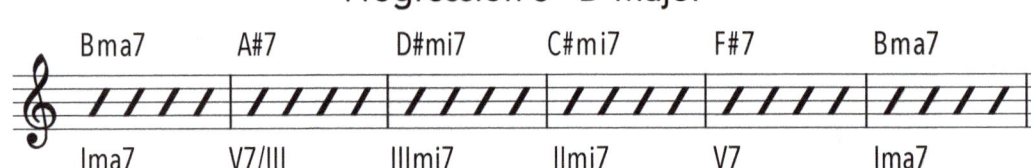

Progression 6 - D Minor

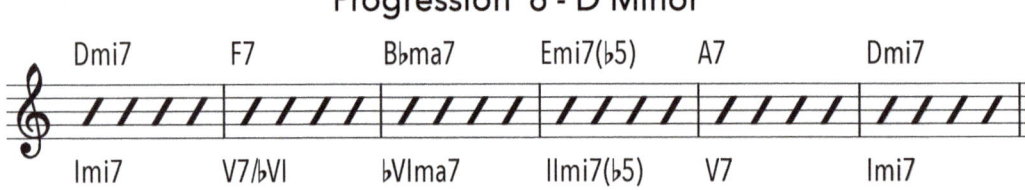

Progression 7 - G Minor

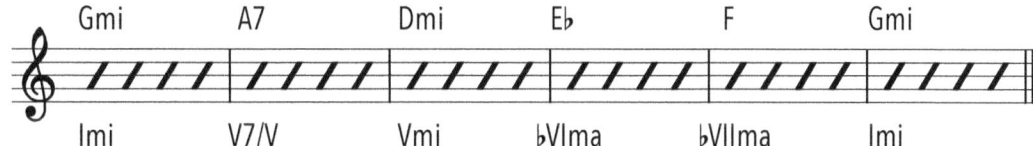

Progression 8 - F Minor

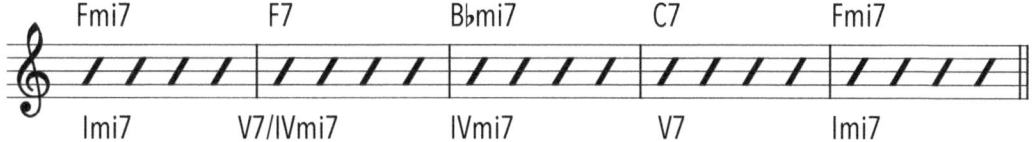

Progression 9 - B♭ Minor

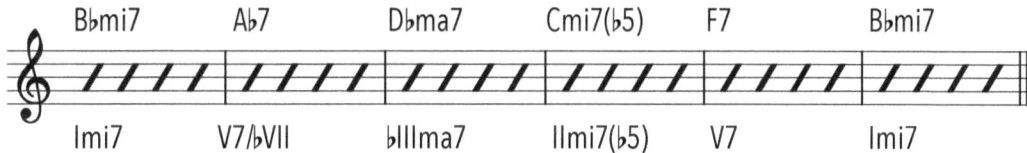

Progression 10 - D Minor

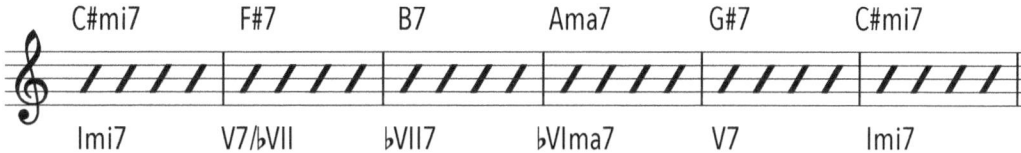

Unit 10 Theory - Progression Analysis - Group 2

Progression 1 - C Major

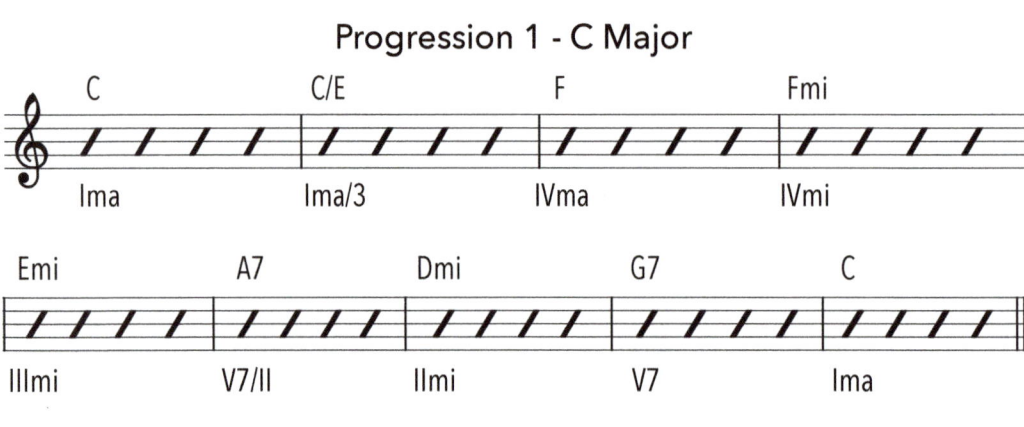

Progression 2 - A Minor

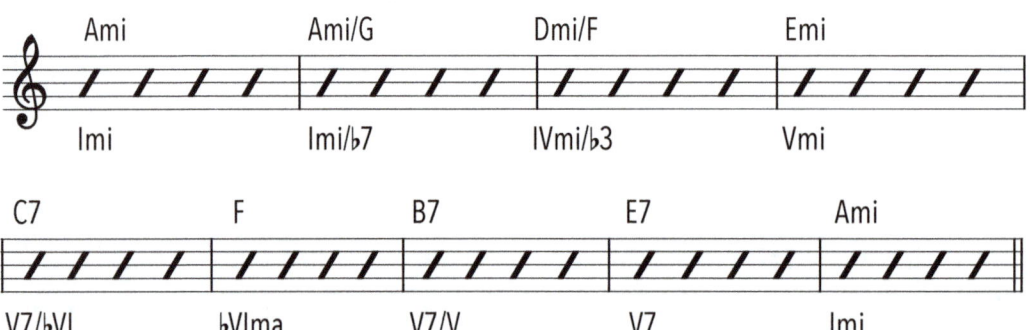

Progression 3 - D Major

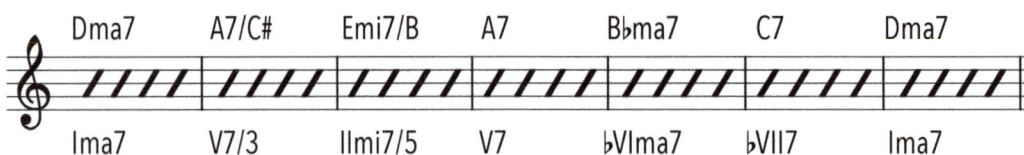

Progression 4 - E Major

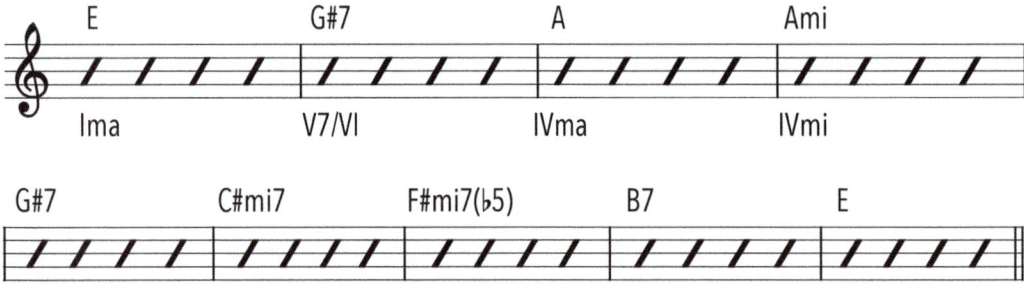

Progression 5 - F Minor

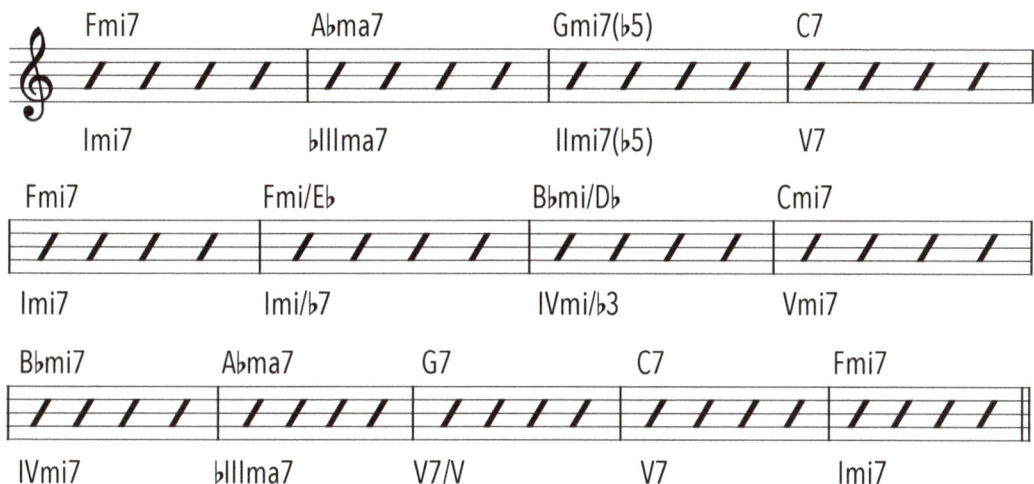

Progression 6 - Bb Minor

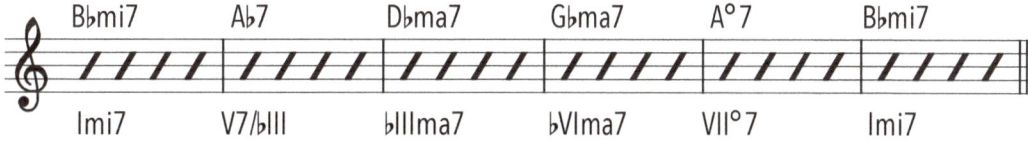

Progression 7 - Ab Major

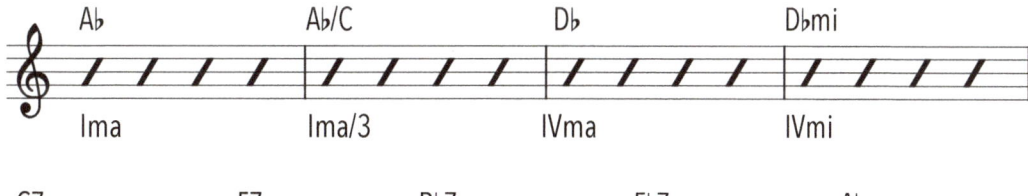
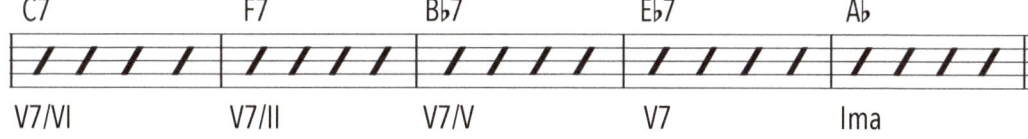

Progression 8 - G Minor

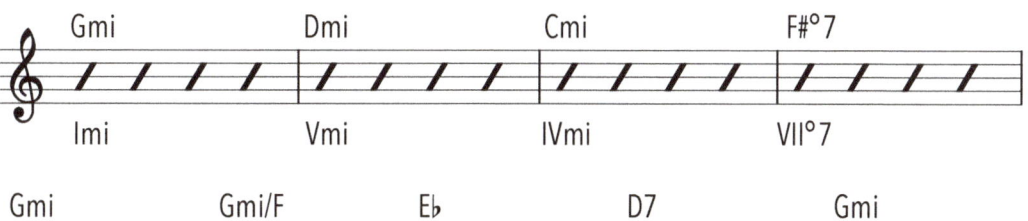
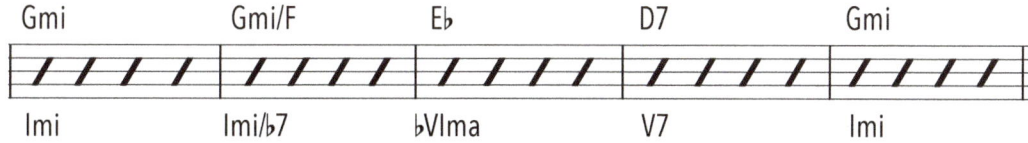

Progression 9 - B Major

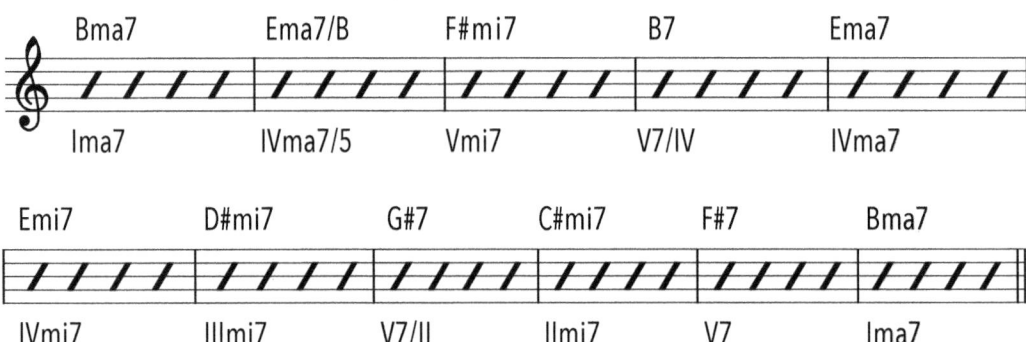

Progression 10 - B Minor

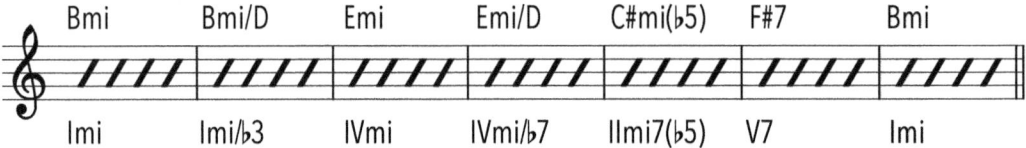

Unit 10 Chart Reading - Answer Key

DS al Coda

- Intro 4 bars played twice
- 'A' with first ending
- 'A' with second ending
- 'B'
- 'C'
- Interlude
  to DS
- 'A' and second ending
- 'B'
- 'C'
  To Coda
- Coda and end

DS al Fine

- Intro 4 bars played twice
- 'A' with first ending
- 'A' with second ending
- 'B'
- 'C'
- Interlude
  To DS
- 'A' and second ending
- 'B'
- 'C' w/fine

DS (and on)

- Intro 4 bars played twice
- 'A' with first ending
- 'A' with second ending
- 'B'
- 'C'
  To DS
- 'A' and second ending
- 'B'
- 'C'
- 'D' and end

DC al Coda

- Intro (4 bars)
- 'A' with first ending
- 'A' with second ending
- 'B'
- 'C'

DC (the very top of the song)

- Intro (4 bars)
- 'A' and second ending
- 'B'

To Coda

- Coda and end

DC al Fine

- Intro (4 bars)
- 'A' with first ending
- 'A' with second ending
- 'B'
- 'C'

DC (the very top of the song)

- Intro (4 bars)
- 'A' and second ending
- 'B' w/fine

DC (and on)

- Intro (4 bars)
- 'A' with first ending
- 'A' with second ending
- 'B'
- 'C'

DC (the very top of the song)

- Intro (4 bars)
- 'A' and second ending
- 'B'
- 'C
- 'D' 3x
- 'E' w/fine

Table of Inverted Intervals

INTERVAL	→	INVERSION
Mi2		Ma7
Ma2		Mi7
Mi3		Ma6
Ma3		Mi6
P4		P5
A4		D5
D5		A4
P5		P4
Mi6		Ma3
Ma6		Mi3
Mi7		Ma2
Ma7		Mi2
P8		Unison

Shell Voicings

Pattern IV (6th string)

Major 7	Dominant 7	Minor 7	Minor 7(♭5)
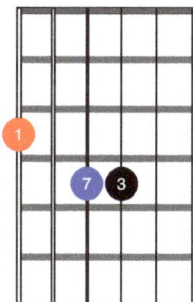	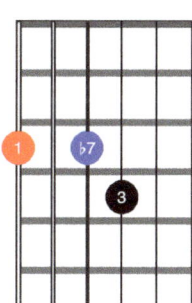	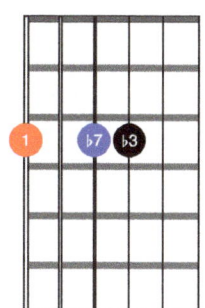	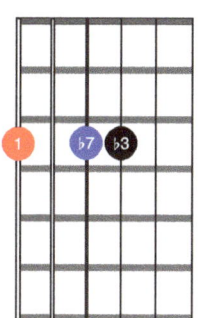

Pattern II (5th string)

Major 7	Dominant 7	Minor 7	Minor 7(♭5)
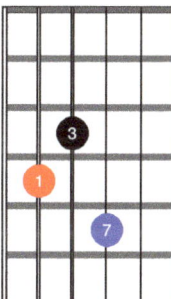	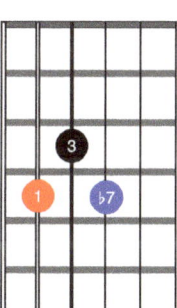	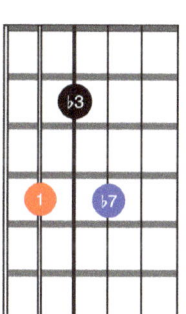	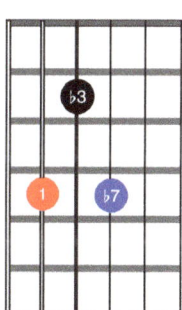

Root Map 1

Root Map 1

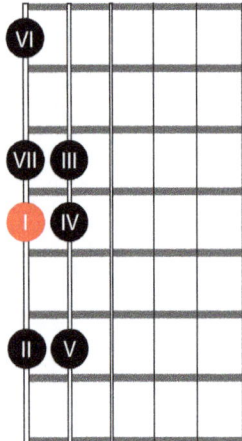

Root Map 1 Shell Voicings

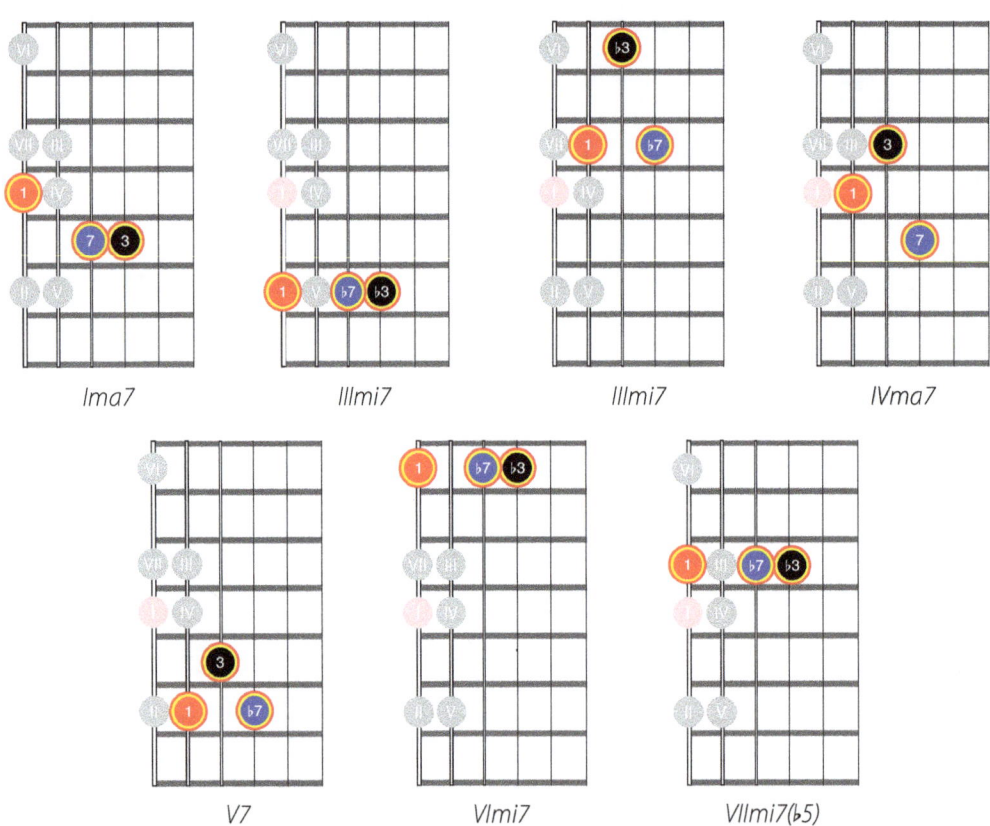

Root Map 2

Root Map 2

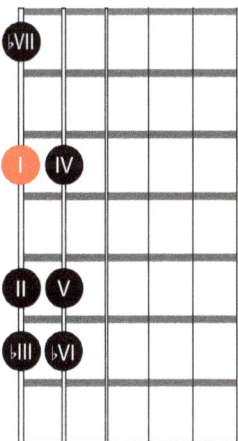

Root Map 2 Shell Voicings

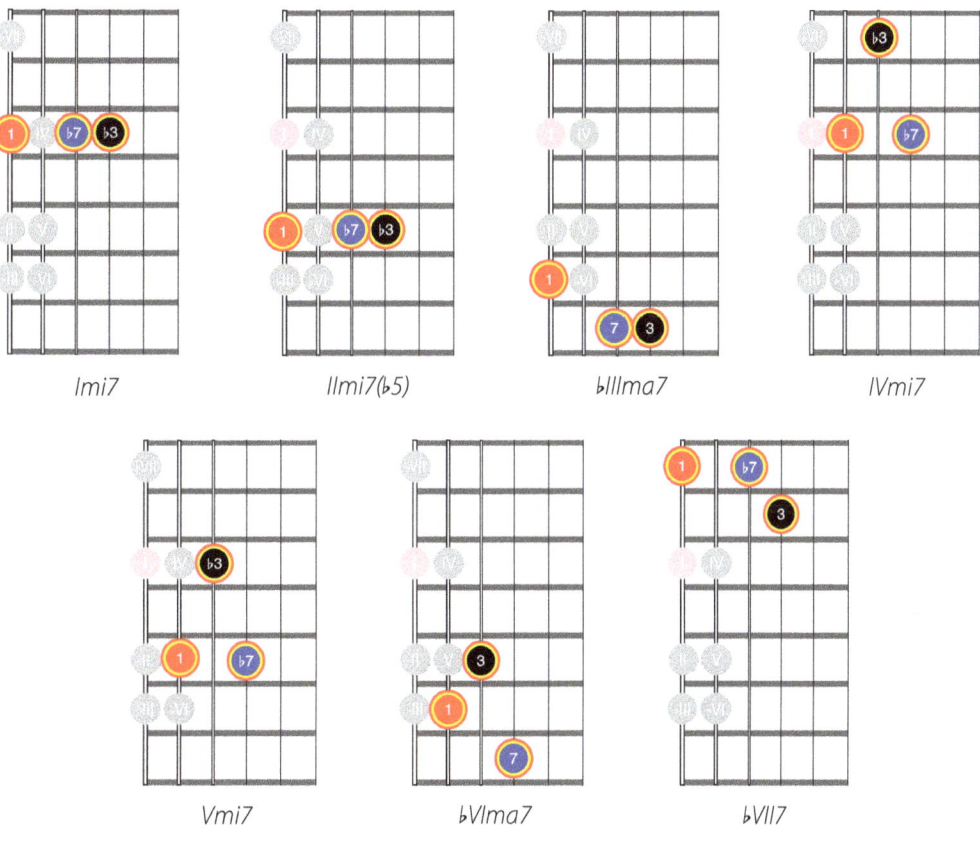

Imi7   IImi7(b5)   bIIIma7   IVmi7

Vmi7   bVIma7   bVII7

Root Map 3

Root Map 3

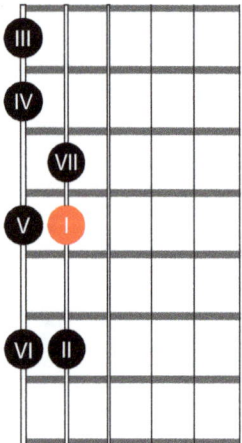

Root Map 3 Shell Voicings

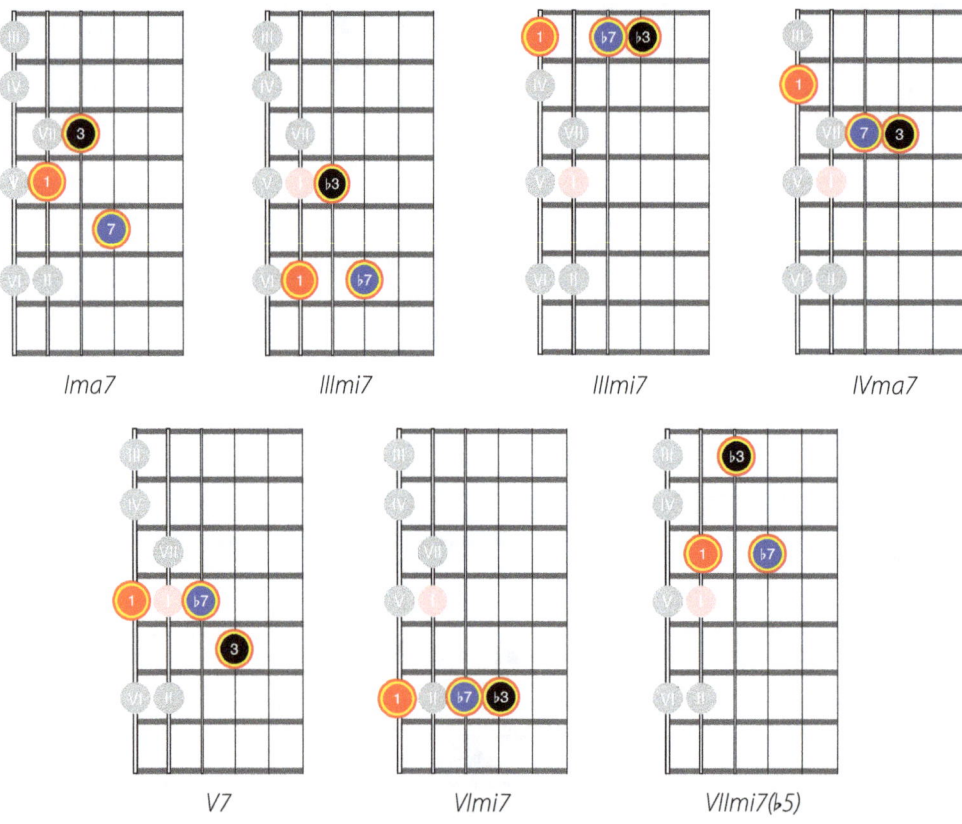

Ima7   IIImi7   IIImi7   IVma7

V7   VImi7   VIImi7(b5)

Root Map 4

Root Map 4

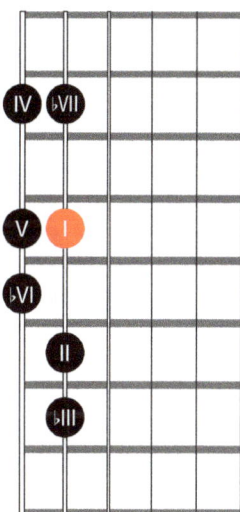

Root Map 4 Shell Voicings

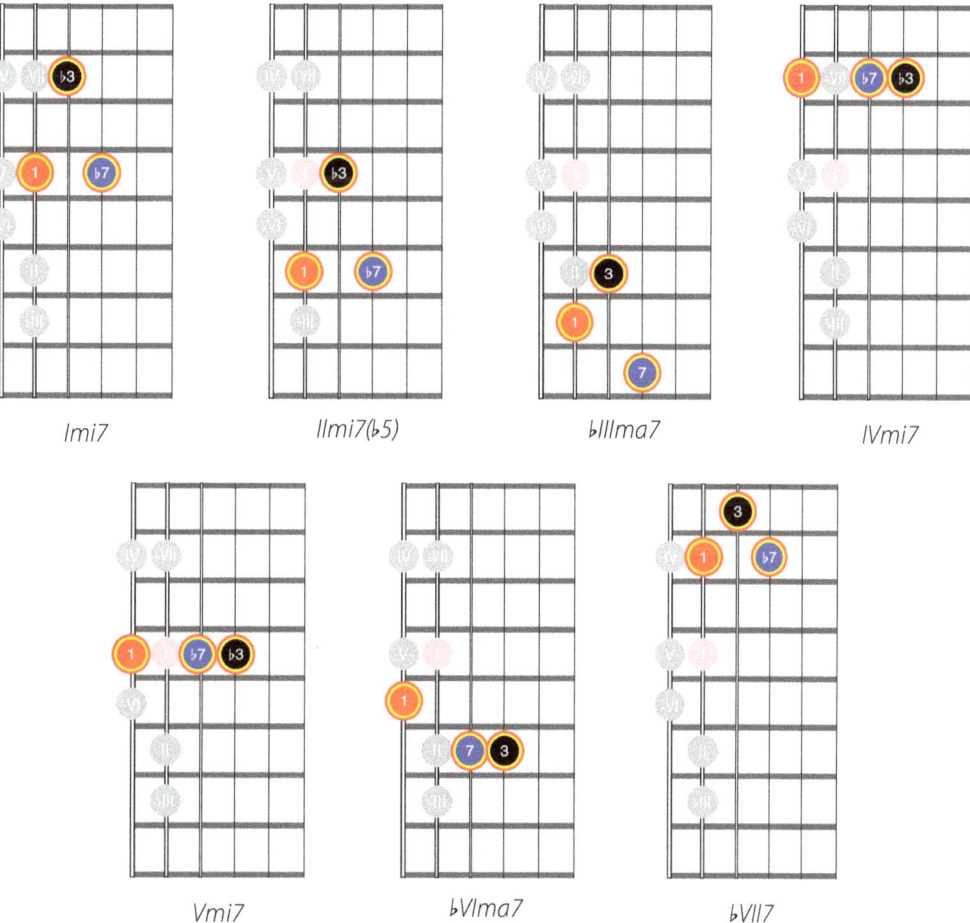

Chords

Pattern II and IV Movable / Barre Chords

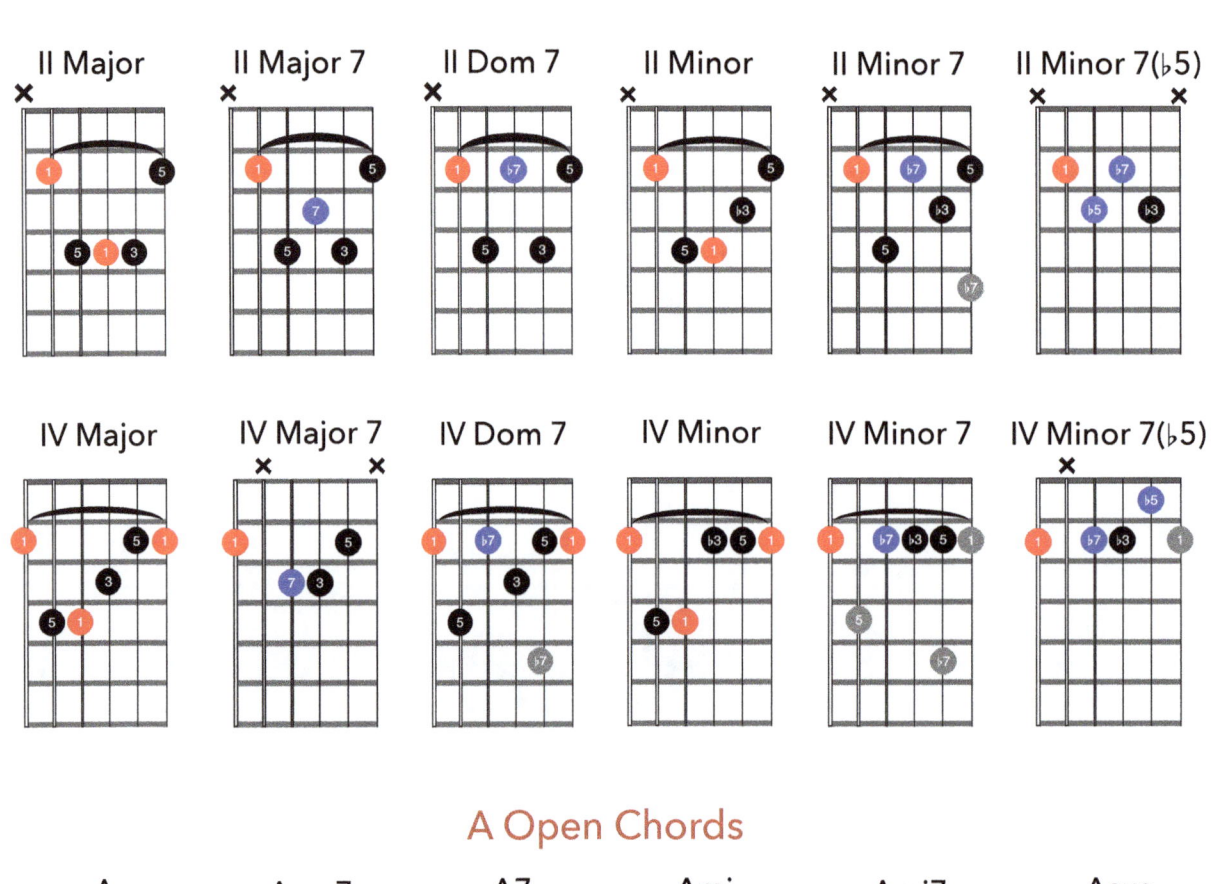

A Open Chords

Inversions

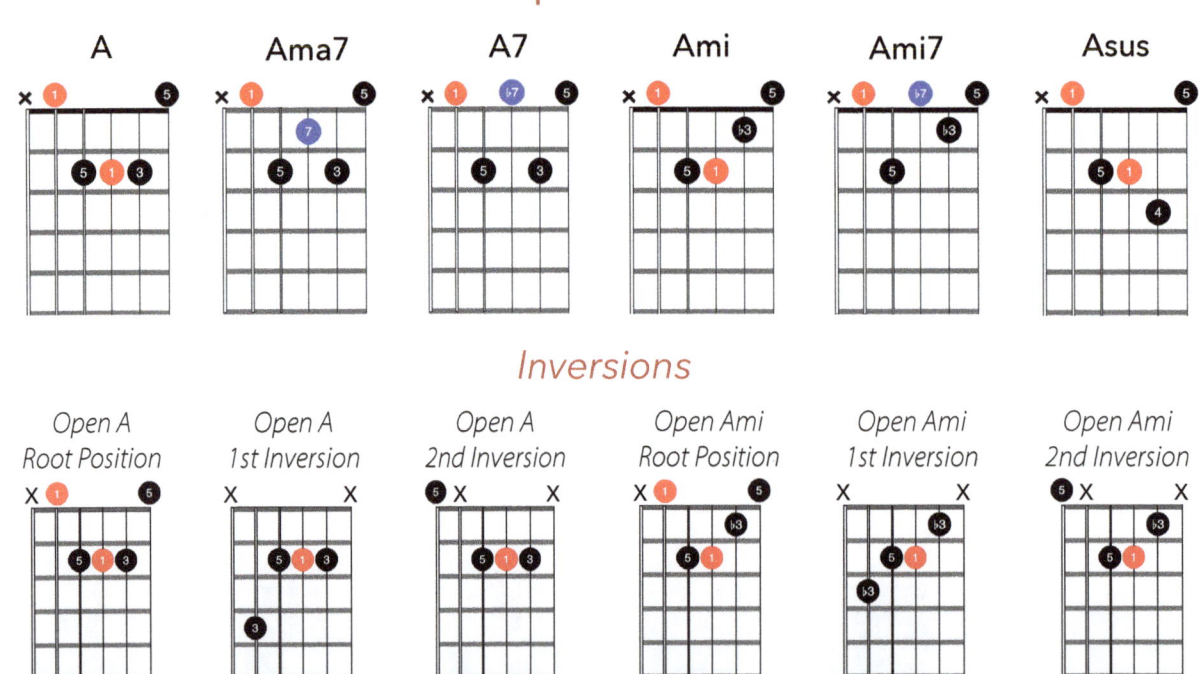

C Open Chords

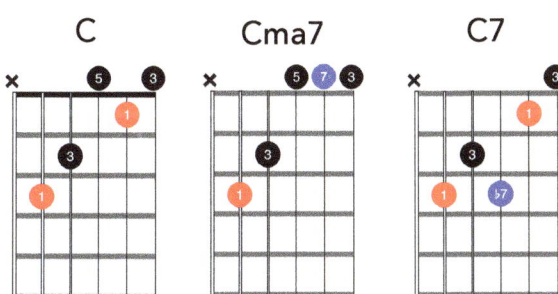
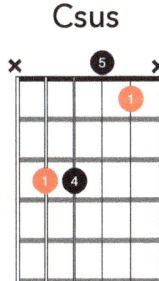

Inversions

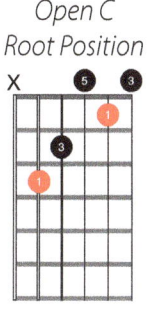
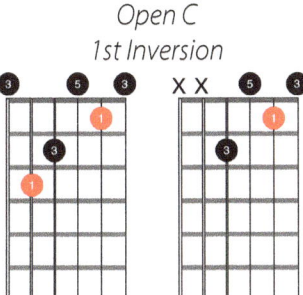
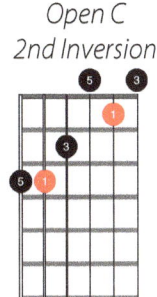

D Open Chords

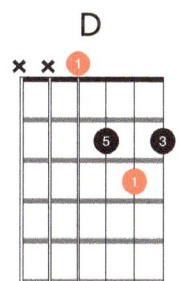
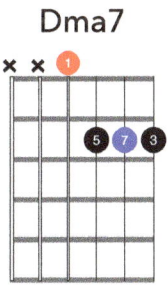
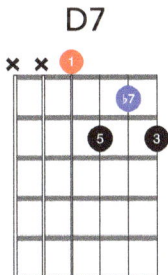
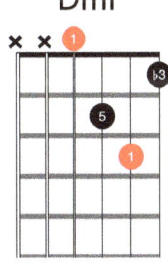
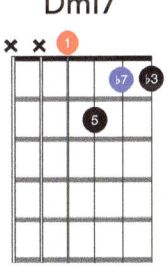
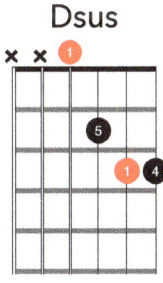

Inversions

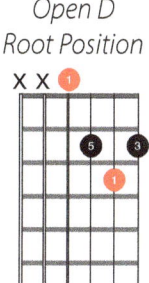
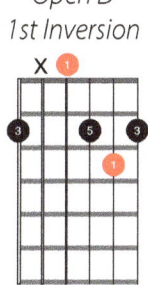
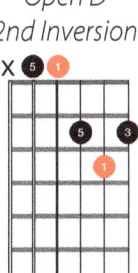
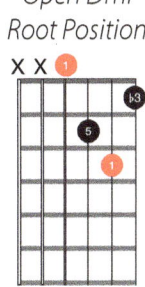
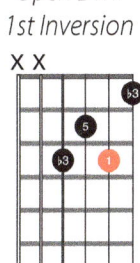
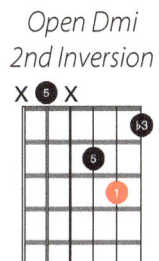

E Open Chords

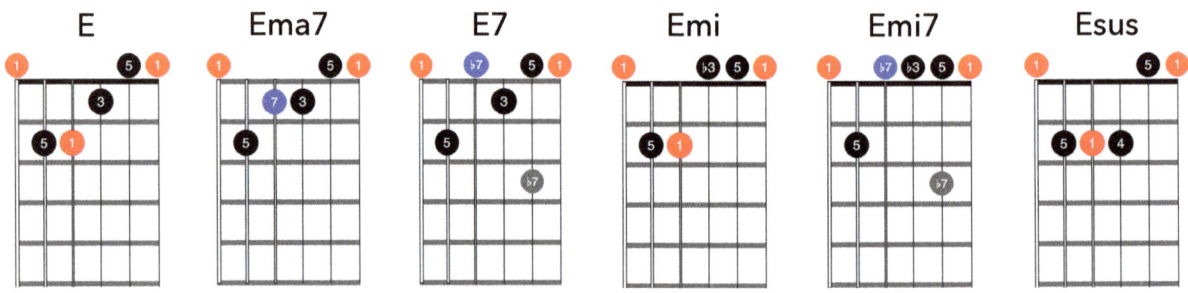

Inversions

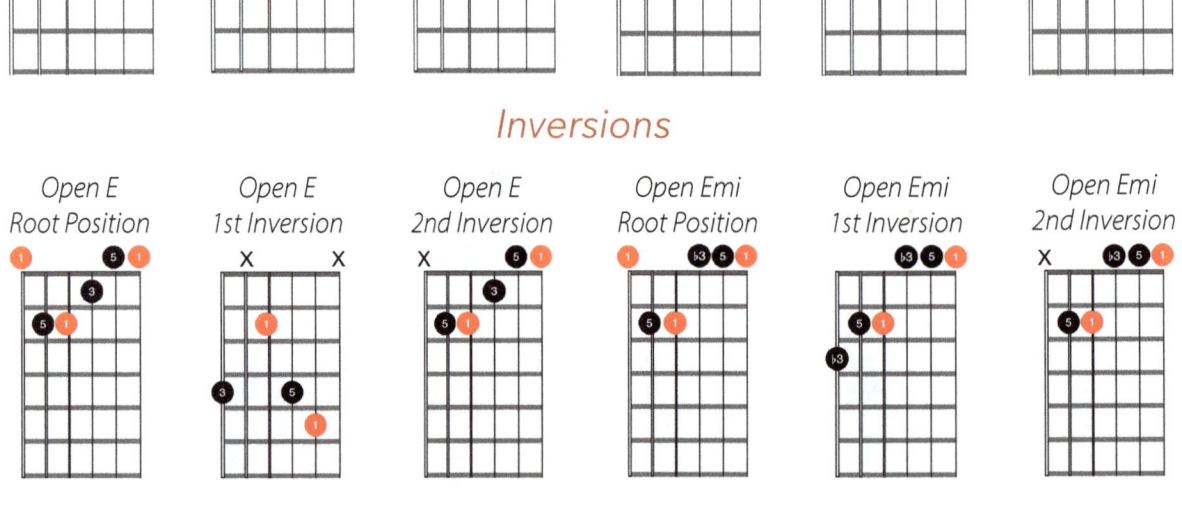

F Open Chords

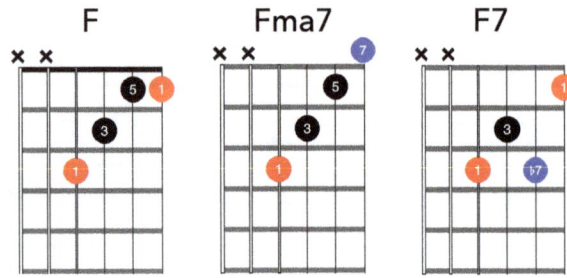

G Open Chords

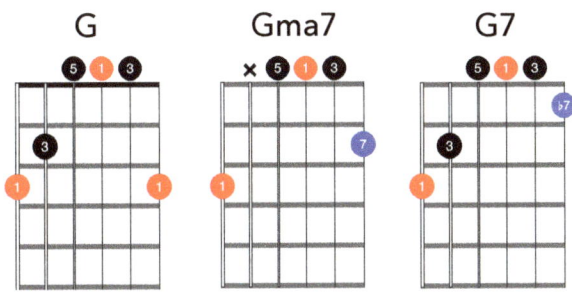 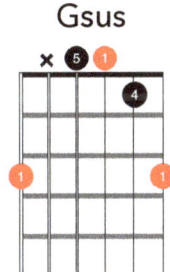

Inversions

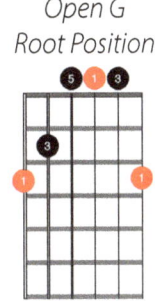 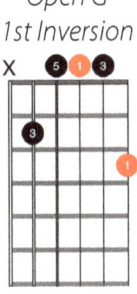 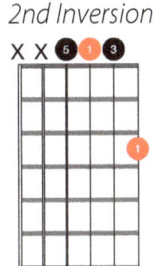

B Open Chords

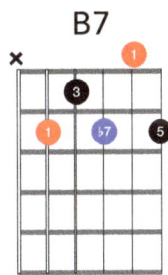

About Joe Elliott

Joe Elliott is an American guitarist, author, composer, and music educator.

Joe's professional experience as an educator includes 23 years of teaching at Musicians Institute (MI) in Hollywood, California, at the Guitar Institute of Technology (GIT). Joe has taught numerous clinics throughout the U.S. While at MI, Joe wrote and edited courses for GIT and MI's Baccalaureate programs. He spent three years as GIT Department Head and nine years as Vice President and Director of Education at Musicians Institute. He spent seven years as the Guitar Department Head and Director of Academic Administration at McNally Smith College of Music in St. Paul, Minnesota. He is currently the co-founder, CEO, and Director of Education of the guitar education website FretboardBiology.com and Music Biology, Inc.

Joe has authored several instructional books for guitar, including *An Introduction to Jazz Guitar Soloing* and *The Fretboard Biology* series of books, and has co-authored *Ear Training* with Carl Schroeder and Keith Wyatt.

Joe has released two solo guitar albums, *Joe's Place* and *Truth Serum*, as well as an instrumental country album, *Country Grit*, is currently a composer for APM Music in Los Angeles, and has composed numerous scores for television and film.

www.ingramcontent.com/pod-product-compliance
Lightning Source LLC
Chambersburg PA
CBHW051329110526

44590CB00032B/4463